Beyond Alliance
Israel in U.S. Foreign Policy

THE INSTITUTE FOR PALESTINE STUDIES SERIES

Muhammad Y. Muslih. *The Origins of Palestinian Nationalism.* 1988.
Justin McCarthy. *The Population of Palestine.* 1990.

THE INSTITUTE FOR PALESTINE STUDIES SERIES

Beyond Alliance
Israel in U.S. Foreign Policy

Camille Mansour
Translated from the French by James A. Cohen

Columbia University Press
New York

Columbia University Press
New York   Chichester, West Sussex

Library of Congress Cataloging-in-Publication Data

Mansur, Kamil
    Beyond alliance: Israel in U.S. Foreign policy /
    Camille Mansour.
        p. cm.
    Includes bibliographical references and index.
    ISBN 0-231-08492-7 (alk. paper)
    1. United States—Foreign relations—Israel.
2. Israel—Foreign relations—United States. I. Title.
E183.8.I7M34   1994
327.7305694—dc20   93-28046
                                                      CIP
  ⊗

Casebound editions of Columbia University Press
books are Smyth-sewn and printed on permanent
and durable acid-free paper.

Printed in the United States of America

c 10 9 8 7 6 5 4 3 2 1

Contents

Preface

It was in Beirut in the mid-1970s that I started following the relations between the United States and Israel. As a researcher at the Institute for Palestine Studies living in a city that then embodied in many ways the core of the Arab-Israeli conflict, I felt that understanding the foundation of the U.S.-Israeli special relationship was necessary if I were to grasp the dynamics of the conflict itself.

From the start, I had put spontaneously aside simplistic explanations, such as making Israel an obedient tool of America or making U.S. administration a servant of the Jewish lobby. I was already faced, of course, with more subtle assertions: if support for Israel did not serve U.S. interests, U.S. policy in the Middle East would have been different; if the lobby was not so powerful, U.S. policy would have been different. The problem was that these two assertions, while probably correct if taken separately, appeared to exclude each other and were anyway insufficient because they could not explain how and to what extent American interests or the lobby influenced U.S. policy toward Israel and the Middle East. I felt the need of an approach that could at the same time assess the fulfillment of U.S. strategic interests in the Middle East and lead to an integrated explanation accounting for the solidity of the U.S.-Israeli ties, the strength of the lobby, and strategic considerations. I hope that the result of my search, which gives precedence to U.S. culture in the framework of its stature as a world power, provides a satisfactory explanation.

As a result of the search, which has continued on and off for several years, I have been able to meet and talk with many people. I would like first to evoke the memory of two friends, the late Riad Ashkar and Marwan Buheiry, with whom I had many thorough discussions on the topic but to whom life has been unfair far too early. I would like also to thank, either for the exchange of ideas about the subject of this book, for the location of sources, or for facilitating the process of publication, Leslie Bialler, Jody Boudreault, Linda Butler, James Cohen, Antoine Gennaoui, Alain Joxe, Samir Kassir, Herbert Kelman, Rashid Khalidi, Walid Khalidi, Jean Leca, Philip Mattar, Mona Nsouli, Elizabeth Picard, Mahmoud Soueid, Kate Wittenberg, and many others.

Camille Mansour
September 1993

General Introduction

For most observers, the relationship between the United States and Israel could be described as special and privileged. The intensity of interaction between the two countries at both the governmental and societal levels, the breadth and the intimacy of their cooperation, and American support to Israel in its multiple forms (economic, military, diplomatic and verbal), are manifestations of solid and perhaps unbreakable ties. The way in which periodic snags are managed, a mixture of exaggeration and negation of possible divergences, and the fear, so often expressed, of a degradation in the climate of relations between the two countries that in fact never occurs, confirm the unique character of the bond. But if the expression of this relation can be captured and described, albeit not without great difficulty, the dynamics and the deeper nature of the relationship, that is, its very foundations, are more difficult still to elucidate.

The question of the basis of the American-Israeli relationship is posed not only to analysts, but also, and more concretely, to political actors. For the Israelis, the way in which the United States perceives and experiences this relationship is determinant because it involves their well-being and their destiny. For the states and the peoples of the Middle East, and even for a wider circle of states, American-Israeli relations constitute an essential factor in their status, their stature, and their future. This is so because a conflict experienced as existential pits Israel against its neighbors and thus provokes, in varying degrees, the intervention of outside powers on the side of one of the parties in this strategically important region. Whether one considers the Israeli-Arab conflict in its historical, military, political, diplomatic, economic, psychological, or even its demographic dimension, the impact of the special American-Israeli relationship is always important, if not crucial. This relationship appears to be so privileged that one can consider the United States itself to be, in many ways, a party to the Israeli-Arab conflict. This role cannot be attributed with the same assurance to other "involved" outside forces, such as the ex-Soviet Union or certain Western European countries.

For the future development of the region, the correlation between the Israeli-Arab conflict and American-Israeli relations is so close (although its terms are not so clear) that the Israelis, the Americans, and the Arabs as well, have long since ceased to intervene in any of these spheres without considering its potential effects on the others. For each of these parties, to confront the problems related to the conflict—for example, the questions of balance of forces, or the choice between war and peace—necessitates considering, as well, the consequences of one's decisions on the quality of American-Israeli relations. Conversely, wishing to protect or develop any given aspect of these relations to the detriment of any other, or believing in the possibility of their becoming strained and acting in consequence, imply being ready to deal with the positive or negative effects of one's choices on the balance of forces in the conflict.

Thus, American-Israeli relations may and often do present, for each party, and depending on the political action envisioned or pursued, great opportunities or serious constraints. If one adds that each party perceives these relations and their potential consequences in accordance with its ideology, its rationality, and its needs, one will easily understand the multiplicity, not to say the confusion, of resulting explanations. Thus, one or another of the following explanations is advanced: Israel is a strategic asset for the United States; American and Israeli strategic interests essentially converge; the United States feels bound to the Jewish state by a moral commitment; the Jewish-American lobby is all-powerful and dictates American policy; Israel is a base for American imperialism.

Faced with this broad range of interpretations and in light of the undeniably central character of American-Israeli relations, one feels the necessity to understand their basis accurately and objectively. The problem, of course, is to find the most adequate approach and guiding thread. To begin by reviewing the content of these relations, then describing their multiple forms over time, and quantitatively evaluating the different forms of exchange that link the two countries—all this would serve more to prove that the relations are privileged, and to establish their "what" and their "how," than to understand the "why" behind them, or their foundations. We will thus not follow this approach, which would rapidly become bogged down in proving what is obvious for observers and actors, i.e., the privileged character of American-Israeli relations—a subject that has already generated an abundant literature in the United States. It seems more useful to consider the special relationship as an already-established fact and to go directly to the question of "why."

In other words, we must ask from the outset whether the special American-Israeli relationship conforms to a rationality. But which rationality should be taken as a starting point? In our view it is fruitful to approach the relations between the two countries in terms of *instrumental rationality*, such as it may be seen on the American side of the relationship. This perspective, suggested by certain interpretations evoked above, means, first of all, that American-Israeli relations will be considered from the point of view of the American rather than the Israeli actor, for it is the United States that is a world power and that gives Israel its indispensable support in arms, finance, and diplomacy. Our perspective implies as well that the instrumental rationality we shall attempt to infer and verify is an actor's logic, a strategy, that is, in ideal form, a coherent relation between U.S. policy toward Israel and its great-power interests in the world and the Middle East.

We say "in ideal form," because it is not our purpose to claim a priori that American policy is rational, instrumental, coherent, and able to adapt its means to its ends without error. The limits of an actor's rationality constitute a well-known dilemma in research: the analyst, seeking to make the actor's choices intelligible, has no alternative but to assume their rationality as a working hypothesis in order to compare the implications that flow from it with the reality of the behavior being studied. But in doing so, the analyst is often led, almost in spite of himself, to attribute his own rationality to the behavior of the actor (in particular, the hidden, as yet unrevealed, side of this behavior). This is a leap that the analyst must avoid making; we shall raise this problem more concretely in chapter 6.

Keeping this dilemma and the precautions it entails in mind, we shall try to "read" American policy toward Israel according to the strategic-instrumental hypothesis, in order to give it all the chances it deserves while striving at the same time to verify its relevance, establish its possible deficiencies, and even propose complementary or alternative explanations. Similarly, in taking the American decisionmaker's perspective as a starting point, our intention is not to deny the role of the pro-Israeli lobby or that of Israel in the development of the U.S.-Israeli relationship, but rather, in the event that the explanation based on the American decisionmaker's perspective should prove insufficient, to set the stage for assessing the proper importance of the lobby, or of Israel, neither minimizing nor exaggerating these.

We shall thus seek to understand the special character of American-Israeli relations starting from a particular, but apparently determinant pole, that of American strategy. More precisely, we shall seek to determine the place of Israel in American strategic *doctrine*, which implies that we must first of all identify American doctrine regarding Israel and only then examine its explanatory value (as we shall do in the two final chapters, which constitute the third stage of this study). But another question is thereby posed: how is this doctrine to be studied, and how is it to be identified?

Let us first of all examine the term "doctrine." According to Lalande (1976), a doctrine always implies "the idea of a body of organized, coherent truths, most often linked to action—not an isolated or purely theoretical assertion"(definition B). Lalande then quotes G. Pirou: "Science and doctrine have different ends: one observes and explains, the other judges and prescribes. . . . Doctrine needs simple lines and clear-cut biases [*partis pris tranchés*]." From this definition, we retain in particular that a doctrine is a discourse, and this discourse has as its function to guide action while also aiming at coherence. However, this definition raises methodological problems if we seek to take its elements literally and apply them to our object of study, the American decisionmaker (or any collective decisionmaker).

Three major difficulties appear: First, there may not be any one official discourse, but several coexisting ones, given the possible plurality of participants in a decision at a given moment and their turnover, and the fact that the decisionmaker might modify his declarations according to changing conditions. Which declarations, then, are the best suited to expressing the doctrine to be studied? By what criteria can we choose them?

Secondly, there may be a gap between the official discourse and actual policy, either because the latter cannot be legitimated in terms of recognized values and norms, or because of tactical considerations. In their statements decisionmakers must often project an embellished image of what they intend to do in practice, or verbally reconcile what is actually irreconcilable. For the analyst, this may lead, among other things, to doubts about how to qualify the discourse being analyzed: is it the expression of a doctrine which actually guides action or is it only a disguise or rationalization, an expedient to justify one's practice after the fact?

Finally, the number and turnover of decisionmakers, the gap that may separate their discourse from their actual policy, the possible contradictions of the latter, the recourse to justifying expedients— all this can only disturb the coherence of the discourse. The resulting problem is not merely logical in nature and cannot be reduced to the fact that it is impossible to decide in advance which declarations should be chosen for analysis. It also involves the difficulty of uncovering the actual but implicit contradictions of a series of declarations that may be coherent only in appearance. For example, when an American decisionmaker declares successively that the United States (1) considers Israel to be an asset and (2) that it has a moral obligation toward that country, how can it be known whether these two statements, apparently pro-Israeli, are logically linked, merely congruent, or contradictory in their strategic implications?

These difficulties, linked to an overly narrow definition of the term "doctrine," suggest that it is not possible to find an official, ready-made, constituted doctrine, nor to make a coherent and convincing compilation of authorized American declarations that could be described as the strategic doctrine inspiring American decisions concerning Israel. This does not mean that such a doctrine does not exist. But one would have to induce it from American practice rather than deduce it from official declarations. Such a doctrine would thus be in itself "implicit" and it is the analyst's role to extract it from practice or make it explicit. The doctrine, thus induced, would, in accordance with the hypothesis of instrumental rationality advanced above, command American policy toward Israel and would or would not correspond with the official discourse(s). This implicit doctrine would not be rigid; it would evolve by periods, and would accompany changes in political decisions over time and according to circumstances. We will thus assume that such an implicit doctrine exists. But how shall it be studied? How can it be induced from actual policy?

Obviously, a study that extracts doctrine from actual policy must follow the latter's evolution chronologically. But the danger of this approach would be to cause us to slide from reconstructing the historical evolution of the doctrine into tracing a factual history with no guiding criteria. How, indeed, can one choose, among the mass of documents and facts concerning American policy in the Middle East and American-Israeli relations over the past 45 years, those which allow for a direct reconstruction of a doctrine which, because it is implicit, cannot by itself offer keys for its own apprehension? Do we not need criteria to make our choice, and conceptual tools to interpret the elements thus assembled, from the point of view of strategic significance and coherence? An induction cannot be made out of nothing; it requires a conceptual framework at the outset. But where are the concepts to be found?

At this point, a return to the narrow and literal meaning of the term doctrine, that is, the idea of an explicit discourse whose objective is to guide action and achieve coherence, can be of great help. But the point is not to revert to an official, discursive doctrine we now know to be practically nonexistent if understood in terms of coherence and conformity with actual policy. The idea is rather to call on "private" doctrines or advocacies formulated by representative, nonmarginal authors addressing themselves to American decisionmakers regarding the strategic place to be accorded to Israel. The prior recourse to advocacies, to private discourses whose aim is to influence political decisions, will constitute, as we shall see, the most convenient path to inducing the implicit American doctrine concerning Israel.

One may be surprised that a study of governmental doctrine starts by examining advocacies that in principle are not subject to being put into practice by their authors, commit only their authors, and can be as diverse and as gratuitous as certain official declarations whose disadvantages we have sought to avoid. We shall see that these principled reservations can be softened because the distance between advocacies and political responsibility is not, in practice, as great as it appears. But we shall also see that this distance is great enough to actually present certain advantages to the analyst.

First, it is by no means our purpose here to refer to the advocacy of authors considered marginal in American political life. In particular, we shall not call on certain Arab-American or black authors whose points of view on the Middle East do not belong—or not yet—to acceptable opinion. We shall limit ourselves to those authors whose opinions are considered "respectable" by members of the American political elite—those authors whose opinions on the Middle East already enjoy a favorable bias in American culture and do not provoke automatic exclusion. This respectability is of course not a value in itself, but it does mean that the spectrum of possible disagreements between the different advocacies to be considered is not unlimited. It is, in any event, the minimal necessary condition for exercising influence on decisionmakers.

The scope of this influence is remarkable in the case of the United States because of the functioning of its political system. The system's openness; the diffuse character of the decision-making process due to the checks and balances among the different branches of power; the role of the president, frequently that of arbiter and manager of bureaucratic differences; the relatively rapid turnover of high officials in the administration—all these factors create a large space for advocacy from the private sector (for example: Smith 1991). Political science researchers belonging to universities or research centers often play the role of consultants to decision-making centers. There is a constant back-and-forth movement between the administration and politics on the one hand, and research and the university on the other. We shall note this movement, in the section of this study devoted to the advocacies, when the prior or subsequent official functions of given authors are mentioned.

This osmosis between research and policy-making in the United States means that advocacy by establishment authors influences decisionmakers, with a legitimate claim to do so. But it also means that they are themselves inspired by the same decisionmakers, that they gravitate around them and cannot, except within certain limits, deviate from actual policy. For in so doing they would lose their influence, and certain would even lose the hope of acceding, or returning, to governmental functions. Decision-makers are themselves divided among several sensibilities, hesitating among contradictory decisions and often seeking to reconcile them. That makes possible the expression of multiple advocacies which, while clearly divergent, are not, when each is taken separately, too far-removed from governmental actions. Returning to the idea of the advocacies' gravitating around decisionmakers, one might portray the two groups as constituting two concentric circles (the decision-makers represented, of course, by the smaller circle), while the gulf separating an advocacy from "centrist" governmental practice is always smaller than that separating two opposed advocacies.

The authors' claim to orient governmental action, their often tangible influence on the decisionmakers in the framework of the American system and their concern to maintain their disagreements with the decisionmakers within reasonable limits, thus lead us to the idea that in practice, analyzing these advocacies is not a gratuitous exercise. On the contrary, such analysis presents precious advantages for apprehending the implicit American doctrine. These advantages derive from the fact that it is the very distance between the advocacies and effective policy that makes possible a debate and allows the "discursive" effort to find its expression in the interpretation of this policy. More concretely, we may highlight the advantage of turning to advocacies and the futility of searching for an official discursive doctrine in the narrow sense by referring directly to the central advocacy examined in this study and which represents a mandatory reference point for the entire discussion based on instrumental rationality: the idea that Israel constitutes a strategic asset for the United States.

Let us take as an example, because of its author's importance, an "opinion" published by the *Washington Post* on August 15, 1979 and devoted entirely to the idea of asset. The article was signed by Ronald Reagan, who was then preparing to become candidate for the presidency of the United States. It stated, in part: "our own position would be weaker without the political and military assets Israel provides. . . . The fall of Iran has increased Israel's value as perhaps the only remaining strategic asset in the region on which the United States can truly rely. . . . Israel has the democratic will, national cohesion, technological capacity and military fiber to stand forth as America's trusted ally."

Reagan's advocacy was not one of a kind. As we shall see in this study, the idea of Israel as a strategic asset has been, over the past 25 years, the object of a multitude of favorable writings, and the constellation of ideas to which it has given rise has even led it to become an integrated doctrine. It is only the idea that this "private" doctrine commands effective American policy that poses a problem. We shall of course have occasion to see how Ronald Reagan, when he became president, tried to follow a policy inspired by that doctrine, in accordance with his campaign positions. And clearly we may say that American policymakers have on several occasions since 1967 asserted the idea of an Israeli strategic asset. But one may ask whether the successive American administrations, even Reagan's, have not sometimes followed policies that went against this idea, although they have never gone to the length of overtly negating it.

It is authors close to the American administration, or at least full-fledged members of the American establishment, who have taken it upon themselves to negate the idea of asset. To the extent that these authors, convinced in varying degrees that Israel is a strategic burden or liability to the United States, express a real trend or real frictions in American policy, they contribute to showing that it is not sufficient to limit oneself to official discourse in order to bring a doctrine to light. Their advocacies against the doctrine of Israel as an asset must thus be taken into consideration. Let us simply say that while each of these advocacies taken separately may display great coherence, when taken all together they do not constitute the basis of an integrated "counter-doctrine," as we shall observe in chapter 2. This is because, contrary to the idea of asset, the assertion that Israel is a burden for the United States does not automatically imply the policy to be proposed.

In any event, these divergences among the advocacies (including the doctrine of asset) can only provoke an enlightening debate. The authors of the advocacies have no direct responsibility in decision-making. They therefore do not have to justify the existing policy. They do not need to use "diplomatic" language when addressing themselves to Israel or the Arabs. They can allow themselves to be frank and direct when proclaiming their support for a governmental decision or their reasons for disapproving it. Moreover, since the advocacies are less subject to changes in the conjuncture and to the tactical meanders of decisionmakers in their official declarations, they have a more durable and stable character, which facilitates their apprehension by the analyst. When events refute certain of their viewpoints, the authors who plead a cause before decision-makers may wait for longer-term developments to confirm their own views, even if that implies, in the meantime, keeping a low profile or losing a part of their influence on decisionmakers.

Since these authors are less vulnerable to the vicissitudes of day-to-day events, their arguments are more systematic and structured, and more coherent. Additionally, since they do not have to respect sensitive diplomatic considerations—less so, in any case, than decisionmakers—they present for the analyst the merit of expressing,

better than the decisionmakers themselves, the strategic significance of official policy or of their own proposed options. Since they
seek to defend or refute a given idea, attitude or political decision,
they are led to make explicit its logical implications, sometimes
taking them to the extreme, to make distinctions that are not
always obvious at first glance, to make often useful conceptual clar-
ifications, and to offer criteria for defining the nature of a given decision or for judging the coherence of a given policy. Of course, they
are thus led to exaggerate, to see serious contradictions in the ambiguities of governmental policy, and to assert their total disagreement with the opposing advocacies, but at least these ambiguities
and disagreements are brought to light rather than remaining latent
and hence ignored. It is up to the researcher, at a later stage, to evaluate the ambiguities or contradictions thus brought to the surface
and to measure their actual dimensions in official policy.

In short, the advocacies provide, both in themselves and via the
effort of analysis and conceptualization they provoke among
researchers, certain keys, categories, and conceptual tools for comprehending and interpreting actual American strategic policy. With
categories and tools elaborated in this manner, it should be possible
to resolve the methodological difficulty explained above, that is,
selecting, among the mass of documents and facts, the significant
and constitutive elements of implicit American doctrine concerning Israel and its evolution in the past 45 years. That is why the
analysis of the advocacies occupies the first two chapters, followed
by a history of the implicit doctrine as it can be induced from actual policy, which is to be treated in chapters 3–5.

At this stage, one may ask why we have not chosen to draw our
conceptual tools from existing research on the relations of cooperation and alliance between two states of unequal power, instead of
constructing them from the advocacies. One could indeed argue
that questions such as those suggested by the attempt to understand
Israel's place in American doctrine are not new and have already
been treated: Why does a world power aid a weaker or peripheral
state? Is the cost of the aid compensated for by some benefits? Are
the latter of the same nature or of a different nature from the costs?
Does support to a small state involve risks for the great power in
terms of global or regional security? Who profits most from the relationship? Is the latter a means for the great power to control the
dependent state? Does the existence of the relationship increase or
diminish the two partners' margin for maneuver, or their mutual

margin with respect to third parties (Bar-Siman-Tov 1980; Hassner 1966; Keohane 1971; Liska 1968; Park 1975; Rothstein 1968)?

There is no doubt that the analyses and comparisons of cases and situations to which these questions have given rise are quite useful. But a literature review or a theorization based on the literature concerning the strategic ties between two states of unequal power would have been too general a preamble for the American-Israeli case, and inapplicable in certain aspects. We have preferred to be content with the general distinction, drawn above, between asset and burden, using it as an initial key to approaching the American-Israeli case (through the debate about it provoked by the advocacies) and progressively exposing the relevant conceptual categories. And as we advance toward more complex distinctions, we will refer when needed to what is directly useful in the literature.

It should be added that the study of the advocacies is of more than just methodological interest. Its usefulness will be perceived in the two final chapters, which examine the explanatory value of governmental doctrine. We will ask in particular whether the instrumental explanation is valid and whether American strategic doctrine concerning Israel originates in considerations of American regional interest, or instead in a dynamic and in demands internal to American society. In the latter case, the advocacies may take their place as modes of expression of these societal demands.

In any event, chapters 6 and 7 will lead us to verify, among other questions, whether imperialism, rationality in foreign policy decision-making, the pro-Israeli lobby, or American ideology and culture constitute, separately or together, satisfactory explanations for the American-Israeli special relationship and American strategic doctrine concerning Israel. We will propose an explanation articulated on several levels and involving both the internal dynamic and strategic interest.

The great number of factors that must be taken into consideration to account for American strategic doctrine and to study its explanatory value have led us to leave aside two subjects that deserve substantial development but which, in our judgment, can be separated from this study: first, American-Israeli cooperation outside the Middle East (in particular in Africa and Latin America) and secondly, the incidence of Israeli nuclear power on relations between the two countries. The latter point will be raised only incidentally.

This study was at an advanced stage when the Eastern Bloc started to crumble. We have tried, each time it has seemed necessary, to take into account this major development which has upset nearly a half-century of certainty in world and Middle East history. It is possible that this upheaval has caused Israel's status in American strategic doctrine to be significantly and enduringly called into question. However, as far as we can judge today, the approach followed in this study does not seem in itself to be upset by the lessons to be drawn from the dismantling of the Soviet empire and the launching of the Madrid peace process—and is in some ways confirmed by these.

Beyond Alliance
Israel in U.S. Foreign Policy

Beyond Alliance
Israel in U.S. Foreign Policy

1 The Doctrine of Israel as a Strategic Asset

The authors examined in these first two chapters belong to the "Establishment" and are thus in a position to influence decision-makers and contribute to the debate about the strategic role of Israel. There are two such groups: those who advocate taking advantage of Israel's status as a strategic asset for the United States; and those who consider Israel a liability and propose to limit the damage it may cause to American interests by offering it a guarantee.

Since our main object in studying these two schools is to shed light on their internal logic and to draw conceptual distinctions from them, we shall not be concerned at this stage with their truth-content or validity. For the same reason, we shall follow a topical rather than a chronological approach in presenting them. This raises, however, the question of how the different arguments of both schools are related to the dimension of time. It seems, first, that time intervenes as a supplier of illustrations from the more or less recent past: an author will select a given event relating to the Middle East, Israel, or American policy to illustrate his or her argument. Secondly, and more importantly, time constitutes the particular matrix in which an advocacy is spelled out; it can thus appear either as a favorable moment for the advocacy's credibility, encouraging its expression in numerous and elaborate writings or, on the contrary, as an unpropitious moment in which the school's arguments will be expressed only in isolated and relatively impoverished form; there can also, of course, be intermediate circumstances. Obviously we will dwell mostly on the favorable moments of each of these two schools of thought, but our purpose will be less to analyze particular historical conjunctures than to understand each set of arguments. For the doctrine of strategic asset, the most favorable moment is the early 1980s, thanks to the events of Iran and Afghanistan, the proclamation of the Carter doctrine and the rise of Reaganism. For the guarantee proposals, the most favorable moment followed the 1973 war and the oil embargo, because of the shocks provoked by these events in Israel and in the United States.

The Services Attributed to Israel

The exponents of the doctrine of strategic asset attribute to Israel diverse services. In order to classify these (and they are often presented in disorderly fashion by the authors), we shall begin with the most material types—the more technical and secondary ones—and proceed to examine the more important, strategic and intangible ones.

Geographic Location

The advantages of Israel's geographic location are emphasized by all the defenders of the idea of strategic asset. For Michael Handel (1983:80), a Harvard researcher specialized in Israeli strategic problems, Israel is "an ideal staging base for operations" in any necessary direction that can "easily be reached by shorter sea-lanes through the Mediterranean." According to Geoffrey Kemp (1981:373), a Tufts professor who became a member of the National Security Council under Reagan, the use of Israeli territory as a site for prepositioning military equipment would allow an American intervention force to face a contingency involving simultaneously the Persian Gulf and NATO. The geographical advantages of the Israeli territory as a prepositioning site with respect to other places have been described in great detail by Steven Rosen (1982), who, in addition to his own contributions on the subject, has coordinated a series of studies on Israel as an asset for the pro-Israeli lobbying organization AIPAC (American Israel Public Affairs Committee).

For Rosen, the most significant variable in the "defense" of a region such as the Persian Gulf is distance, since the United States is 9,000 miles away by air. The closest American base, Diego Garcia in the Indian Ocean, is 3,000 miles away. The improvements that could be made in airlifting capacity from the United States to the Gulf would be quite expensive and would have only a marginal effect. The ideal solution would be to find sites where equipment could be stored permanently and to which troops could be rapidly flown in time of crisis. Rosen excludes the choice of sites such as Kenya (Mombasa), Somalia (Berbera), or Oman (Masirah), although they are close to the Gulf. These sites, which had already been retained by the Rapid Deployment Force in 1980, do not meet with Rosen's approval because they are not suitable "to a 'swing force' that could be deployed *either* to Europe or the Gulf" (Ibid.:3).

The idea that emerges from Rosen's quantified comparisons is that Israel (as well as Egypt) offers the optimal advantage as a base for a swing force. In a scenario of European conflict, Israel is well placed, just after Turkey. Airlifting a mechanized division from Tel Aviv to Munich would take 11 days, but 24 days would be required to carry the same load from the east coast of the United States to the German city. Moreover, it would take 11 days to airlift a mechanized division from Tel Aviv to Dhahran, but it would take two and a half months, to transport it, using the same equipment, from the east coast of the United States (Ibid.:7–8). However, General Paul Kelly, first chief commander of the Rapid Deployment Force, estimated in August 1980 that the time necessary to deploy a division in the Gulf is less than two weeks (Hanks 1982:43).

In terms of cost, the choice of Israel as a staging base would allow a savings of nearly $10 billion, according to Rosen. This sum, he claims, is equal to the procurement costs of the additional airlifting equipment (C-5A aircraft, for example) that would be needed to make transport as rapid from the east coast of the United States as from Israel (Rosen 1982:11).

Rosen's study appears to be the one, or one of several, that the Pentagon's Program Analysis and Evaluation Office asked the Rand Corporation to carry out in 1981 with a view to designating the most favorable countries that could offer logistics support to a U.S. rapid deployment force (Stork 1982:8–9). But it is above all a strong argument for an Israeli role in any American intervention force in the Middle East (Shipler 1981; Tamir 1988: 218–220). Its technical and quantitative appearance are meant to give it an objective, rigorous, nonpartisan and even nonpolitical character. AIPAC has published other studies in the same vein (see, for example, Carus 1983).

Another of these (Indyk et al. 1983) took up the problem of fuel supplies for the hundreds of aircraft that would have to intervene in the Gulf. Among the three authors of this study, it is worth noting that Martin Indyk would later become the director of the Washington Institute for Near East Policy, whose pro-Israeli orientation is well-known. For these authors, fuel cannot be stocked in tanker vessels because these are too vulnerable; it must be done on land, and here again, the choice of Israel would be competitive from the point of view of distance and cost (Indyk et al. 1983:10–11).

We may conclude the geographical argumentation by quoting the appeal contained in a *New York Times* advertisement on October 13, 1982 under the title "Faith in Israel Strengthens America": "If U.S. interests in the Middle East were threatened," the ad reads, "it would take months to mount a significant presence there. With Israel as an ally, it would take only a few days."

Infrastructure and Logistics

If, from the geographical point of view, Egypt and Israel appear to offer largely the same advantages, only Israel is left in the running when infrastructure is taken into account. As Steven Spiegel, UCLA professor of Political Science, stresses (1980:48), that country is known to possess "the best and most advanced facilities in the area, the best-trained personnel." For Joseph Churba, who had worked as an adviser to U.S. Air Force intelligence, Israel "has first-line support facilities which can provide maintenance and preparedness for American forces critically short of such capacities." More precisely, Israeli ports "are fully capable of servicing and supporting every ship in the Sixth Fleet, up to and including CVNs" (Churba 1980:360). They "can handle any loads in a short period of time" and Israeli airfields are "suitable for all types of civilian and military aircraft, including all of the necessary logistical support" (Handel 1983:80). Aside from their "outstanding" medical facilities that could aid in caring for American personnel in case of emergency (Spiegel 1983:51; Stork 1982:12; Wingerter 1985:83), Israel offers the most modern facilities for stocking munitions and spare parts (Phillips 1986).

Since Israel uses the same types of weapons as the United States, the maintenance and repair services Israel can render are also emphasized (McNaugher 1985:56). Concerning the U.S. Air Force in particular, its recourse to Israeli maintenance services would allow it to improve the rate of readiness of its aircraft, a rate that apparently did not exceed 63 percent in 1980 (Indyk et al. 1983:28). Spiegel estimates that the Israelis "have the facilities and the trained manpower to maintain U.S. equipment at a 20–30 percent higher stage of readiness than is currently the case" (Spiegel 1983:51).

All in all, as Handel explains, the Americans could use Israeli air, naval, or ground bases "either for direct military, intelligence, electronic warfare, reconnaissance, or any other support operations or as intermediary second-echelon bases for organization, supplies and maintenance." They could also install or use in Israel "radar stations, ground satellite and communication centers, forward or intermediary command communications and control systems" (Handel 1983:82).

Defense Capability

Israel's military capabilities allow the authors to emphasize the country's possible contribution to the protection of an American intervention force in the Middle East. This is held to be true because, in the words of Eugene Rostow (1977:37), former Under-Secretary of State under Johnson and member of the Committee on the Present Danger who later joined the Reagan administration, Israel "is the only sure access point we have between Western Korea and Japan." More precisely, Israel, contrary to other countries that offer facilities to an American intervention force (such as Kenya, Oman, or even Egypt) (Churba 1980:358–359), is reputed to be capable of ensuring the defense of this force. Israel's domination of the air and its ability to protect its own air space can shield any American intervention force that uses Israeli facilities against any air attack (Lakoff 1987:82). "The same applies," writes Rosen, "to security against large-scale guerrilla operations, which the Israelis have brought almost completely under control." Anywhere but Israel, the United States would have to worry about protecting by itself the facilities and prepositioning sites it uses (Rosen 1982:5).

It may be noted that these arguments contradict the "tripwire" idea (Grayson 1982:58; Haffa 1984:146; Hanks 1982:48; Newhouse 1971:44) that is often invoked in connection with the presence of American armed forces in an allied country: in order to deter a potential aggressor, a symbolic military presence is judged sufficient and there is no need for an offensive potential or even a defensive one. The enemy must know that in attacking the country in question, he will not fail to confront American soldiers, that is, the prestige of a superpower and its commitments toward its allies. The tripwire notion was even used to qualify the presence—albeit substantial—of American troops in Europe. In the present case, it is Israel that acts as the protector as it were, and the United States as the protected party!

The following argument is significant in this regard. In a letter addressed to the *New York Times* on October 2, 1979, Admiral Elmo Zumwalt wrote that American strategists "rely on Israel's armed forces to . . . *guarantee* the U.S. Sixth Fleet air superiority despite the Soviet Mediterranean fleet."

Experimentation, Research and Development, Intelligence

Israeli military experience furnishes defenders of the doctrine of strategic asset with another series of arguments, the main lines of which are as follows. The Israelis have real combat experience under conditions identical to those an American force of intervention would encounter regarding the terrain, the climate and the performance of potential enemies. They have thus developed tactics of interception and aerial duel as well as tactics adapted to desert operations (Handel 1983: 83). Spiegel (1983:55; 1986:480) has drawn up what he calls a partial list of "changes" introduced into combat thanks to Israel: "the decreased use of searchlights and the increased use of thermal sights for night fighting; the increased use of tanks and armored personnel carriers (APC's) in tandem; improvement in command, control and communication, facilitating the coordination of air, land and sea operations down to the unit level."

American experts were able to inspect Soviet T-62 and T-72 tanks and Mig-23 and Mig-25 aircraft or their remains captured by the Israelis; they were also able to study Israeli intelligence concerning the combat tactics either taught to Arab armies by the Soviet Union (Handel 1983:83–84; Spiegel 1983:53; Spiegel 1986:479) or used directly by Soviet troops, as was the case during the war of attrition of 1970, when Soviet pilots confronted Israeli pilots over Egyptian skies (Glick 1982:154).

The Israeli army's experience and the information it can supply about the performance of American weapons systems are said to be very useful for the improvement and reconception of these arms, the development of high-technology intelligence-gathering equipment and, more generally, the orienting of R&D in the United States (Spiegel 1983:53; 1986:480; Indyk et al. 1983:2).

Israeli R&D is itself said to be quite profitable to the United States thanks to "the close integration of Israeli inventors with U.S. companies" (Spiegel 1986:483). The following examples are cited in this respect: Israeli suggestions concerning the platform of the TOW anti-tank missile system; the repairing of helicopter rotor blades (Handel 1983:83); the modification of M-48 and M-60 tanks (Spiegel 1983:54–55). Israeli procedures in R&D, it is claimed, are faster, more flexible, less bureaucratic and less costly than in the United States. As a result, the participation of Israeli companies in American military contracts would allow the United States to obtain, in the words of AIPAC Director Thomas Dine (1987:97), "a quality product for a lower price" in the high-technology areas where Israel has gained competence.

With such Israeli expertise available, American taxpayers would realize great savings. The Israeli contribution would more than off-set American aid. For Spiegel (1983:54–55), "if Israeli experiences were worth only 2 percent of the annual U.S. defense budget, that would amount to over $4 billion" (also Indyk et al. 1983:27). George J. Keegan, former head of U.S. Air Force intelligence, estimates that "Israel's contribution was worth $1000 for every dollar's worth of aid we have granted her" (quoted by Glick 1982:155). Further, the Israeli army is indirectly, through its reputation, a source of profits for the American military industry by convincing potential buyers to decide on a type of weapon that has already been successfully tested by Israel. And beyond this, Israel profits the United States in an even more subtle way because, according to Spiegel (1983:54), "Israel's combat experiences have led to the improvement of American equipment, potentially saving American lives in the process"! Presumably, then, Israeli lives are risked to save American ones . . . We may add that for Edward Luttwak (1989:46), strategic studies specialist, the emergence of the post-nuclear era and the possibility that wars may break out regardless of East-West relations, enhances the importance of "what Israel has to offer, namely real battlefield knowledge and technology adapted to the battlefield."

Israel's contribution to political intelligence is yet another argument to justify that state's role as a strategic asset for the United States in the Middle East. Many Israelis come from different countries in the region, which "gives them a better knowledge of languages, mentality and other factors necessary for a better analysis and interpretation of information collected in the region" (Handel 1983:83). Churba (1980:360) considers the Israeli intelligence apparatus to be "the best source of hard military and political information." The Israelis are thus seen as the experts, the "Orientalists" of the Middle East, in the sense defined by Edward Saïd (1978; also Hentsch 1987): they are at once knowledgeable about the terrain and imbued with Western civilization. They are the ones who can claim to understand Arab mentalities, their political processes, their "irrationality." The assessments they communicate to Washington are thus of inestimable value. More prosaically, Israeli intelligence services are said to have warned the Americans several times of threats to Egyptian and Saudi leaders (Spiegel 1983:51). In the area of intelligence, then, Israeli-American cooperation is thought to have allowed the United States to economize on training and to deploy fewer intelligence operatives and use fewer facilities (Spiegel 1986:476).

Intervention Capability

The Israeli contributions mentioned up to now are of a technical nature; they are subsidiary and, in the best of cases, operational. Moving now to a higher plane, we shall consider the function attributed to Israel's own intervention capability in the Middle Eastern theater. This capability must be understood in its two dimensions, deterrence and coercion, with more emphasis on the former than on the latter.

The importance of Israeli military power for the United States is celebrated by all the authors considered. For Harvey Sicherman (1983:69–69), a special assistant to Secretary of State Alexander Haig in 1981–82 who later joined James Baker's staff in 1989, Israel's effectiveness makes it "a highly desirable associate." For George Keegan, a former major-general, Israel is "a powerful stabilizing force" (quoted in Reich 1980:91); for Churba (1980:358), it constitutes an indispensable complement to the rhetoric and "bluff" of American threats; and for Robert McFarlane (1989:3), National Security adviser to Ronald Reagan between 1983 and 1985, Israel is an ally that helps to deter "non-nuclear threats." Ray Cline, former assistant director of the CIA and former director of the State Department's intelligence and research service, ranks the power of the Jewish state as 18th in the world, taking into account several nonmilitary factors including surface area, population, and economy; however, he ranks its operational capacity in fourth place, after China but before the European powers. This, combined with a number one ranking in coherence of national strategy and force of national will, leads Cline (1980:136, 173, 183, 187) to include Israel in what he calls an "all-ocean alliance" led by the United States and including Canada, the United Kingdom, France, Germany, Italy, Japan, Australia, New Zealand and Taiwan.

To substantiate their claims, the authors may resort to emphasizing the negative consequences of Israeli military inferiority. The result of such inferiority would be "regional instability, erosion of credibility among allies, encouragement to adversaries to test further American credibility in other regions ." (Churba 1977:33). The fall of Israel would "further weaken the moderate Arab states, such as Jordan and Saudi Arabia . . . , would probably facilitate Arab radical pressures which have been destabilizing factors in the Persian Gulf" (Reich 1980:75–76).

To support their thesis about the services Israel can render thanks to its military power, the exponents of the doctrine of strategic asset refer to examples drawn from recent history. Let us cite the most significant of these examples, before proceeding to examine the magnitude of the strategic contribution attributed to the Jewish state.

Israel is credited, before 1967, with having "prevented Egypt under Nasser from conquering Saudi Arabia and the Persian Gulf states" (Rostow 1977:37). The victory of an Israel supported by the United States in June 1967 is considered to have struck a blow against "Arab aggression" which otherwise "might have led to a larger conflict affecting American interests or involving the United States in a confrontation with the Soviet Union" (Reich 1980:75). Since at least 1967, Israel is thought to have served as the protecting shield against which "the attentions and energies of the Arab radicals" have been diverted instead of concentrating themselves on the overturning of pro-Western regimes in the oil states (Churba 1977:33). However, it is the Jordanian events of September 1970 that constitute, for all these authors, the mandatory reference point in establishing the idea of Israel as a strategic asset.

Israeli American coordination and Israel's warnings to Damascus are considered to have saved King Hussein's regime from a Syrian invasion (Churba 1977:32; Reich 1980:75; Spiegel 1983:75; Glick 1982:154; Indyk et al. 1983:23; Handel 1983:82–83). For all these authors, the Israeli military deployment "spared American leaders the terrible choice of either injecting their own military forces into the region or abandoning to Soviet-supported armies our Jordanian allies" (Zumwalt in Churba 1977:15). However, the 1973 war and its immediate aftermath clearly made the reference to a credible Israeli strategic contribution more problematic. Only in the 1980s could concrete cases, such as the destruction of the Iraqi nuclear reactor (June 1981) or the weakening of the PLO and Syria and of Soviet influence during the 1982 invasion of Lebanon, be cited (Churba 1977:32; Spiegel 1983:51; Handel 1983:84; *Near East Report* 6/18/82:121).

It matters little at this point to assess whether the services attributed to Israel in the above cases are real and effective. Let us note, however, that these cases concern, directly and principally, only the countries of the Israeli-Arab front. But what about the other threats to Western regional interests? Of course, the authors do extend the Israeli strategic contribution to two other fields much larger than that of the conflict: the protection of Western oil interests and the readiness to face a direct Soviet military intervention (at a time when such an intervention was deemed possible). Thus, Handel (1983:84) speaks of Israeli power as being "one of the best guarantees for the protection and continuation of oil supplies in the future," while Amos Perlmutter (1983:71) writes that Israel "could act as a surrogate to check Iraq" if it threatened Saudi Arabia and the Gulf emirates. During the long period of East-West confrontation, the authors tried to imagine all the possible contributions that Israeli air and naval forces could make to the common effort against the Soviet Union in the Mediterranean and on the southern flank of NATO (Glick 1982:155–156; Churba 1980:360; Snyder 1985:127; Handel 1983:81; Kemp 1981:376). Spiegel even spoke (1983:51) of Israel as a "deterrent against Soviet plans for an invasion of the Persian Gulf or for activities in the Mediterranean." But let us stress that the role attributed to Israel in these two fields remained a matter of conjecture, since it was not supported by any concrete examples. The collapse of the Soviet Union renders pointless any further discussion of the Israeli role against an intervention by Moscow. Moreover, while the invasion of Kuwait in August 1990 and the war against Iraq in January, 1991 did not allow the authors to confirm Israel's strategic role in the Gulf, it must be added that this role was reaffirmed in the months that followed (*Near East Report* 3/25/91:52; 5/6/91:79).

The Ladder of Israeli Services

We have tried up to now to classify the services attributed to Israel by the strategic asset doctrine along a ladder from the most technical or operational to the most strategic. Like any attempt at classification, this one perhaps draws distinctions and establishes a hierarchy that are not justifiable in every respect. In particular, the level at which we have placed Israel's defensive capability (a rather low ranking in the scale) may seem debatable; it may seem more correct to place it just below Israel's intervention capability. But in making our choice we sought to account consecutively for the entire set of complementary elements (geographical location, infrastructure and logistics, defensive capability) that could justify, for the doctrine, an Israeli role in support of an American intervention force.

The following figure (figure 1.1) represents the ladder of services attributed (and attributable) to Israel, once defense capability has been "promoted" to the level it seems to merit. In this hierarchy, which goes from the most technical and operational to the most strategic, each level or rung must be considered as assuming the availability of the lower ones.

Another point should be made concerning the ladder of services attributable to Israel. These services can be distinguished according to whether they are initiated by the United States or by Israel. We have here the two poles of a distinction whose implications must now be made explicit. We would locate at the first pole the idea of an Israel that, thanks to the threat or actual use of its intrinsic strength, would consequently contribute to the defense and protection of American interests in the Middle East. This would suggest an active, dynamic, relatively autonomous role for the Israeli actor.

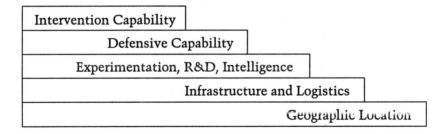

Figure 1.1
Ladder of Services Attributed to Israel

For convenience, we would say that for the authors Israel represents here an *intrinsic* asset. At the second pole, we would see an Israel that would, more modestly, simply offer military facilities to the American armed forces in order to allow these forces to intervene rapidly and successfully in the Middle East theater. Here, the Israeli contribution is more passive, static, and auxiliary. We would say in this case that Israel constitutes an *extrinsic* asset.

These two poles may be identified, respectively, with the top and the bottom of the ladder. The place where the status of Israel would be located on the ladder would depend on the nature of the services attributed to that country by a given author. In order to better grasp the correlation between intrinsic asset, extrinsic asset, and the different intermediate stages, we propose to formalize it algebraically (with the usual warning that such a formalization is not explanatory but simply a means of representation). In order to do this, we shall superimpose the following graph (graph 1.1) on the earlier figure.

Let x represent the idea of extrinsic asset and y, that of intrinsic asset. The value of x grows to the degree that the autonomous role of Israel diminishes, until the point where it offers only its territory to an American intervention force, at which point Israel is minimally an intrinsic asset and maximally an extrinsic one. Conversely, the value of y grows to the extent that one includes in it higher and higher stages in the scale of services rendered; this implies that the value of y is congruent with the accumulated value of services (accumulated, because each stage includes, as we sug-

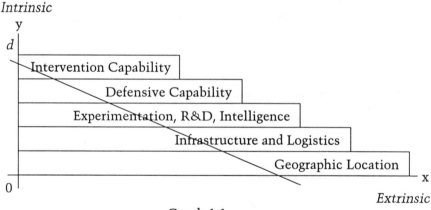

Graph 1.1
Ladder of Services Attributed to Israel

gested above, the inferior ones). In other words, the more Israel is considered as participating in the American intervention force by providing its territory, next its infrastructure, next its logistics, next contributing to the defense of this force, and finally launching joint operations with it, the more Israel rises in stages toward the idea of intrinsic asset. The value of y is maximal if the United States, without itself intervening, counts on Israeli coercion or deterrence.

To illustrate our point, let us refer to the example of Iran. During World War II, Iran was an extrinsic asset to the allies in their war against Germany. Consequently, Shah Reza's endorsement of the use of his territory by the allies was a secondary matter; moreover, when this endorsement was not forthcoming, Reza was simply cast aside. Later, in the 1970s, when his son was in power, Iran's y value (as an intrinsic asset to the United States) in the Gulf region was relatively high (Iran then being considered the "policeman" of the Gulf). But when set against the Soviet Union, Iran's y value was not as high: Iran was, in this situation, an extrinsic asset of the United States (a higher x value) because of American observation posts pointed toward Soviet territory and because of Iran's minimal military capacities against the Soviet Union.

It cannot be deduced from the foregoing, however, that y is inversely proportional to x, yielding the equation $y = f(1/x)$. Indeed, this would give an infinite value to one of the variables while the other tended toward zero, and this is clearly not the case. To simplify greatly, that is, by according each nonaccumulated stage the same weight a, and assuming a maximum number b of stages, we would obtain the linear equation $y = b(a-x)$ represented by a straight line D. On this line, a is the parameter representing the maximal value that x can attain when y tends toward zero (that is, the "value" of Israel's geographic location for the United States); and b is the multiplying coefficient of a when the top stage is reached (that is, when x tends toward zero and when y reaches the value ab, that is, the maximal accumulated value of the services Israel can render).

It must be emphasized that the above corresponds to a formalized representation of the strategic asset doctrine only if we assume that y and x simultaneously have positive values (implying that y is less or equal to the maximum ab, and that x is also less or equal to a). This assumption is necessary because the services attributed to Israel oscillate between the maximal theses of extrinsic asset and intrinsic asset, that is, are located in the quarter delimited by the two axes Ox and Oy. It would be interesting, however, to ask what a negative value for y or x would mean. We shall consider this point further on.

Let us also note that the authors have a tendency to identify Israel with the top stage (a maximal y or intrinsic asset) and to avoid reducing that state to an extrinsic asset (maximal x but minimal y). Thus, when they speak of Israel's contribution to an American intervention force, they always go beyond the stage of Israel's geographic location and highlight its other stages (infrastructure, ability to defend the intervention force itself). The Ox axis would constitute the pole they would most seek to move away from in order to come closer to Oy. But in this case, one might ask why they do not adhere more closely to the ascending axis constituted by Oy. Why do they sometimes see fit to detach themselves from it, even slightly, when, as we have seen, exaggeration is not the least of their failings? The reason is that the arguments of these authors, in order to be credible, must often take into account the realities of the moment. At the beginning of the 1980s, these realities included the establishment of the Rapid Deployment Force (RDF) and the administration's efforts to find bases and facilities for it in Southwest Asia. The defenders of the strategic asset doctrine thus had to position themselves on this new agenda, in order for Israel not to be excluded to the benefit of other countries (such as Egypt or Saudi Arabia), making Israel strategically useless. It was therefore mandatory to elaborate, for the first time in detail, the services that Israel could render to an American intervention force, and more precisely, to the RDF.

For the strategic asset doctrine, the idea of Israel as an extrinsic asset is better than that of an Israel no longer recognized as an asset at all. Only by integrating Israel into the RDF project could the authors profit conceptually from the advantages that only Israel was supposed to offer: not only a better geographic location but also superb facilities, excellent maintenance, and an unmatched aptitude to assure the RDF's defense. In other words, only by accepting the undesired idea of extrinsic asset could they hope to climb the rungs up to the stage of intrinsic asset. If American leaders officially and publicly accepted the use of Israeli facilities, Israel would then enjoy a strategic status that was certainly intermediate, but in any case tangible, and preferable to a maximal glorification that could in fact be no more than lip service.

The Political Implications

While up to now we have centered our attention on the services rendered by Israel thanks—and thanks only—to its geographic position and its military capabilities, we must now examine the political and policy implications which logically flow from these.

The Exclusiveness of Israeli-American Ties

If the exponents of the strategic asset doctrine do not hesitate to praise the services that Israel would render to the United States, it is because they base these services on the idea of Israeli-American identity, that is, on the indestructible ties that bind Israel to the West and to the United States. Israel, as civil society or as government, is considered a permanent friend of the United States; one cannot conceive its leaving the latter's sphere of influence or having with the Americans no more than a "temporary convergence of interests" (Indyk et al. 1983:13).

To emphasize the nature of the relationship between the two countries, the authors insist on their specificity and their exclusive character. Indeed, if Israel is to play a role in the Middle East, the other countries of the region must not enjoy ties of the same nature. The countries in question are, of course, those reputed to be friends of the United States, since the gulf separating anti-American regimes from Israel does not even need to be pointed out. For the strategic asset doctrine, the association of pro-Western states of the Middle East with the United States belongs only to the ephemeral order of "instrumentality" whereas Israel's association belongs to the realm of durable "identity." Israel is seen as "virtually a U.S. outpost in a dangerous sea of Mideast states" (Cline 1980:172, 187). For example, the countries of the Persian Gulf, unlike Israel, are not "organic components of the West" (Churba 1980:358). According to the Committee on U.S. Interests in the Middle East, there can be no "moral equivalency" between Israel, "a proven, valuable, democratic friend and ally of the United States," and its Arab enemies (*New York Times* advertisement 2/26/92; 3/5/92). It must be pointed out that this committee, constituted in February 1992 to protest against President Bush's policy toward Israel in the peace process and his refusal of a loan guarantee for $10 billion requested by Israel in order to integrate the ex-Soviet Jewish immigrants, comprised about 40 public figures who had formerly been members of Congress or had occupied high positions in the State Department or the Pentagon, among them Elliott Abrams and Alan Keyes, former Assistant Secretaries of State, John Lehman, former Secretary of the Navy, Richard Perle, former Assistant Secretary of Defense, and Eugene Rostow, former Under-Secretary of State.

In order to explain the doubtful character of pro-Americanism in the region, the authors refer to Islam, Arabism, or nonalignment and to the Arab regimes' fear of being seen as cooperating with American "imperialism" (Churba 1980:356–357; Handel 1983:81; Indyk et al. 1983:13). This applies to all the states of the region except Egypt (Indyk et al. 1983:17; Spiegel 1983:52). Robert Tucker, a well-known figure of American conservatism who took part in Ronald Reagan's electoral campaign as a foreign policy adviser, adds the following point, concerning the case of Saudi Arabia: "Destitute of the sinews of power save for one, surrounded on all sides by hungry wolves, increasingly dependent on foreign workers to run its economy and on foreign mercenaries to make up its armed forces, the Saudi regime is afraid of its own shadow—and not without reason" (Tucker 1981:35). Thus, states that, for reasons of ideology or internal insecurity, hesitate to display their positive attitude toward American strategic interests, or are ashamed or fearful of doing so, cannot constitute reliable assets. To supply arms to such countries is, as the Iranian example showed, dangerous for the regimes concerned, for the United States, and for Israel (Churba 1980:355).

By comparison, Israel would be, for the United States, "the most dependable ally a country could possibly have" (Glick 1982:158). Its democratic regime is a guarantee of stability and "predictability" (Handel 1983:81; Rosen 1982:4). Agreements with Israel, "unlike those with other countries in the area, will not be precipitously reversed" (Spiegel 1980:408). Moreover, a general consensus at all levels exists there regarding the pro-American orientation, whoever may be the leaders of the major parties and whatever governmental coalitions are in power (Cline 1980:187). During the era of East-West competition, the same consensus existed among the Israelis concerning their readiness to support "a strengthening of the United States' role in the region, an enhancement of the U.S.' ability to deter and, if need be, to defeat Soviet aggression" (Rosen 1982:4). Thus, for all the authors who promote the strategic asset doctrine, there is, between Israel and the United States, not only a community of values but also a community of strategic interests (Churba 1977:15, 29; Handel 1983:82; Indyk et al. 1983:13).

Several remarks need to be made regarding this affirmation of the community of values and interests between the two countries. First of all, while the authors insist, as we have seen, on Israel's attachment to American values, they are nevertheless loath to use what would be the reciprocal argument, that is, to explain the necessity of American support to the Jewish state by these same values. This attitude is symbolized by Tucker (1981:32) when he refuses to base the ties between the United States and Israel on a "moral commitment" of the former toward the latter, because that would imply Israeli vulnerability and dependence, and consequently Israel's inability to defend Western interests. The other authors, even when they cite U.S. moral attachment to Israel as one of the foundations of the special relationship between the two countries, prefer to give priority to the fact that the United States must support Israel because it is in its strategic interest to do so. The fear exists of a conflict between the idea of Israel as a "moral burden" for the U.S. and that of Israel as a strategic asset. The doctrine has a manifest tendency to "instrumentalize" Israel.

Second, the idea of a community of interests leads us inevitably to raise the question of possible Israeli-American divergences. One must, in this regard, distinguish between two possibilities. The first would consist in Israeli reservations about rendering one or another service to Washington. An example is provided by Tel Aviv's lack of enthusiasm toward the Reagan administration's wish, expressed in late 1983, for a more active Israeli intervention policy in Lebanon to support the American contingent, which was then experiencing difficulties in Beirut. The second possibility would be, conversely, an American reservation about Israeli military intervention in the Middle East. And here, of course, the examples abound since 1967. How can we situate the arguments of the strategic asset doctrine with respect to these two possibilities?

The first possibility, that is, the possible Israeli reservations about its "instrumentalization" by the United States, seems to occur to the exponents of the doctrine only rarely, and then indirectly and defensively. Spiegel, in an article written with Gerald Steinberg, denies, for example, considering Israel "in its relation with Moscow . . . as a proxy for Washington   Israel contributes to Western security *in the process of guaranteeing its own security and survival*" (Steinberg and Spiegel 1987:41, authors' emphasis; also Lakoff 1987:86). Churba (1980:358–59), after having denied considering Israel as "a surrogate or proxy" of Washington, recognizes that "Israel's sensitivity to casualties" constitutes a legitimate limitation of its role as a "military partner" of the United States. But since strategic cooperation between the two countries has an essentially deterring effect, "the outbreak of hostilities" is improbable. Generally, however, the authors, including Churba himself in other writings (1977:34), do not express such hesitations.

The second possibility, that is, American reservations about Israeli activism, is even more strongly denied or rather refused by the authors. When Israel makes use of its military superiority in the region, it is not because of "militarism," but rather to assure its survival and defend the "true" interests of the United States. And if disagreements were to break out on this subject with the American administration, these would not be real divergences of interest; the responsibility for them would lie with Washington. The exponents of the doctrine of strategic asset thus find themselves closer to the Israeli position than to that of their own government. If, as William O'Brien, professor of Political Science at Georgetown entreats (1982:98), the Americans finally decide to understand that "*their* security and the security of the Free World are threatened by the PLO and Syria in Lebanon, for example, they may be more tolerant of Israeli 'militarism.' "

If we were now to place the possible reservations of each country regarding the activism of the other on a continuum from intrinsic asset to extrinsic asset as presented above, we would obtain the results shown in figure 1.2, below.

To interpret this figure, let us first point out that the correlations between categories must be read vertically and that each line (indicated by a Roman numeral) contains the two poles of a single category. As we go from the center toward the pole of Israel as an intrinsic asset (I), the degree of Israeli activism (III) grows while Israeli-American cooperation (II) diminishes. When Israeli activism reaches its maximum, it may give rise to reservations by the United States (V), due to fear for American interests in the region. But if, on the contrary, it is American activism that grows (IV), it is because Israel is considered more and more like a mere extrinsic asset (I): the United States utilizes ("instrumentalizes") Israel perfectly, asks precise services of it and expects them to be carried out, even to the detriment of Israel's own interests. This maximal pole of American activism (IV) corresponds, of course, to Israeli reservations (V). The maximal strategic coordination between the two countries is located in the central area, halfway between the two ideas of intrinsic

Israeli Overflow	Intrinsic Asset	(I)		Extrinsic Asset	U.S. Overflow
Nil	Minimal	(II) STRATEGIC COORDINATION Maximal		Minimal	Nil
Maximal		(III) ISRAELI ACTIVISM Medium		Minimal	Nil
Nil	Minimal	(IV) U.S. ACTIVISM Medium			Maximal
U.S. Reservations		(V)		Israeli Reservations	

Figure 1.2
**Israel as an Asset for the United States
and Israeli-American Cooperation**

and extrinsic asset (I), that is, at the meeting point between Israeli activism (III) and American activism (IV) of medium intensity.

Figure 1.2 allows us to take another step in our analysis. It will be noted that the poles representing reservations on the part of one of the two countries (V) and maximal Israeli (III) or American (IV) activity, "overflow" the limits of the idea of asset (I) and minimal strategic coordination (II). The reason is that intrinsic Israeli activism may "overflow" to such a degree that the United States may find that Israel risks losing its characteristics that cause it to be an asset. Starting with a certain maximum, what had been an intrinsic asset may turn into a burden and become dangerous. Conversely, if American activism in the region is pursued at Israel's expense and in spite of Israeli reservations, here again the Jewish state has become a burden for the United States.

The overflow at the two extremes may now be incorporated into graph 1.1 shown above. In graph 1.2, the overflow of Israeli activism beyond the idea of intrinsic asset, into the area of "danger" for American interests where Israel becomes a burden, is located in the x'Oy quarter. It should be noted that this is "verified" in the equation we examined above, $y = b\ (a\text{-}x)$, because when y exceeds a certain value ab, x then assumes a negative value. As a concrete example, we may take former Defense Minister Ariel Sharon's strategic design in the early 1980s, which suggested the establishment of a barrier between the United States and the region by an Israel that had become the only regional power. Sharon's "adventurism" is so marked that the risk of negative effects for American interests becomes too great.

Considering now the other extreme, an "overflowing" American activism would reach the $y'Ox$ quarter; it is now y that takes on a negative value. This is the case when the United States can no longer use Israel because the latter no longer wants to be used or cannot be used any longer. It is possible to imagine two hypotheses in which American activism provokes Israeli reservations or refusal: first, the case in which the American armed forces want to use the Israeli territory or facilities without taking Israel's interests into consideration (territory as military staging ground); and second, the opposite case, in which Washington, seeking a rapprochement with

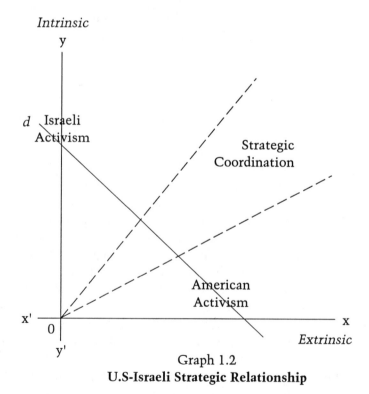

Graph 1.2
U.S-Israeli Strategic Relationship

the Arabs, puts pressure on Tel Aviv to withdraw from the occupied territories (territory as political staging ground). While the first case is improbable and constitutes no more than a logical hypothesis implied by the idea of extrinsic asset, the second case has at certain times since 1973 been close to reality.

Two remarks must be made in conclusion. First, the authors, as we have seen above, refuse to admit this idea of overflow. Further, it is clear that these divergences and mutual reservations concern above all the Israeli-Arab conflict and the problem of its settlement. It is to that conflict that we now turn.

The Israeli-Arab Conflict and the Idea of Strategic Asset

It will have been noted up to now that the idea of Israel as an asset is inseparable in many ways from the Israeli-Arab conflict. If, for the United States, Israel possesses such a well-developed infrastructure, enjoys such a strong military capability (defensive and offensive), and has such a great experience of weapons and intelligence, this is no doubt "thanks" to the situation of conflict that pits Israel against several states in the region. Naturally, the exponents of the asset doctrine will refuse to admit that they seek to manipulate the conflict or exacerbate it in the aim of strengthening a "fortress Israel" in the service of the United States. But it is nonetheless true that, even while making this overly general assertion, they will seek to protect the congruence between their faith in this fortress and their judgments about the development of the conflict, the attempts to settle it, and its effect on the very idea of strategic asset. There is very likely a structural relation between the conflict and the idea of asset, and we must now elucidate it.

Let us begin with the effect of the conflict on Israel's strategic role. This question is the object of a debate between the defenders of the asset idea and those who believe that Israel is a burden. For the latter, the conflict, even if it has contributed to turning Israel into a military fortress, has nonetheless had unfavorable consequences for the United States. The Arabs, although they too can make of the conflict an opportunity to learn modern warfare, will nevertheless blame Washington for the increase in Israeli aggressiveness toward them. They might, by reaction, choose to distance themselves from the United States. As we shall see in the following chapter, the critics of the asset doctrine do not understand how one can call for the promotion of American-Israeli strategic cooperation if the pro-

American countries that this cooperation is supposed to assist are offended or weakened by it and if other Arab countries conclude that they must ally with other powers (such as the Soviet Union before its collapse) to ensure their defense.

This argumentation is, of course, refuted by the asset doctrine. Israel's strategic role, and in particular American-Israeli strategic cooperation, cannot, from the point of view of the doctrine, be challenged by what the Arab countries think of it. The "strategic benefits" of cooperation compensate largely for its "political costs." An extension of American-Israeli cooperation would have a minimal marginal cost, because Arab public opinion already holds it as self-evident that Washington is "in league" with Tel Aviv. Furthermore, as Steven Rosen explains, "since the very founding of the Jewish state, the U.S. has played both sides of the street successfully. . . . It is probably even the case that the U.S. has had more rather than less influence with the Arabs exactly because it also has had (most of the time) influence with Israel too" (Rosen 1982:5–6; also Indyk et al. 1983:22–23). Sadat's change of attitude toward the Americans took place in spite, or perhaps even because of, the American-Israeli connection (Spiegel 1983:52).

The defenders of the asset doctrine do recognize that, "in deference to Arab sensitivities," or out of a certain desire for effectiveness, Washington and Tel Aviv must be discreet about the extent of their cooperation (Ibid.; Handel 1983:82; Sicherman 1983:68–69). This is so because the private attitude of the pro-American Arab regimes is thought to be different from their public denunciations (Glick 1982:157). However, other authors such as William O'Brien (1982:97–98) believe that "it would be better to confront the Arab world with the fact of an explicit, permanent U.S.-Israeli alliance." The pro-American Arabs need Washington too much to be able to distance themselves. Whether or not they make up for their public declarations with a more positive attitude in private, they lack credibility when they condemn American-Israeli cooperation. In the opinion of Indyk et al. (1983:23), a responsible power such as the United States cannot allow its policy to be dictated by a logic according to which "the conservative Arabs" wish to be defended, but from "over the horizon," "not from bases on their territory and not from facilities provided by Israel either." To accept this would be a "form of appeasement." These ideas are confirmed, in Spiegel's view (1990–91:16), by the aftermath of the Iraqi invasion of Kuwait in August 1990: "The unprecedented

Saudi willingness to accept American assistance and troops proves that close relations between the United States and Israel will not be a decisive impediment when Arab regimes believe their survival is at stake." Spiegel adds, further on, that discretion in American-Israeli strategic cooperation will always be called for (Ibid.:18).

If, in the eyes of the defenders of the doctrine of asset, the Arabs have pretended to distance themselves from Washington because of the latter's special relationship with Israel, their real motive is different: it is to extract concessions from the United States (Churba 1980:359), particularly in the area of a settlement of the Israeli-Arab conflict. However, we can cite an example in which the Arab conservatives did more than just pretend to condemn the American-Israeli relationship: we are alluding, of course, to their use of the oil weapon during the war of 1973. It is known that the oil embargo brought about an American policy (of which Kissinger was the main architect) that oscillated between threats of intervention against countries of the Gulf and a certain willingness to take their demands into account (Buheiry 1980:13–18). This episode was the occasion, for the defenders of the idea of Israel as asset, to strenuously deny any linkage between the conflict and oil (Handel 1983:84; Tucker 1981:31); this denial was reiterated even more vigorously after the invasion of Kuwait by Iraq in August, 1990. Let us note that this denial operates in only one direction, that is, only to the extent that oil is considered an Arab weapon or asset for the settlement of the conflict. The denial does not occur in the opposite direction, that is, when it is Israel that is called upon as the asset to play a role in the strategic oil zone. There is linkage here, but it is only implicit.

It thus appears that the strategic asset doctrine leads its defenders to exorcise any suggestion that the enduring conflict pitting Israel against its Arab neighbors would transform the former into a liability. If the authors minimize or deny the fact that the pro-American Arab regimes are reluctant to be identified with American-Israeli cooperation, and if they reject the link between the conflict and oil, this is to show the vanity of any attempt to protect American interests in the Middle East at Israel's expense. And it is probably with much bitterness that Spiegel observes: "Countries like Saudi Arabia and Kuwait, which offer friendship but will not cooperate with U.S. defense or diplomatic efforts, are regarded as crucial allies whereas Israel—which offers facilities and services—is pro-

gressively treated as a pariah, a candidate for economic sanctions
and political alienation" (Spiegel 1983:55).

It should be noted that this discussion about the consequence of
the relationship between the Arab-Israeli conflict and the asset idea
concerns only the Arab states that are close to the United States.
The authors are loath to take up the same discussion concerning
anti-American regimes. That these regimes have chosen to break off
with Washington and to ally, for instance, with Moscow, in order
precisely to face an Israel supported by the United States, is not
debated or even admitted by the authors. They are content to state
that the problems of the region and shifting alliances "would have
arisen even if Israel had never existed" (Tucker 1981:31; also Churba 1977:20). Far from being a "particular set of problems, *sui gener-
is*" (W. O'Brien 1982:96) that prevent the protection of American
interests in the Middle East, Israel is generally and indistinctly perceived as being the solution, the permanent key to the protection of
these interests.

If, for the strategic asset doctrine, the Israeli-Arab conflict must
not interfere with American-Israeli strategic cooperation, this
should mean that its settlement is not a priority for American policy. And this is indeed the attitude that the defenders of the doctrine
actually adopt (Churba 1980:354). For Tucker (1981:29, 31), emphasizing Israel's role as a strategic asset for the United States goes
along with "the downgrading of the Arab-Israeli conflict in the scale
of American priorities," for "if Israel represented our most critical
remaining strategic asset in the region, it was foolhardy to press a
course of action that would have the effect of weakening this asset."
W. O'Brien (1982:97), who declares that "the security of Israel and
of the region comes before the resolution of the Palestinian question," also explains that "it would be difficult for serious defense
analysts to agree that the place of Israel in Middle East defense be
held in abeyance until such time as the Arab-Israeli conflict has
been settled to the satisfaction of the Palestinians and their supporters. Obviously, threats to Middle East security and stability
exist today and obviously, they are already being met in substantial
part by Israel, also today."

This type of reasoning is constant over time and manifests itself
each time the administration tries to move toward a settlement.
One of the reasons why the defenders of the doctrine appear to
oppose a settlement is that the process leading up to it would necessarily imply Israeli territorial concessions, and thus a greater vul-

nerability in geographical terms (Handel 1983:84–85). This in turn would lessen "its military value to the United States." The Americans would even be putting their own security in danger if they promised "to guarantee and secure Israel without sufficient defensive depth on the ground" (Churba 1977:16, 104–107). Although the question of withdrawal from the Sinai now has no more than a historical significance, we may note that the authors were not able to prevent themselves from expressing regret that the implementation of this withdrawal would not be accompanied by granting the American forces the right to use the bases of Eitam and Etzion, built on the peninsula by the Israelis; they would have to be destroyed (Churba 1980:360; Spiegel 1980:407; Tucker 1981:35). Geoffrey Kemp even asked in 1980, prior to being named to the National Security Council in the Reagan administration, "whether now is the ideal time for Israeli withdrawals from other occupied territories, just as these assets are growing in value" (1980:74).

The same logic could be verified more than 10 years later, during the period that followed the military intervention against Iraq in 1991. Charles Krauthammer, a *Washington Post* editorialist, accuses the American leaders (1991) of "shouting" the slogan "land for peace" and demanding "that Israel, the only organic American ally in the region (meaning a country that no coup could ever shake from its friendship with the United States), gamble its existence at a conference at which that slogan is to be the centerpiece." A few months later, the new Committee on U.S. Interests in the Middle East, which claims its raison d'être and its public positions to be based solely on American strategic interest, declared: "American officials should not make the dangerous error of underestimating Israel's view of the strategic importance of the West Bank, Gaza and the Golan Heights under present and foreseeable circumstances. . . . It would be unwise for the U.S. to take a country (Israel) now in a position to defend itself, and even to help us in certain regional contingencies, and turn it into a state that relies on the U.S. for its defense" (Statement in *New York Times* 2/26/92; 3/5/92).

In summary, it would seem that the authors give priority to Israel's strategic role and seek to preserve it, come what may, even if this means sacrificing the settlement process. We see this as coherent with the rest of the positions adopted by the doctrine's defenders. If we attempt now to portray the correlations between the idea of asset and conflict, we will obtain figure 1.3 below, which may be compared with the previous one. Just as in figure 1.2, the correlations must be read vertically. Since the authors place themselves within the strategic asset perspective, the extremes represented here constitute implications that they do not admit or seek to avoid. The idea of burden or danger that would result from Israeli "militarism" is of course not accepted. The idea of a comprehensive settlement of the conflict is not attractive because it would mean that Israel is no longer an asset but indeed a burden for the United States. We may add, finally, that we have qualified the idea of extrinsic asset as "political" in order to distinguish it from another usage in the preceding section. In this case, it means above all the American use of territories occupied by Israel as a political staging ground for a rapprochement with an Arab country (as in Kissinger's policy after the 1973 war, for example). Earlier, it meant above all the use of Israeli territory as a military staging ground for an American intervention in the region.

Another clarification is necessary here. The "coherence" between the idea of asset and the conflict, which is troubling in more than one way because it implies taking advantage of a country by the very fact that it is perpetually at war, is not present in all the authors we have consulted. Certain authors, such as Harvey Sicherman (1978:98), are not opposed to a process of settlement if the United States, instead of mobilizing to put pressure on Israel, remains in the background and accepts an "intermediary" role, while of course supporting "Israeli military supremacy." The dissonance is even greater in the case of Glick (1982:152–153), for not only does his position combine the idea of Israel as an asset with withdrawal from the occupied territories and the solution of the Palestinian question, be it in the form of a Palestinian state, but he

Burden	Asset (Strategic) Intrinsic	Asset Political Extrinsic	Burden
Israeli Activism		American Initiative	
Military Adventurism	No Settlement Process	Partial Settlement Process	Comprehensive Settlement Process

Figure 1.3
Israel as Asset or Burden and the Israeli-Arab Conflict

further proposes the establishment of American bases in Israel that would serve both to intervene in "hot spots" in the Middle East and to guarantee the survival of Israel in the framework of a comprehensive settlement of the conflict.

What reinforces the feeling that Glick's position is located outside the logical implications of the strategic asset doctrine is his call for an American guarantee to Israel. If Israel needs to have its survival guaranteed, with American bases, in the framework of a final settlement, can it maintain its own deterrence capability in order to play the role of intrinsic asset? And if its territory is used, because of an autonomous choice by the United States, as a staging ground for military interventions in the Middle East, is Israel's role not reduced to that of a mere extrinsic asset? We shall take up this debate in the next chapter, where we indeed observe that the idea of guarantee, proposed by those who believe that Israel is a liability, is firmly rejected by the defenders of the idea of strategic asset.

Identifying the Threat

The Israeli-Arab conflict thus constitutes the framework within which the doctrine of strategic asset may grow and develop. Nothing, of course, prohibits one from trying to imagine the future of the idea of asset in the hypothetical context of a global settlement, that is, Israel living in peace with its neighbors. But the authors rarely reach this point, perhaps for fear of having to negate the very idea of asset. In any event, the conflict continues and constitutes the permanent condition that gives meaning to their doctrine. This, as we have seen, has implications for the prospect of a settlement and withdrawal from the Arab territories, and so must also imply, for the authors, a certain idea of the nature of the threat against which the Israeli asset is supposed to act in the service of the United States. On the basis of what we have so far discovered, we shall try to identify what, according to the doctrine, is considered a threat.

The hostility between Israel and the Arabs means that Israel considers the Arab states (excepting Egypt since the peace treaty, and pending other such agreements), as enemies, and vice versa. While there is a great disparity in the degrees and forms of the conflict with Israel (ranging from a mere juridical dispute to actual war), depending on the country in question and its geographical distance from the battlefield, Israel's enemies may be radical or moderate states and they may be anti-American, neutralist, or pro-American. In other words, if certain of Israel's enemies can (in the extreme case) be considered as enemies of the United States, others are apparently its friends and others still are neither friends nor enemies. How, then, can one identify the threat against which the Israeli asset is supposed to protect the United States? Can this threat be perceived in the same way in Tel Aviv and in Washington?

For the authors, the threat is first of all the precarious situation of the United States' friends in the Arab world, their unreliability, and their internal societal and political problems. Israel's role would consist of protecting these regimes not only against other, more radical Arabs, but also, perhaps, against themselves, that is, against their own weakness and their own anti-Israeli attitude. It is as if the instability of the terrain on which the pro-American regimes evolve and their antagonism to Israel constituted the real threats to American interests in the Middle East. The question of whether their friendship for the United States protects them against Israel is of course not the authors' first concern. For them, in short, the exclusiveness of the role and place of Israel should lead the United States to adopt the Israeli perception of what constitutes common interests and the regional threat: the enemy of Israel cannot be a true friend of the United States; Washington's interests cannot be different from those of Tel Aviv.

Concerning those states that are not considered friends of the United States, the exponents of the doctrine of strategic asset—who are writing, it should be recalled, mainly in the context of East-West competition—tend spontaneously to see them as under Soviet influence. They no doubt inflate the influence of the USSR and succumb, as L. Carl Brown would put it (1984:212–213), to the "syndrome" of attributing all the troubles of the Middle East to the manipulative ill-will of an outside power. This inflation is related to a certain reductionism regarding the dynamics of the region; the authors ignore the intrinsic Arab causes that could have facilitated the perceived Soviet influence. Two reasons may help to explain the authors' insistence on Soviet aggression and the reductive role of instrument or mere surrogate they assign to the Arab regimes. First, when American authors—moreover, conservative ones—are addressing other Americans, they have no other ideological alternative: Norman Podhoretz (1980:348–351), editor of _Commentary_, is representative in this regard. Secondly, coherence and the inflation of the Israelis' strategic role impose, as it were, the recourse to the Soviet danger. Spiegel confirms this interpretation after the fact when he states (1990/1991:21) that "the prime impact of the end of the Cold War as it affects U.S.-Israeli relations has been to rob Americans of a missionary focus."

Although the majority of the authors tended, during the Cold War, to minimize the intraregional threats and integrate them into the threat originating from outside the region instead of distinguishing them, Robert Tucker, for one, does not fail to tackle the issue. Writing ten years before the American intervention in Iraq, he analyzes the Carter doctrine promulgated in January 1980, which expressed American determination to intervene if an "outside force" attempted to take control of the Gulf region. Tucker (1981:29) notes that this doctrine does not reply to the problems posed by "the threat to American interests that might arise from forces *inside* the Gulf" (our emphasis). In this regard Tucker makes an interesting distinction between the most serious danger and the most probable one: since the Carter doctrine "was directed only to the Soviet Union, though not to the states of the Gulf, it addressed the more serious threat to access while leaving in abeyance the more likely threat to access" (Ibid.:30). In another passage (Ibid.:31), Tucker, well known for his "tough" anti-Soviet stance, adds: "In fact, much of the erosion of Western interests in the Gulf in the 1970s had little if anything to do with the Soviet Union but had been the result of a misguided American and Western policy of appeasing the Arab states."

With Tucker, we practically have a recognition of the Arabs as autonomous actors. Whether they are pro-American or not is of little importance. What is important is that all the Arab regimes belong to another camp, or rather another world, which is not that of Israel or the United States. These regimes, whatever their political orientation, thus constitute the threat that Israel confronts and can further confront successfully. Although the other authors are not as explicit as Tucker about the relation between the notions of Soviet threat and Arab threat, we believe they share the same perspective and the same logic.

These reflections, which minimize the role of the Soviet threat even when East-West competition was the prevailing environment, are more relevant still to the current situation in which this competition is a thing of the past. It is likely that for the defenders of the idea of strategic asset, intraregional threats, such as the "Arab-Muslim" one, still require a strategic role for an Israel capable of confronting them. For Spiegel (1990–1991:17), the end of the Cold War by no means abolishes the necessity of American-Israeli strategic cooperation to counter "the spread of Islamic fundamentalism"; but it means that from now on "the United States and Israel have the same regional adversary: radically anti-Western Arab states." The position adopted in February 1992 by the Committee on U.S. Interests in the Middle East is even stronger: "As friendly as the United States is with many Arab states, when it comes to the Arab-Israeli conflict, the United States must be squarely on the side of the Israelis." This is so because "American support for freedom, democracy and Western values over totalitarianism, tyranny and anti-Western ideologies should be the rule for U.S. policy, including in the Middle East" (Statement in *New York Times* 2/26/92).

We may ask, finally, whether the role attributed to Israel in acting against the threats described here does not involve contradictory implications in the final analysis. Indeed, in the majority of cases in which the authors attribute to Israel the merit of having struck hard blows against "radical" forces of states (the PLO, Syria or Egypt) or defended pro-American regimes (Lebanon, Jordan), we may legitimately ask whether Israel was not itself the cause of the problems it contributed to resolving. This is not the place to express doubts about the veracity of any given contribution at a given moment (such as during the Jordanian crisis of September 1970), but rather to observe that many "problems" that Israel is reputed to have resolved originated in the Israeli-Arab conflict or in Israeli actions themselves. If Soviet influence gained so much strength in Syria and Egypt after the 1967 war, was this not due to the victory of the Israeli strategic asset in this war? If the Palestinian movement almost succeeded in overturning the Hachemite kingdom between 1967 and 1970, and if it was a factor in the Lebanese civil war, was that not also a result of the Israeli victory of 1967, the multiple little military "victories" of Israel's reprisals beyond its borders and, going back further in time, the nonsolution of the refugee problem and the Palestinian national question since 1948? If Syria sought to intervene in Lebanon or Jordan and was able to do so, was this not largely for reasons linked to the Israeli-Arab conflict? In other words, do Israel's actions not constitute, precisely, the very threat against which it must, at a later stage, protect the United States?

The authors remain silent, of course, about these possible chains of causation . . .

Conclusion

What conclusions may be drawn from this examination of the services attributed to Israel and their explicit or implicit implications for the idea of strategic asset? Or more precisely, what are the coherence and the function of this doctrine?

Most of the authors articulate their position with a great show of coherence, but they pursue it to the point of exaggeration and simplification. This is because the idea of strategic asset appears to require a certain exclusiveness; once it has been affirmed, it cannot coexist with any other thesis. This exclusive character causes the authors to extend the role of Israel to a field much larger than the Israeli-Arab conflict; to attribute to the Israeli army qualities without equal in the Middle East and even in the rest of the world; to deny to any other Middle Eastern actor the possibility of being or becoming an asset for the United States, and even to consider such actors a threat and to argue as if the continuation of the Israeli-Arab conflict were preferable to the loss of asset status for Israel.

However, this exclusiveness, when taken to the extreme, leads the authors to ignore or at least deny Israel's share of responsibility in the region's political or military developments that are detrimental to American interests. Generally speaking, we may say that questions such as the contradiction among these interests depending on whether they are short-, middle- or long-term, the primacy of the military or the diplomatic instrument, the reasons (relative to Israel) for the instability of certain Arab regimes and the precarious nature of Arab-American relations—are questions that are hardly ever raised explicitly. The authors seem to answer them by preferring the solidity of Israel's strategic rock to the slippery terrain of politics; by relying on the persuasive force of the military instrument rather than the weakness of diplomatic argument; by favoring short-term certainty over deceptive and unpredictable circumstances of the distant future; and by considering that Arabs who take distance from Washington cannot really have any legitimate complaints against the Americans . . .

The logic of the idea of strategic asset also supposes, on the part of the authors, the belief in (or desire for) the maintaining of such a state of instability and weakness in the Arab world, and such a high degree of militarization of Israel, that even the latter would probably be uncomfortable with these conditions and with their long-term implications. One champion of Israel (Wildavsky 1977:7), for whom the United States' support to the Jewish state is essentially the result of a moral and cultural identity between the two countries rather than of any military role Israel may play, does not hesitate to accuse, in the following terms, the defenders of the doctrine of strategic asset:

> Some people, perhaps too friendly to Israel for its own good, view Israel as strategically important, thus constituting ipso facto a vital American national interest. . . . Israel becomes a strategic interest by providing the United States with bases for its troops and nuclear weapons. With friends like this, however, Israel would need few enemies, saving itself, so to speak, only to become an occupied country. The rationale for its very existence—the struggle for cultural identity and independent national life—would be lost in its defense.

Pushed to the extreme, the idea of Israel as a strategic asset would thus carry within it its own negation. A question then arises: if the idea of being an asset is so fraught with risks for Israel over the long term, why do authors who consider themselves friends of Israel, and why do Israeli leaders in their contacts with Washington continue to celebrate the idea of asset? In other words, what is the function of this idea in their argumentation?

It seems to us that the essential function of the doctrine of strategic asset is to constitute a counterweight to the idea of dependence. The importance of the military and economic aid the United States now furnishes annually to Israel need hardly be stressed. The same goes for support in the political and diplomatic areas. In general, the donor (as well as the observer) might expect that such a situation would lead to a state of indebtedness, a certain loss of autonomy in political decision-making on the part of the dependent state and its alignment with the protecting great power. We know that this is not the case in American-Israeli relations, for it is often the United States that aligns itself with Israeli positions regarding the Middle East, and there are some American authors who condemn their own administration's attempts to put pressure on Israel. Our purpose here is not to seek the causes of this phenomenon, which are complex and variable over time, but rather to understand their ideological justification or legitimation. Here is where the idea of asset plays an important role.

If Israel renders immeasurable services to the United States, the ideas of dependence and indebtedness undergo a total reversal. According to the doctrine, it is not Israel that depends on a few billion dollars annually—an insignificant sum for a power like the

United States—but rather the United States that depends on Israeli services. The natural conclusion is that pressure on Israel is ill-advised and Israeli concessions in the conflict or on the Palestinian question would be mistaken and even dangerous.

This refusal of the implications of the idea of Israeli dependence on the United States is so strong that the authors go to great lengths, at each new stage of the Middle East situation, to find the appropriate argumentation most favorable to Israel. Prior to 1973, this meant, above all, emphasizing the role Israel played against Soviet intervention in the war of attrition over the Suez Canal and against Syria in the Jordanian crisis of September 1970. After the 1973 war, the argumentation became somewhat harder to develop because of the difficulties then experienced by the Israeli army. It is significant, in this regard, that less than a year after the October war, Tucker (1975:41), who goes beyond most authors in his awareness of the implications of the twin ideas of asset and dependence and who, no longer able to defend the former as vigorously as before, nor admit the latter (because of the state of indebtedness that flows from it), came to propose an Israeli nuclear strategy in order precisely to establish limits "to a dependent relationship that is ultimately in the interests of neither state."

Little by little, however, with the concluding of the disengagement agreements on the Egyptian and Syrian fronts at Kissinger's initiative, and with the diminishing pressure for a settlement of the Israeli-Arab conflict, the idea of the Israeli asset found its defenders again. It was once again possible for the advocates of the doctrine to attribute to Israel, if only timidly, a role in defending American oil interests. Later still, with the fading of the idea of the Arab oil weapon (that is, the weakening of the pro-American oil-rich regimes), the Iranian revolution and the Soviet intervention in Afghanistan, the idea of strategic asset regained its former vigor. It was possible to emphasize Israel's stability and its potential role in the defense of the oil regimes and the prevention of Soviet interventionism. From this flowed the appeal not to overarm deeply unstable Arab regimes, such as Saudi Arabia, and not to seek a solution to the Palestinian question, which was denied the status of being the main cause of instability in the Arab world.

Another stage was reached when the Rapid Deployment Force was placed on the American agenda. The authors now had to elucidate the advantages Israel could offer to the RDF. This made it possible, as we indicated at the end of the previous section, not only to preserve the idea of asset, but also to pave the way for several important practical advantages for Israel. A prepositioning of American arms in Israel was the equivalent of an instant airlift toward that country in the event of an Israeli-Arab war. Israeli facilities for the RDF could also bring about joint maneuvers, that is, supplementary training for the Israeli army; these facilities would have to be developed qualitatively and quantitatively to satisfy American needs, which would mean another appreciable gain for the Israeli army (Indyk et al. 1983:6).

The Iraqi invasion of Kuwait and the war that followed under American leadership did not, to say the least, glorify Israel's strategic role. The invasion of Kuwait could be taken to mean that Israeli deterrence had failed. The military operations of January-February 1991 against Iraq could be seen as meaning that Israel was indebted to the United States rather than the opposite. But with the end of the war, the doctrine of strategic asset (symbolized by the aforementioned Committee on U.S. Interests in the Middle East) could stress anew the importance of Israel's strategic role. However, new challenges were to put the asset doctrine on the defensive: the collapse of the Soviet empire and the initiation of the peace process in Madrid in October 1991.

2 | A Doctrine of Israel as a Burden?

Opposite to the strategic asset doctrine is that of Israel as a burden to the United States. We shall now rapidly explore the main arguments of this thesis before observing that it is more fruitful, for understanding the terms of the debate, to focus on the study of the arguments in favor of granting an American guarantee to Israel.

From the Idea of Burden to the Idea of Guarantee

The idea of burden suggests that Israel hinders the development of American interests in the Middle East, either because it is perceived as too "adventurist" or because it is considered politically weak—even if militarily strong—or again, because it is perceived as condemned in the long term to lose its military superiority. We shall see how, nearly perfectly parallel with the doctrine of asset, certain authors go about establishing that Israel is a liability for the United States.

For former Assistant Secretary of State Parker Hart, writing in 1972 (quoted in Reich 1977:425–426), Israel

> offers no substitute and is not at the present time a contributor to area stability. Militarily powerful as it now is and may yet become, its strength can no more be at the service of the United States or NATO than would be that of an Arab country. In case of an East-

West war, Israel, for reasons of geography and profound interest in the fate of Soviet Jewry, would have to seek neutrality. Its gunsights are directed for the foreseeable future toward hostile Arab societies with which it is strongly in the strategic interest of NATO and America to have at least tolerable relations. . . . The point is emphasized because Israel is so often referred to in election hyperbole as 'America's best ally in the Middle East'. To the broad American public this is portrayed as a welcome readiness of Israel to fight for America's cause in the Middle East, without need of American troops. This concept was a distortion of realities.

Writing more than ten years later, Anthony Cordesman (1984:979), defense specialist who had served in the State Department and the Pentagon, noted that the American-Israeli strategic relationship in the 1980s

> is militarily purposeless and hopelessly unstable without an Arab-Israeli peace, and any U.S. use of Israel as a base of USCENTCOM forces would do the West far more harm than good. The end result of any U.S. use of Israel to deal with a contingency in any Arab state would be to destroy the legitimacy of all Arab regimes friendly to the U.S. and to kill any U.S. hope of strategic partnership with the Gulf states.

George Ball, former Under-Secretary of State, also replies to the arguments of the asset doctrine. "First," he writes (1984:128–130),

> the United States cannot cooperate militarily with Israel without irreparably damaging its relations with the Arab states. . . . Second, Israel's physical limitations deny its utility as a significant strategic asset. . . . Quite clearly, it is Israel, not the United States, that would benefit from an alliance relation . . . Third, there is no way Israeli military power can effectively be deployed beyond its own immediate neighborhood . . . Fourth, the proposal for a military alliance with Israel misses the central strategic point: the real menace to the Middle East is not external aggression but the political fragility of most of the Arab nations and their vulnerability to subversion and destabilization. . . . Fifth, advocates of an alliance with Israel make much of the contention that Israel provides America with invaluable intelligence information and the results of combat experience in disclosing the weaknesses and capabilities of our advanced weapons. Yet, isn't that the least the Israelis can do?

More recently still, Harry Shaw, former head of the military assistance branch of the Office of Management and Budget, wrote, under the revealing title "Strategic Dissensus" (1985/86:125): "Exaggerated claims of Israel's capabilities and willingness to act as a strategic surrogate for America in the Middle East . . . confuse and distort the differences in the two countries' interests, responsibilities, and capabilities and hamper America's efforts to protect its interests when Israeli actions threaten them." Shaw writes further (ibid.:140) that "the intimate relationship between the United States and Israel implied by 'strategic partnership' undercuts close U.S. relations with friendly Arab states and inhibits the U.S. ability to respond to opportunities for improved relations with other Arab countries, such as Syria and Iraq." For Cheryl Rubenberg (1986:2) the U.S.-Israeli relationship "has impeded the efforts of the United States to further the stability of pro-American governments throughout the Middle East and has led to less than optimal conditions concerning American access to markets, raw materials, and investment opportunities."

We conclude this rapid survey with Graham Fuller, a researcher at Rand Corporation and formerly of the CIA, writing toward the end of 1990. Fuller recognizes that the American-Israeli strategic alliance had a meaning during the Cold War as a means of confronting the Soviet Union, adding, however, that the Iraqi invasion of Kuwait demonstrates the strategic irrelevance of Israel for the United States concerning inter-Arab crises. For Fuller (1990/1991:31–33), "the U.S. strategic alliance with Israel is both an antiquated tool to fashion order and a limited, short-sighted approach to regional crisis." The alliance, when all is said and done, serves "the strategic interests of no one—not America, Israel, or the Arabs."

Here, then, are the major arguments related to the idea of Israel as a burden. We may observe that they are simply the exact opposite of the theses put forward by the asset doctrine; that is, they are mainly negative and do not constitute in themselves an advocacy for any precise policy. Nor would the use of logical deduction allow us to imagine, convincingly, the policy proposals of the defenders of the burden idea, for such reasoning would result in a call to abandon Israel. And although this is indeed a plausible option for some, it is not an acceptable proposition for authors who are members of the Establishment and who gravitate around foreign-policy decision-makers. For these authors, other considerations, which will be made clear below, must be added to the implications of the idea of Israel as burden in order to derive from them proposals for action. A careful reading of their work reveals, perhaps unexpectedly, that a significant portion of their proposals consists of giving Israel one or another form of guarantee. We may note, very rapidly for the moment, that these proposals, whose declared goal is to protect Israel, seek to control it in order to limit the regional damage the Jewish state, as a burden, might provoke.

We think it is appropriate and fruitful to adopt the idea of guarantee as an axis for this chapter. This choice should allow us not only to verify and analyze its complex relations with the ideas of burden, protection, and control, but also, as we shall observe, to discover the terms of the debate—which are interesting both conceptually and in view of the stakes involved—with the asset doctrine. However, before proceeding to analyze these authors' propositions, we must think about the main questions posed by the idea of guarantee. Let us start with the broad definition of guarantee given by Alan Dowty (1974:7): a guarantee is "the acceptance by a state of a commitment to protect—by force unless otherwise specified— another and weaker state's independence, territorial integrity, or other specified attributes." The guarantee thus implies two elements: a promise and an obligation.

As a *promise*, the guarantee is inseparable from the question of whether it requires an official form, a constitutional procedure, a certain solemn character that might convince others of its solidity, its permanence. This is not the place to engage in a juridical study of the relative authority of American guarantees contained respectively in declarations by the executive, executive agreements (or agreements in simplified form), executive agreements endorsed by Congress, and treaties, or of the distribution of authority between the executive branch and the Senate in matters of war, following a constitutionally valid guarantee (Pomerance 1974). What is important here is to note that this juridical discussion raises a primarily political question, that of the credibility of American promises; it is indeed the credibility question that the authors will have to face and answer.

Posing the problem in terms of credibility allows us to situate the question of formalism of commitments in a broader framework. We must realize, indeed, that the constitutional authority of a promise is only one indicator among others of the existence of a commitment toward another country. Even the most valid constitutional form is surely not a sufficient condition, and may not even be a necessary one, to affirm the credibility of a commitment. A commitment is a promise made today regarding what might happen tomorrow. Even the most carefully prepared treaty, covering all the contingencies of the future, remains only an act corresponding to yesterday's and today's interests. It is not terribly difficult, when conditions and interests have changed, to find valid juridical paths of escape to avoid respecting one's earlier commitments (Pelcovits 1976:19–30).

To gauge the solidity of a commitment, one would therefore have to verify other indicators. Among these we may note, following Terry Deibel: physical criteria, of a military nature, such as the stationing of troops in a given country; of an economic nature, such as the dependence of the guarantor state on an important resource of that country (such as oil); or again of a personal nature, such as the presence of one's country's own citizens on the territory; "behavioral" criteria, such as the durable intensity of political interaction between the two countries or the volume of economic and military assistance over a long period of time; or psychological criteria, such as identification by public opinion or a portion of the population with the given country (Deibel 1980:10–11; also Hassner 1966:23; Paul 1973:8–11; Schelling 1960:134ff). Thus, for example, the strength of the U.S. commitment toward Europe did not spring so much from the letter of the Atlantic pact of 1949 as from the fact that the United States was implicated in the affairs of the continent by its dominant participation in the integrated command and by the stationing of its troops.

We know that there is no full-fledged formal treaty binding the United States to the defense of the Jewish state. However, the durable character of several indicators among those we have just cited would suggest that an informal American guarantee is already a reality (Pomerance 1974:13; Huth and Russet 1984). If the conviction of the authors were that such a guarantee already exists de facto, what would their proposals for guarantee change or add? What meaning should be attributed to the appeal to codify relations between the United States and Israel (and conversely, to the refusal by other authors of such a codification)?

Let us now turn to the commitment as an obligation, that is, to its content. The content of a commitment is often determined by the conditions of its granting, but above all by its conditions of implementation. We agree with Deibel (1980:7) that this "is directly related to the character and the specificity of the 'if' and the 'then,' the triggering cause requiring action by the committed party and the response it is pledged to make" (Deibel's emphasis). What are the threatening events that constitute the precipitating cause of the implementation of the guarantee? Is it generalized war? War on a single front? A guerrilla movement from the outside? Internal subversion? Must the threatening event originate from an extraregional power? Or from a local ally of the latter? From anyone, even it is an ally of the United States? Is the response of the guarantor automatic, or is it left to his discretion?

These questions must naturally be transposed and applied to the Israeli situation. But it is also necessary to consider the specificity of this situation: any guarantee of the survival and territorial integrity of the Jewish state must face the problem of the "historic" conflict opposing Israel and the Arabs. Further, because of Israel's occupation of Arab territories and the juridical indetermination of Israeli borders, the guarantee of survival cannot ignore the problem of delimiting the borders and separating what is guaranteed from what is not. As a result, the question of the Israeli-Arab conflict must be at the heart of any guarantee proposal. And since we already know that many of those who consider Israel a burden propose the idea of a guarantee only to pave the way for a settlement and an Israeli withdrawal, we shall begin by centering the discussion on this point of view (which we shall call, for convenience, the proposal of "guarantee linked to settlement" or GLS), before considering other variants of the idea of guarantee.

The Debate over a Guarantee Linked to a Settlement (GLS)

The Idea of GLS

It was during the years 1974–75 that the idea of GLS was proposed and its implications most widely explored, because of the shock inflicted on Israel by the 1973 war and American involvement in the settlement process. For the period prior to 1973, we need only evoke the views of Senator J. William Fulbright who, in August 1970, sought to make an American guarantee to Israel the keystone— rather than a complementary ingredient—of a settlement of the conflict. He proposed that in exchange for a withdrawal from the territories occupied during the 1967 war, Israel obtain an international guarantee from the United Nations and a bilateral guarantee from the United States (*Congressional Record* 8/24/70: 29805). In 1972, the senator was more explicit (1972:147) when he suggested, once again in exchange for an Israeli withdrawal, that the United

States commit itself "to use force if necessary, in accordance with its constitutional processes, to assist Israel against any violation of its 1967 borders, as adjusted, which it could not repel itself."

After the 1973 war, Fulbright (1975:23), who was no longer a senator, returned to the fray and proposed, in an article with a revealing title—"Getting Tough with Israel"—to soften Israeli intransigence regarding the territories by offering "an explicit, binding American treaty guarantee of Israel." But in this post-1973 period, Fulbright was now only one of several personalities who put forward this notion. Among the others were Senators Charles Percy and John Sparkman (Draper 1975:38); Zbigniew Brzezinski, then a professor at Columbia University (Brzezinski 1974:7; Brzezinski et al. 1975:12); John Hargrove (in *Washington Post* 1/14/75); William Quandt, a future member of the National Security Council (Quandt 1975:48); Charles Yost, former Ambassador to the United Nations (Bruzonsky 1976:79); George Ball (1975:6); and William Griffith, professor at M.I.T. As an example, we may cite Griffith (1975:72, 75), who called for a "prompt and decisive" American action to settle the conflict and demanded the signing of a formal military pact with Israel in order to demonstrate that "we would regard an attack on Israel proper as an attack on the U.S. and that we would send American troops to defend Israel . . . But defending its conquests is quite another matter" (see also Battle 1974:117–118).

It should be noted that all these personalities belonged to the core of the American political establishment. Their point of view is confirmed by the content of the then-celebrated Brookings Report on the conditions for peace in the Middle East, published in December 1975 by a study group made up of those who had occupied, or were soon to occupy official functions, such as Yost, Brzezinski, Bowie, and Quandt. However, the idea of a GLS is not limited to this "golden era"; it persists even today and seems to be invoked each time the settlement process implying an Israeli withdrawal returns to the agenda. In this regard we may cite the repeated proposals of George Ball (1977; 1979–80; 1984:127), Richard Rosecrance (1980:35), Harry Shaw (1985/86:141) and Quandt (1988:385–386). Finally, we may quote James Reston (1989), *New York Times* editorialist, who, in the political climate provoked by the Palestinian uprising and the PLO's peace initiative, proposed that the United States grant Israel a security treaty, if they wanted that country to accept the formula of "land for peace."

For the authors who propose an American guarantee in exchange for Israeli withdrawal, the principal motivation is the idea that American interests in the Middle East make it necessary to take Arab demands into account. Depending on the moment when they write, the point is either to prevent a destabilization of the pro-American regimes, a "Balkanization" of the Middle East, a return of the Soviet Union, another war, another oil embargo, or a rift among Western allies (Griffith 1975:72; Bruzonsky 1976:87–88). Under certain circumstances, and in particular during the period 1974–75, the authors consider that Arab frustration provoked by the Israeli occupation has reached a point where they may take combined measures involving a military, economic, and diplomatic linkage. This does not necessarily mean that the authors perceive Israel, in these circumstances, as having lost its superiority, but it does mean that for them, time is not on Israel's side and may lead to considerable dangers (Brzezinski et al. 1975:7–8; Ball 1977:464–465).

Clearly, the promoters of the GLS have no special sympathy for Israel and even criticize its intransigence. If they completely exclude the option of abandoning Israel, it is for reasons of internal politics (the spontaneous pro-Israeli sentiment of the American polity, the pro-Israeli lobby, etc.) and in order to protect American prestige internationally. It is interesting to note that the same authors who see in Israel a strategic burden recognize as a given, as a stable and inevitable state of things, the indestructible attachment of their country to the Jewish state. For these authors, there is already a "long-standing commitment" on the part of the United States toward Israel (Griffith 1975:75); that country already "enjoys such a guarantee," without which it would have collapsed long ago (Brzezinski 1974:9). This de facto guarantee has been established "in a cumulative manner" by official declarations (Ball 1978:22) and has been reinforced by the fact that "our word and even our national honor are involved as completely as they would be by duly ratified treaties" (Fulbright 1972:217). The United States was now "the ultimate guarantor of Israel's security" (Cordesman 1984:943) and the alliance between the two countries would be "unique in American history" and would constitute "by far our strongest and most comprehensive international commitment" (Bergus 1988:203).

For the authors who propose the GLS, this inescapable de facto guarantee manifested by enormous grants of weapons and money and by diplomatic support is not satisfactory because it is not paid for by Israel in return (Ball 1977:468; 1979–1980:246–247). In other words, for them Israel has all the advantages of a guarantee, that is, a real commitment by the United States to come to Israel's support, without having to bear any of the concomitant obligations, i.e., the inherent limits for any protégé and for any object of guarantee (geographical and political limits). That is why the authors see a formalized guarantee as positive. Since they cannot call for the abandonment of Israel, for internal as well as external reasons, these authors believe that by offering a codified American commitment, they can require something in return, that is, a withdrawal from the occupied territories and a solution to the Palestinian problem. The guarantee becomes a compensation, and a conditional one; the formalization makes it a means of pressure and control. When Fulbright proposed an American-Israeli treaty of security, he wrote that the suggestion "is made not in the belief that we would be contracting a new obligation, but, quite frankly, for the purpose of codifying and limiting a de-facto obligation" (1972:217–218) whose uncertain character "appears to have driven Israel to greater militancy and inflexibility in her attitude toward the Arabs" (ibid.:135). The formal guarantee, a means of control, would also make it possible to show that the pressure the United States might wish to exercise on Israel is not the sign of an anti-Israeli attitude but that it is proposed, rather, for Israel's own good. George Ball's article of 1977, which we have already quoted, was entitled: "How to Save Israel in Spite of Herself."

The authors prefer, however, to emphasize the idea of compensation more strongly than that of pressure. They thus try to demonstrate the advantages for Israel of a formalized guarantee. Such a guarantee would "enhance the existing U.S.-Israeli relationship and have the added advantage of making the consequences of any aggression against Israel much more serious" (Brzezinski 1974:9). A formalized guarantee "would constitute a clear sign to the Arabs that we mean business and therefore that they can never destroy or dismantle Israel" (Griffith 1975:75). The existence of this country "within fair and defensible borders" would become a really "vital interest" for the U.S. (Reston 1989). To these formal signs that would enhance the credibility of the guarantee, certain authors have added others: the participation of the (ex-)Soviet Union; the stationing of American troops or American-Soviet troops after the settlement of the conflict (Brzezinski 1974:9; Ball 1979–1980:254).

The credibility of an American guarantee under the conditions evoked above raises the question of its deterrent effect on other parties and in particular the Arabs. The authors seem to believe that the idea of guarantee is dissuasive enough to make the Arabs put an end to their struggle against Israel and even attractive enough—since it is linked to an Israeli withdrawal—to obtain their cooperation. The assumptions they make in this regard are significant. Without totally ignoring the risks inherent in their proposal, they assume that the Arab countries are ready to coexist with Israel (Bruzonsky 1976:85–86); that the GLS model will strengthen the pro-American moderate forces in the region; and that it is in the Soviet Union's interest to contribute to the GLS (Brzezinski et al. 1975:10–13). There is surely a pragmatism in this reasoning and even, as Bruzonsky (1976:86) has written, an "optimism" regarding Arab objectives—one that is not shared, as we will see further on, by those who believe that the real source of deterrence lies in Israel's intrinsic power.

The Refusal of the GLS

It is useful at this point to examine the counter-arguments offered by the opponents of the idea of GLS. We may assume that they would be recruited among Israel's most fervent supporters and the strongest champions of the asset doctrine. The main argument they develop is, paradoxically, the same as the guarantee's defenders: the fact that it is an instrument of control over Israel. But what is a necessity for one side is an object of denunciation for the other. While the proponents of the GLS see control as a desirable objective both for American interests and for Israel (even if it is against the latter's will), the opponents look upon it with disdain. Tucker (1975:35) characterizes the guarantee as "a manipulative device for forcing Israel into a more tractable position." Theodore Draper (1975:42), historian and specialist of international affairs, calls it a "gimmick." For Draper, "the consequences of attempting to impose a one-sided settlement on Israel, covered up by a less-than-convincing guarantee, could be traumatic for both Israel and the United States." Sicherman (1978:91–93) notes that the logic underlying the idea of guarantee justifies its refusal, for "the very process of imposing a settlement and then compensating withdrawal" is motivated by the Arab threat to American interests. This could only "undermine the confidence Israel could repose in a subsequent American guarantee," especially since such a GLS "will not eliminate some of the major dangers to American interests in the Middle East."

For the opponents of the guarantee, the proposal is a substitute for an authentic settlement of the Israeli-Arab conflict (Bruzonsky 1976:74). An American mediation conducted under these conditions would mean that the settlement sought for would consist largely of an arrangement between the United States and Israel and, in the best of cases, of another arrangement as well between the United States and the Arab states. As Draper explains (1975:38–41), if a guarantee "becomes critical to a settlement, the next step is to impose those terms which are agreeable to the guarantor. As a result, it becomes more important for the contending parties to negotiate with the guarantor than among themselves." The result would be that "the Arabs will give as much or as little as they want to give, the United States will in some manner pay off for them, and Israel will get whatever the Arabs and the United States together choose to give." The guarantee, as Tucker notes (1975:36), "presumably opens the way for the return of the occupied territories and the eventual creation of a Palestinian state, though the deeper sources of the Arab-Israeli conflict are expected to persist." Finally, in the words of Allen Lesser (1975:579), an official of the Zionist Organization of America (ZOA), a guarantee, instead of bringing peace, would force Israel to return to the Arabs "the land they lost in a war they started."

In the eyes of the guarantee's opponents, unilateral territorial concessions by Israel are not the only potential danger of a guarantee granted too lightly. For, as Sicherman explains (1978:91), the GLS would also entail risks to Israeli security: "A great power, allied with a small state, will coerce the latter into a less defensible position in order to protect its own interests threatened by a small state's enemies; the small state will then be 'guaranteed' against fatal indefensibility by the full faith and credit of its powerful ally." In the words of Charles Krauthammer (1991), the GLS thus has as its goal to compensate Israel for its "U.S.-imposed weakness." The Jewish state "would be left waving a meaningless guarantee in the face of hostile Arab armies" (Lesser 1975:579) massed all along its shrunken and thus indefensible borders (Tucker 1975:36). As Churba explains (1977:107), the risk of war would increase because "any diminution in the concrete strength on the ground of an ally or other guaranteed power—such as, for example, Czechoslovakia in 1938—only increases by a dangerous factor the propensity of an enemy power to test that guarantee." The GLS would thus result, as well, in heightened Israeli psychological dependence toward the United States (Tucker 1975:37). To assign the defense of the Jewish state to the United States "would smother Israel as it smothered Vietnam," writes Draper (1975:41), while "its will to survive is its veritable guarantee."

One last argument is used by the detractors: what would be the use of a formalized guarantee if, as the promoters of the GLS themselves already emphasize, Israel already enjoyed a de facto guarantee? As Tucker asks (1975:35), if the United States "will not permit Israel to be destroyed, why should an explicit commitment to this effect now prove so important?" Expressing his skepticism about the more constraining character of a formal guarantee, Draper (1975:38, 42) concludes: "When we are told that Israel has, in effect, always had an American guarantee but should get another one, we have a right to wonder whether the proposal can be taken seriously."

Up to now, we have centered our attention on the criticisms formulated against the political implications of the GLS rather than against the conditions for implementing a guarantee as a formal American commitment. Regarding these conditions, the detractors accuse the proponents of not having thought seriously about the "credibility of the guarantee to others" or about "many difficult problems its implementation may be expected to raise" (Tucker 1975:35; Draper 1975:40).

Among these problems, the detractors mention first of all the constitutional obstacles. For Tucker (1975:37), if the guarantee represents a serious commitment, "it must expect to encounter great difficulty in obtaining congressional approval. Certainly, it would not be approved at all unless the Senate knew at the time of ratification what it was approving." For Draper (1975:39–40), it would not be easy, after the experience of Vietnam and Cambodia, to negotiate a detailed treaty that Congress would approve; and "it would be even more difficult to get Congress to declare war for the sole purpose of making good a guarantee."

Moreover, for the detractors, any guarantee is weak unless it is automatic, that is, unless it defines precise measures, particularly of a military order, that the guarantor must take under precise given circumstances. Here, the authors take pleasure in showing the failure of different historical experiences of guarantee, and in particular the failure of what they see as the American "guarantee" made to Israel in 1957 regarding the right of free and innocent passage in the Gulf of Aqaba. They also take pleasure in stressing the vagueness of the conditions attached to the implementation of a GLS and in asking whether the United States would indeed be ready to intervene militarily against the Arabs—that is, in expressing doubts about American determination and deterrent power (Tucker 1975:35–37; Draper 1975:39–40). The detractors' doubts are reinforced by the fact that the idea of guarantee does not involve a significant presence of American armed forces in Israel. In Tucker's view (1975:37), a credible guarantee should involve the deployment of "substantial American forces in and around the territory of the guaranteed state." For Draper (1975:40), a guarantee cannot be effective if it boils down to a stationing of a merely symbolic force of the "trip-wire" type, for such a force "would not be able to defend itself adequately, let alone Israel." An attack against this force, resulting in American casualties, would move public opinion "before we knew how far we wanted to commit ourselves to a real war." A credible guarantee would thus necessitate a force "perhaps as large as the Israeli force." Draper adds: "One shudders at the thought of thousands of American troops . . . stationed permanently in Israel, their logistical bases six thousand miles or more away."

The proponents of the idea of GLS do not pay sufficient attention to the potentially dangerous consequences of a serious guarantee, which is confirmed, for the detractors, by the proponents' overly hasty recourse to the argument of the Israeli army's effectiveness. Draper (1975:38), criticizing Griffith for having stated that Israel should henceforth depend, not only on its own forces but also "partially" on an American guarantee, states: "A guarantee 'in part' is a contradiction; a guarantee is totally effective or it is no guarantee." For Tucker (1975:37), the idea of an authentic American guarantee cannot logically coexist with the idea of Israeli military capability: one can only be the substitute for the other. If not, the guarantee proposal is a fraud, even if unconsciously so. It would be a fraud if Israel, after having returned the occupied territories in exchange for a guarantee, could rely only on its own forces and not on those of the American army.

The Significance of the Debate

What can be made of this debate between proponents and critics of the GLS idea? It is easy enough to observe that the detractors' argumentation regarding the conditions that should be attached to a guarantee consists essentially of counterposing the idea of an absolute, idealized guarantee to the sort actually contained in the

GLS proposal. By placing themselves in the perspective of "all or nothing," they seem to be engaging in a more coherent exercise than the "accommodationist" discourse of the defenders of the GLS— perhaps because the latter are less interested in the precise require- ments of a guarantee to Israel than by the idea—in itself rather vague as well—of a settlement of the conflict. Because of this nec- essary link with the idea of a settlement, it is often difficult to know whether the guarantee proposal aims first at guaranteeing Israeli security or at guaranteeing a settlement, or even at guaranteeing the Arab states against Israeli expansion.

While the detractors are more coherent, however, they are not necessarily more realistic. While they articulate, in opposing the GLS, the requirements of an absolute guarantee, they refrain from actually proposing one. They give the impression of wanting to keep American policy in a passive state, or, in Stanley Hoffman's formu- la (1975:407–408), to "merely provide Israel with weapons without pressing toward a settlement." Such a policy is not always possible, because of the dangers lurking in the Middle Eastern situation (the possibility of new wars and new confrontations with the Soviet Union, or risks of dissension within the Western alliance).

It was precisely because certain political analysts (leaving aside decisionmakers such as Kissinger, architect of the "step-by-step" approach) sought to take these risks into account that they tried, through the GLS idea, to conciliate the inevitable obligation of spe- cial American-Israeli relations with the necessary elements of an American policy toward the Arabs. If these authors, in proposing the GLS, are indeed not very coherent, or do not share a pro-Israeli sen- sibility, at least they advance a substantive proposal when they affirm their wish to guarantee Israel's security in order to facilitate a settlement. We might say that their arguments reply to a different type of coherence whose pragmatic orientation—not necessarily realism—is its essential ingredient.

The detractors, in spite of their undeniable polemical skill, do not propose a real alternative to a policy of passivity toward Israel or to the vague and incommensurable de facto guarantee. Of course, Draper (1975:43) calls for American support to UN Resolu- tion 242 and does not exclude "some form of guarantee as long as the parties concerned wanted it after reaching an agreement among themselves on the substantive issues." And Tucker (1975:38ff) indeed proposes a radical solution when, to prevent a situation in which Israel would be even more dependent on the United States for its survival, he advises Israel to adopt an openly declared nuclear strategy. But these suggestions are addressed more to the Jewish state than to the American administration whose options they are discussing.

To conclude this discussion of the coherence and realism of the idea of GLS, we may note that the detractors justify their attitude with a coherent but rigid system of hypotheses about reality—a system that their attitude cannot but subsequently confirm. Let us take an example. *Hypothesis*: the Arabs cannot be prepared for a compromise with Israel; *action*: Israel and the United States must not, in this case, make concessions to their demands; *outcome*: the Arabs become even less ready for a compromise, which verifies the hypothesis *post facto*, whether it was true or false at the start. In other words, the detractors engage in what Robert Merton (1957:421ff) called "self-fulfilling prophecies." As for the defenders of the GLS, they wager, in an apparently fairly flexible manner, on the dynamic of reality and hope that a policy in accordance with their proposal will bring about a dynamic favorable to American interests; they appear ready to correct their course if their wagers are not verified. We have here, quite probably, the classic opposition between doctrinaires and pragmatists.

It is useful to note that the detractors of the idea of GLS belong to the ranks of those who see in Israel a strategic asset of the United States. There is indeed no doubt that in both cases we see a similar pro-Israeli sensibility and an identical, strongly negative vision of Arabs in general; we see the same confidence in the virtue of arms and in particular Israeli deterrence; the same suspicion of diplomacy and the same fear of a "drift" in American policy—a fear provoked by the tiniest and most insignificant signs. Finally, there is a similar concern not to make Israel have to pay the price of its dependence toward the United States. But in order to express this concern, the argumentation employed adapts itself to the conjuncture. When regional or internal conditions are favorable (as during the 1967–1973 period or during the 1980s), the proponents of the doctrine of asset may go on the offensive and explain that compensation for Israeli dependence resides largely in the services it renders to Washington. When, on the other hand, the conditions are unfavorable to the Israeli strategic role (as after the shock of 1973 or each time the American administration becomes active in the process of settling the conflict), they return to a defensive stance. To justify their refusal of the various proposals for a GLS that locate compensation for Israeli dependence in American control, they are reduced to denouncing the contradictions of these proposals.

What is truly at stake in the debate between defenders and opponents of the GLS thus seems to be the form of compensation for Israeli dependence (Bruzonsky 1976:98–100). In other words, it is not so much the idea of American commitment to Israel that causes disagreement, but rather the state of indebtedness in which Israel is placed vis-à-vis the United States by the guarantee. The detractors cannot, of course, oppose an American commitment if it means continuous support to Israel and the protection of that country in time of need or danger. On the contrary: they did not fail, for instance, to criticize Kissinger for his tardiness in setting up an airlift to Israel during the 1973 war. However, there are varying degrees within the idea of American commitment. Diplomatic support, routine annual economic or military aid, emergency military aid, and direct protection by armed intervention all occupy different levels of support. Regular aid may be justified by the idea of asset, that is, by the role Israel plays for the United States; emergency aid implies on the contrary a state of danger for Israel, that is, a situation where its role in the Middle East cannot be glorified. For those who uphold the asset doctrine, it is obviously preferable that Israel appear to be requiring minimal support and playing a maximal role. That is why they tend to avoid the idea of guarantee and above all that of codified guarantee (which suggests too much Israeli indebtedness) and prefer the argument of American support, which is much more neutral.

A guarantee without the name, an American commitment to Israel, an indestructible link, the absence of a reference to an Israeli counterobligation—is this not the de facto guarantee denounced by the promoters of the GLS as too vague and incommensurable? It is as if the defenders of the asset doctrine not only rejected the implications of a codified guarantee but also perceived the implicit merits of the de facto guarantee too well to lose them by making them explicit. Though it is a condition *sine qua non* of a potential Israeli role in the Middle East, the de facto guarantee must, paradoxically, be kept out of sight in order to make possible the argumentation in favor of the valorization of this role. The respective implications of the ideas of burden and asset, from the perspective of American support to Israel, may be summarized in figure 2.1.

If Israeli indebtedness is the true stake of the debate between defenders and opponents of the GLS, and if we place these two groups on opposite poles, the question we may now raise is whether some authors have proposed variants of the guarantee that are located between the two poles and that succeed in either avoiding or clearly limiting Israeli indebtedness. What type of guarantee do these variants offer to Israel and what type of compensation do they demand in return? Does the balance between what Israel gives and what it receives work, in each case considered, to Israel's favor, and is it likely to satisfy the detractors? It is these variants that we must now consider.

The Variants of the Idea of Guarantee

In this section we will examine the different guarantee proposals other than the GLS. Since the latter is located at the opposite end of the spectrum from the idea of asset, which is itself an extreme pole, we will verify whether these variants have as their object—or at least have the effect—of reducing the distance between the defenders and the opponents of the GLS.

The Guarantee as Moral Commitment

Along the spectrum of guarantee proposals, some are concerned neither with American strategic interests nor with controlling Israel's freedom of maneuver. Instead they are concerned mostly with the survival of Israel and base their argumentation on the necessity of a moral commitment by the United States toward the Jewish state. Professor Richard Ullman, former member of the National Security

Israel, Strategic Burden	*Israel, Strategic Asset*
I. Support	
Pragmatic and Conditional	Doctrinaire and Unconditional
II. Guarantee Linked to Settlement (G.L.S.)	
Proposed	Refused
III. De Facto Guarantee	
Codified to Emphasize Israeli Indebtedness	Kept Implicit to Deny Israeli Indebtedness

Figure 2.1
The Nature of American Support to Israel

Council, and Aaron Wildavsky, professor of political science, are representatives of this point of view. We shall now consider their respective proposals.

Richard Ullman (1975b:21, 27–28) proposes that the United States offer Israel a guarantee similar to the one that binds it to West Germany or to South Korea—a "military alliance" that would involve stationing American troops on Israeli territory. He further suggests that the American guarantee be sealed before the settlement of the conflict while still being linked to it, so that the Israelis feel sufficiently confident and withdraw, "the quo for the quid," from "essentially all of the territory occupied in 1967." Without dwelling on the details of the proposal, we may note that Ullman's placement of Israeli indebtedness in the idea of withdrawal from the occupied Arab territories apparently puts him close to the GLS idea. His proposal seems to differ from it only in that he calls for the permanent stationing of American troops, in order to reinforce the credibility of the U.S. commitment.

Although Ullman's proposal has been refuted by the opponents of the GLS, it only provokes moderate reservations on their part (Draper 1975:38, 43). This is so because Ullman is motivated by considerations that have little to do with those behind the GLS idea. He indeed takes a resolutely pro-Israeli perspective and is more concerned with the protection of Israel than with American accommodation with the Arabs. If he proposes a guarantee, it is not in order to control Israel, but rather in order that Israel's "survival and security" become "a non-issue" in inter-Arab politics and in order to "send a signal to Israel's neighbors that the forces behind Israel's defense would be, in effect, inexhaustible" (1975b:19, 28). And if he suggests withdrawal from the occupied territories, it is not to put pressure on Israel but rather to allow that country to avoid the risks and dangers of a new war. The defenders of the GLS also fear the risks of war, but they are mainly concerned with American interests in the region.

Ullman thus intends to find the best American policy that would be good for Israel itself rather than for American interests. He goes so far as to assert (1975a:291) that "there are no overriding American interests at stake in Israel's survival as a state." He believes that even when the balance of forces is in favor of the Arabs (as it was just after the 1973 war), taking into account only strategic interests could lead to the conclusion that "the United States should no longer attempt to prevent the inevitable from happening." But such a policy, he states (ibid.:292–293), is not in accordance with U.S. diplomacy, because the latter "is not and never has been 'Metter-nichean.' " Its mission, on the contrary, is to serve "transcendental values." In this perspective, American attachment to Israel must be founded on "moral and cultural bases," and these cannot be ignored without causing "serious damage to our national self-esteem."

Like Ullman, the defenders of the GLS did not believe that Israel was a factor in the promotion of American interests in the Middle East but asserted, rather, that it was a burden. However, if they failed to conclude from this that Israel must be abandoned, it was not out of love for the Jewish state but because they consider, as we have seen, that their country's support to Israel is an inevitable "given" based on past investments (and hence a question of inter-national prestige) and internal American realities. But for Ullman, the basis of support to Israel is less a given than an "imperative," less an established fact than a moral obligation. This is so because Ullman fears that the American discourse on values has become cheapened and cynical (1975a:293), that American support to Israel has depended on the strength of "ethnic and religious linkages" alone (ibid.:294) and that the de facto guarantee is "ambiguous" and "vague" (ibid.:295; 1975b:33)

We may deduce from the preceding remarks that, compared to the "pragmatic" orientation of the defenders of the GLS, Ullman's perspective may be characterized as "idealistic." Israel may be a burden, but that is of little importance, since the United States is morally bound to guarantee its survival. Ultimately this argument would mean that the ideas of strategic asset and burden are no longer relevant. Similarly, American control and Israeli indebted-ness no longer have meaning. Ullman's position could thus be char-acterized as idealistic compared not only to the GLS, but also to the asset doctrine orientation, which we have called "doctrinaire." Let us not forget that although the proponents of the asset doctrine share with Ullman a pro-Israeli sensibility, they find it necessary to justify a policy favorable to Israel with strategic arguments. To this extent, it is no longer sufficient to consider Ullman's proposition, at least in its furthest implications, as simply an intermediate term between the two poles of GLS and the asset doctrine; it is preferable to see it as a third pole, that of "moral commitment," irreducible to the other two (see figure 2.2 below).

The idea of moral commitment as constituting a third pole is per-haps expressed most explicitly and "purely" by Aaron Wildavsky.

While rejecting, as we have seen at the end of the last chapter, the idea that Israel is a strategic asset for the United States since that would not be a sign of true friendship toward the Jewish state, Wildavsky does not affirm that Israel is a strategic burden. He pleads (1977:7, 11) in favor of an American commitment that would ensure Israel's survival but that would neither take the form of a treaty nor replace a process by which the parties concerned would arrive by themselves at a peaceful settlement. What is most interesting here is the justification for this commitment. For Wildavsky, the United States must guarantee Israel's security because it is a question of "national interest," but this interest is not at all to be understood in the sense of a strategic role for the Jewish state. Israel, as an object of American national interest, is a sort of "moral asset." It is worth quoting Wildavsky (ibid.:13) at some length:

> America's national interest in the security and prosperity of Israel rests on this: any moral argument which condemns Israel applies equally to America itself and any cultural argument against Israel applies to all of Western civilization. In Israel we Americans are brought face to face with our own origins. By acting as if there were no American national interest in Israel, the United States would simultaneously be rejecting its own religious, moral, political and

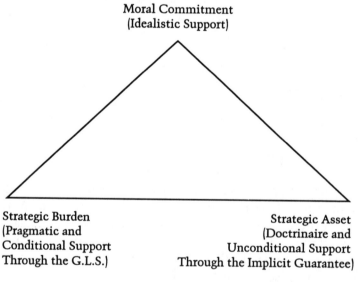

Moral Commitment
(Idealistic Support)

Strategic Burden
(Pragmatic and
Conditional Support
Through the G.L.S.)

Strategic Asset
(Doctrinaire and
Unconditional Support
Through the Implicit Guarantee)

Figure 2.2
The Nature of American Support to Israel

cultural identity. America has a national interest in Israel precisely because no other nation invokes at one and the same time so many basic American values.

Interestingly, Wildavsky adds (ibid.:12) that he does not consider these American values as representing "universal moral principles" but as valid "because the United States believes they are good ones." In particular, the legitimacy of Israel must be measured by American standards. The following example is revealing of the author's "Americanocentrism": "If Israel is deemed unworthy because its founders displaced native inhabitants, how much greater must have been our offenses in regard to Indians and Mexicans" (ibid.:6). And if Israel is criticized, it is because it represents, for the Third World, imbued with the values of the anticolonial and national liberation movements, "a different kind of culture—Western culture in a non-Western area of the world." For Wildavsky, "whether anyone likes it or not, Israel is of, by, and for the West . . . Unlike Vietnam or Korea or Angola or Jamaica or wherever you want, Israel is not part of the periphery but contains the core of the West. For better or for worse, Israel is us" (ibid.:12).

Is Wildavsky's cultural perspective different from that of the defenders of the doctrine of asset? Recall that they, too, insist on Israel's Western identity, but for them, this is an argument among others to establish the community of American-Israeli interests at a strategic level. They are not inclined to derive from the argument of cultural identity between the two countries the idea of an American moral commitment toward Israel. Further, an insistence on the argument of moral commitment is, as Tucker suggests (1981:32), antithetical to the idea of strategic asset. Rostow (quoted in Reich 1977:425) is even more explicit on this point: "The United States does not support Israel out of sentiment, or out of sympathy, or because of the supposed influence of a Jewish lobby. . . . The United States is supporting Israel in order to protect the vital national interests of the United States, and of its allies and friends in Europe, the Middle East and Asia."

It is as if the defenders of the asset doctrine had the same attitude toward moral obligation as they have toward the idea of guarantee: one should be satisfied that Israel takes advantage of this U.S. moral obligation, but one should not talk about it, except in terms of support to Israel and in terms of a community of values, for fear of admitting the idea of Israeli indebtedness or American control. For Wildavsky, on the contrary, material and strategic calculation is counterproductive and irrelevant to the debate: moral obligation is a superior interest that pertains to the very "being" of the United States and not to its bookkeeping in terms of assets and liabilities. Understood in this manner, moral obligation cannot carry with it the idea of Israeli indebtedness or American control.

For Wildavsky, this applies in particular to the question of the settlement of the Israeli-Arab conflict. If the object of moral commitment is Israel's survival, this means mobilizing the means to assure that survival: the American guarantee is one of these, but the settlement of the Israeli-Arab conflict is another. Insofar as they flow from a moral commitment, American efforts in favor of a settlement cannot but be congruent with the survival and welfare of Israel, even if they lead to Israeli concessions to the Arabs. Of course, the asset doctrine sees in this only an excessively costly compensation demanded of Israel, but the champions of moral obligation can reply that a peace process is to be valued in itself and that a succession of wars, even when victorious for Israel, is not a viable alternative. In this regard, Wildavsky fears (1977:11–12) that Israel's aptitude, more psychological than military, "to go on confronting adverse conditions," has been overestimated.

Wildavsky's and Ullman's argumentations related to the idea of a moral commitment, the strategic asset doctrine, and the idea of the GLS constitute different modes of articulation between strategy and culture, between interests and values. (a) For Ullman, if interests and values are in conflict, the latter must prevail: Israel may be a strategic burden, but the United States must remain tied to that country by moral obligation. (b) Although Wildavsky, like Ullman, gives priority to culture, he expresses his point of view in a slightly different manner (1977:9). For him, every strategy appears to derive exclusively from culture, even if that implies sacrifices. Rather than speak of Israel as a strategic asset or burden, it is better to speak of a moral asset. The difference in perspective between Ullman and Wildavsky is represented in figure 2.3, which complements the earlier figure 2.2. (c) The doctrine of asset seems to assume a spontaneous congruence between culture and material interests and to exclude a conflict between the two. Israel is at once a strategic asset and part of the cultural world of the West. (d) As for the GLS, it implies, fittingly, a pragmatic attempt at accommodation in the possible conflict between interests and values, with a certain primacy accorded to the former: although it is a burden, Israel, which benefits from a sense of identification in public opinion, is protected, but under certain conditions.

In any case, Wildavsky's perspective confirms the interest, raised by Ullman's proposal, in postulating moral commitment as the third point of a triangle which also includes the poles of asset and GLS. It would certainly be possible to class Ullman and even Wildavsky in an intermediate position between these two poles, closer in fact to the latter than the former. But moral commitment as foundation of the guarantee of Israel's survival is a criterion that remains irreducible to the idea of GLS, the primary function of which is to safeguard American interests in the Middle East. We need hardly emphasize that the poles we have presented represent the three ideas in their maximal coherence; actual argumentations may borrow elements of some or all three.

The Intermediate Guarantee

We have identified three forms of guarantee among the proposals that have tried to define an intermediate strategic line between the defenders and the opponents of the GLS: the functional guarantee, the guarantee through admitting Israel to NATO, and the guarantee linked to strategic cooperation.

The functional guarantee (or quasi-guarantee) has been proposed by N. A. Pelcovits, a former high official of the Department of

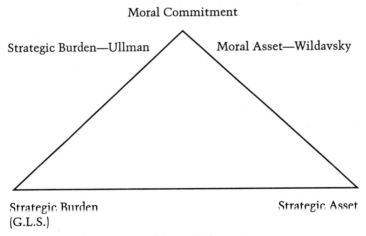

Moral Commitment

Strategic Burden—Ullman   Moral Asset—Wildavsky

Strategic Burden   Strategic Asset
(G.L.S.)

Figure 2.3
The Nature of American Support to Israel

Defense. This author agrees with the opponents of the GLS (1976:2)
that the idea of guarantee is usually proposed by personalities "not
noted for warm feelings toward Israel"; but he affirms, on the other
hand, that he does not wish to succumb to the "negative reflex" provoked by "the mere sound of the word [guarantee]." For Pelcovits,
an absolute guarantee does not exist and "the form of a guarantee is
not the paramount consideration" (ibid.: 21). The most "hermetic"
guarantee, that is, the one whose codification is the most elaborate
and whose mechanism of implementation is the most automatic,
would encounter the most opposition among members of Congress
and would require the most concessions on Israel's part. A security
treaty, in a form comparable to the NATO treaty or to that linking
the United States to South Korea or Japan, would have the disadvantage for Tel Aviv of stressing the "patron-client" relationship,
that is, once again, the idea of indebtedness, while Israel in fact does
not need American troops on its territory (ibid.:22, 25). What the
author wants to suggest is that Tel Aviv has an interest in obtaining
less than a treaty, but more than a de facto guarantee.

For Pelcovits, this intermediate form would consist of a series of
American-Israeli arrangements and agreements on military and economic aid, consultation, and cooperation. An American commitment would be made to assure the regularity of military aid in order
to protect Israel's military power relative to its neighbors. A joint
declaration of the two houses of Congress would be added in to reaffirm that the policy of aid to Israel is governed by both strategic and
moral considerations (ibid.:24, 27). Is this proposal conditioned on
the settlement of the Israeli-Arab conflict? For Pelcovits, the settlement must contain intrinsic security arrangements among the parties; discussion about guarantees must not begin until after the end
of negotiations. At this stage, Israel would be offered the above-
mentioned assurances and an international guarantee in the framework of the UN would crown the achievement (ibid.:19–20). There
is thus a link—at least an implicit one—between the settlement and
the American assurances, but this link does not necessarily work to
Israel's disadvantage, at least if one judges by the model that
inspires Pelcovits, which is the American-Israeli Memorandum of
September 1975, attached to the Sinai accord (to be analyzed in
chapter 4).

All in all, Pelcovits's proposal, by offering Israel something
"functionally akin to" a guarantee (ibid.:27), by requiring from Israel
only minimal compensations, by allowing controversy within the

American administration and Congress to be limited, by not making American assurances depend on third parties, by aiming to safeguard Israeli military superiority, and by stressing the idea of cooperation and consultation—by thus appearing to give Israel a role of its own—comes close to addressing the concerns expressed by the opponents of the GLS. In this functional guarantee or "quasi-guarantee," Israel is required to concede more than in a de facto guarantee, but less than in a juridically binding one. But what Israel obtains in the way of an American commitment in its favor seems to be, conversely, more than in a de facto guarantee but less than in a codified one. The quasi-guarantee might thus constitute for Israel the optimal choice in the face of two opposing interests in a worrisome but not threatening Middle Eastern situation. This would mean that in a "comfortable" Middle Eastern situation for Israel, the Israelis could be content with the support implied by the de facto guarantee. Conversely, in a threatening situation, Israel would need the most formal guarantee possible.

The second form of intermediate guarantee is proposed by Alvin Rubinstein, a specialist of Soviet Middle Eastern policy. This author, writing in the spring of 1978, pleads in favor of admitting Israel to NATO. This admission would take place in exchange for an Israeli withdrawal from the occupied territories (but excluding the establishment of a Palestinian state), in the framework of a "formal peace settlement" from which the Soviet Union would be explicitly left out. Israel's belonging to NATO would mean that it would enjoy "a formal treaty guaranteeing its independence, security and territorial integrity within adjusted and recognized borders—not just from the United States, but also from the entire Atlantic alliance." This would have the effect of ending the cycle of Israeli-Arab wars, since every attack against Israel "would automatically involve NATO." Since joining NATO would be tied to a settlement of the conflict, it would strengthen the position of the West in the Arab world. Moreover, Israel "would have regular access to the most advanced weaponry as a matter of normal alliance procedure and not as a perennial act of favoritism or largesse. Israel would be an ally, not a ward" (Rubinstein 1978:91–92).

It is unlikely that Rubinstein's proposal, with the link it establishes between the settlement and the granting of admission into NATO (ibid.:91), would be subjected to the same criticisms that are addressed to the GLS by its detractors. By placing his proposal in a global framework, and by seeking to integrate Israel in an already-established institution in which the countries tied to the United States enjoy more of an ally status than one of dependent wards (such as South Vietnam before its fall, or even South Korea) and by rejecting the prospect of a Palestinian state in spite of the Israeli withdrawal, Rubinstein offers the Jewish state compensations that should appear substantial in the eyes of the opponents of the GLS. The idea of Israel as a strategic asset of the United States is not expressed, but a large step is made in this direction. Israel's belonging to NATO suggests recognition and even elevation of its strategic status rather than reduction of Israel to a status of protected state.

The guarantee linked to American-Israeli strategic cooperation is the third form of intermediate guarantee. Bruce Kuniholm of Duke University, who has worked for the planning bureau of the State Department, pressed Israel (1983:712) to make concessions in the West Bank and stated: "Security arrangements and United States guarantees . . . could compensate for the loss of strategic depth on the West Bank." This was not a terribly new idea, but Kuniholm added: "Those guarantees could be made more credible by an Israeli stake in the Western alliance (air bases, prepositioned stocks, land-based air power, and a role in defending strategic maritime areas) which could establish the principle of interdependence between the United States and Israel." As a result, not only is the peace process linked to the guarantee offer, but also the offer of strategic cooperation. This means as well that guarantee and asset, although both conditional, are incorporated into the idea of interdependence, as if this idea served to partially "neutralize" the implications of Israeli dependence. It should be noted in this regard that Kuniholm refers in his proposal to the opinion expressed in 1981 by Israeli analyst Shai Feldman, who justified the necessity of an Israeli-American interdependence and an Israeli role in the Western alliance by noting that an American guarantee, if it were the sole compensation for an Israeli withdrawal from the West Bank and Gaza, would be unacceptable: it would "institutionalize dependence—with a debilitating effect on the nation's morale" (Feldman 1981:767). Feldman's suggestion was taken up again in 1985 by another American author, James Ray, who proposed that the Jewish state be offered "a formal alliance guaranteeing American military support if Israel is attacked" (1985:91, 98) and suggested a role for Israel in the Western alliance.

Let us, finally, cite Harry Shaw, whom we have already mentioned at the beginning of this chapter. This author (1985–86:141) subordinates the granting of a clear American commitment "in treaty form" to Israel's survival to that country's clear definition of its borders. For him, the strategic interest of the United States resides in Israel's ability to defend itself against its enemies in the region, and also in Israel's readiness to reach an accommodation with its neighbors. But while criticizing the exaggerations of the doctrine of asset regarding Israel's strategic role, he appears, rather ambiguously, to approve the use of Israeli facilities (prepositioning of equipment, maintenance and repair, medical facilities) (ibid.:131). Here again, we have a type of intermediate guarantee.

What conclusions can be drawn about the intermediate guarantee, in the three forms we have examined? Their "grafting" of elements borrowed from the asset doctrine raises difficulties for the analyst. Indeed, the discourse, which contains both elements from the asset doctrine and the guarantee proposal, appears to lack coherence and it is sometimes difficult to know whether it is protecting a threatened Israel or taking advantage of a threatening Israel that predominates in any given proposal. In order to decide whether a proposal belongs to the intermediate guarantee category or to the doctrine of asset, we might apply what could be called the criterion of *conditionality*. If, in a given argumentation, the recognition of a strategic role for Israel is conditioned by or linked to its acceptance of a settlement of the conflict and a withdrawal from the occupied territories, we then have an intermediary guarantee. If the recognition of Israel's strategic role is unconditional and already granted, we are dealing with a proposal based on the doctrine of asset.

It was with this criterion in mind that we classed Edward Glick (1982:152–153) among the proponents of the doctrine of asset, even though he also proposed a peace settlement including the establishment of a Palestinian state (without linking it to the recognition of the Israeli asset) and the concluding of an American-Israeli treaty of assistance. Following the same criterion, we would classify in the intermediate guarantee category the rather ambiguous argumentation of Grayson (1982:58) who, considering the possible sites for an American force of intervention, writes: "The only locations where a permanent deployment can be envisaged are in Saudi Arabia, and, conceivably, in Israel. Deployment in Israel could become necessary to persuade Israel to make concessions for a Palestine settlement, which it could otherwise not accept."

Is the intermediate guarantee, or the grafting of elements of the doctrine of asset onto the GLS, no more than lip service paid to the idea of Israeli-American strategic cooperation, as was in fashion in the 1980s under the Reagan administration? This may sometimes be the case. But the intermediate guarantee perhaps also illustrates the possible latent function of the whole idea of guarantee. In other words, the guarantee that should serve to assure the survival and territorial integrity of Israel, that is, its defense, can suddenly serve to assign it a role of regional intervention, once it is assured of protection. The specific contribution of those who proposed the admission of Israel to NATO or certain forms of intermediate guarantee would thus be to perceive strategic cooperation as a possible outcome of the GLS and even integrate it into their proposals. By so doing, they surely cause their proposals to lose something of their coherence, but they perhaps also gain a degree of acceptability from the detractors of the GLS. Even Anthony Cordesman, who, as we have seen, does not spare his criticism of Israel and the doctrine of asset, writes (1984:982): "If Israel eventually can reach a peace settlement, Israel's relations with the U.S. will eventually be translated from a moral obligation to a strategic asset worth far more than the cost of any increases in U.S. aid."

Can we take this hypothesis even further and attribute to the GLS what we had attributed to the doctrine of asset? For the latter, it seemed more satisfying for Israel to take advantage of the de facto guarantee or the moral obligation than to talk about these, the point being to avoid a state of indebtedness toward the United States. For the promoters of the GLS, would it not be preferable, conversely, to take advantage of Israel's military strength without recognizing this advantage and even claiming that Israel is today a burden, the point being to better control the Jewish state and not to alienate the Arabs without reason? It is difficult to dismiss this interpretation entirely. Leonard Binder (1984:442), for one, subscribes to it.

In any case, Israeli-American strategic cooperation, which accompanies the proposals of intermediate guarantee, embraces the idea of "mutuality" concerning the obligations and services each country can offer the other. Normally, the reference to this idea, as in the expressions "mutual security pact" or "mutual defense treaty," is intended to signify a role for both partners in each other's defense. However, the use of the term does not suffice to assure mutuality. There may, indeed, be a confusion of language. Certain authors propose what appears to conform altogether to the idea of GLS (thus, a unilateral commitment), but call it a mutual security treaty. This is the case, in particular, of Nadav Safran (1974), who, while emphasizing the necessity of an American commitment toward Israel, excluding its territorial conquests, proposes a "mutual defense treaty" but never refers to the idea of reciprocity (see also Pelcovits 1976:21–22).

Leaving aside the cases of language abuse, it must be recognized that the proposals for guarantee linked to strategic cooperation explicitly emphasize the idea of American-Israeli mutuality. But how can the idea of mutuality be consistent with the disparity in means between the two countries, or at least be integrated into the more general framework of strategic relations between a great power and a small state? To answer this question, it seems useful to distinguish between "central" and "peripheral" treaties. The first are those that, between 1945 and 1990, tied each of the two great powers to their European allies in the framework of the global conflict between the two blocs. Since 1990, these treaties could be described as "global" in the case of the ties that bind the remaining superpower, the United States, with its European allies. The "peripheral" treaties are those of a more traditional nature, which tie a power (and not necessarily one of the superpowers) to a weaker state. The idea of mutuality would seem to be more pertinent to central (and now global) treaties than to those we have defined as peripheral.

Israeli author Yoram Dinstein (1980:400) seems to be referring to central treaties when he writes: "Military alliances, like mutual aid treaties, are founded on the principle of reciprocity. A Big Power like the United States does not merely provide a nuclear umbrella for its allies; it also benefits from their active support (contribution of armed forces) and passive assistance (permission to use military bases)." Let us note in passing that the expressions "active support" and "passive assistance" correspond to the distinction between intrinsic and extrinsic asset as defined in the previous chapter. Pomerance (1974:19), on the other hand, appears to refer to the idea of peripheral treaty (and negation of mutuality) when evaluating the concept of "mutual security pact": "Between a great and small power, such a pact is, in effect, equivalent to a guarantee by the former to the latter."

If this distinction between the two categories of treaties (the "central" ones, which have a mutual character, and the "peripheral" ones, which are one-directional) is pertinent, we will not be surprised to observe that the authors who propose the granting of a guarantee linked to strategic American-Israeli cooperation seek to give the idea of mutuality maximal credibility by assigning Israel a status comparable to that of a NATO country. Conversely, the absence of the idea of mutuality in the GLS proposals (given their negation of an Israeli strategic role) appears congruent with an attitude of muteness regarding a possible NATO-type status for Israel. In the guarantee as a moral commitment, the idea of strategic mutuality between the United States and Israel would not be relevant— we might ask here whether the Jewish state does not enjoy, "culturally," a status analogous to that of a NATO country.

In the case of the asset doctrine, how do the idea of mutuality and the possibility of a NATO-type status for Israel fit in? For this doctrine, Israel deserves to enjoy a status at least equal to that of a European member of NATO, but the mutuality is "reversed," since Israel is presented as rendering more services to the United States than it receives. The mutuality is in fact only implicit, for there are reservations about recognizing the American de facto guarantee and codifying strategic cooperation in a treaty which would be a reminder of Israeli indebtedness. What the proponents of the asset doctrine in fact propose is a real American-Israeli alliance, but without the signing of a defense treaty (Dinstein 1980:399).

Conclusion

Our discussion of the multiple forms that may be taken by the idea of guarantee, and the multiple interpretations to which a single form may sometimes give rise, confirms that the idea of an American guarantee to Israel does not constitute a systematic and coherent set of theses that could reply to the doctrine of asset. Only the GLS, in which Israel is treated as a burden requiring American control and some recognition of Israeli indebtedness, can be considered as the polar opposite of the idea of asset. If we bring in the third pole (moral obligation), which is situated outside the axis of strategic considerations, we have a triangle that may be considered as delimiting the field of possible argumentations regarding the place that should be assigned to Israel in American policy.

We may now add to figure 2.3 above the three forms of intermediate guarantee we have presented here. As we move from left to right in our new figure 2.4, we find them between the GLS and the idea of asset in the following order: first, the functional guarantee;

next the guarantee via the admission of Israel to NATO; and finally the guarantee tied to strategic cooperation. Note that all these argumentations, even the most extreme ones, located at the poles, express support to Israel, even if it is not to the same degree. It is from the point of view of strategic implications that this spectrum of positions is most differentiated and its contrasts are most striking.

Is there a correlation between the nature of these argumentations and their authors' place in the Establishment? We have tried to note, whenever possible, the prior or ulterior functions held by the author we were referring to. Very roughly, we can say that the promoters of the GLS gravitate traditionally around the Department of State, whereas the defenders of the asset doctrine often accept the arguments of the pro-Israeli lobby; they are often close to members of Congress and are sometimes even their legislative aides; and in the 1980s some of them were on the National Security Council under Reagan or even in the State Department under the Bush administration. It is impossible to associate the Defense Department with one or another tendency, though in the circles close to it there seems recently to have been a turn toward the idea of asset.

We trust that the work accomplished up to now, in terms of

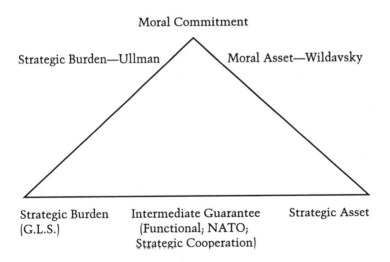

Figure 2.4
The Nature of American Support to Israel

description, classification, and internal critique of the different advocacies, will provide us with the concepts and distinctions necessary for tracing and understanding the evolution of official American doctrine concerning the place assigned to Israel over the past 45 years.

3 | Forging a Strategic Role for Israel, 1948–1973

What needs to be considered in the next three chapters is the evolution of American governmental doctrine as we may induce it from the history of American policy in the past 45 years. In order to construct this doctrine, or rather reconstruct it, we do not propose, in what follows, to describe in minute detail the history of American policy toward Israel. Our primary objective is not to expose manifestations of American diplomatic or financial support from 1948 to 1992, nor to trace the signs of lukewarmness in the relationship, although these will certainly be pointed out when needed. What is more important, as the analysis of the advocacies showed, is to detect indications of American willingness to sell arms to Israel (at least up to 1967), to defend the country, guarantee its existence, assign it a strategic role, allow it full freedom to take major initiatives, or, on the contrary, to control these or even dictate important decisions. We shall base our analysis largely on now-available archive material, in some cases directly and in others via authors who have used it, and on the memoirs of political leaders, while avoiding the use of what appears as the *post facto* justifications of their actions. We shall try as well to avoid the innumerable public declarations they made while in power, since these express not so much their doctrine at a given moment as the image they wish to project of it. The only official texts of which we shall make use are those that have the strength of a commitment, that is, in effect, almost exclusively the American-Israeli agreements.

Clearly such a study requires a periodization. Although, in each period presented (in particular the first one, from 1948–1973), no doctrinal unity is always identifiable and although one must distinguish sub-periods, the overall subdivision we propose is the following: 1948–1973 (chapter 3); 1973–1980 (chapter 4); and 1981–1992 (chapter 5).

From 1948 to 1973 very few things remained constant in American strategy toward Israel. The 1967 war appears to constitute the major break: before that time, the United States had supported Israel's existence and welfare for reasons apparently unrelated to self-interest; after it Israel became important in the United States' strategic calculations. Although we agree that the war of June 1967 constitutes a turning point, we will try to show that the idea of a hiatus between the two sub-periods must be relativized. The strategic content of Israeli-American relations took form very gradually, element by element, from the 1950s on; and we will try to identify these elements as they emerged.

The Slow Emergence of the Strategic Relationship, 1948–1967

The Years Leading Up to the Suez Crisis

Our investigation begins just after the founding of the state of Israel. It seems pointless to study the preceding period, since there are no credible sources indicating that U.S. support to the creation of a Jewish state corresponded to a voluntaristic strategic objective. Let us note in passing, for the 1947–1948 period, which is now abundantly documented, that the sources indicate, rather, a complex and hesitant management of the Palestine crisis and a fear of seeing the Palestine partition plan result in negative consequences for the United States. Thus, in January–February 1948 (between the vote of the partition plan at the UN General Assembly and the proclamation of the state of Israel), the U.S. administration (the Department of Defense and to a lesser extent the Department of State), warned, in its internal reports, against direct American participation in the enforcement of the partition on the ground. According to these reports, the result would be a demand for equivalent participation by the Soviet Union, Arab hostility to the United States to the benefit of Moscow, a loss of Anglo-American military facilities in the Middle East, the loss of trade concessions, and risks for U.S. security (FRUS 1948:549–552, 632).

We must not, however, exaggerate the significance of these bureaucratic reports. They expressed more an opposition to the idea of sending an American armed force than to diplomatic support for the creation of a Jewish state, which was being imposed in any event by the military strength of the Zionists, with or without a partition plan. Moreover, the strategic argumentation developed in these reports was merely hypothetical: in the climate of East-West tension and emotional mobilization of American public opinion in favor of the Zionist program, the press took it upon itself to show that any American reservations about supporting this program would only benefit Moscow. Further, the U.S. role in the Middle East was not yet considered a substitute, but only a complement, to the responsibilities of the British. In short, the double debate of that time—secret and public—did not involve the idea that the establishment of Israel would inevitably harm U.S. strategic interests. However, what the debate indicates for us today is that American support for the creation of Israel was not expressly integrated into a U.S. "project" or blueprint for the Middle East. This by no means signifies that the strategic debate within the administration was pointless and did not weigh on Truman's policy (Neff 1988; Evensen 1992). It had led the president to follow a median line between the mobilization of American public opinion and the fear of a Soviet advance in the Middle East; to rule out an American military intervention in Palestine; and to support an official military embargo directed toward the Middle East.

Immediately after the establishment of Israel, American apprehensions regarding the new state were mixed with new hopes. A secret memorandum addressed by the Secretary of Defense to the National Security Council on May 16, 1949 (NSC 47), entitled "United States Strategic Interests in Israel" (FRUS 1949:1009–1012), sums up these fears and hopes. Regarding the former, the memorandum evokes the possibility "for Communist penetration through Jewish immigration," the official Israeli policy of "neutrality in the 'cold war'" (a principle known in Hebrew as *î-hizdahût*, or nonidentification), and Tel Aviv's temptation to accept friendly Soviet overtures in order to face its Arab enemies helped by the British. However, the memorandum strongly moderates these fears by explaining that Israel has "close ties with the United

States" because of the latter's "large and influential Jewish minority" and that Israeli leaders have assured, in private, that "their sym-
pathies lie with the West," but that it was necessary for them to
take a public position of neutrality in order "to facilitate the emigration to Israel of Jews now in the 'Iron Curtain' countries." Finally the document notes that the U.S. attitude toward the emergence
of "an independent Jewish nation" after "bitter conflict with the
neighboring Arab states," can be considered as favorable to Israel
(FRUS 1949:1011; also Grose 1983:302; Green 1984:23–24).

But the strategic role attributed to the new state also merits our
attention. In the memorandum, the strategic importance of Israel is
based on that country's "central location in the Eastern Mediter-
ranean-Middle East area." Despite certain reservations of a technical order about the military facilities that Israel could provide, the
memorandum considers that "air installations would be most useful in the interdiction of the lines of communication from the USSR
to the Middle East oil resources with medium and short-range aircraft." Great value is also attributed to the potential contribution of
the Israeli armed forces: "Should Israel ally herself with the Western democracies in the event of war with the USSR, full advantage
could be taken of defensive positions in that country and of Israel's
forces for the defense of the Cairo-Suez area and for land operations
to defend or to recapture the Middle East oil facilities." For the
authors of the memorandum, "Israel may become a danger or an
asset depending upon the nature of her future relations with the
Soviets and with the Western democracies." Finally, the memorandum recommends working to prevent any domination of Israel by
the USSR; strengthening Anglo-Israeli relations in order to allow for
a common Anglo-American military approach regarding objectives
that concern Israel; reconciling Israeli-Arab differences "at least to
the extent that Israel and the Arab states would act in concert to
oppose Soviet aggression"; and, if a pact along the lines of the
Atlantic treaty is created, bringing Israel into it alongside the Arab
states, "providing the participation of Saudi Arabia and Iran is not
precluded by such action" (FRUS 1949:1012).

What significance can be attributed to this memorandum from
the point of view of the strategic role attributed to Israel? The document seems to lay the foundations of an American doctrine for the
1949–1956 period, even if certain of its recommendations proved
inoperative. This doctrine (and it was to be refined in other documents of the period) may be considered from two standpoints:

Israel's direct relation to the anti-Soviet struggle, and the effect of the regional Arab environment on the Jewish state's strategic contribution.

Regarding the first point, let us note that at the moment when American strategic doctrine of containment and installation of bases in the perimeter of the Soviet bloc was coming into being, American military officials saw in Israel, above all, an extrinsic asset. Not only was the Israeli territory considered from this point of view, but its armed forces as well, since they were envisioned only as forces subject to Western command in the event of an armed conflict with the Soviet Union in the Middle East. In November 1952, an internal report by the Chairman of the U.S. Joint Chiefs of Staff estimated that of the 19 divisions the West would need to counter a Soviet attack in the Middle East, Israel could provide two within three years, alongside Turkey's 10, and two apiece from Great Britain and Iraq. Moreover, it was calculated that the contribution of the Israeli Air Force could reach 80 planes, while that of Turkey was estimated at 75 (FRUS 1952–1954:321). A more immediate and less hypothetical contribution to the anti-Soviet effort should also be mentioned here: cooperation between the intelligence services of the two countries, thanks to the Haganah's old networks in the East European countries and the Soviet Union, and thanks to information that Jewish immigrants from these countries could provide. An agreement on this point appears to have been concluded in October, 1951 (Bialer 1992:251). This "under-the-table cooperation," in Peter Grose's expression (1983:302), caused the American intelligence services to be "more sympathetic to the Jewish state than either the State Department or the Pentagon" (see also Cockburn and Cockburn 1991:8, 41).

Matters were different regarding the second point, that is, the effects of the regional environment on Israel's strategic contribution. In the 1949 memorandum and the internal documents of the following years, Israel was given no positive role to play vis-à-vis the Arab world; its hostile relations with the Arabs even made its role a negative one. The United States, while favorable to the new state, did not yet seek to exercise pressure on the Arab states *thanks to* Israel, but sought rather to persuade them to take part in an anti-Soviet security system *in spite of* Israel. If Israel is to be aided and strengthened, then so must be the Arab states, and the two sides must be reconciled in order that they might combat the USSR rather than each other. From the American military point of view, according to the Joint Chiefs of Staff in 1950, there was no "fundamental difference between the defense situation in Israel and in other Near East states" (FRUS 1950:134); furthermore, "the Middle East in war is of importance second only to Europe" (FRUS 1951:98).

Developments in the first half of the 1950s were to reveal the extent of American efforts directed both to the Arab states and to Israel, but also the difficulty, if not the impossibility, of reconciling these efforts. In this study we will evoke only those developments necessary for comprehending the strategic role attributed then to Israel. Concerning, first of all, American policy regarding arms sales, it must be noted that following the U.N. Security Council resolution of August 11, 1949 which ended the embargo on arms shipments to the Middle East, the United States decided to sell weapons to the states of the region within the limits of their legitimate security needs, and thus to avoid an arms race. Licenses for the export of weapons (probably light ones) to Israel and the Arab states were granted (FRUS 1950:132). This official policy was confirmed on May 25, 1950 in a "tripartite declaration" expressing the common will of the United States, Great Britain, and France to limit the arms race between the Arab states and Israel, even while arming both parties so as to let them "play their part in the defense of the area as a whole" (*Department of State Bulletin* 6.5.50:886). The declaration also opposed any violation of the armistice lines.

We must add, however, that in spite of the official impartiality of the tripartite declaration and the low level of American arms sales to Israel, the United States had, in practice, begun to lean favorably toward the Jewish state. Israeli sources make it clear, for example, that toward the middle of the year 1950, there were already more than a hundred Israelis receiving military training in the United States, while the experts and professionals of the Israeli army included "an extremely high percentage of American Jews" (Bialer 1990:222). At a more fundamental level, President Truman, on May 19, 1950, just a few days before the tripartite declaration, adopted the National Security Council report 65/3, which recommended that "sympathetic consideration" be given "to Israel's application for export licenses for defensive military equipment sufficient to discourage attack from beyond its borders" (FRUS 1950:166). In fact, it was following Israeli protests concerning military supplies sent by the British to Egypt, in the framework of the strategic partnership between these two countries, that Truman approved the idea of the tripartite declaration. The United States was seeking to maintain

Israel's regional deterrence capacity, even though the U.S. did not consider the Jewish state an asset vis-à-vis the Arab world and even though it wished for an Israeli-Arab reconciliation with a view toward a common anti-Soviet mobilization.

Such a mobilization rose urgently to the top of the agenda with the Korean crisis of June 1950. In particular, Israel was pressed by Washington to clarify its position on this question. On July 2, the Israeli government decided to take the American side in the conflict, thus putting an end to the policy of "nonidentification" with either the East or the West (Brecher 1974:13–17). Israeli leaders then considered the possibility of an "outright alliance with the West" (Safran 1978:339). In fact, the Israeli Foreign Minister Moshe Sharrett even proposed, in a confidential letter to the U.S. Secretary of Defense George Marshall dated December 23, 1950, what came to be known as Operation Stockpile. The United States was invited to establish supply depots in Israel in order to constitute a strategic reserve of basic supplies (such as grains, foodstuffs, oil, raw materials for industry) which would be American property but which Israel could use according to its needs; to supply arms to Israel; and to provide technical assistance and material aid to the Israel arms industry (*Ma'ariv* 12/11/81; Bialer 1990:230–231, 242–243; Gazit 1987:89). Let us note that this proposal coincided with Ben-Gurion's well-known ambition of convincing Washington to make of Israel "the base, the workshop and the granary" of the Middle East (Bar-Zohar 1978:194).

Washington, for its part, was not interested in such proposals. Once again, it had to mobilize the entire region against the Soviet Union. It appeared increasingly clear that the mobilization should take the form of a regional pact led by the United States and Great Britain, and including, at the outset, Egypt and possibly Iraq—two countries already having strategic ties with London. The project for this pact was known, in October 1951, as Middle East Command and in June 1952 as Middle East Defense Organization. Israel's joining either of these was out of the question, for the Israelis as well as for the Americans. The Israelis, who sought, as in Operation Stockpile, a form of bilateral cooperation that would bring tangible and immediate dividends with no binding commitment on their part, saw only disadvantages in a regional pact, since it would serve mainly to arm the Arab states and would further alienate Moscow with very little in return (Bialer 1990:249–250; FRUS 1952–1954:198). As for the Americans, even as they promised Israel to take its interests into account when planning for regional defense (Eytan 1958:142), they perceived more and more that inviting Israel into a system of collective security would make impossible the already difficult adherence of the Arab countries (FRUS 1952–1954:253; Yaniv 1987:53–54).

The events that followed in the Middle East, including the anti-monarchist coup in Egypt in July 1952, the building up of anti-Western sentiment, the signs of internal instability and the rise of Israeli-Arab tensions, reduced to naught any hope of a Western-led pact regrouping the Arab states. As was noted in the National Security Council document 155/1 dated July 14, 1953 ("United States Objectives and Policies with Respect to the Near East"), "the current danger to the security of the free world arises not so much from the threat of direct Soviet military attack as from a continuation of the present unfavorable trends. Unless those trends are reversed, the Near East may well be lost to the West within the next few years" (FRUS 1952–1954:400; Gendzier 1989:24–25). The American administration, under the recently elected President Eisenhower, was convinced that before constituting a regional security organization it was first necessary to assure its "political base." An attitude of greater firmness toward Israel was adopted. Thus, in September 1953, the United States secretly suspended all economic aid to Tel Aviv in order to force Israel to desist from unilaterally diverting water from the Jordan River. A month later, this suspension was announced publicly, following the bloody raid organized by the commander of Special Unit 101, Ariel Sharon, in the Jordanian village of Kibya.

With the emergence of Iraq in American strategic calculations following an arms delivery agreement in April 1954 and the (exaggerated) Israeli fear of a similar development with Egypt as a result of the July 1954 agreement concerning the evacuation of British troops, Israel saw the regional environment evolving unfavorably to its interests. Its government, led since January 1954 by Ben-Gurion's successor, Moshe Sharett, finally resolved in August of that year to explore the possibility of obtaining from Washington a security guarantee, that is, American "protection." An official request to this effect was made on April 11, 1955 (Bialer 1990:261–268, Eban 1977:184; Brecher 1974:17, 26; Bar-Zohar 1978:192–195). Let us note that this new approach, which corresponded to Sharett's will to develop a relatively prudent policy toward the Arabs, came after Israel under Ben-Gurion had failed to impose itself as a strategic asset to the United States in the region and had shown its reticence to becoming an extrinsic asset in the struggle against the USSR. Secretary of State John Foster Dulles's answer was given to Israeli ambassador Abba Eban on April 16: the United States accepted the idea in principle, but it would be conditional to progress in settling the Israeli-Arab conflict (Bialer 1990:269–270; Bar-Siman-Tov 1988:343). Abba Eban (1977:184) reports a conversation with Dulles in August 1955, in which the latter said that the United States "could not guarantee temporary armistice lines." In an important speech delivered on the 26th of the same month, Dulles proclaimed that in order to make possible a definitive settlement of the Israeli-Arab conflict, the United States was ready to "join in formal treaty engagements to prevent or thwart any effort by either side to alter by force the boundaries between Israel and its Arab neighbors" (*Department of State Bulletin* 9/5/55:378–380). The conditional guarantee that Dulles was ready to grant was indeed what we called, in the previous chapter, the guarantee linked to settlement (GLS).

For Israel, however, the cost of an American guarantee was exorbitant. Indeed, when Dulles, in the same speech, listed the problems that a settlement would have to resolve as a matter of priority, that is, mutual fear, the refugee problem, and the establishment of borders, he suggested that Israel make concessions on the latter two points. Furthermore, the Israeli leaders (Ben-Gurion above all, who had returned to government as Defense Minister in February 1955) realized that the immediate effect of their approach, even before the conclusion of a guarantee agreement, would be to limit the Israeli army's margin for maneuver in the policy of reprisals beyond Israeli borders. They concluded that the pursuit of efforts to achieve a guarantee treaty would be harmful (Bialer 1990:271). It should be stressed, however, that the conditional character of the American guarantee did not imply the absence of an informal and de facto guarantee to Israel. American documents of the era are full of remarks suggesting that protecting Israel was a matter of official concern. The Israeli archives reveal the following message from Dulles to the Israeli Foreign Ministry: "Even without a formal link, which we will reach when the time comes, Israel should trust that the U.S.A. will not abandon her" (ibid.:273).

Another indication lies in the manner in which Washington justified its refusal to take part officially in the Baghdad Pact, while at the same time sponsoring it. In a meeting at the White House called by Eisenhower in March 1956, John Foster Dulles declared: "The United States cannot join the Baghdad Pact without giving some security guarantee to Israel, and if we were to do so, our action would quickly knock out Iraq" (Spiegel 1985:67; also FRUS 1955–1957:294). Dulles's assertion implied both a concern for the protection of Israel and a reticence, based on regional considerations, to translate this concern into an official and unconditional guarantee to the Jewish state.

Events in the Middle East culminating in the Suez crisis were soon to modify several American assumptions concerning Israel and the region. Above all, the question of the arms race was posed. President Nasser's announcement, on September 27, 1955, of an arms delivery agreement between Egypt and Czechoslovakia was indeed to destroy one of the foundations of the tripartite declaration of 1950, that is, control of the arms race—a control that had up to now been assured, to a certain extent, by the West's monopoly of arms sales in the Israeli-Arab zone. In particular, it appears that Israel did not purchase or receive any heavy weaponry from the United States between 1952 and 1955, in spite of the U.S.-Israel Agreement on Mutual Defense Assistance, concluded on July 23, 1952. It is sometimes thought that American leaders did not modify their basic policy following the Egyptian-Czech agreement, since they maintained their earlier refusal to sell arms to Israel, perhaps considering that Nasser should not be pushed any further toward the Soviet Union. But this perception is exaggerated, if not erroneous. A first indication of this is the rising American suspicion of Egypt, now accused of "playing off East against West by blackmailing both" (Eisenhower 1965:31–32). This suspicion manifested itself above all in the official American refusal to contribute to the financing of the Aswan Dam in July 1956.

A second indication involves the question of Israeli armament. Although Israel indeed continued to be refused American arms sales, it is important to note that in the United States' view, Egypt "would be decisively defeated" in the event of war with Israel (Neff 1981:43; also FRUS 1955–1957:107). It should also be noted that Israel used both France and Canada as sources of supplies, without objection from Washington (Reich 1977:65), or even with Washington's approval and encouragement. Eban (1977:197) could thus write: "The paradox of Dulles' position was reinforced by the fact that he had no objection to other countries giving Israel arms. Actually he would have liked this to happen." Eban and others cite the example of 24 Canadian-made F-86 planes that were originally reserved for the U.S. Army but were then allocated to Israel; they note as well that Washington decided to renounce, in Israel's favor, the NATO priority for French Mystère planes (Eban 1977:197, 200–201; Ball 1979/80:232; Safran 1978:354; Rubin 1981:227, 230; Kennen 1981:130). Furthermore, throughout the 1950s Washington allowed the transfer of technical know-how to the Israeli arms industry. According to Ephraim Inbar (1982/83:47), "the U.S. preferred not to sell Israel weapons and offered, instead, access to arms production technology."

It must finally be noted that while Israel found it possible to wage a more activist Arab policy by establishing a strategic partnership with France as early as the spring of 1956, its cooperation with the United States at the level of intelligence services did not cease. Thus, in April of that year, the Mossad was the first agency to hand over to the CIA a copy of the famous secret speech by Khrushchev to the 20th Congress of the Communist Party of the Soviet Union, delivered two months earlier. It even appears that the Israelis obtained, in compensation for this favor, the signing of a formal CIA-Mossad agreement on the swapping of intelligence concerning the Arab world (Neff 1981:246).

The Suez War and its Consequences

Beyond the question of arms, it was the Suez war in the fall of 1956 and its consequences that confronted the United States with a major challenge. Until the last moment, Washington was in ignorance of Israel's decision to wage war (as well as the site of the war). On October 28, the day before the Israeli attack against Egypt, President Eisenhower, who was by now worried by the Israeli mobilization and who apparently believed that it was directed against Jordan, in spite of some indications to the contrary, sent a message of moderation to Ben-Gurion (Bar-Zohar 1978:244–245; Spiegel 1985:74; Cockburn and Cockburn 1991:65–67). It indeed appears that the Israeli leaders carefully hid their preparations from the American intelligence services and had not sought directly to obtain Washington's approval—even tacit approval—of their military objectives. This is not to say that such approval was not an Israeli concern; in fact, they expressed such concern in preparatory meetings with French officials (Dayan 1976:157), but they apparently felt that the French and the British could form, vis-à-vis their great American ally, a buffer that would absorb the shocks of any American reservations.

However, the war was to demonstrate that France and Great Britain constituted neither a buffer between Washington and Tel Aviv, nor a screen between Washington and the region. The pressures exerted by the Eisenhower administration on Great Britain, France, and especially Israel, for a rapid withdrawal from the Suez Canal zone and the Sinai are well known. Several remarks should be noted regarding this point. Eban (1977:217) relates that during a meeting held October 30, 1956 between Eisenhower and the American Jewish leader Abba Hillel Silver, and whose content was intended to be communicated to Ben-Gurion, the American President insisted on the necessity of an Israeli retreat and warned that, even though there may have been a momentary convergence of interests between Israel, France, and Great Britain, "Israel's power and future are in fact bound up with the United States." Come what may, the Jewish state occupied a special place in American strategy, and it was in order to preserve that place that Ben-Gurion negotiated the retreat.

The United States did not only employ threats in this negotiation. Isser Harel, the chief of Mossad at that time, explains that the U.S. administration, during the Suez crisis, used the contacts between the respective intelligence services as a substitute for political and diplomatic channels (Cockburn and Cockburn 1991:68). Cockburn and Cockburn also suggest (1991:87) that Israel might have obtained, among other compensations for its withdrawal from the Sinai, the express authorization to "divert" enriched uranium from the Apollo factory in Pennsylvania for its nuclear program (then under way in cooperation with France).

As concerns diplomatic compensations, let us note Washington's assurance to Tel Aviv regarding the right of its ships to sail through the Gulf of Aqaba after its retreat from the Sinai. In spite of Israeli insistence, the United States refused to go beyond a formula contained in an exchange of correspondence, according to which the Gulf of Aqaba "comprehends" international waters and that no state had the right to impede "free and innocent passage" through the Gulf. The United States added that it was ready to exercise this right and to join with others in ensuring its general recognition (Reich 1977:33). As Spiegel notes (1985:79), this was far from an "absolute guarantee, such as a security treaty with the U.S.," which Eisenhower considered to be the true Israeli objective. Another source asserted, however, when the Gulf of Aqaba crisis broke out ten years later, that a secret guarantee had been given to Tel Aviv in 1957 (Heren 1970:162–163).

It was not the question of assurances concerning the freedom of passage through the Gulf of Aqaba that distinguished the years 1957–1967, even if this question was to prove explosive at the end of the period. The real challenge of this post-Suez period for American policy in the Middle East was the Franco-British political failure, which created a vacuum that was in danger of being filled by the USSR, which could now anticipate deliberate political choices by, e.g., Egypt and Syria. As early as 1955, Nasser had shown it was possible to have a policy independent from the West and to draw closer to Moscow. Arab nationalism was increasingly perceived by Washington as having a destabilizing effect on the pro-Western regimes and as containing many objectives that coincided with those of the Soviet Union (Wright 1984:645; Gendzier 1989:28; Heikal 1988). In order to combat the potential influence of Moscow and the spread of Nasserism, the United States began to integrate the configuration of intraregional alliances and conflicts into East-West competition. In other words, Israel and conservative Arab states interested in the status quo were lined up on the American side while the opposite camp was thought to include not only the USSR but also those forces—Nasserism above all—seen as favorable to change. This does not mean that American policy during the 1957–1967 period was constantly directed against Nasserism, but rather that it worked toward neutralizing the "revisionist" components of Nasserist policy toward the Middle East, attempting at times to "co-opt" Nasserism, but often combating it as well.

How does the Israel factor figure into this reclassification? First of all, the Eisenhower doctrine, announced in January 1957, promised to aid any Middle Eastern country that fell victim to an outside aggression or internal subversion; for the first time Israel was included in an American regional security arrangement (Safran 1978:372). Secondly, Washington from this point on began to take Israeli apprehensions seriously, since Israel had now proven that it could translate its apprehensions into military exploits. In a more positive light, Israeli military force and its pro-Western orientation were valued in American regional policy. A January 1958 memorandum of the National Security Council notes that the "logical corollary" of opposition to radical Arab nationalism "would be to support Israel as the only strong pro-West power left in the Near

East" (quoted in Chomsky 1984:21; also Wright 1984:646). More explicitly, as George Ball explained (1979/1980:234), "Dulles decided that a strong Israel could, by holding down the bulk of Egypt's armed forces, restrict Nasser's freedom of action." This is confirmed by Eban (1977:263) when he speaks of the instituting of regular consultations between Washington and Tel Aviv: "The U.S. was obviously coming to regard Israel not as a burden to be chivalrously sustained, but as an asset in the global and ideological balance."

Eban's strategic evaluation of the consultation between the two countries is probably exaggerated, at least for the period running from the late 1950s to the early 1960s. The documents concerning Israeli-American exchanges during the Lebanese civil war of 1958 and the anti-monarchist coup in Iraq on July 14 of the same year (events that occurred a few months after the Syrian-Egyptian union), suggest rather that Israel was looking at once for American protection against the apparently triumphant Nasser regime and strategic cooperation, without either of them being defined formally in a treaty. Welcoming with "relief" (FRUS 1958–1960:69) the arrival of American troops in Lebanon and British troops in Jordan on July 15 (and allowing the aircraft that transported the latter to fly over its territory), Israeli leaders demanded "assurances that if Israel got into difficulties like Lebanon's, we would give them help" (ibid.:73). In response, U.S. leaders explained to the Israelis that the example of their military intervention in Lebanon, based on the Eisenhower doctrine, should suffice to reassure them. But they were ready to take an extra step since, on July 25, Eisenhower addressed a letter to Ben-Gurion in which he stated that Israel could "be confident of United States interest in the integrity and independence of Israel" (ibid.:74). This letter, which apparently did not satisfy the Israeli Premier (ibid.:85), nonetheless meant that a conditional guarantee implying Israeli concessions in the settlement of the conflict was no longer on the Eisenhower administration's agenda. Eisenhower's letter was followed on August 1 by another, signed by Dulles, which asserted: "We believe that Israel should be in a position to deter an attempt at aggression by indigenous forces, and are prepared to examine the military implications of this problem with an open mind" (ibid.:78).

It appears that for the American leaders, strategic cooperation with Israel in this period had to stay limited in form and substance. It is difficult, however, given currently available sources, to know the full extent of strategic cooperation implied by this American perception of Israel. Let us note, however, that in his biography of Ben-Gurion, Michael Bar-Zohar gives an interesting example of such cooperation. Reacting to the Lebanese events and the republican coup d'Etat in Iraq in July 1958, Ben-Gurion solicited, toward the end of that month, "political, financial and moral" encouragement from the United States for the establishment of a "peripheral alliance" regrouping Israel, Iran, Turkey and Ethiopia—an alliance that would not necessarily be "formal and public," but that could "stand up steadfastly against Soviet aggression through Nasser" and even "save the freedom of Lebanon" and perhaps that of Syria as well. Bar-Zohar (1978:263–264) notes that Dulles's answer came in August 1958: the answer was favorable, for Israel was encouraged to establish a "peripheral pact." This is probably the same letter dated August 1 that we mentioned above, but from which 15 lines, not yet declassified and most probably concerning the "peripheral alliance," have been deleted. A permanent triangular link between the secret services of Israel, Turkey, and Iran was probably formally constituted at the end of 1958 (Cockburn and Cockburn 1991:100).

As concerns the politics of arms sales, the United States was now more favorable to Israeli demands, but it wanted to satisfy these only partially. It appears that from 1958 to 1960 the Americans agreed to supply about 100 antitank recoilless rifles, about 20 S-58 Sikorsky helicopters, and early warning electronic equipment against air raids. However, they did not cede to a request for Hawk antiaircraft missiles (FRUS 1958–1960:98, 306–307, 359). The Eisenhower administration sought to avoid an arms race, which it saw as futile because of Israeli superiority and because of Nasser's apparent ability to respond and take part in a race thanks to the Soviet Union. In any case, the United States preferred that France, as in 1956, take the responsibility for arming Israel, and even provided "hidden economic aid to help Israel buy arms," according to Haim Herzog, then a minister in the Israeli embassy in Washington (ibid.:298).

There are few changes of a strategic nature to be noted at the beginning of the Kennedy administration in January 1961. It is nonetheless interesting to observe Kennedy's concern to induce the Israelis to show a moderate and sympathetic attitude toward the United States' regional and global preoccupations and its possible overtures to the Arabs. It is perhaps in this light that one can understand the essence of what Kennedy (quoted in Gazit 1983:112) told Golda Meir, then Israeli Foreign Minister, during her visit to the United States in December 1962:

The United States has a special relationship with Israel in the Middle East really comparable only to that which it has with Britain over a wide range of world affairs. But for us to play properly the role we are called upon to play, we cannot afford the luxury of identifying Israel—or Pakistan, or certain other countries—as our exclusive friends, hewing the line of close and intimate allies (for we feel that about Israel though it is not a formal ally) and letting other countries go. . . . Our interest is best served if there is a group of sovereign countries associated with the West. We are in a position, then, to make clear to the Arabs that we will maintain our friendship with Israel and our security guarantees.

Kennedy added: "I think it is quite clear that in case of an invasion the United States would come to the support of Israel. We have that capacity and it is growing" (ibid.:113). The President concluded:

Israel, the United States and the free world all have difficult survival problems. We would like Israeli recognition that this partnership which we have with it produces strains for the United States in the Middle East. . . . We would hope Israel could proceed in such a way as to lessen collision between us. . . . What we want from Israel arises because our relationship is a two-way street.

Israel's privileged position vis-à-vis the United States is asserted here with force, albeit without publicity. A strategic role for Israel is not mentioned, except perhaps indirectly in the comparison with Great Britain. The existence of a sort of nonformalized American guarantee is recalled, and a *quid pro quo*, Israel's moderation, is demanded. Gazit (1983:46–47) considers that this is equivalent to an "executive defense commitment." To substantiate this opinion, he notes that Kennedy's verbal engagement was confirmed in writing in a letter to Levi Eshkol, then Prime Minister, on October 2, 1963. However, this letter remained confidential. It is worth noting that the guarantee evoked by Kennedy is doubly ambiguous in a way that is now familiar to us. First, the guarantee is said to protect Israel in case of invasion (which implies a weakness), but it also seeks to moderate Israel (which implies strength). Secondly, the guarantee expresses an already-existing de facto commitment (which does not in principle require an Israeli quid pro quo), but by the very fact that it is uttered by the President, even confidentially, a quid pro quo is demanded. It is because of this double ambiguity that the idea of guarantee can coexist with the notion of Israel as an asset in American perception.

We must return, in this pre-1967 period, to the question of American arms sales to Israel, because a significant additional step was taken starting in 1962. In the summer of that year, Kennedy finally acceded to the Israeli request concerning the sale of Hawk antiaircraft missiles to Israel because his administration considered that the Western allies of the United States could offer no equivalent alternative that "would satisfy Israel's legitimate security needs" (Spiegel 1985:107; Reich 1977:40). Interestingly, this decision was preceded in July of the same year by an Israeli-American meeting whose purpose was to examine the balance of forces between Israel and the Arab states. This appears to have been the first meeting of its kind since the founding of Israel, and it was to be followed by another in the fall of 1963 (Gazit 1983:45; Spiegel 1985:109). In February 1965, the Johnson administration decided to supply Israel with 200 Patton tanks after an arms deal with West Germany had been made public (40 tanks had already been delivered) and canceled in the face of Arab protests. In February 1966, an American-Israeli agreement was concluded for the supply of 48 Skyhawk bombers (Spiegel 1985:132–134). All this makes relative—without contradicting it—the idea of French (or European) preponderance in arms supplies to Israel before 1967; it indicates a trend that was to become even more marked after the 1967 war: the United States wanted to be able to offer arms to Israel, directly and openly, in order to compensate for those it had given to Jordan and those the USSR had supplied to Egypt, Syria and Iraq.

We may conclude this overview of the emergence of the American-Israeli strategic relationship prior to 1967 with the observation that few American leaders then realized what kind of dynamic could be unleashed if the United States had exclusive recourse to Israeli military superiority. Let us note, however, the March 1963 memorandum addressed by a high CIA official, Sherman Kent, to his superiors regarding the effects of Israel's military superiority and its possible possession of the atomic bomb. In this document Kent reckons that if Israel felt surer of itself, it "would become more rather than less tough" toward its neighbors. These neighbors would then call on Soviet assistance. So far there is nothing new in the analysis. But Kent adds that this assistance would then allow the Israelis to assert that their country is "clearly the only worthwhile friend of the U.S. in the area" (Cockburn and Cockburn 1991:90). The underlying logic of the asset doctrine is hereby exposed.

Toward the 1967 War

It is often said that the special relationship between the United States and Israel, or at least the strategic dimension of these, began only after the 1967 war. It is true that the rapid and crushing victory by the Jewish state represented a sort of hiatus following which it was perceived as an undisputed regional power defying all the Arab countries together. In particular, Israel appeared to have broken the regional influence of the two "radical" countries of the front, Egypt and Syria, and proven that their military strength had been artificially inflated (perhaps by the leaders of the three countries simultaneously, and for different reasons in each case); it had proven as well that Soviet arms and Soviet prestige had not provided effective support. But however important this turning point in Israel's regional position may have been, it was not an abrupt leap in terms of Israel's place in American strategy. It is, rather, a progressive consolidation that had begun, as we have seen, well before the war of 1967, and was revealed and confirmed by the very process that led Israel to decide to initiate hostilities on the morning of June 5, 1967.

We will now evaluate the role played by Israeli-American relations in Israel's decision to go to war. In accordance with the method we have followed throughout this chapter, we will neither attempt to describe all the negotiations between the two countries during the weeks preceding the armed conflict nor consider the Israeli, Soviet, Arab or U.N. role in the aggravation of the crisis. (For example, Israeli threats against Syria, Soviet alarmism and Soviet warnings of a "defensive" character to Egypt (Slater 1991:566), the hurried withdrawal of U.N. peacekeeping forces, Egypt's decision to close the Gulf of Aqaba to ships headed for Eilat, or the Israeli military mobilization). Rather, we shall look for possible indications of an American "green light" in response to Israeli solicitations.

If these solicitations, after Egypt's announced measures, had as their objective to obtain an essentially American support, nothing could be more normal, since only the United States was capable of neutralizing the Soviet Union in an Arab-Israeli confrontation; it was the United States that had given Israel considerable economic and military aid, as well as "assurances" in 1957 concerning the freedom of navigation in the Gulf of Aqaba. For Israel it was necessary to avoid at all costs the experience of the 1956 war, waged without consulting Washington. Indeed, American warnings had been clear on this point. In a telegram to Prime Minister Levi Eshkol on May 17, President Johnson (1971:290) declared that he could not "accept any responsibilities on behalf of the United States for situations which arise as the result of action on which we are not consulted." When Johnson received Abba Eban, then Foreign Minister, a few days later, he said on three occasions that "Israel will not be alone unless it decides to go alone" (ibid.:293; Eban 1977:358; Quandt 1977:53).

This response by Johnson was not without its ambiguities, however, since it was difficult for the president, in this crisis situation, to go beyond a reiteration of the traditional American commitment toward Israel. In a secret memorandum dated May 19, entitled "U.S. Commitments to Israel," Walt Rostow, Johnson's National Security Adviser, had summed up for Johnson the state of the commitment: " 'Our main formal public commitment toward Israel,' Rostow wrote, underlining 'formal public commitment,' had been expressed by President John F. Kennedy during a press conference on May 8, 1963 when he said: 'We support the security of both Israel and her neighbors' " (Neff 1984:77). Although it was clear, as Neff explains, that American support concerned in fact Israeli security and not that of the Arab states (ibid.:78), Abba Eban had been asked to obtain much more than that.

Indeed, as soon as Eban arrived in Washington, he received urgent instructions from Tel Aviv to ask for a formal American guarantee, since the Israeli general staff, who had on May 23 excluded the possibility of an Egyptian-Syrian attack, now considered it, two days later—and to Eban's great astonishment—to be an imminent danger. The message from Tel Aviv read: "Israel faces a grave danger of general attack by Egypt and Syria. In this situation, implementation of the American commitment is vital—in declaration and action— immediately, repeat, immediately, meaning a declaration by the U.S. government that any attack on Israel is equivalent to an attack on the United States. The concrete expression of this declaration will be specific orders to U.S. forces in the region that they are to combine operations with the IDF against any possible Arab attack on Israel" (ibid.:131–132).

The U.S. administration was not, of course, ready to commit itself to this extent. Politically, it supported the Israeli point of view regarding the gravity of the Egyptian decisions and the principle of freedom of navigation in the Gulf of Aqaba, but it was undecided as to the measures it could take, for example, to challenge the blockade along with other maritime powers (Quandt 1977:40–41). Above all, however, it was convinced that Egypt had no intention of initiating hostilities (Neff 1984:136) and suspected the Israelis of engaging in artful maneuvers aimed at forcing its hand. This was true because it estimated, based on the prevailing intelligence view, that, whichever country attacked first, the Israeli army would need only "five to seven days" to win. General Earl Wheeler, Chairman of the Joint Chiefs of Staff, reported that when Johnson expressed his skepticism at such an "optimistic" estimate, the re-evaluations the different intelligence services were ordered to perform could go no longer than ten days for an Israeli victory (Spiegel 1985:141; also Green 1984:199–200). For the U.S. administration, therefore, it was best to play for time, let diplomacy progress, and obtain Israeli moderation.

If the Israeli government, in particular Prime Minister Eshkol and Foreign Minister Eban, appeared ready to play the diplomatic card, this was not true of the army and of certain factions of the Labor Party. One might even surmise that Eshkol's alarmist attitude was the product of internal Israeli manipulations whose objective was to obtain an American green light (Brecher 1980:130–131; Spiegel 1985:138). It was not Eshkol, in fact, who originated the urgent message we mentioned above: it was Rabin, the Chief of Staff, whose intention was "to seek a nearly impossible commitment from the United States, and failing to achieve it, give the generals ammunition to pressure the politicians to approve the initiation of hostilities" (Neff 1984:148).

The true objective of the Israeli general staff in this approach to Washington was thus not to obtain a formal guarantee. Moshe Dayan, who because of repeated and heavy pressure on Eshkol became Defense Minister on June 1, expresses in his memoirs his dissatisfaction with this backhanded approach. Speaking of the meeting between Eban and Johnson, he notes (1976:263) that its object was apparently not free Israeli navigation, but "an American guarantee to Israel against attack by the Arab armies." Dayan goes on to express his refusal of such a "defensive" attitude, that is, "America's support for Israel as a victim," since what had to be obtained was "American support for an Israel that launched an attack in order to break the Egyptian blockade" (see also Teveth 1972:330–331).

Here we see a clear expression of the terms of the debate between the defenders and the opponents of the idea of a guarantee. The idea that Dayan wanted to sell to Washington was that of a menacing Israel, not that of a threatened one. However, this dichotomy is exaggerated by Dayan because the U.S. administration, in seeking to make Israel more moderate, had from the beginning correctly evaluated the supremacy of the Jewish state and understood that the Israeli political-military system, if not Eshkol himself, sought to engage in an ambitious armed action. Whatever the case may have been, the Americans, whose resources were absorbed by the Vietnam war, were less and less willing to take charge by themselves, through diplomacy or through force, of the reopening of the Gulf of Aqaba, and thus more and more willing by the day to unleash the Israelis (Spiegel 1985:139; Green 1984:197).

In order to verify this state of mind that was beginning to form within the administration, the Israeli government sent not a diplomat, but the chief of special services, Meir Amit, on a quick trip to Washington on May 30 (Dayan 1976:273; Quandt 1977:56; Neff 1984:176). Amit met Secretary of Defense MacNamara and officials of the Pentagon and the CIA "whose views were different from White House policy" (Brecher 1980: 153). Here is what Dayan related (1976:273) concerning Amit's report submitted upon returning to Israel on June 3: "His private conclusion was that the U.S. would do nothing to open the straits . . . but would also do nothing if we went to war. There was even a possibility that the U.S. might help us in the political sphere" (also Brecher 1980:157). Israel Lior, Eshkol's military secretary, goes even further and attributes to Amit the following sentence: "I am given to understand . . . that the Americans would bless us if we were to break Nasser in pieces" (quoted in Cockburn and Cockburn 1991:145; Black and Morris 1991:120–121). Abba Eban (1977:384–385), speaking no doubt of the same mission by Amit (indicating only that a "high official" was involved), employed similar terms, adding that he had received on June 1 a "document" that had a "decisive effect" on his attitude. In this document, "an American known for his close contact with government thinking" but not yet identified by sources, was said to have described the prevailing situation in Washington as follows: "If the measures being taken by the United States prove ineffective, the United States would now back Israel." Thanks to this new information, Eban reports that he then contacted the Chief of Staff Itzhak Rabin and the chief of military intelligence Aharon Yariv and gave them what he himself describes as "the diplomatic green light" (ibid.:386).

These indications of the fairly favorable attitude of the American administration prior to the Israeli attack are of course confirmed by the events that followed, that is, by the American policy of support from the moment the hostilities began. But other sources, mainly of American origin, seek to maintain the notion of an American distance with respect to the Israeli initiative. These sources present the thesis of the "go-ahead" as only one option among others, recommended by the Pentagon and also (the paradox is only apparent) by the American ambassadors in the Arab countries (Spiegel 1985:144, 147; Quandt 1977:57). For these ambassadors, writes Spiegel (1985:147), "it would be more favorable to American relations with the Arabs and the Russians for the Israelis to act on their own" (also Quandt 1977:69). Spiegel notes, however, that "there is no evidence that Johnson accepted this view."

One could indeed find in Johnson's memoirs evidence to support Spiegel's interpretation. Johnson wrote, for example (1971:297): "I can understand that men might decide to act on their own. Nonetheless, I have never concealed my regret that Israel decided to move when it did. I always made it equally clear, however, to the Russians and to every other nation, that I did not accept the oversimplified charge of Israeli aggression." However, this rather ambiguous regret expressed by Johnson following the Israeli military initiative is greatly attenuated by what he is reported to have said before the start of the hostilities. Following his meeting with Eban, he told his closest advisers that he had "failed" in his attempts to convince the Israelis not to attack (Quandt 1977:54; Spiegel 1985:142). Moreover, Johnson was warned by his intelligence services on June 2 of the imminence of the Israeli attack; an American Jewish leader, Abe Feinberg, took care to confirm the imminence of the event the following day (Neff 1984:190–191).

Parallel to Johnson's being informed about the Israeli military initiative, it should be noted that the messages he sent to Nasser through official or unofficial envoys seem to have had the objective of "camouflaging" this knowledge. Mahmoud Riad, Egyptian Foreign Minister in 1967, reveals in his memoirs (1981:50–52) that he believed the American president's assurances that Israel would not attack. Riad adds that he understood too late the "great operation of deception" that Johnson's messages represented. And Stephen Green (1984:204–211) describes in great detail an American assistance in the form of reconnaissance flights by RF-4C aircraft over Arab territories from the morning of June 5 until the 12th. The mission is said to have been planned as early as the 3rd. While Green does not attribute this information to any specific written or oral source, George Lenczowski cites "declassified" documents from the Lyndon Baines Johnson Library in Austin, Texas, in affirming that as early as May 23 the president secretly authorized supplying Israel by air with a variety of arms systems, even while announcing an embargo on arms shipments to the Middle East (Lenczowski 1990:110).

It is only normal that American decisionmakers and historians, apart from Green and Lenczowski, be little inclined to accredit the idea of American approval, and even less that of an encouragement of the Israeli military initiative by the administration. However, one senses in Johnson's attitude a resignation, a certain passivity, that would have inevitably changed into their opposite, that is, into a threat of sanctions, if the opening of hostilities by Israel had been perceived by the administration as possibly causing grave damage to American interests in the region. For the Israelis and for observers seeking to reconstruct the facts, what is (or should be) important is to know whether the administration sought at all costs to prevent the Israeli initiative, to flash a "red light" and to hold Israel in check. In the absence of threats of sanctions, the Israelis apparently found themselves at a crossroads where a green light was in evidence, that is, they were free to advance *if they wished*. It was precisely to pierce through the subtlety of the American attitude that the Israeli government sent Amit on his mission to the Pentagon and the CIA on May 30. Moshe Bitan, official in charge of American affairs in the Israeli Foreign Ministry, stated in an interview (Brecher 1980:153) several years later that "we could not ask Johnson directly; he would have had to say no. But we had to know." Precisely because it concluded (thanks to its multiple lines of communications with Washington) that the green light existed, or that there was at least no red light, Israel decided on June 4 to launch its attack the following day, counting, of course, and correctly so, on the subsequent political support of the United States.

What conclusion can be drawn from the 1967 crisis regarding Israeli-American strategic relations? The development of the crisis and its dénouement in the war denote the prior existence of a privileged relation between the two countries. An understanding, negotiated by Amit, on the objectives of the war and on certain forms of military assistance for the duration of the fighting, is not to be excluded, even though it is not yet firmly established by the sources

(Cockburn and Cockburn 1991:146–147). But even if this understanding were verified, the war was not an American decision in which Israel figured as a mere instrument. Provoked by a series of events during May in which the Arab countries played their part (not to mention historical roots that go back decades), the attack of June 5 was fundamentally an Israeli decision that Washington did not seriously wish to prevent and, finally, allowed to be taken. Washington apparently had no essential conflicts of interest with the initiatives of a country firmly entrenched in the Western camp and whose regional supremacy allowed it to do without a guarantee of protection, except in the case of a direct Soviet intervention (Green 1984:219), as American warnings to the USSR during the war proved. For Washington, it was better for Israel to act on its own initiative, that is, as an intrinsic actor (if not an asset), for this allowed the United States not to appear to be frontally opposing the entire Arab world: it is always easier to appear to be moderating an impetuous ally than to appear to be inciting a docile instrument to act (in this case, against Arab nationalism and against states armed by Moscow). If, in spite of this, accusations of collusion are raised, this is considered a lesser risk than those involved in a direct American intervention either to protect Israel or to protect its own interests.

Israel's Lightning Ascension to Strategic Status, 1967–1973

The 1967 War and its Immediate Consequences

The American attitude during the six days of war is well known. The main concern of the administration during the hostilities was not the nature of official and popular Arab reactions to the American stance, but rather the possibility of Soviet interference. There was no real crisis between the two superpowers, except perhaps on June 9 and 10, when the Soviets warned that they would be obliged to intervene if Israeli troops did not halt their advance toward Damascus. In reply, Johnson, who did not seem to be opposed to the idea of Israel's "punishing" Syria, ordered the 6th Fleet to move close to the Syrian coast (Spiegel 1985:151; Quandt 1977:63). But as soon as the Israeli army occupied the Golan Heights, the cease-fire took effect and the impending superpower crisis disappeared.

The episode of the Israeli attack on June 8 against the American spy-ship *Liberty* requires comment. Although the circumstances of this attack are still not yet fully clear, there is no doubt today that it was no mere Israeli error (Green 1984:212–242; Ennes 1979). If the apparent facility with which the Israeli military could decide to sink an ally's ship seems astonishing, it should not be forgotten that the *Liberty* was capable of intercepting all Israeli communications and could thus hinder Tel Aviv's freedom of maneuver, particularly regarding the extent of its advance into Syrian territory (an advance which had not yet begun on June 8). Although elements of the episode remain unexplained, one sees here a tendency that would manifest itself frequently in the following years: Israel insists on acting alone within the framework of an overall strategic convergence with the United States, with actors inside the American system (Congress and the pro-Israeli lobby) taking care to reduce the tensions that might arise between the two countries.

Just after the June war, Johnson decided not to follow the same course as Eisenhower (Quandt 1977:63), who had imposed on Israel a withdrawal from the Sinai by obtaining from Egypt assurances at the military level (a freezing of the front, acceptance of United Nations troops, the de facto reopening of the Gulf of Aqaba), but without requiring of Egypt any basic political concessions affecting the Israeli-Arab dispute. For Johnson, who did not feel pressed for time, the object was to take advantage of Israel's conquest of new territories in order to demand that the Arab states drop once and for all the Palestinian question, which they had proclaimed to be their sacred cause throughout the previous 20 years (Slonim 1974:9–13). Johnson's attitude would prevail through the remainder of his term and into Nixon's, until the war of 1973. Throughout this period, the official American position regarding a settlement was expressed directly or through participation in international initiatives: Johnson's speech on the principle of peace on June 19, 1967; Resolution 242 of the United Nations Security Council on November 22, 1967; conversations between the two superpowers and the four major powers in 1969 during Nixon's first year of office; Secretary of State Rogers's initiative in June-July, 1970; and finally, the Rogers Plan of December 9, 1970.

Although Washington did not rally to Israel's theses about the settlement of the conflict, its position (involving minor, not major border modifications, an end to the state of belligerence rather than normal, peaceful relations, indirect and not necessarily direct negotiations) was still far from the concessions the Arab states felt they were in a position to make after their defeat. In fact, even if the administration sometimes made a step toward certain Arab demands, its "de facto permissiveness" (Spiegel 1985:153) toward Israeli actions (such as the annexing of Jerusalem in July 1967 and increasingly bloody reprisal missions in the following years) did nothing to advance the settlement process. In addition, Washington progressively became Israel's sole supplier of weapons and economic aid: in January 1968, Johnson promised officially to maintain Israel's military defense capacity "under active and sympathetic examination" (*Department of State Bulletin* 2.5.68:174); and in October 1968 he announced his approval of the sale to Israel of 50 Phantom F-4 fighter planes (Quandt 1977:67; Bard 1988).

The Two "Tracks" of American Policy

After this historical review we can now analyze its bearing on official American doctrine regarding Israel. In the days following the June war, the United States faced a new Middle East landscape. Israel appeared for the foreseeable future as the only real power in the Arab-Israeli zone; time seemed to be working for a consolidation of Israeli supremacy. Whereas before the war Egypt and Syria were perceived as capable of destabilizing the pro-American Arab regimes, now they were in need of these regimes' diplomatic and financial support. The new situation created by the Israeli victory was judged to be greatly preferable to one in which Nasser, having avoided war, would have seen his power in the region increase markedly. Further, Israel had inflicted severe defeats on two states that were, if not allies of Moscow, at least armed by it. By furnishing information about the Soviet weaponry captured during the war and by closing Soviet supply lines to Hanoi via the Suez Canal, the Israelis seemed to be contributing to American security (Spiegel 1985:152, 159). In the eyes of many American officials, Israel had become an asset (Yaniv 1987:155).

Reality was, however, somewhat more complicated than this simplistic assessment. If it is true that the energies of the "radical" Arab countries could no longer be channeled into upsetting the conservative ones, and that these energies, although lessened, were directed toward the unshakable rock of Israel, it was nonetheless clear that the struggle against Israel could now become the theme of a tangible Arab consensus that superseded the "Arab cold war" of the preceding years (Kerr 1971). Whereas before the war the liberation of Palestine was more of a profession of faith than the organization of effective means to an end, the recovery of the newly occupied territories now appeared as the top priority to which everything else had to be subordinated. In this perspective, the Soviet Union alone was perceived as being able to offer the alternative of military reconstruction and military pressure, while the United States appeared to be the only power capable of persuading Israel to evacuate the new occupied territories. To the extent that the Israeli victory was likely to provoke the Arabs' return to the military option, closer Arab relations with Moscow, popular anti-American sentiment, the renaissance of a "radical" Palestinian movement and the risk of an uncontrolled Soviet-American escalation, this victory was in fact negative in its consequences for American interests (i.e., Israel was a burden). But to the extent that Israel could still strike against pro-Soviet Arab radicalism and that the Arab countries, Egypt in particular, could realize the futility of the military option and Soviet aid and thus try the diplomatic path leading inevitably to Washington, the Israeli victory had served the long-term interests of the United States (i.e., Israel was an asset).

These two possible courses of events in the Middle East, one hoped for and the other feared, were equally impossible to predict over the middle term. It was this uncertainty that made possible the coexistence within the American administration, and sometimes within the minds of individual decisionmakers, of two different outlooks. Those who above all feared the first possibility called for giving top priority to American efforts to settle the conflict via a certain compromise with the Arabs in order to help the "moderates" against the "radicals" and to encourage potential moderates; in this case, Israel would receive, in exchange for the territories, a formal guarantee of security which would be "an insurance against sudden shifts in the Arab position" (Yaniv 1987:153). Those who were confident in Israel as an asset warned against "appeasement" of the Arabs and tended to support Israel's conditions for peace; in their eyes, an unwritten American-Israeli alliance already existed (ibid.:156–157). Both tendencies within the administration called for Arab concessions, the maintenance of Israeli military superiority, and economic and military assistance to Israel, but there were disagreements as to the extent of these concessions and as to whether assistance to Israel should be linked to specific gestures on Israel's part. The internal competition of these two outlooks and their convergence on certain points made American policy in the post-1967 period a tissue of ambiguities: sometimes it seemed to follow the second track (Israel as asset), at other times it seemed to be on both tracks at once, and sometimes it appeared to be on a borderline between the two. However, the preponderant position after 1967 conformed to the vision of Israel as an asset. The reasons for this are both ideological and practical.

Ideologically, as the preceding chapters have shown, the doctrine of Israel as an asset, which imbued public opinion, won over the pro-Israeli lobby and Congress and affected the administration, had the advantage of being based on simple, consensual ideas such as the exclusiveness of Israeli-American ties, the value of assisting Israel, Arab fickleness with regard to the United States, and the struggle against the Soviet Union; it deduced from these ideas more debatable but difficult-to-challenge assertions: the community of interests between Israel and the United States, the imperative of firmness with regard to the Arabs and the Soviets, the futility of any compromise with them, and so on. Preaching conciliation, even when one believes in it, is hardly ever popular.

On the practical level, an American policy that did not recognize Israel as an asset, that tried, through conciliation, to prevent the Arabs' use of the military option and the reinforcement of the Soviet Union in the Middle East, would have been very difficult to effectuate. It would have implied, for American officials, the very active pursuit of a settlement, involving pressure on a strong and confident Israel to pull out of its newly conquered territories without obtaining satisfaction on all the conditions it now felt able to impose on the Arabs. In exchange for such pressure, that policy would have offered Israel an American or international guarantee that the Jewish state felt it could actually do without, which in turn would have exposed American policymakers to the criticism of the vigilant pro-Israeli lobby and of Congress, thus risking electoral defeat. Finally, the U.S. policymakers would have been attempting all this without being sure that Israel would comply, that the Arabs would follow, and that the Soviets would leave this path open. On the other hand, for the U.S. officials to believe in Israel's strength and its ability to nullify Soviet influence and the Arab military option required no active policy on their part; they needed only to bow to the powerful arguments of the lobby and of Congress, to count on Israel's regional strength, that is, to do nothing but supply economic aid and arms to Israel.

Consequently, as long as potential developments in the Middle East appeared relatively uncertain and did not allow exclusive recourse to either of the two tracks, a *policy congruent with the status of Israel as an asset* was the one that would have the upper hand in Washington. We are indeed saying a policy congruent with Israeli status as an asset, and not a policy based on the idea of Israel as an asset. If we are making this distinction, it is to stress that the decisionmaker does not need to believe in this idea in order for Israel to benefit from the consequences that flow from it (generous and unconditional aid). The decisionmaker may think that Israeli activism is the real cause of the growing strength of the Soviet Union in the Middle East; he may issue numerous declarations about the necessity of a settlement, be thoroughly convinced of this in his heart, and even take some steps in this direction. But since policy is often made up of expedient measures rather than of decisions deduced logically from a rational strategy, he may have no other alternative than to grant unconditional aid to Israel. This would be the case not only for internal reasons (the lobby, Congress), but also because the decisionmaker would fear that a policy of American pressure on Israel in time of crisis would suggest to Arab radicals that their alliance with Moscow would pay after all. In this situation, the result of different constraints on the administration leads to a policy which is, in effect, not in contradiction with the status of Israel as an asset.

This should help us understand and perhaps even resolve the ambiguity of the official American doctrine concerning Israel in the post-1967 period. On the first track, we observe initiatives for a settlement that are more timid than serious. On the second track, we observe the continuation of broadly unconditional aid to an Israel that enjoys a clear regional superiority. The timid initiatives for a settlement would thus implicitly constitute an inexpensive insurance premium for the future in the event that the main track—Israel as an asset—turned out to be counterproductive. Even if the two tracks followed by the administration were in apparent contradiction, they served the same cause. Nothing symbolizes this apparent dichotomy and its real significance better than the tension on U.S. Middle East policy between Nixon's Secretary of State William Rogers and the National Security Adviser Henry Kissinger during the 1969–1970 period. Let us examine this tension more closely.

The Two Tracks in Action Under Nixon, 1969–1970

Rogers's efforts during Nixon's first term as President were devoted to conceiving a settlement process that would interest Nasser's Egypt. From a "bureaucratic" point of view, Rogers had all the advantages on his side. Nixon (1978:477), in fact, assigned the Middle East question to his Secretary of State and excluded Kissinger from it while assigning him other crucial foreign policy questions. The President even seemed to share Rogers's point of view regarding the necessity of a settlement in order to weaken Soviet influence in the Middle East. For Nixon, the war of June, 1967 had not been a defeat for the USSR, as many in Washington had seen it; in fact, the Soviets "became the Arabs' friend and the U.S. their enemy" (Quoted in Kissinger 1979:564). At the very beginning of his term, on January 27, 1969, Nixon declared that the Middle East situation was "a powder keg, very explosive," that needed to be defused "because the next explosion in the Mideast, I believe, could involve very well a confrontation between the nuclear powers" (*Department of State Bulletin* 2/17/69:142–143; Nixon 1978:477). Commenting on a memorandum submitted by Kissinger in late 1969, the President is reported to have noted: "I am beginning to think we have to consider taking strong steps unilaterally to save Israel from her own destruction" (Kissinger 1979:372–373).

It was this apparent support by Nixon to Rogers's approach that allowed the latter, with the aid of his assistant Joseph Sisco, to present several initiatives in 1969 and 1970 that sketched out the contours of a settlement and obtained a cease-fire in the long and bloody war of attrition that pitted Egypt against Israel from March 1969 to July 1970. However, the well-known failure of Rogers to get an Israeli-Arab negotiation started leads us to minimize the significance and the importance of his diplomatic activism, particularly since his failure appears to have been wished for or expected by Kissinger and even by Nixon himself (Nixon 1978:479).

Nixon, indeed, used a double language in referring to Rogers's initiatives. In his memoirs, Kissinger (1979:348) claims that the President, in assigning the Middle East question to the State Department, "calculated that almost any active policy would fail." In a similar manner, Nixon clearly implied, in his contacts with the American Jewish community in the fall of 1969, that he "would see to it that nothing came of the very initiatives he was authorizing" (Kissinger 1979:372). A few weeks later, Nixon "ordered that private assurance be given to Mrs. Meir . . . that we would go no further and that we would not press our proposal" (i.e., the Rogers Plan) (ibid.:376). However, it is at the level of the very foundation of American policy toward the Middle East that Nixon's double language is most significant.

If, for Nixon, the Israeli-Arab conflict had to be settled because it was the means by which the Soviet Union was reinforcing its influence in the Middle East, it was also necessary, in the meantime, to face the Soviet leaders vigorously and firmly. In a memorandum that, according to his memoirs (1978:481) he "dictated" to Kissinger in the spring of 1970, the President stated that "Israel is for us the only state in the Mideast which is pro-freedom and an effective opponent to Soviet expansion." Criticizing those senators who were impatient to increase American aid to Israel and at the same time called themselves "doves" with respect to Vietnam, Nixon asserts that they would run away when "any conflict in the Mideast stares them straight in the face." As for Nixon himself, he felt that "Mrs. Meir, Rabin et. al. must trust R.N. [Richard Nixon] completely. He does not want to see Israel go down the drain and makes an absolute commitment that he will see to it that Israel always has 'an edge.' " However, according to Kissinger (1979:371), Nixon justified the need for this superiority on the grounds that "he did not want the United States to have to fight Israel's battles."

Let us now turn to Kissinger himself. He seems to have disavowed from the start Rogers's and the State Department's haste: "The bureaucracy wanted to embark on substantive talks as rapidly as possible because it feared that a deteriorating situation would increase Soviet influence. I thought delay was on the whole in our interest because it enabled us to demonstrate even to radical Arabs that we were indispensable to any progress and that it could not be extorted from us by Soviet pressure" (ibid.:354, 376, 378). Throughout 1969 and 1970, Kissinger says he believed that the "deadlock" in the settlement process worked in favor of the United States (ibid.:368; Kalb and Kalb 1974:217) and that "we should not be panicked by radical rhetoric" (Kissinger 1979:559).

More clearly than Nixon, Kissinger asserts that he always thought that any initiative along the lines of the Rogers strategy was bound to fail. More significant still is his conclusion that this failure was equivalent to the adoption of his own strategy. He writes: "Nixon understood well enough that the diplomacy would go nowhere; whenever it threatened a blowup he would usually follow

my advice to abort it. And the final irony was that the resulting policy of fits and starts, of tantalizing initiatives later aborted, was the
functional equivalent of what I wanted to achieve by design"
(ibid.:372).

It is, however, well known that, during 1969–1970 at least, this
American policy, that Kissinger called the "functional equivalent"
of his own ideas, was unable to prevent the influence of the Soviet
Union from growing in the Middle East and taking the form of a
more direct Soviet participation in the aerial defense of Egypt (from
the ground or by aerial interception) between March and July 1970.
This participation threatened the balance of forces between Israel
and Egypt for the first time; and in any event it forced Israel to cease
its in-depth bombings within Egypt and to be more circumspect
along the Canal. This process of reinforcement of Soviet influence
is recognized by Kissinger (ibid.:344, 569, 576), he who had advocated a wait-and-see policy in the settlement process and firmness
toward the Soviet Union. Is this not tantamount to recognizing the
vanity of his strategy?

Beyond Kissinger's obvious attempts at self-justification, it
should be noted that for him, from a certain point on, "the question
of what causes a Soviet move becomes irrelevant; American policy
must deal with its consequences, not with its causes" (ibid.:569).
More precisely, with reference to the Soviet Union's sending of military personnel to Egypt in March 1970, the National Security
Adviser states: "Our agencies blamed Israel for the tension along the
Suez Canal, arguing—not without evidence—that Israel had provoked the Soviet reaction by its deep penetration raids. Their 'solution' to the Soviet military move was to press Israel to be more flexible. . . . Whatever one's view about greater Israeli flexibility, we
now had first to face down the Soviets and the Arab radicals. Otherwise, Israeli concessions would be perceived as resulting from the
introduction of Soviet military personnel" (ibid.:570–571). Facing
down the USSR, in this precise case, meant, for Kissinger, as he publicly declared on July 26, 1970, "to *expel the Soviet military presence,* not so much the advisers, but the combat pilots and the combat personnel, before they become so firmly established" (ibid.:580,
Kissinger's emphasis).

However, Kissinger's strategy lessons, which still make fascinat-
ing reading today, did not govern U.S. policy toward Egypt in 1970
and did not discourage Rogers from working toward the effective
end of the war of attrition on the Israeli-Egyptian front, in spite of

Soviet military presence in Egypt, nor did they prevent the Soviets and the Egyptians from taking advantage of the cease-fire of August 7, 1970 to advance SAM-2 and SAM-3 missile bases toward the Suez Canal; these were missiles whose impressive effectiveness was to be demonstrated during the first days of the 1973 war. Kissinger can of course claim that the administration's conversion to his call for firmness toward the Soviet Union would achieve its goal two years later (when Soviet experts were expelled by Sadat in July 1972) (Kalb and Kalb 1974:223), but for the moment, a pro-Israeli policy in the Israeli-Egyptian theater had failed, proving both counterproductive and strategically dangerous (Stein 1987:338–340).

Whatever the case may be, Soviet intervention on the side of Egypt was the occasion for Kissinger to participate more actively—to the detriment of Rogers and Sisco, of course—in the elaboration of American Middle East policy. He instituted frequent consultations with Israeli Ambassador Rabin, who could thereby bypass the State Department to obtain from the President a more favorable treatment toward Israel (Kalb and Kalb 1974:219). The Kissinger-Rabin consultation manifested itself in particular during the Palestinian-Jordanian-Syrian crisis of September 1970. Since the doctrine of strategic asset considers the role played by Israel during this crisis as the model of strategic services that it can render to the United States, it is worthwhile to examine this crisis more closely.

The Jordanian Crisis of September 1970

With the Jordanian crisis, it is no longer necessary—if indeed it was so before—to treat Rogers's and Kissinger's points of view separately, as if they constituted two autonomous strategies within a bicephalous administration. Kissinger's predominance, particularly under crisis circumstances, allows us to return to a more global consideration of American policy, even if some divergences continued to manifest themselves within the administration (Safran 1978:448–449). For Kissinger, and thus now for the administration, it was urgent to have the Jordanian regime emerge victorious from its inevitable test of strength with the fedayin, in order to redeem the American failure in Egypt and to prevent another possible reinforcement of Soviet influence (Nixon 1978:483). But here, contrary to the circumstances prevailing in the Israeli-Egyptian war of attrition, an American display of force involving no immediate risk of direct confrontation with the Soviet Union was possible.

Let us recall first of all that on September 16 and 17, the Jordanian army launched its major offensive to restore its authority throughout the kingdom and on September 18 and 19, two Syrian brigades crossed the border to support the fedayin in difficulty. During the two days that followed, the Hachemite regime believed that its situation, already grave, would become desperate if the Syrians decided to escalate their intervention and push all the way to Amman. Also, the crisis brought about an American military deployment in the Mediterranean and an Israeli mobilization on the Golan Heights. Although the Jordanian army vanquished the Syrian contingent on its own strength and forced it to retreat on September 22, one should nonetheless consider the role played by the American and Israeli military preparations and American-Israeli coordination in this dénouement.

We must ask first of all whether the Israeli role was envisioned by Washington as a substitute for a direct American intervention. Two facts argue against this notion: first, the ostentatious military preparations by U.S. forces themselves (Kissinger 1979:605, 614, 622; Kalb and Kalb 1974:231) and secondly, the intentional leak of an informal declaration by Nixon according to which the United States was "prepared to intervene directly in the Jordanian war should Syria and Iraq enter the conflict and tip the military balance against government forces loyal to Hussein" (quoted in Quandt 1977:114; Kissinger 1979:614–615). It appears as well that Nixon was not favorable, at the outset, to Israel's participation in an eventual American intervention (Kissinger 1979:606–612). This was not, however, the essence of the recommendations by the Washington Special Actions Group, an interdepartmental crisis task force led by Kissinger. Already, just prior to the great Jordanian confrontation, the Group had concluded as follows, according to Kissinger in his memoirs (1979:605–606):

> Nobody relished another military involvement while several hundred thousand Americans were still fighting in Southeast Asia. We would have to commit our entire strategic reserve and supply it by air; we would become vulnerable to a Soviet thrust elsewhere. Operations would be difficult to sustain. . . . The longer the war continued, the more complicated our positions would become. If Israel intervened in Jordan on its own, we would be conducting parallel military operations for different objectives. Even worse for our position in the Arab world and our prestige, if we got into difficulties we might have to ask Israel to bail us out.

For all these reasons, I thought it desirable for our long-term interest to separate our military actions from those of Israel. My view was that American forces should be used for the evacuation of Americans because this could be done quickly and represented an immediate American interest; but in case of a major conflict provoked by an Iraqi or Syrian move, I favored letting the countries most immediately concerned take the principal responsibility. Since I considered an Israeli response to an Iraqi or Syrian move almost certain, I thought the best use of our power in that contingency was to deter Soviet intervention against Israel. A consensus developed around these propositions.

The American deployment and alert, ordered on September 9 (ibid.:614, 622; Quandt 1977:113), were more of a bluff (Garfinkle 1985) than a serious disposition to fight. The preparations by a reticent Pentagon had as their goal more to show the Soviet Union how seriously the United States was interested in the fate of King Hussein than to directly deter the regional actors (Palestinians, Syrians and Iraqis). As proof, the Syrian intervention took place after the commencement of a portion of these preparations and after the above-mentioned Nixon declaration. While this does not mean the gravity of the American deployment should be minimized, it should nevertheless be considered as more a political than a military warning, and more a global than a regional one.

Direct and local deterrence in the Jordanian crisis—if indeed there was one—would be furnished by Israel. But Israel would not threaten intervention only because Washington prevailed on it to do so; one cannot insist enough on the intrinsic, manifest, and declared interest of Israel in safeguarding, at its borders, the status quo favorable to it, and in preventing the victory in Amman of much more activist enemies, the Palestinians and the Syrians (Carl Brown 1984:211–212). Because he perceived this clearly, Kissinger understood that, regionally, it was sufficient to count on Israel, while at the same time making it quite clear to the Soviet Union that its interference against a possible Israeli action in a pro-Western zone such as Jordan would not be allowed. If this attitude involved the risk of an East-West escalation, the responsibility of this risk would be borne by the USSR. This was quite different from the case of the Egyptian front, where the Americans could not encourage Israel to escalate combat against Soviet combat personnel, because they would have had to assume responsibility for it, along with the Israelis.

In any event, as soon as Syrian troops entered Jordan, Kissinger persuaded Nixon that direct military intervention was not a credible option and that their policy would have to be coordinated with Israel's in order for a possible Israeli action to be controlled (Dowty 1984:158), and as fruitful as possible from the standpoint of both parties' interest. It should not be thought that the United States needed to rein in an Israel that would have serenely considered triggering a chain of events involving not just the Jordanian front but also the Egyptian and Syrian fronts. For Israel—a regional power to be sure, but one that could not have already "assimilated" its territorial acquisitions of 1967—this would have meant another war only three years after the June conflict, not to speak of the costly war of attrition that had only recently given way to a precarious cease-fire. Consequently, for Israel, vanquishing the Syrian intervention if deterrence proved insufficient meant limiting itself to a "surgical" operation only within Jordan (Kissinger 1979:628; Quandt 1977:117). The relative prudence of the Jewish state (in strategic terms of course, not in the perception of the Arabs), in addition to the common Israeli-American interest in protecting the Hachemite regime, had as a corollary Israel's own inclination to coordinate its action with Washington (Garfinkle 1985:136).

American-Israeli coordination did indeed take place through Rabin and Kissinger. The prudence with which this coordination was conducted is suggested by the following exchange between the two men, as reported by Rabin in his memoirs (1979:187):

" 'Do you advise Israel to do it?' I pressed.

" 'Yes', he said, 'subject to your own considerations.' "

While they preferred Israeli aerial attacks on Syrian tanks in Jordan, the Americans also gave their approval in principle to a ground action in that country, but they asked that its actual execution depend on prior American approval (Kissinger 1979:626). It is evident, however, that for the Israelis, the coordination could not be limited to this accord in principle and that Washington also had to supply, as Rabin noted (1979:188), supplementary weapons and give them "written" guarantee and "cover" in the case of an escalation (extension of the hostilities to the Egyptian front, Soviet participation in the fighting on that front, or on Syrian territory). If the Israeli request for arms could easily be satisfied, the request for a guarantee appears not to have been so simple (Dowty 1984:173). Of course, authors such as Marvin and Bernard Kalb (1974:238) venture to speak of a "historic" and "extraordinary" (but verbal) agreement, in the following terms: "If Israel would move against Syrian forces in Jordan; and if Egyptian or *Soviet* forces then moved against Israel, the United States would intervene against *both*" (their emphasis). But first-hand sources (Nixon, Kissinger, Rabin) are silent or quite reserved on this point (Kissinger 1979:626–627).

Does this mean that writers like the Kalbs have exaggerated the range and the force of American assurances, or does it mean, on the contrary, that the main actors are not yet ready to speak frankly about such a sensitive question? We would conclude, for our part, based on the study of the different sources, that significant assurances were given to the Israelis—but assurances that were oral, prudent, more "morally" than juridically binding, conditional, and subject to revision. The most clear and most certain indication of this was the message addressed by the United States to Israel the day after the crisis, on September 25, that is, at a point when the possibility of testing these assurances had lapsed: "We believe that the steps Israel took have contributed measurably to that withdrawal [of Syrian troops]. We appreciate the prompt and positive Israeli response to our approach. Because circumstances will be different if there is another attack, we consider that all aspects of the exchanges between us with regard to this Syrian invasion of Jordan are no longer applicable, and we understand that Israel agrees. If a new situation arises, there will have to be a fresh exchange" (Kissinger 1979:631).

We can conclude our study of the Jordanian crisis only on a note of ambiguity. The scope of the American assurances cannot be evaluated with precision because no escalation actually occurred. Similarly, it is difficult to gauge to what extent American and Israeli military preparations contributed to Hussein's success by bolstering the king's determination and dissuading the Syrians. Aside from the eminently unverifiable nature of the effect of deterrence in a crisis (the role of bluff), one should not minimize the other factors favorable to the Hachemite dynasty: the recent slight drop in Nasser's enthusiasm toward the Palestinians, who had just criticized his acceptance of the Rogers initiative; internal Palestinian dissension; internal struggles in Syria and opposition by Hafez Assad, the chief of the Syrian air force (who was to become head of state two months later), to his country's intervention; the moderating role of the Soviet Union vis-à-vis Damascus; and the intrinsic strength of the Jordanian army (Quandt 1977:124–125).

But what is most important here are the strategic lessons that were learned from these events concerning Israeli-American rela-

tions. The American officials, Kissinger in particular, not only minimized the conjunctural factors that were at first favorable to Hussein, but also exaggerated the positive character of the Israeli role in
the Middle East and in East-West competition (Neff 1987). Two
arguments tend, however, to weigh against their assessment. First,
it should be noted that much of the instability and the inter-Arab
struggles for influence were due to intrinsic conditions of the region
and not to the East-West opposition, even if that opposition naturally grafts itself onto the regional situation. It should also be noted
that this instability and these struggles for influence, occurring in a
region so close to Israel, are often linked (and in the case of the Jordanian crisis, were definitely linked) to the Arab-Israeli conflict
itself: for the Americans, Israel was in the paradoxical position of
being an asset by alleviating threats to its own and American interests—threats, however, that it may have itself originally provoked
through its situation of conflict with the Arabs.

Conclusion

Whatever ambiguities we may find in the Jordanian crisis, it is no
exaggeration to say that it marked a turning point in the American
administration's perception of the role of Israel. From then on, the
Jewish state was considered as a strategic asset. And if the Soviet-
Egyptian military cooperation of the spring and summer of 1970
could still belie this perception of Israel's value at the moment
when the Jordanian crisis reached its peak, the death of President
Nasser, the extension of the cease-fire on the Canal for an indeterminate period, the expulsion of the Soviet experts by Sadat in July
1972, and the establishment of secret contacts between Egypt and
the White House were to confirm the idea that a policy of support
to Israel is, after all, profitable (Kissinger 1982:204–205; Safran
1978:464–465).

One might ask whether the place assigned to Israel at this point
was really different from the earlier period. We believe that there is
a real difference, which resides in the fact that after September 1970,
American perception and actual American policy came to coincide.
Prior to the Jordanian crisis, American policy decisions were in harmony with the status of Israel as an asset, although the principal
decisionmakers within the executive branch did not necessarily
believe in this status. After the crisis, the White House, under the
driving force of Kissinger and in spite of certain doubts on the part

of Nixon, tended to minimize the possibility of the harmful character of Israeli actions and to translate its belief in Israel's strategic
importance into the conscious adoption of the following orientations (Spiegel 1985:211; Quandt 1977:126–127): guaranteeing
Israel's deterrence, supplying weapons on a long-term basis, promising not to force Israel into a settlement process that did not meet
with the Israelis' approval, making "futile" Rogers's continuing
efforts (Kissinger 1982:202) and reducing them to the pursuit of partial agreements. What had been the result of contradictory pressures
and constraints now became a largely conscious policy.

Thus, for example, the pressure of the pro-Israeli lobby now
became useless, because the administration was itself convinced of
the strategic importance of the weapons asked for by Israel
(Kissinger 1982:202–203). Moreover, in December 1971, when
Golda Meir visited Washington, the first long-term American-
Israeli military supply agreement was signed (Spiegel 1985:211); this
meant that the arms sales contracts were no longer ad hoc (Gazit
1983:32). In quantitative terms, the contrast was striking between
fiscal years 1970, when American military credits to Israel stood at
$30 million, and 1971, when they soared to $545 million (Quandt
1977:163).

In addition, a confidential agreement concerning the exchange of
military information, the "Master Defense Development Data
Exchange Agreement," was signed in December 1970. The existence of this agreement was revealed in June 1983 in a report issued
by the General Accounting Office. The agreement aimed to encourage and facilitate the exchange of information concerning "the surveillance equipment, electronic warfare, air-to-air and air-to-surface
weapons, and engineering" (Stork and Wenger 1983:29; Wingerter
1985:86). The date of the signing, just after the Jordanian crisis, is
perhaps no more than a coincidence, but it certainly took place
against the background of a common perception that a new era of
strategic cooperation was beginning between the two countries.

Nonetheless, aside from the jump in arms supplies, the difference
between the period before 1970 and the period after that date was
more significant at the level of perception and professed doctrine
than at the level of actual American policy toward Israel and the
Arab countries. If the actual policy did not change much, this was,
at bottom, because it had presented in both periods, in Safran's
words (1978:418), "the rare merit of being bold in aim and conservative in means." American policy remained audacious in its objec-

tive because it risked its own interests by betting on Israel alone—
under some constraints prior to 1970 and by choice after that date.
It remained conservative in means because it was content to count
on those of a third party rather than using its own means to protect
its interests. Thus, for example, it refused—more under constraint
than by choice—to intervene militarily to defend the Hachemite
regime (September 1970) or even to defend Israel's interests (May
1967 in the Gulf of Aqaba). Was this not the substance of the Nixon
doctrine, expressed at Guam in July 1969, in justification of the
pullout of troops from Vietnam ("Vietnamization of the war")? In
any event, up to October 1973 the American wager on Israel, either
conjunctural or planned, seemed to bear fruit. The October war
started by Egypt and Syria would upset its implications.

4 | Israel's Recovery After the October War, 1973–1980

From the eve of the 1973 war to the day after the Israeli-Egyptian peace treaty of 1979, Israel's status in American policy went from an unbelievable high point to an unexpected nadir and then gradually rose by fits and starts, without ever regaining its earlier level. We shall examine two subperiods; the first covers the 1973 war and its consequences through 1976, and the second begins with the Carter administration.

The Shock of the War and its Strategic Consequences, 1973–1976

Before 1973, the role attributed to Israel assumed that it would not have to face a major war in the foreseeable future. This was thought to be the case because Israel's military superiority was considered great enough to deter the Arabs from waging a battle to recover the occupied territories and that this superiority, in addition to the territorial conditions prevailing after 1967 (comfortable buffer zones in the Sinai, the Golan and on the West Bank), eliminated the need for Israel to initiate hostilities like those of 1967.

This confidence in its own power led Israel to stipulate conditions for a settlement that the Arab countries, and in particular Sadat's Egypt, considered unacceptable. But this confidence also led

Israel, in 1973, to undertake, beyond the usual acts of reprisal following Syrian or Palestinian operations, certain actions, such as the
destruction of a civilian aircraft lost in a storm above the Sinai in
February of that year, that could be perceived by the Arab countries,
Egypt in particular, only as provocations. If all this (the idea of Israel
as an asset, Israeli peace conditions, and Israeli actions) constituted
an expression of Israeli power, it also contributed to a contrary
dynamic that manifested itself in Egyptian-Syrian military preparations and the actual attack on the afternoon of October 6.

The 1973 War

The Significance of the War's Outbreak: The very fact that Egypt
and Syria had dared to undertake these preparations already meant,
several weeks before the actual opening of hostilities, that Israeli
deterrence had failed, no matter who was to be the winner in the
new conflict. However, the Israelis and the Americans did not realize this failure until the moment the war broke out, since the abundant information their intelligence had provided regarding Egyptian
and Syrian preparations had not succeeded in upsetting their pre-
conceived notions. By Kissinger's own admission (1982:467), "We
had become too complacent about our own assumptions. We knew
everything but understood too little."

It is also significant that the Israelis decided, on the evening of
October 5, when they finally discovered the imminence of the Arab
military initiative, not to lead a preemptive strike but instead to
wait for the enemy to come to them. On October 5, the Israeli government sent the White House a message to this effect, requesting
that Kissinger, who since August had been Secretary of State,
"inform the Soviet Union and the Arabs that Israel intended no pre-
emptive strike; if Arab military preparations were for defensive purposes they were therefore unnecessary; at the same time Israel
would react with firmness and great strength if the Arabs initiated
a war" (Kissinger 1982:466, 477; also Insight Team 1974:58–59;
Dayan 1976:460–461). Note that this contradicted Israeli military
doctrine about the conditions required for a decision to make war.
According to this doctrine, war was to be waged in enemy territory
and was to be either preventive (it would take place before the
enemy's armed forces reached a given level of strength), or preemptive (it would occur just before the enemy launched an attack). But
on October 5, Israel had internalized the major implications of being

an asset—blind confidence in its strength in the region—so well that it did not behave in accordance with its own classical doctrine of war, which is a doctrine of the "worst-case" scenario (Safran 1978:285–286). Moreover, the decision to consult Washington and not to take responsibility for starting the conflict meant that the de facto alliance between the two countries involved, at this precise moment, the same constraints of a de jure alliance (Yaniv 1987:214).

If, when the hostilities began, Kissinger expected a "rapid Israeli victory" (Kissinger 1982:455), he also understood that the Egyptian-Syrian initiative constituted one expression of the intolerable character, for the Arabs, of the 1967–73 status quo and their ability to translate this attitude into military action. We may add that Kissinger (1982:468) perceived that this action, because it was suicidal, had the potential to mobilize the most "moderate" Arabs, to polarize the entire Middle East, to cause Moscow to emerge as "the Arabs' savior," and thus to endanger the American-Soviet détente. For the new Secretary of State, who now held real power in foreign policy in the midst of the Watergate crisis, a series of factors were united that made it necessary for fighting to stop "after Israel reversed the initial Arab gains but before it inflicted a total defeat on its enemies" (Safran 1978:478; Quandt 1977:172–173). Kissinger (1982:468), who believed that Israeli needed 72 hours to recover the ground lost the first day, wanted only to demonstrate to the Arabs "the futility of the military option."

To allow Israel only a limited victory (Safran 1978:478) meant that the American administration sought from this point on to take the Arabs' point of view into account, not just rhetorically but operationally as well, in their conflict with Israel. The Arabs in question were not only the "moderates," but also—and perhaps especially—the Arabs armed by the Soviet Union. A statement by Nixon in his memoirs (1978:922) reveals the consensus on this point within the administration on October 7–8: support to Israel had to be given "in such a way that we would not force an irreparable break with the Egyptians, the Syrians and the other Arab nations." In order to detach Cairo and Damascus from Moscow it was necessary to "use the war to start a peace process" (Kissinger 1982:468).

The Course of the War: All these considerations, suggested to the Americans by the Arab war initiative, were to become amplified by developments on the ground during the next three weeks of combat. While Kissinger foresaw having to confront Israel's intransigence, toward October 9–10, i.e., when he would deprive it of total victory, the performance of the Arab armies proved much better than expected: on October 9, the Egyptian army was solidly entrenched on the eastern bank of the Suez Canal and the Syrian army, although it had lost back a part of the ground gained in the previous two days, remained generally intact. Instead of scoring a rapid victory, Israel found itself on October 9–10 "on the threshold of a bitter war of attrition that it could not possibly win given the disparity of manpower" (Kissinger 1982:492). As Kissinger himself declared on October 9, during a meeting with the interdepartmental Washington Special Actions Group, "Israel has suffered a strategic defeat no matter what happens" (ibid.:494). This constituted the second surprise of the war and required "a fundamental reassessment of strategy" (492). For Kissinger, at this stage, "a defeat of Israel by Soviet arms would be a geopolitical disaster for the United States" (493). The new situation, concluded the Secretary of State, required that Israel concentrate on a single front, the Syrian one, and register a clear victory there. This implied, however, that Kissinger was resigned in advance to the Egyptian army's retention, with impunity, of what it had just conquered. For the first time since 1967 (if not before), the United States appeared to recognize that the Arab military option was not "futile."

It was only toward October 12–13, it appears, that Kissinger understood that his apprehensions regarding the transformation of the conflict into a costly war of attrition were coming true. At this point, of course, the Israeli army had advanced beyond its October 5 lines on the Syrian front and moved closer to Damascus, but it had still not succeeded in breaking the Syrian army. More serious, however, was its urgent need for arms, particularly tanks and aircraft (Israel had then probably lost close to 400 tanks and 70 aircraft) (Sheehan 1976:231). The urgency was so great that Golda Meir sent Nixon a message that Safran considers "of truly critical import." Meir is reported to have stated, in substance: "Things have now reached a point where Israel's very existence is endangered. If the United States does not begin immediately to resupply Israel on a massive scale, it might soon be forced to use every means at its disposal to ensure its national survival" (Safran 1978:482–483). Safran, who is generally close to Israeli sources, explains that the Israeli Prime Minister's warning concerned the nuclear option (ibid.:482–483; Green 1988:91; Hersh 1991:225, 299). At the same time, the Jewish state made it known to the administration that it was inclined to accept a cease-fire ordered by the Security Council (Kissinger 1982:509; Brecher 1974:215).

From this point on, Kissinger felt that the United States' wait-and-see attitude, which at first had been based on the *prediction* of a total Israeli victory and later on the *hope* of a clear victory on the Syrian front, had become harmful. Now it was necessary either for the war to end with a prompt cease-fire (and thus with Arab, especially Egyptian, acceptance), or for Israel to receive all the means necessary to impose it on its enemies. The first possibility, which toward October 12–13 expressed a fragile equilibrium of forces and thus implied American prudence, was rejected by Egypt, whose leaders then believed that they could link their acceptance of a cease-fire to an Israeli promise of withdrawal from all the occupied territories. For Kissinger, then, the only remaining option was to send Israel massive aid; this took the form, starting October 14, of a gigantic airlift.

It should be noted here that pro-Israeli personalities blamed Kissinger for having intentionally slowed supplies to Israel during the war, in order to make clear Israel's situation of dependence. This is possible, but the point should not be exaggerated. At first the Secretary of State, like many others, believed that Israeli superiority made it possible to forego a vast arms supply program during the conflict, which had the advantage of not exasperating the Arabs and not vainly endangering détente with the Soviet Union (Sheehan 1976:33). And in fact, during the first week of the war, the United States delivered some F-4 aircraft to Israel and allowed Israel to supply itself with American weapons, stipulating only that Israel had to provide the means of transport (El Al airplanes) (Kissinger 1982:485–486, 492–493). Between the moment when this mode of airlifting proved inadequate because of severe Israeli losses and the firm decision to use the entire potential of American transport aircraft, there were hardly more than 24 hours of hesitation (Safran 1978:481–483; Quandt 1977:179–181).

The lesson that can be drawn from this episode is that for the first time in its existence, Israel found itself in a situation of precarious dependence vis-à-vis the United States. By so urgently asking Washington for arms, the Israeli government did not behave as a strategic asset, but as a protégé that feared—exaggeratedly, perhaps—for its life. The United States decided to help Israel on so large a scale not because Israel was rendering services to the United States, but rather as if the two countries had been linked by a treaty of guarantee. It should also be said, of course, that the alternative presented serious risks for American credibility: other Arab countries, Jordan especially, would have been encouraged to join the war if they had perceived Israel as weak and abandoned; the Soviet Union, which had stepped up its deliveries to Syria and Egypt, would have believed its American rival was impotent; détente, which Kissinger saw as playing in favor of his country, would have instead favored Moscow.

Although the airlift was not a direct American intervention involving American troops, it probably had a "crucial" effect on the Israeli performance, and in particular on Israeli morale (Spiegel 1985:255). Indeed, from October 14 to October 25, American deliveries amounted to "approximately 11,000 tons of equipment, forty F-40 Phantoms, thirty-six A-4 Skyhawks and twelve C-130 transports" (Quandt 1977:185). It should be added, however, that these deliveries provoked, in return, the third surprise of the war: the oil embargo by the Arab countries friendly to the United States.

The Cease-Fire: What characterizes situations of crisis, when the actors involved are relatively numerous, and when the confrontation of wills takes place through the hazards and vicissitudes of combat, is the difficulty for each party to make appropriate decisions at the appropriate day, even the appropriate hour. This was the case for all the parties involved in the 1973 war, including Washington. When the Israeli army, during the second week of the war, recovered the initiative, crossed the Suez Canal, and placed the Egyptian army in a perilous situation, the question of the best moment for a cease-fire was raised again for the American administration. It is well known that Kissinger, invited to the Soviet Union, left for Moscow on October 20 and reached an agreement with the Soviet leaders in favor of an immediate cease-fire resolution by the UN Security Council. It appears that when this agreement was reached, Kissinger did not know precisely how serious the situation of the Egyptian army was. One may wonder whether, if he had been better informed, he would have hedged in his negotiations with the Soviets in order to buy more time for Israel (Safran 1978:486–487, 492). Kissinger denies this in his memoirs (1982:544), but when he traveled to Tel Aviv on October 22, on his way back from Moscow, the Israeli leaders interpreted some of his remarks to mean that they had some extra time, beyond the official cease-fire, to complete their encircling of the Second and Third Egyptian armies (Golan 1976:84–87).

As is well known, this episode was at the origin of the serious international crisis that followed: Sadat sent urgent messages to Washington and Moscow asking them to intervene, even with troops if necessary, to force Israel to respect the cease-fire; Moscow threatened to intervene and in fact prepared to do so; and Washington declared a "stage 3 alert" to deter the Soviet Union (Quandt 1977:195–197). Although the Soviet leaders retracted their threat, the Americans, in order to resolve the crisis, had to decide, in compensation, to put pressure on Israel to avoid forcing the surrender and humiliation of the Third Egyptian army. "We had supported Israel throughout the war," writes Kissinger (1982:602), "for many historical, moral and strategic reasons. And we had just run the risk of war with the Soviet Union, amidst the domestic crisis of Watergate. But our shared interests did not embrace the elimination of the Third Army." The Secretary of State also reports a communiqué he sent to the Israeli ambassador on October 26, in the President's name (1982:609): "your course is suicidal. You will not be permitted to destroy this army. You are destroying the possibility of negotiations." Kissinger adds that this stern warning remained secret and was communicated to no other government. Dayan writes (1976:448) that the United States "presented their demand more or less in the form of an ultimatum."

The American attitude during the 1973 war, as our investigation has shown, was characterized by a series of balancing acts resembling those of a tightrope walker. Whether one judges this to be a sign of Kissinger's consummate skill or simply a series of decisions—not always good ones—that barely avoided failure, this balancing exercise in any event expresses a modification in the place of Israel and the Arab world in American policy. The delicate adjustments that occurred throughout the war continued after its end; witness, in particular, the American mediating role in the disengagement agreements on the Egyptian front (January 1974), on the Syrian front (May 1974) and in the second Sinai agreement (September 1975). What, then, are the implications of these adjustments for the place of Israel in American policy?

The New American Strategic Considerations

After the 1973 war, the United States was faced with the new imperative of setting up conditions that would prevent not only the outbreak of another major Israeli-Arab war but also the polarization of the superpowers over the Middle East, while breaking the link between oil and the conflict. All this had would have appeared superfluous until 1973 (Quandt 1977:208; Dowty 1984:281–288). Let us examine this situation more closely.

Previously, a major Israeli-Arab war had appeared improbable in the foreseeable future because the Americans believed that Israel had no need to resort to it and the Arabs would not dare to wage it. But after the October shock, the Israelis were prone to overreact by launching a preventive war in order to avoid being taken by surprise again. The Arabs, who, in spite of their defeat, had just destroyed the myth of Israeli invincibility (Kissinger 1982:561, 619), would "only stand to gain from another war," according to Kissinger's own assessment (Sheehan 1976:235). For the Americans, the prospect of another war—whoever won it militarily—would lead to one or more of the following results, all of them unfavorable to American interests: direct confrontation with the Soviet Union, serious U.S.-Arab and U.S.-European tensions, and renewed use of the oil weapon (Safran 1978:503).

Before October, the American did not fear an international polarization. The United States wanted to prove to Egypt and to Syria that recourse to Moscow would not make them any stronger against Israel, would in fact harm their chances of recovering their occupied territories and would only result in increased American aid to Israel. But when Egypt indicated it had understood this message by expelling Soviet experts in July 1972, Washington did nothing to "reward" it, as if the policy shift of countries that were militarily impotent against Israel was of little importance to the United States. However, now that the Arabs had acquired a certain military credibility and diplomatic stature thanks to the October war, the United States could no longer ignore the direct threat to its interests that would materialize if "central" Arab countries (such as Egypt, and now, Syria) (Kissinger 1982:782) had no other alternative but to seek an alliance with Moscow.

Prior to October, the Americans, with the exception of a few experts, had considered the link between oil and the Israeli-Arab conflict as mere rhetoric (Quandt 1977:13). For the United States, there were—and had to be—two separate strategic zones in the Middle East: that of the Israeli-Arab conflict and the oil zone (Kissinger 1982:871). The latter did not include the former because it was considered that the oil-producing countries, mostly conservative and having only partial control of their wealth, were not concerned by the conflict. Conversely, it had been thought since 1967 that the first zone did not spill over into the second because the frontline countries, concerned with the recovery of their territories, could no longer direct their energies toward the "radicalization" of the conservative oil-exporting countries. After October 1973, the two zones could no longer be separated because the United States' own friends decided to engage in the oil embargo and reduce production in order to pressure it into modifying its attitude toward the conflict.

It is thus clear that in order to respond to these new concerns following the October war, Washington could no longer count solely on the power of the Jewish state. It now had to neutralize the factors harmful to its interests by adopting a "new Arab policy" that took certain Arab demands into account (Sheehan 1976:51). This was all the more necessary since the Arabs—Egypt in particular—indicated they were ready to restore or improve their relations with Washington and give diplomacy its chance to operate. Does this mean that at a certain moment the American officials considered dropping Israel in order to satisfy Arab demands? No, because apart from internal American factors, the idea of a weak and isolated Israel held out only disadvantages to the United States. It would undermine its international credibility, encourage Arab "intransigence," and help create a "desperado" attitude in Israel, which could manifest itself through the fear and obstinate refusal of any concession in the settlement process, possible recourse to the nuclear threat, and the temptation to destroy Arab oil wells in order to point the "oil weapon" back toward its users.

On the other hand, preserving Israeli military supremacy did not appear to be an impossible task. Although the idea that Israel's future could be based on the force of arms now gave rise to pessimistic projections, it was agreed that Israeli superiority was not threatened. One should indeed distinguish between the balance of forces valid at a given moment, which was *in fact* favorable to Israel ("striking power") and the balance of forces in the long run, which was only *in principle* favorable to the Arabs ("staying power"), since it depended on their determination, their consistency, and their technological progress (Safran 1978:500–502). If this hypothetical reversal of the balance of forces could occur in the future, present Israeli superiority and the quality of Israeli-American relations could still serve Washington by showing the Arabs that their military option was very costly and that it was preferable for them to moderate their demands (Quandt 1977:201–202). The

American administration thus had to locate its new policy between the conflicting requirements of taking Arab demands into account and preserving Israeli strength. In the best of cases the essence of the United States' "new Arab policy" was "a commitment to the Arabs that so long as they understood the United States would not abandon Israel, Washington would truly wield its power to regain Arab rights" (Sheehan 1976:51). Actually, in Kissinger's mind and in his practice, it meant even less: the point was not to help the Arabs to recover their rights, but simply to try to defuse the explosive aspects of their demands, in such a way as to promote American interests while getting Israel to make a minimum of concessions.

These considerations took concrete form in what came to be known as Kissinger's "step-by-step" approach. While declaring himself favorable to a comprehensive settlement, Kissinger (1982:615) always refused to sketch out its contours or to work toward it, because this meant dropping Israel. Instead, the Secretary of State used all his talents to celebrate spectacularly the small steps he accomplished (such as the calling of the Geneva conference in December 1973 and the recovery of a few strips of Arab territory under the title of "disengagement") and to make the process last as long as possible. As Steven Spiegel (1985:227) puts it so well: "Success depended on devising a never-ending succession of effective tactics." As opposed to a rapid overall settlement, the long duration of the process presented the following advantages: (a) it made it possible to keep the Arabs in the position of petitioner for the longest time possible vis-à-vis the country that held the key to the settlement, the United States; (b) it forced the Arabs to pay Washington the highest possible price in exchange for the recovery of a few acres of land: ending the embargo, resuming diplomatic relations (in the case of Egypt and Syria), causing a climate of suspicion between Moscow and the Arab countries, and opening markets to American interests; (c) it might neutralize the Arabs' capacity to express operationally the intolerable character of their situation, since by privileging one Arab front at the expense of another and by postponing the hardest questions (such as the Palestinian one), it provoked inter-Arab divisions; and (d) it allowed Israel to recover little by little from the shock of war and to gauge the precise consequences of each of Kissinger's "steps" in order to better react to the next one (Kissinger 1982:1056; Sheehan 1976:114–115).

The "Step-by-Step" Approach and Israeli-American Tensions

Certain aspects of Kissinger's approach were contained in what he is reported (Sheehan 1976:161–162) to have told Israeli leaders in March 1975 when they provoked the failure of the first attempt at negotiation toward the second Sinai agreement (Sinai II):

> We've attempted to reconcile our support for you with our other interests in the Middle East, so that you wouldn't have to make your decisions all at once. . . . Our strategy was to save you from dealing with all these pressures all at once. If that was salami tactics—if we had wanted the 1967 borders, we could do it with all of world opinion and considerable domestic opinion behind us. . . . Compared to that, 10 kilometers is trivial. . . . It's tragic to see people dooming themselves to a course of unbelievable peril.

For the Israeli leaders, this line of argument was not convincing, because a series of partial retreats could place the country in a more and more vulnerable situation without diminishing Arab and international pressure (Kissinger 1982:789).

The strategic implications of Kissinger's step-by-step policy and of the differences between Israel and the United States over this approach are worth examining. For the Israelis, the policy meant that Kissinger was attempting to transfer tangible assets from the Israeli portfolio into Arab hands in exchange for an improvement of the American position in the region; Israel seemed to be receiving nothing more than "intangible"—and easily revocable—promises from the Arabs (Safran 1978:508–509). This idea is expressed clearly by Kissinger in his memoirs (1982:1046): "Once during the shuttle when I pointed out the strategic stakes, Golda [Meir] responded emotionally that she was not prepared to pay for even very important American objectives in Israeli coin." In other words, instead of reinforcing Israel's autonomous role, the United States was perhaps using Israel geographically and politically as an *extrinsic asset*, in spite of and at the expense of the Israelis, in order to draw closer to the Arabs.

It is significant in this regard that Israel's unconditional partisans in Washington referred precisely to this argument, after the failure of March 1975, in order to criticize Kissinger and rally a majority of the Senate to their point of view (Ben-Zvi 1984:17 19; Sheehan 1976:166). Indeed, in an open letter addressed to the President on May 21, 1975, 76 Senators expressed themselves in these terms (*Congressional Record* 5/22/75, S. 8933):

We believe that a strong Israel constitutes the most reliable barrier to domination of the area by outside parties. . . . We urge you to make it clear, as we do, that the United States, acting in its own national interests, stands firmly with Israel in the search for peace in future negotiations, and that this premise is the basis of the current reassessment of U.S. policy in the Middle East.

Israeli fears, as subsequent events would show, were exaggerated. As we observed above, the long duration of the process offered advantages to Israel, not just to the United States. The Americans could explain that a strengthening of their influence in the region to the detriment of the Soviet Union was in Israel's own interest. As for the Jewish state's strategic role, it was the war itself that had called it into question, not the limited withdrawals required by step-by-step diplomacy. This policy, on the contrary, was likely to offer Israel the best chance of recovering, little by little, the strategic role that the war had upset (Kissinger 1982:620–623). Consequently, Israel had the choice of either (a) refusing Kissinger's tactics and condemning itself to be considered a burden by Washington—a situation that could open the door to even greater American pressure in the future, or (b) resigning itself to being, temporarily and incidentally, an extrinsic asset, by undertaking minimal withdrawals and using its own reluctance on this issue to bargain for the best possible American compensations.

For the Israeli leaders to be able to use their own reticence in the negotiation tactics, they had to know how not to go too far. A certain balance had to be maintained between obstinacy and the need for military and economic aid. This is illustrated, on the American side, by what President Ford (who had replaced Nixon in August 1974) and Kissinger themselves had to say regarding American-Israeli tension in the spring of 1975. Ford states in his memoirs (1979:244–245):

> For the past twenty-five years, the philosophical underpinning of U.S. policy toward Israel had been our conviction—and certainly my own—that if we gave Israel an ample supply of economic aid and weapons, she would feel strong and confident, more flexible and more willing to discuss a lasting peace. . . . The Israelis were stronger militarily than all their Arab neighbors combined, yet peace was no closer than it had ever been. So I began to question the rationale for our policy. I wanted the Israelis to recognize that there had to be some quid pro quo.

As for Kissinger, he is reported to have told people close to him in early 1975: "I ask Rabin to make concessions, and he says he can't because Israel is weak. So I give him more arms, and he says he doesn't need to make concessions because Israel is strong" (Sheehan 1976:200).

It should not be thought, however, that Israeli reluctance to make concessions necessarily challenged the United States' Middle Eastern strategy. This reticence could also be useful to Washington in its negotiations with the Arabs. It is interesting in this regard to recall what Kissinger writes in his memoirs (1982:483–484):

> Israel is dependent on the United States as no other country is on a friendly power. . . . Israel sees in intransigence the sole hope for preserving its dignity in a one-sided relationship. It feels instinctively that one admission of weakness, one concession granted without a struggle, will lead to an endless catalogue of demands . . . And yet Israel's obstinacy, maddening as it can be, serves the purposes of both our countries best. A subservient client would soon face an accumulation of ever-growing pressures. It would tempt Israel's neighbors to escalate their demands. It would saddle us with the opprobrium for every deadlock.

In another passage (1057), the former Secretary of State pursues this idea: "Our strategy depended on being the only country capable of eliciting Israeli concessions, but also on our doing it within a context where this was perceived to be a difficult task."

The privileged relations between the United States and Israel thus did not exclude certain tests of strength between them, consisting of expressions of Israeli reticence, pro-Israeli intervention by members of the Senate, and threats (veiled or otherwise), accompanied by conditional promises by the administration (Ford 1979:286–288; Ben-Zvi 1984:17–19). The important thing for each of the two governments was to know when to stop. The best example is provided by the events following the failure (mentioned above) of the March 1975 negotiations on the second Sinai agreement: a threat by the administration to block military aid, to engage in a "reassessment" of its Middle Eastern policy and to adopt an overall approach to a settlement; Israel's mobilization of its friends in Washington, reciprocal concessions made not only by the United States and Israel, but also by Egypt (Quandt 1977:271–273); and sufficient common ground for a second round of negotiations in August and the conclusion of an interim agreement on the Sinai in September 1975 (Ford 1979:308–309).

The Sinai Agreement and the American-Israeli Memorandum of 1975

It is important to consider here the nature of the concessions the Israelis requested of the United States at the time of the signing of the interim agreement on the Sinai. Apparently, Tel Aviv submitted draft agreements to the administration that, according to an associate of Kissinger, "were simply incredible. They amounted to a formal political and military alliance between Israel and the United States. They would have granted Israel an outright veto over future American policy in the Middle East" (Sheehan 1976:178). Israel finally obtained less than this, but what it obtained was nonetheless considerable. Kissinger had to agree to the idea that "American civilian personnel" would be responsible for electronic surveillance in the buffer zone separating the new Israeli-Egyptian lines, which meant a physical commitment by Americans in a conflict zone only a few months after the débâcle of Saigon (April 1975). More significant still was the American-Israeli Memorandum of Agreement signed, as a supplement to the Israeli-Egyptian agreement proper, by Kissinger and the Israeli Foreign Minister Yigal Allon on September 1, 1975. Let us examine the major clauses of this memorandum (text in *Washington Post* 9/16/75).

Article 1 contains the U.S. commitment to be fully responsive "within the limits of its resources and Congressional authorization and appropriation, on an ongoing and long-term basis," to Israeli defense and energy requirements and to the needs of its economy. Article 10 declares that "in view of the United States' long-standing commitment to the survival and security of Israel, the United States' government will view with particular gravity threats to Israel's security or sovereignty by a world power." The same article stipulates that in such an event, the U.S. government will "consult promptly with the Government of Israel with respect to what support, diplomatic or otherwise, or assistance, it can lend to Israel in accordance with its constitutional practices." Article 11 expresses the intention of the two parties to conclude within two months a "contingency plan for a military supply operation to Israel in an emergency situation." A "secret addendum" to the memorandum stresses the U.S. determination to "maintain Israel's defensive strength through the supply of advanced types of equipment, such as the F-16 aircraft" and expresses American willingness "to undertake a joint study of high technology, including the Pershing ground-to-ground missiles with conventional warheads, with a view to giving a positive response." To all this should be added a second memorandum, of a diplomatic nature, concerning a possible reconvening of the Geneva conference. In this text (*New York Times* 9/18/75), the administration promised, in particular, not to recognize and not to negotiate with the PLO so long as that organization did not accept Security Council Resolutions 242 and 338.

What significance should be attributed to these American commitments, referred to as "assurances"? Above all, they do not appear congruent with the idea of Israel as an asset. The reference to supplying Israel in an emergency situation emphasizes the notion of Israeli dependence. The beginning of Article 10 appears, through a bilateral agreement, to give an official weight to the American commitment—hitherto a de facto one—to Israeli security and survival. Without being designated explicitly, the Soviet Union is considered to be the country apt to endanger the Jewish state. Notably, American protection that resulted from this agreement does not have the same implications as those of the protection Israel enjoyed during the 1967–73 period. Prior to 1973, the United States did not have to protect an Israel fearful of the Soviet Union, but could be content to neutralize a possible Soviet riposte to Israeli activism on the Egyptian or Syrian fronts.

However, one should not exaggerate the notion that the assurances included in the 1975 memorandum imply Israeli weakness and tend to negate the idea of Israel as an asset. First of all, the memorandum does not contain explicit assurances against what constitutes the most immediate danger to Israel, that is, Arab hostility. It does not seem that Israel asked for an American guarantee against such hostility. The reference to the threat of a great power is, from this standpoint, a convenient substitute: with or without this reference, one cannot easily imagine a deliberate Soviet intervention into Israeli territory, and even less easily a passive American response to such an intervention (Spiegel 1985:302). Moreover, the possibility, evoked in the addendum, of a delivery of Pershing missiles—a possibility that was not realized—was perhaps intended only to embarrass pro-Israeli Senators, an outbidding tactic worthy of Kissinger (Sheehan 1976:191–192; Quandt 1977:279). Finally, the memorandum was not a formal treaty; it was only a "simplified executive agreement," and certain of its clauses dependent on Congressional authorization were nothing more than declarations of intention. Spiegel believes that the main American political concession in the memorandum is the one concerning the PLO (Spiegel 1985:302).

Note that this situation, in which Israel asks for assurances linked to the settlement process, rather than the United States offering them, had not been specifically anticipated, either by the defenders of the "asset" doctrine or by the promoters of the GLS (guarantee linked to a settlement). The former feared—and the latter welcomed—an American offer of guarantee because both the former and the latter located it at the starting point of American pressure intended to extract the most possible concessions from Israel in favor of the Arabs. With the memorandum, the guarantee is not situated at the beginning of a comprehensive Israeli-Arab negotiation process, but at the end point of a partial negotiation in which Israeli concessions are already inevitable. Although Israel seems to be in the traditionally unenviable position of petitioner, it is in fact Israel that, through its request for guarantees, demands the maximum number of concessions in exchange for its withdrawal of a few kilometers in the vast expanse of the Sinai, to the Mitla and Jiddi passes. The guarantee at this stage becomes a card in Israeli hands rather than the reverse: the Jewish state thus succeeds in balancing, to its advantage, the necessary concessions to Egypt with the substantial assurances asked of the United States. Even if one considers certain American promises contained in the memorandum to be essentially rhetorical, Israel in fact maintains or acquires certain tangible advantages: the adjournment for an indeterminate period of the Geneva conference, the exclusion of the PLO, the consolidation of the pro-American orientation of Egypt, the separation of Egyptian and Israeli forces by American technicians, the continuation of political coordination with Washington, sophisticated weaponry, and the possibility of retaining an independent military option in the future, that is, of recovering the status of asset (Sheehan 1976:192).

The idea that the memorandum of 1975 relates, in its implications, only marginally to the GLS is again confirmed by the attitude of Kissinger in the period following the 1973 war and up to shortly before the interim agreement on the Sinai. The Secretary of State, excluding, as we have seen, a comprehensive settlement process, used the idea of guarantee with extreme caution throughout this period so as not to excite the Israelis unnecessarily (Bruzonsky 1976:74–75). To a question about guarantees that was posed to him in November 1973, Kissinger had replied (1982:878):

We have not yet given any particular guarantees. However, I would assume that if the peace negotiations succeed, there will be a very serious problem, especially for Israel, of how its security can be assured under conditions when the final border will certainly be different from the cease-fire lines and when withdrawals are involved as Security Council Resolution 242 provides.

Between 1973 and 1975, Kissinger had refused to go beyond this oracular phrase. It is known, however, that the idea of a guarantee combined with that of a comprehensive settlement was considered as a possible option by the administration within the framework of the "re-assessment" in the spring of 1975 (Ben-Zvi 1984:18). But the fact that this possibility was raised precisely during a period of American-Israeli tension shows that its main function was that of a warning to the Israelis as to what would happen if they did not show more flexibility. Kissinger's success in concluding the interim Sinai agreement allowed the Israelis to avoid the disadvantages of prior conditions placed on a GLS and to propose the memorandum. It seems clear that American policy reflected, at this precise moment, an intermediate position in the debate between the partisans and the opponents of the GLS solution. The idea that corresponds most closely to the meaning of the 1975 memorandum might be that of the functional guarantee or quasi-guarantee as we have observed in Pelcovits.

Step-by-Step Diplomacy: The Loss of Momentum

With the interim agreement of 1975, Kissinger's step-by-step policy is considered to have reached its conclusion (Spiegel 1985:310). In the Sinai there was no longer a strategically significant line between the passes and the former Egyptian-Palestinian borders; the Golan was too small a territory to allow for an intermediate stage; the Palestinian territories of the West Bank and the Gaza Strip were too fraught with ideological and emotional significance to make a partial withdrawal agreement possible without predetermining the orientation and the final result of the entire process. A consensus developed progressively within and around the administration regarding the necessity of a comprehensive approach. Among the signs of this were the Saunders document (named after the Deputy Secretary for Near-Eastern Affairs) in November 1975 (Buheiry 1978; Quandt 1977:278); the Brookings Report of December 1975; and the non-use by the U.S. of its veto right against the PLO's first participation in a Security Council debate in January 1976. But inter-Arab divisions following on the Sinai agreement, the Lebanese civil war, and the American presidential race put off until 1977 any concrete action based on the comprehensive approach.

But before 1977 arrived, the developments in the Lebanese civil war in 1975–76 suggested that Israeli deterrence, glorified in 1970 at the time of the Jordanian crisis, could no longer be considered as automatic. Prior to 1973, a Syrian intervention in Lebanon, whatever its pretext, would have been perceived as a threat to the status quo protected by Israel and thus provoked an American-Israeli response. In the post-1973 period, however, the stature acquired by Syria, the new "sophistication" of its leaders in the East-West balancing game, and the lasting effects for Israel of the shock of 1973, made the mechanism of Israeli deterrence more complex and less credible, leading to an American-Israeli acquiescence to the entry of the Syrian army into Lebanon. Of course, unlike in 1970 the declared goal of Damascus was not to protect the PLO but to control it; and of course, Israel posed certain conditions for its acquiescence: no extension to southern Lebanon of the Syrian deployment and no installation of an anti-aircraft defense system (Rabin 1979:280). But, one may ask: do Syria's sophistication and Israel's acquiescence not demonstrate that Syria, as well as Egypt, had now become a partner in dialogue for the United States and Israel—one with whom it was necessary to deal at the strategic level, and who could no longer be deterred by mere military threat? It does seem, after all, that the role attributed to Israel by the strategic asset doctrine regarding the first stage of the Lebanese civil war was exaggerated and simplistic.

The Difficult Recovery of Israel's Strategic Role, 1977–1980

Carter's Comprehensive Approach

Arab reconciliation and the "proclamation" of the end of the Lebanese war, achieved at the Arab summits of Riyadh and Cairo in October 1976, occurring just before the American presidential election of November, brought the idea of a comprehensive approach to the settlement of the Israeli-Arab conflict back onto the agenda. This prospect seemed all the more serious considering that the new president was Jimmy Carter, a Democrat linked to the Trilateral Commission, who chose his advisers from among the members of that group (such as Walter Mondale, Cyrus Vance, Zbigniew

Brzezinski, and Harold Brown) as well as from among the participants in the Brookings Report, known proponents of the GLS
(Brzezinski 1983:49; Spiegel 1985:327).

The place assigned to Israel by the new administration in its Middle Eastern policy cannot be separated from the global vision it
espoused that had earned it victory in the presidential election. For
the Carter team, it was necessary to draw the right lessons from the
"moralization" of public opinion after the Watergate scandal and
from public repugnance at the idea of foreign military intervention
after the failure in Vietnam. Influenced by the thinking of the Trilateral Commission, the Carter administration saw it as important
to develop political and economic cooperation between the United
States, Western Europe, and Japan; to continue the policy of détente
with the Soviet Union, and promote economic relations with that
country; and to adapt to the possibility of a multipolar international system (involving a confirmation of the opening toward China),
which would give each party a role corresponding to its stature.

This vision of the "world order" (Hoffmann 1980) meant recognizing the Third world's "legitimate" share in economic and political benefits and seeking to settle regional conflicts. Such a policy, it
was thought, could create objective conditions in the countries of
the South for moderate and adaptive regimes to emerge and gain
strength, causing "radical" forces to grow spontaneously weaker,
Soviet influence naturally to diminish, and the image of the United
States, as a pacific power that encouraged political participation and
economic and social progress, to improve (Brzezinski 1983:53–55;
Spiegel 1985:318–319). Concerning the Middle East in particular, it
flowed from the foregoing that the essential needs of each party
would have to be considered with sympathy: security and peace for
Israel, a "form" of self-determination for the Palestinian people, and
the recovery of territories for the Arab states (Carter 1982:276–277).
Such ideas were indeed in conformity with the recommendations of
the Brookings Report mentioned above (Spiegel 1985:323).

It should not be thought, however, that this orientation by Carter
was altogether new. Kissinger, in his Arab and oil policies after
1973, had already shown that a compromise was necessary and that
it was no longer possible to rely on deterrence alone or on military
intervention to resolve problems in the Third World. The Arabs'
performances during the 1973 war had confirmed the lessons of
Vietnam, according to which many Third World countries could no
longer be deterred by the symbolic deployment of a few thousand

Marines (as in Lebanon in 1958) and that gunboat diplomacy now had to attain another order of magnitude—tens if not hundreds of thousands of troops—in order to be effective. But the difference between Kissinger and Carter resided in the fact that the former felt compelled to compromise in situations where it was inevitable, such as Vietnam and in the Arab world, and only in those situations, whereas the latter seemed to believe that compromise was a desirable principle for protecting American interests and that it could be applied everywhere. That is why Kissinger clothed his resignation to compromise with the Arabs in a diplomacy that may have been highly spectacular but was poor in tangible gains for the Arabs given their new international stature, whereas Carter, with his idea of a comprehensive Middle East settlement, displayed a general disposition to compromise.

What did this vision imply for Israel's place in the new American policy? By seeking the objective of an overall settlement of the conflict, Carter did not appear to commit himself to pursuing what Kissinger had begun after 1973, that is, progressively reconstructing Israel's status as a strategic asset. Indeed, if Carter were to succeed in ensuring lasting security for Israel via peace treaties calling for the end of the state of belligerence as well as normal diplomatic and economic relations between Israel and its neighbors, the Jewish state itself would feel less of a need (or desire) to resort to force in order to protect its own regional interests and thus claim, rightly or wrongly, to be protecting those of the United States. Further, if Carter were to succeed in resolving the Palestinian question, the problem that poisoned Arab-American relations in a fundamental way, then the Arabs would no longer turn toward Moscow (Carter 1982:205; Brzezinski 1983:83) and would have no reservations about developing close ties with Washington; the United States would thus no longer need the contribution—such an unstable and risky one—of the Israeli strategic asset.

Of course, Carter did say in his memoirs (1982:274–275) that he shared with other Americans the idea that Israel was a "strategic asset." But the context (ibid.:277) suggests that he was only paying lip service to the notion and was seeking above all to provide a justification for considering the Palestinian question at the outset of his term:

> Since I had made our nation's commitment to human rights a central tenet of our foreign policy, it was impossible for me to ignore the very serious problems on the West Bank. The continued deprivation

of Palestinian rights was not only used as the primary lever against Israel, but was contrary to the basic moral and ethical principles of both our countries.

Spiegel notes also (1985:326) that in spite of the presence of "genuine supporters of Israel" among Carter's advisers, "the administration's foreign policy decision-making structure was distinguished by the absence of any senior official who saw Israel as a valuable ally of the United States."

In this perspective, which doubtless corresponded during the first nine months of 1977 to an unrealistic confidence on the part of Carter and his advisers in their own capacity to impose a "moderate" and stable order on the Middle East through a comprehensive settlement of the Israeli-Arab and Israeli-Palestinian conflicts, the question of an American guarantee to Israel could not but arise. However, available American sources about the developments of this year offer very little on this subject. William Quandt, who at that time belonged to the National Security Council, writes (1986:59) that "Carter was prepared to consider how the United States could bolster Israeli security, up to and including a U.S.-Israeli defense pact as part of an overall settlement." Quandt further notes that just before the first visit to Washington of the new Israeli Prime Minister Menachem Begin in July 1977, Brzezinski suggested in an internal administration debate that if Begin made concessions, "he should be rewarded, perhaps even with the offer of a full-fledged military alliance" (ibid.:75).

It is difficult on the basis of these quotations alone to know the precise meaning given to the terms "defense pact" and "military alliance." In the minds of the actors, did it mean a "unilateral" guarantee, a "mutual" treaty, a "peripheral" or a "central" alliance? It is likely that, at the beginning of Carter's term at least, the first of the meanings—unilateral guarantee—was the one retained. Begin's attitude during his Washington visit confirms this interpretation. Indeed, Begin presented Carter "a lengthy document detailing all the strategic benefits that the United States gained from its ties to Israel" (Quandt 1986:81). Through this document, which consisted mainly of a list of Soviet military equipment captured by the Israelis and turned over to Washington, Begin meant to tell President Carter that there was no need for an American guarantee, that "aid to Israeli was not charity, but a sound investment for which good value was given in return" (ibid.:81).

A clearer idea may be gained, however, from what Moshe Dayan,

Foreign Minister of the Begin government, reported about his meetings with American leaders during the second half of 1977 and his responses to their proposals. Here is what Dayan (1981: 56) wrote about the "possibility of an American guarantee" raised by Cyrus Vance, Secretary of State, during a meeting held in Washington on September 19:

> It was the American purpose to get us to withdraw, and to cover the consequent risks to Israel's security by providing insurance through a guarantee. My reply to Vance . . . was . . . that . . . my government would consider the American proposal when it was received . . . I added my personal view that I thought we—like the countries of Europe—needed a U.S. guarantee only against Soviet aggression. We could manage with the Arabs ourselves.

When Dayan met with Carter that same day, the subject of guarantees was also raised. The Israeli minister reports (1981:162) that in response to his question about the American disposition to granting a NATO-type guarantee, Carter answered that the United States "had no firm decision as yet." Quandt (1986:129) confirms this version but places it on October 4 and adds an interesting detail: that Dayan explained to Carter that Israel "would be interested in being treated like a NATO ally and would even offer the United States bases in Israel." It should be noted that Dayan's attitude represented a notable change with respect to his ideas prior to 1973, when he had asserted that Israeli should forego a defense treaty with the United States (Yaniv 1987:215).

The Failure of the Comprehensive Approach

It was with vigor that Dayan replied to what seemed a timid and unattractive offer of a GLS, insisting instead on the requirement that an agreement be mutual and that it be an alliance of the NATO type (that is, a central rather than a peripheral alliance); and if he was able to respond in this way it was because, over time, Carter's original intentions regarding an overall settlement had run up against increasingly insurmountable difficulties. Aside from the Arabs' inability to define a unified diplomatic approach toward the Americans, one of the main factors that upset the assumptions of Carter's approach was the defeat of the Labor Party and the victory of the Likud in the May 1977 elections. By this very victory, Israel overcame the trauma of the October, 1973 war.

However, the most immediate and direct blow to this approach was the Dayan-Carter meeting of October 4, 1977, which marked a serious retreat by the administration from a joint Soviet-American communiqué signed three days earlier. It may be recalled that on October 1, the Soviet and American leaders had published a joint declaration expressing the following principles: a comprehensive settlement, an Israeli withdrawal, respect of the legitimate rights of the Palestinian people, normal and peaceful relations, international guarantees with possible American and Soviet participation, and the holding of the Geneva Conference before the month of December with the participation of representatives from the Palestinian people (*Department of State Bulletin* 11/7/77:639–640).

The failure inflicted on the Soviet-American declaration was due to the convergence of three factors: the firm refusal of the Israeli government (Raymond Cohen 1978; Ben-Zvi 1984:29–31), the mobilization of the American Jewish community, and the indignation of the American conservatives who did not understand why the USSR was being brought back into the negotiation process after having been excluded from it throughout the Kissinger period (Spiegel 1985:338). It should be added, however, that what contributed even more to the failure of the declaration (and consequently to the failure of the global approach) was the way in which Carter and his team had managed, in the year 1977, the preparations for the negotiations: a series of hesitations by Carter, contradictions between Brzezinski and Vance, and incompetence in the necessary effort to gain the approval of public opinion (ibid.:316–317). As Robert Springborg explains (1981:805) "Carter either did not fully comprehend the implications of the shift to the comprehensive approach (i.e., that its successful implementation necessitated confrontation with Israel and her American supporters), or if he did, he nevertheless still failed to prepare his administration adequately for that inevitable political battle." Faced with difficulties, the Carter administration would display the same paradoxical mixture of determination and incoherence in Middle East policy as in its overall policy (and in particular on the human rights question) (Hoffmann 1981).

In any event, the first person to draw the conclusions from the paralysis that threatened to come out of the American failure was President Sadat. With his visit to Jerusalem in November, Sadat changed the rules of the game for all the players (including himself) and believed he could institute a different approach from that of the Geneva Conference, as if its reconvening was being prevented merely by questions of procedure. But Sadat's initiative, which was in many ways the result of the Israeli tactical victory over Carter (culminating in the October 4 reversal), once again opened the path to what was the obvious preference of the Begin government (Brzezinski 1983:235–236; Quandt 1986:150, 152), that is, the process of partial settlement inaugurated by Kissinger and which the new American president had thought he could go beyond.

Indeed, the administration lost no time in profiting from its own impasse and the new situation created by Sadat's visit (Springborg 1981:816). If the Egyptian-Israeli settlement was the only result that could be quickly and easily attained, the administration thought it should be pursued without delay to avoid paralysis. As the year 1978 began, Carter "seemed to think the primary strategic objective for the United States was to conclude a peace treaty between Egypt and Israel, not to resolve the Palestinian question" (Quandt 1986:179). But in order to maintain a semblance of coherence with respect to the stated intentions of the earlier period and to limit insofar as possible the political damage this new political course threatened to cause in relations with the other Arab countries, it was necessary to announce that progress had been made on the Palestinian question as well. In other words, the idea was to cover the projected Egyptian-Israeli accord with some type of declaration of principles or of intention. Some journalists at the time, as well as Brzezinski himself, did not hesitate to call this cover "a fig leaf" (*Jerusalem Post* 3/3/76; Brzezinski 1983:236).

After several months of difficult negotiations in which the dramatic effect of Sadat's initiative faded out more and more, American efforts culminated, in September 1978, in the tripartite summit bringing together Carter, Sadat, and Begin at Camp David and the accords bearing the same name. Even here, as Brzezinski admits (1983:273), "the issue of linkage between an Egyptian-Israeli settlement and the West Bank-Gaza negotiations . . . was not resolved, largely because Carter in the end acquiesced to Begin's vaguer formulas." But beyond the question of the linkage between these two aspects of the conflict, we must ask what were the strategic implications of the Camp David process on the place of Israel in the United States' Middle Eastern policy.

The Significance of the Camp David Process

In certain respects the Camp David process meant the possibility for Israel to re-establish the stature it had enjoyed before 1973 when it did not have to face an Arab military option. Thus on the sixth day of the Camp David conclave—September 10, 1978—Carter (1982:373) said to Begin: "It is important to remember that an agreement between Israel and Egypt would preclude any successful attack against your country by other Arab countries." Even if Carter added immediately afterward that the Israeli-Egyptian accord "should be seen only as a first step on the way to agreement with the other Arab countries" (ibid.:373), this in no way changes the main thrust of his argument.

The neutralization of the Arab military option, in a Middle Eastern environment in which only Egypt was linked by a peace treaty to Israel, was likely to restore to Israel its regional intervention capacity and thus its status as an asset to the United States. The idea of a GLS offered to Tel Aviv by Washington would thus no longer have its place in the logic of the process set in motion by Sadat's visit to Jerusalem. Did this mean that the prospect of a GLS would be replaced by the offer of a mutual defense treaty, which was preferred by the Israelis (as Dayan had indicated to his American interlocutors)? It would appear that the U.S. attitude, without being favorable, was somewhat more open to this idea than before. However, the known facts of the case are contradictory.

In a memorandum by William Quandt (1986:193) addressed to Brzezinski in May 1978, it appears that the administration had (probably in the preceding months) "suggested to Israel a bilateral mutual security treaty." Quandt further related in his book about Camp David that during a meeting of the National Security Council in September 1978, Harold Brown, Secretary of Defense, considered "the possibility of a U.S.-Israeli defense treaty as part of an overall settlement."

"Brown argued," writes Quandt, "that such a treaty might have political value in the negotiations, but that it held little attraction for the United States on strictly military grounds. Carter agreed" (ibid.:217–218). Carter himself points out (1982:355) that on September 7, on the third day of the Camp David summit, the question of mutual defense treaties was discussed in a tripartite meeting. The President writes: "Begin wanted them; Sadat encouraged the idea; I was convinced it would be a serious mistake if we were to continue being influential in resolving differences between Israel and her other neighbors. For us to be a formal ally of Israel would make it impossible to mediate between Israel and the Arab nations." Yet

Quandt notes (1986:242) that on the September 15, the eleventh day of the summit, Vance and Brzezinski "for the first time raised with Dayan the possibility of a U.S.-Israeli security treaty as part of an overall settlement. Dayan must have seen this proposal as something of a trap, as offering American protection if only Israel would make further territorial concessions. He therefore showed little interest, and the issue was quietly dropped."

Reading over these few factual indications about a possible defense treaty, we cannot avoid an impression of confusion. How could the signing of such a treaty, in the framework of one and the same process, be both suggested and refused to Israel? Does the idea of such a treaty fit into the framework of an overall settlement as Brown indicated (and therefore make it similar to a GLS) or does it rather refer to an autonomous act to be juxtaposed to a separate Israeli-Egyptian accord, as Carter implied (thus giving it the character of a formal alliance)? This conceptual confusion is perhaps not surprising; it could even be considered as normal because it expresses an intermediate situation between two possibilities that the Camp David process excluded: the idea of a mutual defense treaty, refused by Carter, and the idea of a GLS refused by the Israelis and then practically abandoned by the American president. Between these two possibilities, there was room for intermediate solutions; one could even say that the path seemed open for a possible Israeli recovery of its status of strategic asset, which, let us recall, does not need to be acknowledged within a formal document or even in an official doctrine. In other words, the Camp David process would allow Israel to enjoy a situation comparable to the one prevailing in 1968–69, when its capacity for regional intervention coexisted with the administration's assertion of its intention in theory to work for an overall settlement.

An important difference should be noted, however, between the conditions prevailing in 1968–69 and those of 1978: in the earlier period, the regional context included a "radical" Egypt, close to Moscow, whereas now the foremost Arab state had swung toward Washington. Thus, in the spring of 1978, the administration rewarded Cairo with a promise of delivering fifty F5-E fighter planes in the framework of a "package deal" which also included Israel and Saudi Arabia. (Spiegel 1985:346–347). This was the first time that Egypt had been allocated American weapons; in 1975, Egypt had been authorized to buy some C-130 transport planes as a symbolic acknowledgment of the beginning of military relations. The Camp

David process signified the potential emergence of Egypt as a precious regional ally of the United States and thus as a potential competitor of the Jewish state. According to Brzezinski, for example (1983:236), "Sadat saw in the peace process an opportunity to fashion a new American-Egyptian relationship, one in which Egypt might even displace Israel as America's closest ally in the region." Without committing himself formally in this direction, and fearful, on the eighth day of the summit, of the failure of the negotiations, Carter (1982:384) claims to have told Sadat that his success would make it possible "to release a large portion of the Egyptian armed forces now marshaled along the Suez looking toward Israel. . . . A peace treaty would let his friends in Sudan and Saudi Arabia, as well as his potential enemies in Libya and Ethiopia, know of this new Egyptian capability to act militarily, if necessary" (also Brzezinski 1983:277).

One might ask, however, whether Carter's objective in using this argument was not above all to obtain concessions from Sadat. Brzezinski (1983:274) suggests this might have been the case: "President Sadat, who saw Camp David as an opportunity to collude with the United States against Israel, ended with much of the pressure directed at him. His choices were either to walk out or to agree to whatever we could get the Israelis to accept." For Sadat, to walk out after having come so far was practically to be excluded. After toying with this possibility on September 15, the eleventh day of the summit, Sadat had to face a "very rough" Carter (Quandt 1986:239) who made it clear to him that this "would harm the relationship between Egypt and the United States" (in Carter's milder version) (Carter 1982:392) or "mean an end to the relationship between the United States and Egypt" (in Brzezinski's starker version) (Brzezinski 1983:272). Under these circumstances, the American promise to allow Egypt to play a regional role loses some of its credibility.

Yet whatever Carter's goal may have been (whether his argument was merely an attempt at persuasion, or whether he actually considered attributing a strategic role to Egypt), and whatever concessions Sadat made to Israel during the Camp David summit, it was still too early to evaluate the strategic consequences of a possible summit success on the regional role of Egypt. However, on the other hand, the possibility that Israel could recover its earlier role was based on more likely estimates, since on the front that remained, that is, the eastern front, the ground had been known for a long time. Whatever may have been the case, on the thirteenth day of the

historic summit, success was finally announced via the proclamation of two broad accords (on the framework of an overall settlement and its interim application on the West Bank and in Gaza; and
on the framework for an Israeli-Egyptian peace treaty). But it
became clear over the next several weeks that even the negotiations
toward the text of an Israeli-Egyptian treaty would run into heavy
difficulties and could not be completed within the three-month
time frame envisioned at Camp David.

The Iranian Revolution and the Difficulties of Concluding a Peace Treaty

Without attempting here to treat these difficulties in detail, let us
simply note that they involved the following points: the Israeli government's acceleration of its settlement activity in the occupied
Palestinian territories, the nature of the link between the Israeli-
Egyptian treaty and the negotiation over these territories, the primacy of the treaty over Egypt's commitments toward the Arabs, the
time frame of diplomatic exchanges, and the sale of Sinai oil to
Israel. At the end of 1978, the negotiations were clearly headed into
an impasse (Quandt 1986:268–269; S. Lewis 1988:224). But in January 1979, after such considerable American efforts, the fiasco
appeared more dramatic still than in the preceding months. Arab
opposition to Sadat was showing itself to be stronger than expected;
and the Iranian revolution against the shah, and against his alliance
with the United States, was proclaiming its victory. Camp David,
had it failed, would have been considered as one more victim of an
irresistible anti-American wave. When "the strategic pivot of the
American position in the Persian Gulf area, Iran, was literally crum-
bling before our eyes," writes Brzezinski (1983:279), then "to let the
Camp David accords slip away would be to turn a triumph into disaster, with unforeseeable consequences for the Middle East as a
whole" (also Quandt 1986:290; Spiegel 1985:368–369).

From this moment on, the "style" of the passages relating to the
Israeli-Egyptian treaty changes in tone in the memoirs of both
Carter and Brzezinski (also Quandt 1986:291–292). What comes
across is less the pride (feigned or naïve) in having participated in
peace efforts (however partial), than the admission of a calculated
determination to surmount strategic challenges. Quoting his diary
for January 26, 1979, Carter writes, for example (1982:412), that
because of the impasse in the Israeli-Egyptian negotiations, it was
decided that Defense Secretary Harold Brown would travel to Egypt,

Israel, and Saudi Arabia at the beginning of February: "We'll issue specific instructions to him, because he'll have both military and diplomatic duties to perform." In a note addressed to Sadat in early March (1982:417), Carter stressed that the nuances of language between Israel and Egypt are "minimal when compared to the over-all strategic considerations which you and I must address together." American officials expressed the same viewpoint in the presence of Israeli officials (Dayan 1981:260).

While the new situation created by the Iranian revolution obvi-ously required the American administration to deploy a burst of determination and energy, it also caused the Israeli government to further harden its positions. As early as November 1978, as Dayan stresses (1981:264), "the peace accords were becoming less popular from day to day, with Israel having to give up so much and then being saddled with enormous financial burdens for doing so." With the possible exception of Dayan (Quandt 1986:294), Israeli officials were inclined to think that no country was in a better position than Israel to take the place of the Iranian "pillar." They were therefore less disposed to withdraw from the Sinai and in particular from its air bases, and refused in any case to make the last-minute conces-sions necessary to finalize an agreement. They thought that if they made these final concessions to Egypt, even at the level of termi-nology, this would be tantamount to recognizing that the strategic modifications occurring in the region were taking place to their detriment, or rather, to the detriment of the role they were entitled to. In their relations with the American administration, they in turn laid emphasis on the importance of their strategic role.

Begin's visit to Washington in early March 1979, at Carter's invi-tation, is significant in this respect. Here is how Carter (1982:414) describes their first session together on March 2:

> Begin made a long, rambling statement about the power of Israel's land forces and their readiness to join Egypt in an attack on Libya or to defend Saudi Arabia. He described how, in 1970, Israel had used its army to stop Syria's move into Jordan. He asked for more airplanes and tanks, and suggested that we needed to have a mutual defense agreement. . . . He did not seem especially interested in the terms of the peace talks. His purpose seemed to be to convince us that Israel should be the dominant military power in the area, and that it was our only reliable ally in the Middle East.

Carter adds that he had noted in his diary for March 2 that Begin was "very strong, negative, apparently confident. . . ." (ibid.:414–415).

Quandt (1986:298) points out another detail of this meeting: Begin "even went so far as to offer the United States an airbase in the Sinai that he had already promised to return to Egypt."

If Begin could argue with such force, this was because, according to the judgment formulated in a memorandum by Brzezinski at the time, the Israeli Prime Minister "believed he could afford a failure and Carter could not" (Quandt 1986:298). The President felt obliged in the end to play on his prestige and traveled to Egypt on March 7–13. Without mentioning in detail the final concessions won from Egypt and from Israel (in fact, mostly from the former), we should note the strategic component of the argument Carter used in Jerusalem to persuade the Israelis. Here is Quandt's description (ibid.:306):

> Turning to bilateral U.S.-Israeli relations, Carter maintained that the two countries were equal partners. He added that what the United States did for Israel was more than balanced by what Israel did for the United States, a point that Begin had long been pressing on American audiences and that Carter really did not believe. Israel, he said, was a tremendous strategic asset to the United States, especially if it was at peace with Egypt, the other major regional friend of the United States.

In the course of another meeting, Carter explained to his interlocutors that "Egypt and Israel could work together to prevent the kind of radicalism seen in Iran from spreading to the rest of the region" (ibid.:307).

One might consider Carter's arguments as mere rhetoric whose only real objective was to force Begin's hand in order to gain his support for the Israeli-Egyptian treaty. This is, indeed, what we were inclined to do with respect to American efforts to persuade (or rather to pressure) Sadat during the Camp David summit. But in the present case, we believe that Carter's words, without having to be taken literally, are more than a gratuitous exercise. Because he was in a position of petitioner, what he said to the Israelis to persuade them to sign the treaty with Egypt excluded threats or blackmail. Even if, as Quandt asserts, Carter did not really believe what he was saying, he was nonetheless committing the United States in a certain manner by admitting that it was indebted to Israel rather than being its "creditor." In this manner he was enlarging Israel's margin for maneuver on the eastern front with respect to what it had already become following Camp David. It is significant, for example, that in exchange for a few modifications favorable to Egypt in

the language of the treaty, Israel obtained other favorable amendments, gaining above all two other advantages: an American
promise to append an Israeli-American memorandum to the Israeli-
Egyptian treaty (Yaniv 1987:216); and the breaking of the few tenu-
ous threads that still linked the treaty to the principle of an overall
settlement and to negotiations concerning the West Bank and Gaza
(Quandt 1986:308–310). Aside from the withdrawal from the Sinai,
Tel Aviv was not bound by any other commitment.

The Peace Treaty and Regional Security

What a difference between Carter's program on the Arab-Israeli settlement at the start of his term in office and its outcome two years
later! And what an evolution in Israel's strategic status during that
time! But although the apparent confusion we mentioned above has
diminished somewhat, although the GLS as a means of pressure has
been removed from the U.S. agenda, and although Israel was no
longer considered a burden, and although its status has potentially
risen, this status remains to be defined more precisely. In order to do
so, we must now consider, on the one hand, the strategic significance of the American-Israeli memorandum of agreement signed by
Dayan and Vance on March 26, 1979, the same day the Israeli-Egyptian peace treaty was signed, and on the other hand, the new American regional strategy after the fall of the shah.

The American-Israeli Memorandum of Agreement. In the same way
as for the interim Sinai accord of September 1, 1975, the American-
Israeli Memorandum of Agreement of March 26, 1979 (Dayan
1981:356–357) was annexed to a text signed by a third party (Egypt),
as if, for Israel, it were an integral part of the treaty. But contrary to
the 1975 memorandum, which was in principle secret (but was
leaked two weeks after its signing), the memorandum of 1979 was
public. While the first one had been bitterly negotiated, the second
one seems to have been easily concluded. From the juridical point of
view, the two memoranda were signed at the same level (Foreign
Minister and Secretary of State) and thus had the same authority.
But according to Article 8 of the 1979 text, the new assurances
replace certain expressly enumerated articles of the 1975 one.

The text of the memorandum does not appear to be equivalent in
content to a mutual defense treaty. Carter, in his memoirs
(1982:426), in fact denies having agreed to conclude such a treaty
during his visit to Jerusalem in early March. Contrary to the text of

1975, this one contained no reference, even indirect, to protecting Israel against the Soviet Union. Article 6 contains a promise by the United States, subject to Congressional authorization and appropriation, to endeavor "to be responsive to military and economic assistance requirements of Israel." The most important article, number 3, declares that "if a violation of the Treaty of Peace is deemed to threaten the security of Israel . . . , the United States will be prepared to consider, on an urgent basis, such measures as the strengthening of the United States' presence in the area, the providing of emergency supplies to Israel and the exercise of maritime rights in order to put an end to the violation" (Dayan 1981:356–357).

Aside from the novelty of Washington's willingness to consider a reinforcement of its presence in the region, the 1979 memorandum appears weaker than that of 1975. Contrary to the opinion of Avner Yaniv (1987:216), the 1979 memorandum is not "a more explicit U.S. commitment to Israel than had ever been offered before." The idea of a general guarantee to Israel is not suggested; all one can induce from the memorandum is the fairly circumspect idea of assurances relative to the application of the Israeli-Egyptian treaty. Between 1975 and 1979, the Israeli-American agenda has changed and the status of Israel has been elevated, in spite of Carter's efforts during his first year in office. In the place of a guarantee, what emerged in the center of Israeli-American discussions was the idea of a mutual defense treaty, even if it was still refused by the American administration.

More precisely, a small step in this direction was made by the Americans. On March 19, that is, one week before the signing of the memorandum by Vance and Dayan, another memorandum of Agreement was concluded between the two countries. This text, whose content was revealed in the above-mentioned General Accounting Office report of 1983, was probably signed by Defense Secretary Harold Brown and Israeli Defense Minister Ezer Weizman (U.S. General Accounting Office 1983; Klieman 1985:177). Described by the report as "a major U.S. commitment to stimulate various types of cooperation in research and development," the memorandum, dated March 19, 1979, broadened the agreement on the exchange of military information already in effect since 1970. It also provided a list of 560 categories of military production in which Israeli firms could submit competitive bids on the same basis as NATO countries (U.S. General Accounting Office 1983; Ryan 1987:17).

The New American Regional Orientation. As we have seen above, Article 3 of the memorandum of March 26, 1979 raised the possibility of a reinforced American presence in the region in case of a treaty violation. It would be an error to see in this provision nothing more than a commitment in Israel's favor and to separate it from the new orientation of American policy in the region following the Iranian revolution. Carter's determination to have the Israeli-Egyptian treaty signed was already, as we have seen, a response to the events in Iran, but it was not the only response. In order to face the challenges of the region, the administration also felt it was important to be ready to intervene militarily in the Middle Eastern theater.

Several signs of this orientation can be noted in the first three months of 1979, just prior to the signing of the treaty. We have already mentioned Defense Secretary Brown's visit to the region, and in particular to Saudi Arabia, in February. Brown's mission was to study, with the countries concerned, ways in which the United States could fill the "void" created by the fall of the shah. According to Quandt (1986:294), no one among the President's advisers believed that Saudi Arabia could be a suitable substitute for Iran. David C. Jones, Chairman of the Joint Chiefs of Staff, saw as desirable the formulation of a "Carter doctrine" for the Gulf (and, in fact, such a doctrine would be proclaimed a year later) (ibid.:294–295). Brzezinski, in his memoirs (1983:446), states that on February 28, he submitted to the President a memorandum urging that a "security framework" be elaborated in order to reassert American power and influence in the region. In order to stress the serious nature of this new American attitude, the administration reacted with excess to a crisis between the two Yemens, sending emergency assistance to North Yemen, two AWACS planes to Saudi Arabia, and the aircraft carrier *Constellation* to the Arabian Sea (ibid.:447). Finally, declaring itself ready to create a multinational force to monitor the application of the Israeli-Egyptian treaty in the Sinai in the event that United Nations personnel could not be sent (Quandt 1986:406), Washington confirmed that it would no longer hesitate to deploy its armed forces in the sensitive zones.

The new American readiness to intervene militarily in early 1979 may even explain why the administration did not greatly fear the negative consequences of the Israeli-Egyptian treaty on inter-Arab stability and the internal stability of countries such as Saudi Arabia (A. K. Mansour ([pseud.] 1980). Since 1973, the United States had considered that this stability depended on its capacity to project the image of a country anxious to settle the Palestinian question. In other words, it had relied, either reluctantly (Kissinger) or willingly (the early Carter) on a policy of compromise in order to strengthen the "moderate" regimes and instituted regular consultations with them about progress accomplished or yet to be accomplished. Now that the United States declared itself ready to resort to military means if necessary, it became less hesitant to face the prospect of having to defend militarily the very regimes it was weakening politically by placing them before the fait accompli of a separate treaty. In February, 1979, "somewhat cavalierly, Carter said the Saudis would have nowhere else to go after the treaty was signed. 'They have to work with the United States and Egypt' " (Quandt 1986:297).

It should be added that the administration, in declaring itself ready, in early 1979, to intervene militarily, perceived the regional challenges mainly in terms of instability, whether it originated from Iran or from the consequences of the treaty. The international polarization which, after the 1973 war, had appeared to constitute a serious danger for American interests, was no longer seen as such a threat. Let us recall that in the aftermath of the 1973 war, the United States wanted to avoid polarization because of the fear that Egypt and Syria would swing toward Moscow, that another generalized Israeli-Arab war would break out, and that the oil weapon would be used. But now not only was Egypt solidly anchored in the West, but Syria also preferred a policy of swinging back and forth between the two superpowers and was in any case obliged to maintain a dialogue with the United States, which had allowed it to intervene in Lebanon while at the same time placing it in a precarious situation in that country (thanks to Israel and the militias of Bashir Gemayel). The possibility of an Israeli-Arab war initiated by Syria was excluded. As for the problem of oil, a divided Arab front and weakened oil-producing states were no longer able to use it as a weapon. Oil of course remained an important stake, a strategic factor, but the oil-producing states were now less actors than objects for whom a regional security system would be instituted in order to protect them against their own weakness and instability.

We may now evaluate the effect of these different elements on the place of Israel in American strategy following the Israeli-Egyptian peace treaty of March 1979. We stated above that Israel had succeeded in making the United States recognize that it was not in the position of a petitioner or "debtor" and in thus placing itself in a better position to take advantage once again of an American policy congruent with a strategic asset status. Did the regional security system that the administration sought to put in place confirm this status?

Apparently not, at least as far as the defense of the Gulf was concerned. In seeking to take into its own hands the tasks of defending the Gulf, the United States betrayed a lack of confidence in the Israeli claims expressed, for example, by Begin, during his visit to Washington in early March 1979. By associating Egypt with this defense, the United States confirmed what had only been an argument of convenience at Camp David in September 1978, that is, the intention of making Cairo into a competitor of Tel Aviv. However, while it was not certain that an Arab but isolated Egypt—isolated because of having signed the peace treaty—could constitute a remedy for the potential instability of the Gulf (MacDonald 1984:101), an Israel perceived an enemy by the Arab world was certain to be even less of a remedy. Against internal instability, the Israeli intervention force constituted neither a dissuasive element nor a remedy. Moreover, leaving aside the claims made by some Israeli officials to Washington, it was doubtful that the Israeli government could justify before its own public opinion a military intervention in a region such as the Gulf where its own vital interests as a state were not in question (Lakoff 1987:86).

The American will to handle the Gulf directly thus reflects a reversal of the Nixon doctrine of 1969—the doctrine by which Nixon, hesitant to make the United States assume the higher costs of military intervention, declared that it would count henceforth on regional powers. Although Nixon was mainly expressing his intention to disengage from Vietnam, his doctrine had the particular consequence of raising the status of Israel and Iran in the Middle East. Now, the new American orientation of 1979 meant that Israel could be, at most, an extrinsic asset in the Gulf, in continuous coordination with Washington. We will analyze this possibility below when the American orientation in the region becomes clearer with the Carter doctrine of January 1980. For the moment, Israel as an intrinsic asset found itself confined on its eastern front (Syria, Jordan, the PLO, Lebanon and possibly Iraq). And even here, was not Israel's freedom of maneuver constrained on this front by the fear of destroying the still-precarious gains on the Egyptian front?

The Carter Doctrine

On January 23, 1980, less than a month after the Soviet intervention in Afghanistan, Carter, in his State of the Union address, defined what has come to be called his "doctrine": "An attempt by any outside force to gain control of the Persian Gulf region will be regarded as an assault on the vital interests of the United States and such an assault will be repelled by all means necessary, including military force" (Carter 1980:197). In fact, the President was making official before Congress a shift that had taken place a year before with the Iranian revolution (Brzezinski 1983:444; M. Johnson 1983:8). Historians would note, however, that the genesis of the Carter doctrine goes back to Presidential Directive 18 of August 1977, which called for the setting up of "light, mobile and flexible forces to meet threats in such areas as the Middle East, the Persian Gulf and East Asia" (Haffa 1984:114). In early 1978, this directive was "interpreted as requesting rapid deployment forces capable of intervening in three areas: the Persian Gulf (to protect the oil fields); the Middle East (to protect Israel); and South Korea" (ibid.:124). Even as we note the reference to protecting Israel, which apparently conforms to the idea of a de facto guarantee, we must stress that the Presidential directive remained for a long time at the stage of notes exchanged within the bureaucracy and continued to meet with the "slow reaction" of the Defense Department until 1979 (Brzezinski 1983:456). From this date on, the intervention scenarios privileged one of the three zones: the Gulf.

If the year 1979 can thus be considered as one of reorientation of American strategy in the region, only after the Soviet intervention in Afghanistan would this reorientation take institutional form. This is only normal, for it is easier to justify a policy of intervention, mobilize forces, and allocate resources when the danger perceived comes from aggressive designs attributed to an identifiable state than when it comes from a situation as unpredictable and elusive as the potential internal instability in Arab countries. But in spite of the Afghan events, the challenges to American interests in the Middle East (broadly defined to include the Gulf) remained more intra- than extra-regional.

Even if the Carter doctrine mentions only the threats from outside the region as calling for an American riposte, it therefore seems to have had as its main, not secondary, function, to announce that the United States was ready to intervene militarily to face intraregional dangers such as "internal subversion" (Cordier 1983:59). It is not our purpose here to judge whether this approach is fruitful and well adapted to the situation. Let us simply observe that it constituted the foundation of the Rapid Deployment Force, officially established in March 1980 under the label of Rapid Deployment Joint Task Force (RDJTF) and that its "area of responsibility" covered what Brzezinski called the "arc of crisis," stretching from the Horn of Africa to Iran, from Afghanistan to Pakistan, and through the two Yemens and the Arabian peninsula. The name of "Southwest Asia" was given to this new strategic region, which included neither Egypt nor Jordan nor Israel (Gold 1988:31, 39). The idea of the RDJTF implied that accords be reached with friendly countries that could offer logistical facilities (not necessarily permanent bases) in suitable sites. It is known that these sites included Masirah (Oman), Berbera (Somalia), Mombasa (Kenya), and Ras-Banas (Egypt). In actual practice, Egypt was included in the Force's area of responsibility because of the Ras-Banas site and because of joint American-Egyptian maneuvers that took place in November 1980 and in following years (Gold 1988:38).

This brings us, of course, to the question of whether Israel (which, like Egypt, was placed outside "Southwest Asia"), figures among the countries with which an agreement to provide facilities was concluded or sought during 1980, the last year of Carter's term. Nothing in currently available sources confirms this. Aside from the probable areas of cooperation, which were secret by nature and did not wait for 1980 to exist (exchange of technical, military, and political information), it is difficult to say whether an operational cooperation was provided for in the framework of the RDJTF. What is certain, in any case, is that the Carter administration was reticent—or even refused—to consider using Israeli sites publicly (Kupchan 1987:136–137). Only under Reagan would there be a move toward public cooperation between the two countries.

5 | The Strategic Alliance and the New World Order, 1981–1992

The advent of the Reagan administration in January 1981 marks a new stage in Israel's strategic status—one that would remain stable, overall, during the eight years of Reagan's term of office. It must nonetheless be noted that the period was punctuated by a series of misunderstandings, the most important of which occurred when Israel invaded Lebanon in 1982. The Bush presidency coincided with a radically new situation on the international level (with upheaval in the Eastern bloc) and in the Mideast region (with the Palestinian uprising and the second Gulf war). A new era had begun which could only call into question the place of Israel in U.S. strategic doctrine.

Reagan's Reaffirmation of the Strategic Alliance, 1981–1982

In the presidential elections of 1980, the American electorate shifted from the moralistic attitude born of Vietnam and Watergate toward a "new right" stance (Blumenthal 1986) and toward a more interventionist foreign policy. American voters seemed to prefer that this policy be managed by those who had advocated it for a long time rather than by the Carter administration, which had converted to it only after hesitation and under the threat of erosion of the

United States' global position, for which it was held largely responsible.

The victorious Reagan team had the advantage of being able to present an apparently coherent vision of international relations. Its response to the complicated "regionalism" of its adversaries was a simple and identifiable "globalism" (Kerr 1980). Because, in its assessment, all forms of regional instability and all opposition to pro-American regimes were related to the ideological and strategic East-West struggle, it thus insisted, regarding the Middle East, on the idea of Israel as the United States' main asset in the region (Tucker 1981:30–31). From this vision flowed its downgrading of the idea of an Israeli-Arab settlement and its concern not to confront the Israeli point of view on regional questions (Barrett 1983:264–265). Thus, during a meeting with journalists at the beginning of his first term, Reagan characterized the settlements in the occupied territories as "non-illegal" (the first declaration to this effect by an American leader since the occupation had begun in 1967) and answered "no" to a question about whether he felt sympathy for the Palestinians (*Mideast Observer* 2/15/81). This was a far cry from Carter's attitude early in his term in office.

Many of the representative figures of the doctrine of Israel as a strategic asset mentioned at the beginning of this study, gravitated around Reagan: Robert Tucker, Eugene Rostow, Joseph Churba, Harvey Sicherman, Geoffrey Kemp and others. Of course, Reagan's circle also included more "traditional" Republicans linked to business circles with interests in the Gulf states, such as John Connally, George Shultz, Caspar Weinberger and William Simon (Spiegel 1985:397–398). But the latter were neither pro-Arab nor anti-Israeli. They were more pragmatists than strategists or ideologues; their main concern seemed to have been not to contradict the simplistic or exaggerated rhetoric of the "ideo-strategists" or of the proponents of the "New Right," but to prevent them from drifting too far toward a doctrinaire application of their conceptions in everyday politics. For these people, protecting American interests in Saudi Arabia, in particular, meant that it was necessary to stay on good terms with the Saudi monarchy, an issue the defenders of the doctrine of Israel as a strategic asset in the new administration were not concerned with.

During the first months of Reagan's first term, the common denominator between these two currents took the form of an appeal for a "strategic consensus" among Israel, the United States, and the pro-American Arab regimes (Joyner and Shah 1981:15–24). In February 1981, the new Secretary of State, Alexander Haig, who was close to those who defended the Israeli asset doctrine, explained that this consensus would serve to face up to "the overriding danger," that is, "Soviet inroads into this area" (Spiegel 1985:400). Defense Secretary Caspar Weinberger, closer to the business interests linked to the Gulf states, declared, in September of the same year, that Saudi Arabia's support for the strategic consensus would contribute in an important way to the security of all the states in the region, Israel included (*New York Times* 9/29/81). It should be noted that the priority accorded to Israel and Saudi Arabia in this strategic consensus minimized the regional role of Egypt, demonstrating a lack of sensitivity to that country even though joint American-Egyptian exercises were continuing. (Coker 1983:32).

However, as in the 1950s, any American intention to establish a regional security system that included both Israel and the Arab countries in a single anti-Soviet front could not avoid running into difficulties. On the one hand, the Arabs would refuse to cooperate with the Israeli enemy and even resorted to the argument that the Jewish state was more dangerous than the USSR. On the other hand, Israel refused the idea that a regional security system involved supplying weapons to the Arab countries. Neither the Arab countries close to the United States nor Israel and its supporters wished to subordinate their intra-regional preoccupations, that is, the conflict that divided them, to East-West competition. Each party claimed to Washington that the weakening of Soviet influence involved both concessions by the other party and its own political and military strengthening.

The contradiction inherent in the idea of a strategic consensus for the Middle East manifested itself during the summer and fall of 1981 in the proposed sale of AWACS and F-15's (with additional fuel reservoirs to extend the field of action of the latter) to Riyadh. Circles close to Israel claimed that supplying these aircraft represented a grave danger for Israeli security and was likely to provoke a pre-emptive Israeli attack against Saudi Arabia (Duncan 1982:100–101; McNaugher 1985:120). In order to overcome the opposition of Israel and to prevent an unfavorable vote in Congress, Reagan had to commit himself personally and risk the capital of sympathy he enjoyed with Israel's defenders (Haig 1984:167–193; Reagan 1990:415–416). This may suggest that the policy actually followed was not a mere dogmatic application of the Israeli asset doctrine—a doctrine espoused by Reagan during his electoral campaign and during the first months of his presidency. Haig himself, in a meeting of the National Security Council, had expressed himself only weakly against certain aspects of the sale to Saudi Arabia (Barrett 1983:268). However, the victory the president scored against the unconditional allies of Israel in Congress in this affair in practice brought but few consequences contrary to the privileged status of Tel Aviv in American strategy. This may be explained in the following way.

Saudi Arabia had to accept precise limits concerning the military use and range of the promised aircraft and materiel as well as a commitment to secrecy surrounding its high-technology equipment, a prohibition (barring express agreement otherwise) regarding the transfer to other states of data gathered from the AWACS, and finally, the participation of American technicians in the maintenance and use of the aircraft (Haig 1984:189–190; Barrett 1983:276). While all this had as its declared objective to grant assurances to Israel regarding its security, Israel also obtained direct compensations (in the form of additional F-15s). But the most important compensation of all was the official public "promotion" of Israel's status, through the concluding of a memorandum of strategic cooperation between the two countries. But before analyzing the memorandum, let us note the following excerpt from Reagan's journal, as reported in his memoirs (1990:415), about his meeting with Menachem Begin in early September 1981: "I told him how strongly we felt it [the AWACS sale] could help bring the Saudis into the peace making process. I assured him we were allies. That the partnership benefited us as much as it did Israel and that we would not let a risk to Israel to be created."

The Memorandum of Understanding on Strategic Cooperation, November 1981

The signing of the memorandum, known under the abbreviation of MOU (Memorandum of Understanding), crowned several months of Israeli-American discussions under the new Reagan administration. What the Israelis were proposing, and what Haig probably viewed with favor, were the following provisions: the possibility of organizing joint maneuvers; the use of Israeli bases and facilities by American forces; Israel's taking charge of the aerial protection, maintenance, and inventory of American strategic equipment (the necessary equipment for an armored division) to be stored on its territory and possibly used by the Israeli army in case of emergency; American financing for the production of Markava tanks; and the exchange of military intelligence (Blitzer 1981; Middleton 1981; Sharon 1989:414; Tamir 1988:217–218).

However, it was, astoundingly, the Pentagon that opposed Haig's views and expressed doubts about the utility of Israel for the Rapid Deployment Joint Task Force (RDJTF). For Pentagon officials, indeed, although Israel might constitute an ideal technical asset for the RDJTF, the same was not true politically (Barrett 1983:276). The breadth and depth of the cooperation envisioned, and the very concluding of a formal and public agreement, could depend only on what the administration considered as "tolerable" in the Arab region. For the Pentagon, what was tolerable excluded American-Israeli cooperation in the Gulf, but did include discreet cooperation in the Eastern Mediterranean (Tamir 1988:218). That is why the memorandum signed on November 30, 1981 was only a "diluted version" of the initial project (Spiegel 1985:410): it resulted from a compromise between an enthusiastic Israel and a circumspect administration and represented another compromise between Haig's favorable view and the reticence of Weinberger. It was signed by the latter and by Israeli Defense Minister Ariel Sharon.

The content of the MOU (*Department of State Bulletin* 1.82: 45–46) can be approached from two points of view: the areas and mechanisms of the cooperation it called for and the objective it assigned to that cooperation, that is, identifying the enemy or threat.

From the standpoint of the areas of cooperation, the only commitments the memorandum contains involve military exercises, including naval and airborne maneuvers in the Eastern Mediterranean. Nothing in the way of land maneuvers on the Israeli territory is called for (MacDonald 1984:104), contrary to the joint American-Egyptian maneuvers called "Bright Star" (Pollock 1982:285). The memorandum further mentions the possibility of joint readiness exercises including "access to maintenance facilities and other infrastructures," and cooperation in the area of "pre-positioning" of American military equipment, arms sales, and research and development. But it assigns the detailed study of these points to "working groups" that would report to a "coordination council," the formation of which is called for at an unspecified time. Thus, the memorandum constitutes more of a declaration of intentions than a precise program of cooperation (Kupchan 1987:154; Tamir 1988:220).

Regarding its objective, the memorandum recalls first of all "the longstanding and fruitful cooperation" between the two countries from the standpoint of "mutual security." It expresses the will to institute a "framework for continued consultation and cooperation" in order to face a threat identified as being "caused by the Soviet Union or by Soviet-controlled forces from outside the region introduced into the region." In evoking such forces, the signers probably had in mind the example of the Cuban presence in Angola.

One cannot help comparing the declared objective of the memorandum of 1981 to those of 1975 and 1979. The text of 1975 seeks to protect Israel against an unnamed power which can only be the Soviet Union. That of 1979 is altogether silent on this point; weaker than the earlier text, it suggests even less the idea of an American guarantee to Israel, but it does not yet indicate an Israeli role in the U.S. regional strategy. It is only in the memorandum of 1981 that we find the idea of "mutuality" of services the two parties can render each other. As for the Soviet Union, it is not only named, but also warned to beware of an Israel apparently ready to face up to it. An evident reversal occurred between 1975 and 1981, via what could be considered the logically and chronologically intermediate stage of 1979. The reversal is gigantic in terms of the message the memorandum seeks to deliver. Israel in 1975 (in the same manner as, say, Western Europe since 1945), called for the American umbrella, without officially mentioning the Soviet danger. But in the memorandum of 1981, it is Israel that proposes its services to the United States in order to deter the USSR, explicitly mentioned, from pursuing its Middle Eastern aims, and these are no longer even considered threatening for the Jewish state itself (as is implied in the memorandum of 1975). Western Europe itself never claimed such a status in its relations with Washington.

The declared objective of the MOU is so disproportionate to its simplified form (it is not even a treaty) and to the means and mechanisms it calls for, that its significance is to be sought outside its actual provisions. In our view, the public—nonsecret—character of its signing is its most meaningful aspect; from it, several important conclusions can be drawn:

First, whatever the text asserts to the contrary at the insistence of the American side (Cobban 1991:84), it is the Arab world, much more than direct Soviet intervention, that is targeted by the idea of Israeli-American strategic cooperation in the region. As we have indicated elsewhere in this study, any growth of Soviet influence in the Middle East would have been the product above all of an intraregional situation and in fact the latter is at the center of American-Israeli preoccupations.

Second, if the memorandum suggests the growing importance of the Middle East stake, it also denotes an overall weakening of the Arab states as actors. It is as if, for the signatories, the other countries of the region constituted a series of impotent wills, a vacuum not to be filled by active anti-American or anti-Israeli forces. Never before, in spite of a long period of special Israeli-American relations, had Washington agreed to emphasize, in a bilateral public text, the idea of a strategic regional cooperation with the state always considered an enemy by the Arabs (Pollock 1982:286). Washington's fear of an Arab reaction must therefore have greatly diminished in the course of these years. Only a few precautions of language or form are taken to avoid useless excess. In this vein, the memorandum states that it is not directed against the countries of the region; and in addition Weinberger did not allow photographers to attend its signing (Spiegel 1985:410).

Third, the MOU not only denotes the weakening of the status of the Arab countries in Washington's eyes but also shows that the idea of a settlement of the Israeli-Arab conflict was, in 1981, less than ever an American strategic priority. By signing this text, American leaders appeared to be minimizing Israel's indebtedness and denying that Israel must offer compensations related to the settlement of the conflict with its neighbors.

Fourth, in the face of these relatively important political implications, the fact that the memorandum leaves the mechanisms of strategic cooperation vague becomes secondary. Precise mechanisms of cooperation do not need to be mentioned in a public text in order to be decided upon and put into practice. *Technical* cooperation between the two countries (exchange of information for research and development) is certainly old and enduring; it is without a doubt the consequence of Israeli dependency on American arms since 1967. *Strategic* cooperation depends on the convergence of interests at a given moment (as in the Jordanian crisis of 1970) and much less on previously signed commitments, public or secret. The same is true of *operational* cooperation, as in the case of the RDJTF in time of crisis or armed conflict. If indeed, as certain authors state, "Israel's own arsenal of U.S. weaponry implicitly creates a logistics base there that could be useful in a crisis" (McNaugher 1985:56), it remains that much depends on the extent to which the Arabs will tolerate it at that time as well as on how much Israeli public opinion will tolerate it. Only *joint maneuvers* (which can be classed as halfway between technical and operational cooperation) are explicitly called for in the memorandum; as is the case for technical cooperation, these could have been governed by precise but secret or informal agreements. A public but imprecise accord, which is what the MOU is, cannot guarantee their organization, even though it facilitates them politically.

Since the memorandum was more of a declaration of intention than a program, and since it offered little information on actual cooperation, its value was more symbolic than material, more political than military. Symbolically, its public character marked a decline in the Arab countries' status in Washington. Politically, it signified that Israel owed nothing to the United States; this applied in particular to the question of possible Israeli concessions in a process of settlement of the conflict. Militarily, the memorandum was useless since other, more discreet forms, certain of which probably already existed, were more appropriate.

The Misunderstandings Related to the Memorandum

The analysis of the memorandum would be incomplete without a consideration of its properly Israeli dimension, that is, its congruence with Israeli interests as perceived by the country's leaders. Aside from its tangible advantages (lessons that could be drawn from joint maneuvers and the hope of including American equipment stored in Israel in its own strategic reserves), the proclamation of strategic cooperation with the United States allowed Tel Aviv to project the image of a state enjoying a great breadth of maneuver in the region.

In order to seize this last point, one must place the Begin government's (and in particular Defense Minister Sharon's) haste to sign an agreement of strategic cooperation with the United States in the context of their political orientation during this period. In 1981, Israeli leaders had a no doubt exaggerated confidence in the fruitfulness and usefulness of their army's power in the region. They had indeed been encouraged in this attitude by the new American administration, which they saw as ready to espouse their "militant posture" (Schiff and Ya'ari 1984:31). Quite significantly, for example, Begin is said to have told his colleagues, after meeting with Haig during the latter's visit to Tel Aviv in April: "Ben-Gurion used to say that if you're pursuing a policy that may lead to war, it's vital to have a great power behind you" (ibid.).

Prior to the memorandum, this self-confidence and this reliance on American permissiveness had manifested itself, in the spring of 1981 by a stronger intervention in Lebanon at the side of Bashir Gemayel and against the Syrian order (provoking the "missile crisis" of the Bekaa valley) (Schiff and Ya'ari 1984:34; Herzog 1981; Haber 1981), in June by the destruction of the Osirak nuclear reactor in Baghdad (Perlmutter et al. 1982; Reagan 1990:413), and in July by the severe bombing of a populous district of Beirut, resulting in hundreds of deaths (Schiff and Ya'ari 1984:36–37). Although these last two actions provoked an official American condemnation, and even a suspension for a few weeks of the delivery of F-16 aircraft (at the insistence of Weinberger over Reagan), they nonetheless encountered a "sympathetic" attitude on the part of Haig (Schiff and Ya'ari 1984:63–65; Barrett 1983:270–271; Perlmutter et al. 1982:162–163; Ben-Zvi 1984:33–40) and did not prevent the negotiation and signing of the MOU. It was just after the concluding of the memorandum that the Israeli government sought to establish a wider margin of maneuver in the sphere of its conflict with the Arabs and to define its own regional ambitions, as if these had been implicitly recognized by the memorandum itself (Chadda 1986:161; Yaniv 1987:218).

Thus on December 14, the Knesset decided to apply Israeli law in the occupied Golan (widely interpreted as a de facto annexation). The same day, Sharon was due to expose in a lecture—never delivered, because of the Knesset debate on the Golan, but published in *Ma'ariv* (12/18/81)—the strategic interests of Israel in the 1980s. For the Defense Minister, these interests included of course "the first traditional circle of confrontation countries surrounding Israel" but also "the second circle of exterior Arab countries." However, Sharon added that Israeli strategic interests should henceforth also take into account a "third geographic area" including "countries such as Turkey, Iran and Pakistan and regions such as the Persian Gulf and Africa, in particular the states of North and Central Africa."

It is quite possible that the very geographical excesses of Sharon were a verbal substitute for what it was difficult for him to state otherwise, that is, his will to increase Israel's breadth of maneuver and autonomy of decision with respect to the United States while still remaining its ally. If, for Sharon, as Yaniv explains, "Israel was so powerful that the United States could not do without it" (Yaniv 1987:218), and if, as the Defense Minister himself asserted in the text of his projected lecture, "the United States have progressively recognized" that Israel "is not a burden but an asset" (*Ma'ariv* 12/18/81; Sharon 1989:408–409), it followed that the Jewish state's capacity for intervention should be able to guarantee the pro-Western destiny of the region. In other words, the United States should rely on Israel, and the latter would thus constitute, according to the wishes of Sharon, a kind of protecting shield between the countries of the region and a useless or even imprudent American interference. The Israeli Defense Minister is said to have told a group of officers in 1981: "Americans treat us like an aircraft carrier—a floating base. They don't understand our real significance: we're not one aircraft carrier. We are twenty aircraft carriers. We are much more important than they think. We can take the Middle East with us whenever we go" (Hersh 1991:289). This unrealistic vision was to be applied in at least one case: Sharon's definition of the Israeli objective in Lebanon in the first months of 1982 during the preparation for the invasion of that country.

But before we reach that point, it should be noted that the sudden decision by the Knesset to apply Israeli law in the Golan provoked Washington's suspension of the MOU. For Weinberger, the suspension was one of the "costs" that the Israelis had to bear as a consequence of their initiative. According to Haig (1984:328), Weinberger declared on this occasion: "If there is no real cost to the Israelis, we'll never be able to stop any of their actions."

As a counter-reaction, Begin in turn considered the American suspension of the memorandum as the equivalent to its nullification and addressed to Washington a message in which he came down forcefully against the American "punishment" following each Israeli initiative (Baghdad, Beirut and now the Golan). The message read: "What kind of expression is this: 'punish Israel'? Are we a vassal state of yours? Are we a banana republic?" Begin complained furthermore that the administration was trying to "make Israel a hostage of the memorandum." In reply to the accusation that he had taken the American leaders by surprise, the Prime Minister asserted: "Had Israel told the U.S. about the law (in advance), the U.S. would have said no. We did not want you to say no and then go ahead and apply Israeli law to the Golan Heights. Our intention was not to embarrass you." (*Jerusalem Post* 12/21/81)

After Weinberger, the Israeli Prime Minister thus formulated clearly, although rather crudely, the contradiction, inherent in the idea of strategic asset, between American recognition and Israeli pretension. For Washington, and in particular for the decisionmakers interested in privileging the military-strategic dimension of their policy, to recognize Israel as an asset was to "instrumentalize" that country, even while glorifying the services it rendered and accepting the idea that it owed nothing in spite of the aid it received. There could be no question of the United States letting Israel constitute a screen—or even a protective shield—between the United States and the region. For Tel Aviv on the other hand, to be recognized as an asset was, if not to have the region "awarded" to it exclusively, as in Sharon's doctrine, at least to enjoy a broad autonomy of decision in regional matters. Divergences are thus inevitable.

However, while the two countries always seem to find, in time, a modus vivendi, the potential American-Israeli divergences are often neutralized by quarrels within the administration itself (or between it and the Congress) regarding the meaning and degree of gravity to attribute to Israel's untimely initiatives. This had been the case in particular between Kissinger and Rogers under Nixon, and now between Haig and Weinberger throughout the year 1981. In the episode concerning the Golan Heights as in the destruction of the Iraqi reactor and the bombing of Beirut, Weinberger's "anger" was neutralized to some degree by the "viscerally" pro-Israeli stance of Haig and attenuated by the mere "disappointment" on the part of Reagan regarding Begin's "surprises" (Barrett 1983:277–278). The suspension of the MOU, as a result of these different reactions within the executive branch, would appear to be a diplomatic gesture toward the Arabs to show them that the United States did not approve of the annexation. Although it was the expression of a passing American-Israeli tension, the suspension of the memorandum by no means signified the end of existing cooperation at the technical, operational, or strategic levels between Washington and Tel Aviv (Stork 1982:12). This is compatible with the idea expressed above that effective cooperation was not the province of the memorandum itself.

Toward the Lebanon War

A series of events much more serious than the annexation of the Golan Heights would put to the test the Reagan administration's doctrine regarding Israel's strategic role and the margin of maneuver it could allow to Israel in the Middle East. For Washington, Israeli preparations for the invasion of Lebanon raised the classic but now acute question: would the planned Israeli initiative provoke the weakening of the "radicals" and of Soviet influence and thus lead to a reinforcement of the "moderates" and of American influence, or would it have the opposite effect? Before considering Washington's answer to this question, let us attempt to define the objectives Israel had set for itself in Lebanon.

The 1982 war can be compared to that of 1956 in that it was not fortuitous or accidental. According to the then Israeli commander of the northern region, Amir Drori, the invasion of Lebanon was "the most thoroughly planned war the IDF had ever embarked upon" (Schiff and Ya'ari 1984:54; Tamir 1988:123). As soon as Ariel Sharon was named Defense Minister in the summer of 1981, he began to define Israel's objectives in Lebanon and their operational implications (Sharon 1984:435–437, 445). It is certain that these objectives consisted in destroying the PLO "quasi-state" within the country, expelling the Syrian army, and establishing a Lebanese government protected by Israel (Schiff and Ya'ari 1984:42–43; Spiegel 1985:413; Rabinovich 1984:122, 133). However, Sharon's project also had a much broader regional dimension.

For the Defense Minister, a success in instituting a pro-Israeli order in Lebanon would lead to the weakening of Syria's regional role, a West Bank solution "according to Israeli rules" (Schiff and Ya'ari 1984:43; Tamir 1988:122), and perhaps even, in that event, to Israeli influence in Jordan (Feldman and Rechnitz-Kijner 1984:21–24). It is known that Sharon saw the solution to the Palestinian problem in the establishment of a Palestinian state in Jordan in the place of the Hashemite monarchy, and that he publicly regretted that Israel had not contributed to overturning that regime during the crisis of September, 1970 (*Time* 10/5/81; 3/1/82). According to Schiff and Ya'ari (1984:43), "Sharon explained to his aides that, in his estimation, a successful operation in Lebanon would ensure unchallenged Israeli superiority for thirty years to come, during which time Israel would be free to establish faits accomplis in its best interests." This means that the Lebanese project of the Israeli Defense Minister was not only a goal in itself, but also a first step, or at least a test, within a larger perimeter of regional ambitions, though of course reaching neither Pakistan nor Central Africa.

However, Israeli action in Lebanon, first in its preparatory stages and then at the beginning of its execution, could not be justified in such terms by Sharon in the eyes of Israeli opinion or the U.S. administration. The Defense Minister even kept the members of his own government (with the exception of Begin and Shamir, and even here not always) in the dark about his "great design" (Feldman and Rechnitz-Kijner 1984:25–41; Schiff and Ya'ari 1984:60–61; Tamir 1988:124). In order to retain a sufficient margin for maneuver, he had two different invasion plans prepared: a minimal one which included the conquest only of southern Lebanon and limited itself to an attack against PLO forces, and an optimal one, which called for an extension of the Israeli advance beyond the Beirut-Damascus highway and implied a confrontation with the Syrian army (Schiff and Ya'ari 1984:45; Tamir 1988:118). Up until the first days of the war, Sharon led the members of the government to believe that only the first scenario was being prepared (Feldman and Rechnitz-Kijner 1984:10–11).

The version of Sharon's argument directed toward Washington was probably slightly different. Maneuvering between the two projects, he had to emphasize what was most likely to gain American support: a narrow regional dimension and a broad global one. On the regional level, Sharon avoided exposing his "grand design" for Lebanon, the West Bank, and Jordan but instead stressed the defensive and local character of his action (protecting Galilee), without specifying how far his army would advance in pursuing this goal (Schiff and Ya'ari 1984:73; Tamir 1988:125). At the global level, Israeli leaders explained that a blow dealt to two actors considered to be pro-Soviet—Syria and the PLO—would mean a serious loss of influence for Moscow and a victory for the United States (Weinberger 1990:141).

What attitude could the Americans adopt in response to Sharon's project? Even if the Israeli objective was as limited regionally and as broad in its global import as Sharon claimed, it was not certain that the U.S. administration would acquiesce automatically. Already in the spring of 1981, during the "Syrian missile crisis" in the Bekaa valley, and in the summer of the same year, during the violent Israeli-Palestinian confrontation in southern Lebanon following the bombing of Beirut, the administration, through its special envoy Philip Habib, had intervened with great energy, first to prevent Israel from destroying the Syrian missile bases and then to obtain a cease-fire between Tel Aviv and the PLO that was to last more than ten months. In spite of having rallied Egypt into its camp thanks to the Camp David process and in spite of the pro-Israeli rhetoric of the Reagan administration in the first months of 1981, Washington was still clinging to the same orientation it had held since 1973: avoiding all East-West polarization in the region, not forcing Syria to have an exclusive relationship with the Soviet Union but rather dealing with the Syrians, and maintaining special relations with the Gulf states. The cease-fire of July 1981 requested of the PLO by Habib through the good offices of Saudi Arabia, even suggested that the Palestinian leadership had forced itself on the Reagan administration as an indispensable and relatively strong partner in dialogue—one that could not be simply fought against, because American strategic interests in the region required dealing with it, if only indirectly. (For a view sharply critical of the Reagan administration's steps toward the PLO, see Indyk 1985:199–227.)

This policy continued until May 1982. The administration thus appears to have prevented Tel Aviv, probably on three different occasions (November 1981, February and April 1982) from leading a broad-scale attack on the PLO (Rabinovich 1984:125). This caution and moderating influence on Israel were signs, of course, of hesitation in Washington to choose between confidence in Tel Aviv's actions (the attitude symbolized by Haig), and fear of their negative effects (the view represented by Weinberger and high-ranking officials of the State Department). From May 1982 on, however, the balance in Washington tilted toward growing confidence and diminishing fear. Why was this so? It was not due to the strengthening of Haig's status in interbureaucratic rivalries—in fact, the opposite was true (Spiegel 1985:415–416)—but, as we shall now see, rather to the evolution of the Middle Eastern situation itself.

In Lebanon, the presidential election, important in spite of the weakness of the state, was scheduled for the summer of 1982. Washington opted, it seems, for the candidacy of Bashir Gemayel, but his success was out of the question given the existing internal and regional balance, unless it was imposed by a shock. In the Gulf, Saudi Arabia was now worried by the reversal of the military tide in favor of Iran and against Iraq and no longer felt itself in a good position, as in 1981, to put pressure on the American administration regarding the Israeli-Syrian-Palestinian tensions in the Lebanese theater. Syria was in the midst of a difficult period in its relations with Saudi Arabia and the Soviet Union, after having benefited since 1975—and especially during the missile crisis of 1981—from a paradoxical Saudi-Soviet convergence in its favor—a convergence that had allowed it to engage in dialogue with Washington from a position of strength (Mansour 1982:338–339). Although it was debatable regarding the longer term, the idea prevailed in Washington and Tel Aviv that Saudi Arabia and the Soviet Union both had declining influence in the Mashrek.

A further regional factor is another good reason for the diminishment of American cautiousness on the eve of the events of June 1982: the fact that Israel had, on April 25, brought to a term the final stage of the withdrawal from the Sinai as stipulated by the Israeli-Egyptian peace treaty. From the assassination of Sadat in October 1981 up to that date, Washington sought to avoid the unleashing of forces that might convince Israel, or "give it the excuse" (Spiegel 1985:411; Rabinovich 1984:125; Ryan 1982:35; Reagan 1990:417), not to pull out of the final portion of the peninsula, which would have called the entire treaty into question and plunged the Middle East into an uncontrollable situation (Schiff and Ya'ari 1984:68). The Israeli chief of military intelligence, Yehoshua Saguy, sent to Washington in February to test American reactions regarding a possible invasion of Lebanon, was told, in substance: "Not before the withdrawal from the Sinai" (Quandt 1984:238; Schiff and Ya'ari 1984:68). American emissaries, apparently authorized to do so, appear even to have promised the PLO some "rewards" relative to the peace process in exchange for the PLO's observing the cease-fire until April 25. This was to arouse the sentiment among the Palestinian leaders, when the Israeli invasion broke out, that Washington had deceived them in the sole aim of assuring better conditions for the Israeli withdrawal from the Sinai (Gwertzman 1984; Fraser 1989:163).

In the wake of both the consolidation of the Israeli-Egyptian peace treaty and the deteriorating strategic and political situation in the Arab world, the U.S. administration felt that "the risks inherent in an Israeli operation seemed to be outweighed by the opportunities it might produce" (Rabinovich 1984:125). It was as if the Jewish state, after having restrained itself with great difficulty until April 25, could finally reap, on the eastern front, the strategic dividends of the peace treaty signed three years earlier. Further, after having waited so long, it may have seemed best not to wait any longer: the favorable regional conditions would perhaps not present themselves again, and the presidential election in Lebanon was drawing close. On May 26, Secretary of State Haig declared in a press conference in Chicago that Lebanon had become a danger zone and expressed, astonishingly enough, his belief in a rapid and radical solution: "The time has come to take concerted action in support of both Lebanon's territorial integrity within its internationally recognized borders and a strong central government . . . " (*New York Times* 5/27/82). Does this mean that Washington had acquiesced to Sharon's project, if only in its minimal form? Was there a "green light"? We will attempt to answer this question in the following paragraphs. However, the notion of a "green light," as we noted in our earlier discussion concerning American-Israeli relations on the eve of the 1967 war, is to be handled with care.

It appears indeed that immediately following April 25, the Israeli government was perceived in Washington in a more favorable light than in previous months. In order to "reward" Israel, U.S. leaders discussed among themselves, during the month of May, the possibility of proposing to Tel Aviv different forms of military cooperation, including the reactivation of the memorandum of strategic cooperation of November 1981 (Barrett 1983:279; Haig 1984:335). It was in this favorable climate that the Israeli government approved the "Peace for Galilee" plan (i.e., the smaller version) on May 16 and that General Sharon visited Washington at the end of the month. In his memoirs, Haig (1984:333), who emphasizes that Israeli military preparations were "no longer much of a secret" and that "the United States would probably not be able to stop Israel from attacking" (330), relates that Sharon sketched out before State Department officials the "two possible military campaigns" (335). In spite of his obvious desire not to appear to be endorsing Sharon's plan, the Secretary of State reports that he explained to the latter that "an attack by Israel into Lebanon would have a devastating effect in the United States," "unless there was an internationally recognized provocation, and unless Israeli retaliation was proportionate to any such provocation" (335). These two conditions could of course be interpreted broadly, and no one doubts that the Israeli Defense Minister wished to understand them that way (Schiff and Ya'ari 1984:70).

Israeli sources, for their part, are much more explicit than Haig's memoirs about the favorable attitude the latter showed to Sharon's plan. According to Schiff and Ya'ari (1984:74), the Secretary of State "used the metaphor of a lobotomy—a quick, clean, neutralizing operation in the event that there was no other choice." The two Israeli authors draw the conclusion from the Sharon-Haig encounter that "from Israel's standpoint, this was sufficient. Neither in the Yom Kippur war nor the Six-Day war before it had Israel enjoyed such heartening understanding from Washington." General Tamir, who was present at this meeting, writes (1988:126): "Sharon carried away from the meeting the impression that the United States was not really opposed to Israeli military action in Lebanon and reported to the government accordingly."

One could perhaps object to the foregoing that Alexander Haig, by acquiescing tacitly to Sharon's plan, overstepped the bounds of the official policy of the Reagan administration. This objection could even be justified when one considers that the State Department and the White House expressed, after Sharon had gone, the fear that Haig had not been "discreet enough" with his interlocutor (Schiff and Ya'ari 1984:74). But this objection can be rejected for two reasons. First, the Israeli Defense Minister did not want to feel "concerned" by the "clashing voices" coming from Washington; after all, "Alexander Haig was Secretary of State, and that was authority enough for Sharon" (ibid.). Secondly, the White House decided that Haig must send Begin a letter of clarification whose purpose was to express a more circumspect and restrictive attitude, but this letter, paradoxically, only reinforced Sharon's impressions (ibid.:75–76).

The letter, dated May 28, considered by Schiff and Ya'ari (1984:75) to be a "highly significant document," indeed confirms "the mild tone of the official American admonitions." Tamir (1988:126) describes it as "too lacking in pressure." In spite of the White House's worries, the document contained, according to the description by Schiff and Ya'ari, "no hint of a threat or ultimatum to Israel—a favored technique when Washington wished to head off an undesirable move on Israel's part." The Israeli officials saw in Haig's letter "a cautious diplomatic maneuver—the formal expression of a reservation by which the Americans intended to cover themselves against liability in case Israel got into deeper trouble than it could handle" (Schiff and Ya'ari 1984:75). A British author, Claudia Wright, goes so far as to say (1982:5) that Weinberger and some White House officials had themselves approved the Israeli project of invading Lebanon, and destroying the PLO, as early as May.

Much more clearly than on the eve of the 1967 war, the Israeli leaders were "convinced that Washington had given them a green light" to enter Lebanon (Spiegel 1985:414). "The Green Light" was, by the way, the title Zeev Schiff gave to his article on this subject (1983). In both cases one finds, in spite of the exhortations to be cautious and in spite of the opposition of some American leaders, the necessary "negative" element, that is, the absence of any threat of sanctions. But in 1982, one notes in addition that several American leaders explicitly affirm the strategic role of Israel and had become accustomed over a period of several months to the idea of the inevitable invasion. According to Wright (1982:37) and Ryan (1982:5), the advance American knowledge of the Israeli initiative is attested to by the reinforcement of the American fleet in the Eastern Mediterranean with two additional aircraft carriers (the U.S.S. *Kennedy* and the U.S.S. *Eisenhower*) several days before the invasion.

From the Invasion of Lebanon to Strategic Cooperation, 1982–1989

American knowledge about Israel's plans implies neither precise and harmonious coordination between the two countries, nor docile Israeli execution of a pre-established American plan. For each country, indeed, there remained a good measure of reciprocal uncertainty; for Washington, this concerned above all the scope of the projected Israeli campaign, and for Tel Aviv, the actual American attitude that would emerge in the course of the military operations. Although each country held identical views regarding certain minimal objectives (the military and political weakening of the PLO and the essentially political weakening of Syria and the Soviet Union, thereby creating a more favorable dynamic for Bashir Gemayel in Lebanon), and although Washington, as we have seen, had drawn closer to the Israeli position, having decided to minimize the risks of a limited operation, it was to be expected that divergences over the respective objectives and the assessment of the risks involved would arise if the Israeli initiative exceeded certain limits. What could not be foreseen, however, was that the intensification of American-Israeli strategic cooperation would be one of the more or less direct consequences of the invasion.

The Invasion of Lebanon

The war broke out on June 4, one day after the attempt on the life of the Israeli ambassador in London by a Palestinian group opposed to the PLO leadership (Weinberger 1990:141–142); the actual invasion began on Sunday, June 6. Sharon, who sought to execute the maximalist version of his plan without having it formally ratified by his peers, had to be content at the outset with the official approval of a limited operation that would extend 40 kilometers into the south of Lebanon. Unwilling to define to his general staff his real operational goals (reaching Beirut and the Beirut-Damascus highway), he proceeded in such a way that the war would "unfold stage by stage" (Schiff and Ya'ari 1984:109–110; Feldman and Rechnitz-Kijner 1984:69) following the advances on the terrain, as if the consolidation of a thrust here or the quelling of a resistance there made it urgent each time to make a new, localized move forward.

What was Washington's attitude in response to Sharon's manner of proceeding, which in Israel itself ended up provoking the suspicions and apprehensions of members of the government and opposition leaders? (Tamir 1988:133) In accordance with the method we have adopted up to now, we shall not examine all the political-military developments of the war, but focus only on certain essential moments of American evaluation and decision-making. On June 5, Begin conveyed to Washington his government's decision to execute an operation whose aim was to chase back Palestinian batteries to a distance of 40 kilometers; he asked the United States to inform Damascus that Israeli forces had no intention of confronting the Syrian army in Lebanon, as long as this intention was reciprocal (Haig 1984:337). Reagan, for his part, was content to send a "polite letter" to Begin exhorting him to moderation (Schiff and Ya'ari 1984:116). It was clear that Washington wanted to let Israel act (Khalidi 1986:107) in spite of Reagan's exasperation concerning the moment chosen for the invasion (Barrett 1983:271). On Monday, June 7, Alexander Haig, whom Schiff and Ya'ari (1984:151–152) describe as the "spokesman" within the American administration for the Israeli cause, spoke explicitly, in the presence of journalists, as if the official Israel position was his own.

What Haig did not yet know, or did not appear to know, was that "even as he was speaking, an Israeli armored column was making its way toward the Beirut-Damascus highway in a bid to reduce the Syrian presence in Lebanon to nothing" (ibid.:152). As early as this Monday, then—the second day of the invasion— "two wars were going on in Lebanon: one against the PLO, the other against the Syrians" (ibid.:155). But this "second" war was so far inscribed only in the potential logic of the Israeli troops' movements; it would take another two or three days for the gravity of the situation to be perceived by the U.S. administration and to provoke the apprehension of Haig himself. Between the 8th and the 10th of June, the Syrians and the Israelis engaged in violent combat: air battles (including one that resulted in the destruction of missile bases installed in the Bekaa valley), and land battles (in the Shouf and in the western Bekaa). Philip Habib, Reagan's emissary, negotiated a cease-fire between the two parties and the American president pressed Begin to accept it. It took effect on Friday, June 11.

The American effort toward an Israeli-Syrian cease-fire attests to a definite prudence and even a certain perspicacity. The Soviet Union was expressing its dissatisfaction to Washington and addressing, through the U.S., a warning to Israel (Spiegel 1985:415). Compared to Israel's declared objective, the Israeli-Syrian confrontation was already a spillover that could not be allowed to become more serious. Many Israeli government leaders saw themselves being led into a major war they did not want and which they had not decided upon. On the other hand, as Barrett writes (1983:280), "Moscow's surrogates had suffered a clear defeat in the air and on the ground . . . . Syria was now dickering with the United States over terms . . . According to this school of thought—which Israel's partisans promoted—Israel had again done the West a favor, albeit in a perverse, bloody manner."

Faced with the double consideration of gains already achieved and the potential risks of an escalation, it would have been unthinkable for the administration, including Haig himself (Spiegel 1985:415), to encourage Sharon's anti-Syrian "spillover" in spite of the reservations of most of his peers. As had been the case several times since 1967, Israeli activism as an asset for the United States becomes dangerous beyond a certain point. On June 10 and 11, 1982, it thus seemed preferable to establish a cease-fire and to take advantage of the points already scored against Syria in order to obtain a Syrian and Israeli withdrawal from Lebanon at a later stage, in the framework of a modus vivendi that would work to the advantage—but not to the exclusive advantage—of Israel. But before reaching that point, Washington had to give its attention to the Israeli-Palestinian confrontation in Lebanon.

The Siege of Beirut. For the U.S. administration, the caution it had to exercise in the Syrian dimension of the war had become useless with respect to the Palestinian dimension. The cease-fire of June 11 obtained from Tel Aviv was applicable only to Syria. The Israeli Defense Minister could thus pursue his offensive against the military forces of the PLO and arrive at the gates of Beirut on June 13 without any fear of a negative reaction from Washington (Khalidi 1986:108–109). Instead of being worried that the Israeli army had not respected its fiction of the "40 kilometers" already conquered, Haig (1984:341–342), whose point of view was still dominant within the administration, saw in the extension of Israel's military objective a "great opportunity": the siege of Beirut and the threat of its annihilation could be used to obtain the withdrawal of the forces and institutions of the PLO; and once this had been obtained, along with a Syrian withdrawal, a strong central government could be set up in Lebanon.

Unlike the Israeli-Syrian confrontation, a defeat of the PLO in Beirut through the threat of conquest—but without actual conquest—no longer presented any short-term risk for the United States. Even if Arab capitals had wanted to intervene (which was not the case), and even if Moscow had wished to provide direct aid (which was debatable), the political and military road they would have had to follow to be in a position to effectively support the besieged PLO in Beirut would have obliged them to go through the Syrian strategic rear. But Damascus, as we have seen, sought a policy of damage-limitation. Pressure on Israel to lift the siege was thus not on Washington's agenda, even among the leaders who might have firmly opposed the siege had they known of it beforehand. It appeared, on the contrary, that "if the Administration cracked down on Israel in any tangible way, the PLO might be encouraged to hold out in Beirut indefinitely" (Barrett 1983:280).

The divergences within the administration did not concern the lifting of the siege but rather its tightening. How was it possible both to threaten the PLO with total destruction and avoid conquering Beirut? The balance was not easy to strike between those who favored the first objective and those who feared Israel's possible recourse to conquest. Haig (1984:341–342) sought, of course, to give more credibility to the threat by subscribing to Israel's "psychological warfare" and by encouraging Israel to tighten the siege. For their part, Vice-President George Bush, Caspar Weinberger, and National Security Adviser William Clark sought to assure the Saudi leaders that a conquest of Beirut by force would not gain their approval (ibid.:343; Spiegel 1985:415). As a result, American signals were contradictory, which, as Haig saw it (1984:344–345), nullified his own efforts, weakened the credibility of the annihilation threat, and reinforced the determination of the Palestinians to hold out in the besieged city (also S. Lewis 1988:239).

Not being able to assure the rapid and victorious result he had hoped for with the siege of Beirut (Khalidi 1986:121–123), and criticized by other American leaders for his management of the war as well as for other reasons, Haig was forced to offer the President his letter of resignation on June 24. It could have been thought at this moment that American policy with respect to the Israeli action in Lebanon was changing; the Palestinian leaders in fact saw in this resignation a respite and the possibility of improving their position in negotiations (ibid.:123–124). More than two years after the events, Philip Habib, the president's emissary, revealed in an interview with Rashid Khalidi that "until the former Secretary's departure from the State Department, he [Habib] found it exceedingly hard to move Washington to restrain Israel or to support his own efforts" because it seemed to him that "Sharon had some sort of understanding with Haig over Lebanon" (ibid.:172). And indeed, from June 24 on, the U.S.administration was more reserved regarding the tightening of the Israeli vise around Beirut and tended to exercise more direct control over the evolution of events on the ground.

Once again, however, this stricter control did not at all mean that Washington no longer wanted to use the Israeli action to obtain the weakening of the PLO and its withdrawal from Beirut. While Haig, leaving diplomacy aside, had based his position on Israeli military pressure and its reinforcement (through air, sea, and land bombing of Beirut and attempts to break through Palestinian lines), his successor George Shultz, along with Weinberger and Clark, sought to use their privileged contacts with Saudi Arabia in order to convince the PLO that there was no Arab-American endeavor to end the siege and that its departure was a lesser evil. But in order for that to happen, the Israeli army, without abandoning its positions around Beirut, would have to respect the cease-fire temporarily and allow the negotiations to progress (Reagan 1990:425–427). If they did not move fast enough, there would always be time to loosen the Israelis' reins. A muzzled Sharon, but a Sharon all the same, was the best instrument of the diplomacy followed by the new Secretary of State Shultz and Presidential emissary Habib.

This situation led one Israeli commentator to assert, no doubt in exaggeration: "The Americans have waited, for many years, for an Israeli doctrine that agreed with the strategy of Pax Americana. If Sharon hadn't been born, they would have created him, not just him but the doctrine on which the operation 'Peace in Galilee' is based" (Yatsiv 1982). Without going that far, it can be argued that the fact that Sharon was more maximalist than they were, and was perceived as "crazy," gave the Americans means of pressure on the Arabs and allowed them at the same time to play an attractive role. For, on the one hand, they could threaten, if their conditions were not accepted, to unleash the bloody folly of Sharon, to the point where the situation would become intolerable for the Arabs. But on the other hand, it was the Americans who on numerous occasions imposed cease-fire after cease-fire on Israel following heavy bombings of Beirut; it was the Americans as well who had the power to save the cadres and fighters of the PLO from total extermination. The United States could thus cull the regional and global fruits of a war whose cost they had to bear only marginally. Of course, the Israelis also thought they could reap a harvest from this war, but its fruits were not as attractive as those hoped for by Sharon, since they had to be acquired at the price of relatively high casualties, a tarnished international image for Israel, and a significant internal crisis; furthermore, the Israeli army did not succeed (or at least hesitated) in conquering the city of Beirut in spite of attempts to break through, and in spite of a siege of more than two months' duration.

The Withdrawal of the PLO from Beirut and its Immediate Consequences. The U.S. diplomatic dynamism, combined with Israeli military pressure, led to the "Habib agreement" of August 18 (*Department of State Bulletin* 9/82/2–5) and to the withdrawal of the PLO from Beirut in the days that followed, under the supervision of a multinational force composed of American, Italian, and French contingents. Thus ended a phase of the war in which the sometimes sharp differences between Washington and Tel Aviv had not undermined the perception of common interests—minimal, of course, but nonetheless substantial. However, after the blow struck to Syria and the USSR and after the Palestinian withdrawal, the joint American-Israeli victory carried within it the seeds of a conflict of interest in two important areas: the settlement of the Palestinian question and the nature of the new order in Lebanon.

On the first point, the announcement of the "Reagan plan" concerning the West Bank and Gaza on September 1, just after the final phase of the Palestinians' withdrawal from Beirut, brought a negative response from Israel, being considered by Begin as "America's recompense to Saudi Arabia and Jordan for their part in getting the PLO to leave Beirut" (Schiff and Ya'ari 1984:234; Spiegel 1985:419). Schiff and Ya'ari (1984:294) report that in August, Secretary of State Shultz had declared to Sharon what was in fact to constitute the principal motive of the Reagan plan: "On the Palestinian question,

I feel . . . the president feels . . . that it must be dealt with. The PLO must be scattered and its credibility destroyed. But unless the Palestinian problem is solved, a new PLO will arise. The Soviet Union will be glad to arm them" (also Spiegel 1985:419). Although Washington did not at that time take practical measures to solve the Palestinian problem, its views did not coincide with Sharon's, for whom the destruction of the PLO in Lebanon was the necessary prelude to a purely Israeli solution on the West Bank.

The second potential item of disagreement between the two allies was of more immediate import because it concerned the setting up, in the shortest possible time, of the new Lebanese government. Although the choice of Bashir Gemayel as president was shared by Tel Aviv and Washington (Schiff and Ya'ari 1984:231), the new order to be instituted was not the same for the two capitals. For Begin and Sharon, the aim was to establish a "vassal state," separated from the rest of the Arab world. For the United States, it was rather to set up a strong central state that would follow the example of Egypt by guaranteeing security for Galilee and would also have reasonable relations with the rest of the Arab world, in particular with Saudi Arabia. While the president-elect, in spite of his "debts" toward Israel, leaned toward the American plan, his assassination on September 14, the day after the hasty departure of the multinational force, called both plans into question.

Thus began the second phase of Israel's war in Lebanon. Begin and Sharon, fearing that they would lose the benefits of their Lebanese campaign, frustrated of the maximalist objectives they had originally aspired to achieve, and determined to make the "Reagan plan" fail, decided to conquer Beirut. The U.S. administration for all intents and purposes turned a blind eye to an initiative it had previously sought to prevent (Khalidi 1986:177). This eventuality shocked it less now because from July-August to September, the war had moved away from the "brink of the precipice," that is, the limits of the tolerable for the Arabs. Of course Beirut was still an Arab capital, but it was no longer the "capital" of the PLO. Its occupation by the Israeli army could no longer provoke the same sort of Arab and international indignation, especially since it had taken place only after the human and material obstacles (fighters and fortifications) had been removed. The occupation of Beirut constituted a clear Israeli and American violation of the Habib agreement (Weinberger 1990:151). On this subject, Khalidi reports (1986:176), from his interview with Reagan's emissary: "Asked whether the U.S. had failed to keep its word to the PLO and whether Israel had violated the commitments it had made to the United States when it entered West Beirut, Philip Habib later answered: 'Of course'" (also Quandt 1988:364; S. Lewis 1988:239).

It would take the massacres of Sabra and Shatila, however, for Washington to understand the extent of its carelessness (Spiegel 1985:422). But whereas France and especially Italy felt the obligation to send its contingents back to Beirut to protect the camps, the United States did not consider that it had to pay for its irresponsibility by humanitarian or political measures toward the Palestinians. Of course Washington ordered the U.S. Marines to return to Beirut, but in doing so it sought mostly to take a direct hand in the restoration of the Lebanese state, so as not to lose its gains of the summer and so as to protect its regional interests. What were the implications of these developments for Israel's strategic status in Washington?

The American effort to take matters back in hand after the Sabra and Shatila massacres meant that Washington could no longer count on its Israeli instrument. Never before had it been so clear that the Israeli asset could turn, at its outer limits, into a burden or even a danger for American interests. In order to protect these interests, Washington now had to undertake its own efforts, send in its own troops, and engage its own prestige. As Leonard Binder noted (1983:1), the administration had now adopted a new orientation which consisted of its "apparent willingness to dispense with the use of surrogates and to act directly in the region."

However, in spite of the dynamics provoked by the events of Sabra and Shatila, and in spite of the strategic significance of the American decision to take matters back into their own hands, Israeli-American relations remained close, for three reasons. First, American leaders could not criticize Israel too much because they had had their own share of the responsibility in what had happened, even if it was less direct and grave than that of the Israeli leaders. Secondly, Tel Aviv had rapidly lost its hope in installing a protectorate in Lebanon and quickly gave in to American demands that it withdraw from Beirut. Finally, the political and military defeat of the Palestinians, aggravated by the massacres, remained, in cold logic, a common achievement for the two countries.

There remained, of course, some points of potential friction between Washington and Tel Aviv regarding Lebanon. These concerned above all the terms of the negotiations for an Israeli-

Lebanese peace agreement and the difficulties of operational coordination between the American contingent and the Israeli army, which were deployed face to face at the gates of Beirut (Weinberger 1990:162; Spiegel 1985:424–425; Green 1988:174–180). But this possibility for friction diminished as Washington's incapacity to impose a solution in the Lebanese "quagmire" became apparent. The eventuality of American-Israeli tension gave way gradually to a noticeable rapprochement (facilitated by the resignation of Sharon in February 1983). But what must be noted, above and beyond this familiar scenario of rapprochement, was Washington's willingness to reactivate its strategic cooperation with Israel. It was indeed a paradox that the failure of the Israeli asset in Lebanon, which had provoked a costly American investment, resulted finally in a desire to raise Israel's strategic status. We shall now seek to explain why this occurred.

The Reaffirmation of Strategic Cooperation: An Unexpected Outcome of the Lebanese Quagmire

We shall not consider here the cause of Washington's incapacity to impose an American order in Lebanon. Suffice it to say that its unconditional support to the new president Amin Gemayel and its manner of conducting the Lebanese-Israeli negotiations alienated, little by little, important sectors of the Lebanese people. Syria, although it had received a severe blow politically and militarily during the summer of 1982, gradually regained its initiative and reinforced its military ties to the USSR. In particular, the Soviet Union undertook to install and operate SAM-5 and SAM-13 anti-air batteries and SS-21 rocket launchers (Spiegel 1986:489, 493; Green 1988:228–229). The Israeli army, whose power had proven to be irrelevant in the face of guerrilla operations and the political complexity of Lebanon, understood not only that the Israeli order à la Sharon had been a chimera, but also that the establishment of a central government in Lebanon that could guarantee a peaceful border with Israel was more and more unrealistic. The Lebanese-Israeli agreement of May 17, 1983, concluded as a result of the energetic mediation of the U.S. administration (and in particular Shultz), was to become a dead letter and lead to an upsurge in mobilization against the American contingent, the Israeli army, the Phalangists, and the Lebanese army loyal to Gemayel.

In the summer and fall of 1983, we thus witness an Israel which, for both military and internal political reasons, sought to disengage from the Shouf and from Saida, and a U.S. administration on the defensive after the attacks directed against its embassy in Beirut and against its own military contingent. At this stage, only considerations of prestige prevented the United States from making the decision to withdraw. Instead of competing with each other to impose a settlement in Lebanon, Washington and Tel Aviv were now both facing the prospect of a serious regional failure. And although Israel was at the origin of the United States' setbacks, American leaders had no alternative but to seek operational support from the Israeli army to protect their Marines and to deter Damascus (Chadda 1986:167).

The administration thus attempted in July and August 1983 to convince Tel Aviv not to withdraw its troops from the Shouf, or at least to postpone the withdrawal (Spiegel 1985:426). More significantly still, during the month of October, that is, at a moment when Israeli determination to confront the Syrians had weakened (Novik 1984:29) and when important sectors of Israeli public opinion had "buried notions of acting as an American strategic surrogate" and thought that Israel should only fight "wars of no choice" (Shaw 1985/86:131), Washington considered the idea of resuscitating the agreement on strategic cooperation (MOU) concluded two years earlier and suspended almost immediately thereafter. On October 29, President Reagan adopted National Security Decision Directive (NSDD) number 111, which made "strategic cooperation" with Israel a priority for the administration (Spiegel 1985:427; Madison 1984:161–162; Gwertzman 1983:62–88). It should be noted that one of the most ardent supporters of the presidential directive was Shultz himself: since the failure of the Israeli-Lebanese agreement of May 17, the Secretary of State had an extremely positive image of the role of Tel Aviv in the region. Shultz wanted to "strengthen ties with Israel and make Israel virtually the centerpiece of U.S. policy in the Middle East" (Gelb 1983; Christison 1989:38–39). With NSDD 111 began a new era in strategic cooperation.

The Significance of NSDD 111. American-Israeli meetings were held in November 1983 with a view to implementing NSDD 111. Shamir, who had replaced Begin at the head of the Israeli government, and his Defense Minister, Moshe Arens, made a visit to Washington at the end of that month. A Joint Political-Military Group (JPMG) was created to examine the details of strategic cooperation. The group began working in January 1984. It should be noted, however, that the presidential directive is "classified, and the details of the discussions to implement it have not been made public" (Shaw 1985/86:129). Christopher Madison (1984:158) believes that these discussions covered three areas of military cooperation: "American use of Israeli medical facilities in an emergency, the placement of U.S. military equipment and supplies, including folding hospitals for transport elsewhere in the region during a possible war, and joint contingency planning and of joint military exercises" (also Geyelin 1983).

Although knowledge about directive NSDD 111 and its implementation is scarce and vague, it is nonetheless useful to compare it with the MOU of November 1981. Recalling what we said earlier about this memorandum: its importance was due not to its contents, for its statements were exaggerated, but to the fact that its public character revealed the weakness of the Arab world. We added that actual strategic cooperation between the United States and Israel did not depend on a pretentious declaration of intention, but would best materialize in the form of continued practice and confidential accords. Because of their secret character, the 1983 directive and the discussions which followed it seem more prudent and yet more serious than the memorandum of 1981: they suggest a certain correspondence between the objectives sought and the means envisioned. Madison (1984:158) explains that "this time, diplomats in both countries are taking precautions" and are adopting "a low profile for the discussions"; and that "U.S. officials are not announcing the talks unless asked" (also Shaw 1985/86:129).

The context of 1983 was not, of course, the same as that of 1981. In 1981, it was Israel, under the influence of the Sharon doctrine, that pushed for a strategic agreement in order to gain an American stamp of approval for the Defense Minister's regional aims; and it was the other signatory, Defense Secretary Caspar Weinberger, who was somewhat reluctant. While, in 1983, Weinberger still had certain reservations, the initiative belonged mainly to Washington (under the combined impact of the Department of State and the White House). As for Israel, not only was it disoriented, in the fall of 1983, about its strategic choices as a result of the Lebanon war, but it also feared certain implications of a quasi-official American recognition of its role as an asset. Whereas it should have been rejoicing at having finally attained the role it had sought for so long, Israel's leaders admitted that they were about to win a "prize" that "can be a burden" and that "it may allow Washington to ask them to act on behalf of U.S., not Israeli interests" (Shipler 1983).

But before these negative implications could be confirmed or invalidated by future developments, the immediate repercussions of strategic cooperation, restored to the agenda by NSDD 111, were positive for Israel. For example, the administration decided, in the weeks following the signing of the directive, to transform annual military aid (which stood at close to $1.4 billion in the form of a loan) into a nonreimbursable grant. However, only a closer examination of the content of strategic cooperation and its development between 1984 and 1989 will allow us to shed light on both its implications for Israel and the benefits that the United States stood to gain from it.

The Implementation of Strategic Cooperation, 1983–1989. We shall now examine the major accords that appear to have been concluded between the two countries and the areas of implementation between 1983 and 1989 (that is, up to the first year of the Bush administration, a year which still maintained continuity with the previous period under Reagan). In order to gain a broad view of the question, let us begin by enumerating the accords concluded before 1983. Certain of these have already been examined and we shall mention them only for the sake of reconstructing the historical sequence.

Let us first recall the accord on the exchange of military information in December 1970, known as the "Master Defense Development Data Exchange Agreement." From its origins up to July 1982, 19 annexes, each covering a particular exchange project, had been added to it (U.S. General Accounting Office 1983). Six other annexes may have been signed between July and August 1982, during the siege of Beirut by the Israeli army (Stork and Wenger 1983:29). Next, in November 1971, an agreement was concluded concerning the production in Israel, under American license, of certain items of military equipment (Green 1988:222). A Weapons Systems Evaluation Group was established in November 1973 for the purpose of drawing lessons from the October War (ibid.:222–223). Next came the memorandum of agreement of March 19, 1979, already cited above, concerning cooperation in R&D and the access of Israeli corporations to American military contracts. This memorandum, completed by a "Commitment" by Secretary of State Haig in April 1981, is the basis of the Defense Trade Initiative, which aimed to "enhance Israel's defense production and technological base" (U.S. General Accounting Office 1983). Haig's commitment, which essentially meant the promise to purchase up to $200 million worth of Israeli military equipment annually, was included in the MOU of November 1981. Although the memorandum was suspended by Washington in reaction to the Israeli annexation of the Golan Heights, "the spirit and some activities of the Defense Trade Initiative" were implemented, based on the earlier memorandum of 1979 (ibid.). This list can be completed up to 1983 by the accord of December 1982 on protecting confidential information exchanged between the two countries (the General Security of Information Agreement) (Green 1988:223).

With the NSDD 111 of October 1983, strategic cooperation gained new momentum and took on added dimensions. Above all, the directive ushered in a new climate between the two countries. Here are the results it was to bring in the years to follow.

In March 1984, Israeli Defense Minister Moshe Arens and American Secretary of Defense Caspar Weinberger signed a memorandum of agreement which revised and extended the scope of the 1979 memorandum (ibid.:222–223). The document invoked "agreed principles governing mutual cooperation in R&D, and an exchange of scientists and engineers, as well as procurement and logistic support of selected defense equipment" (Klieman 1985:176). A few months later and during a visit to Tel Aviv, Weinberger announced that Washington had decided to allow Israel access to the technology necessary for producing the Lavi fighter plane, programmed by the Israel army for use in the 1990s (Friedman 1984). However, in August 1987 Washington succeeded in convincing Tel Aviv to abolish the Lavi program, given its exorbitant cost and its overlapping with American programs.

The Strategic Defense Initiative (or "Star Wars") also provided an opportunity for cooperation between the two countries. When, in March 1985, Washington officially invited its allies to take part in a research program deriving from the initiative, Israel was among the invited states, alongside the members of NATO, Japan, and Australia (*Le Monde* 3/7 and 3/28/85). The advantages that Israel could hope to gain from its participation in the American program were not only financial, but also technological, especially in the area of research on systems for intercepting conventional ground-to-ground missiles such as the SS-21, which was a part of the Syrian arsenal (Starr 1986; Brooks 1986). A memorandum of agreement concerning cooperation in this area was signed in May 1986 (Green 1988:224).

In February, 1987, President Reagan declared that Israel, like other countries, had been elevated to the rank of "major non-NATO ally for purposes of cooperation in certain aspects of military research and development" (*American Foreign Policy Current Documents 1987–88*:228). This declaration took on a contractual form in December 1987 with the signing of a memorandum of agreement by Defense Secretary Frank Carlucci (who had just replaced Weinberger) and Israeli Defense Minister Yitzhak Rabin. The memorandum further limited the restrictions on Israel's purchase of American military equipment and allowed Israeli companies to compete on an equal footing with American companies or those of NATO countries for military R&D contracts (*International Herald Tribune* 12/16/87; Cobban 1991:89).

Another memorandum of agreement, signed in April 1988 for a five-year period, renewable, adds nothing substantial to the earlier agreements, but sums up the frameworks and areas of cooperation between the two countries: (a) the Joint Political-Military Group, which meets twice a year and engages in "joint cooperative efforts such as combined planning, joint exercises, and logistics"; (b) the Joint Security Assistance Planning Group, which meets once a year and reviews Israel's requests for assistance "in light of current threat assessments," and American budgetary capacities and industrial, technological, and R&D cooperation; (c) the Joint Economic Development Group, which meets twice a year and studies the problems of growth and self-reliance of the Israeli economy, as well as Israel's assistance needs in this area (text in *Journal of Palestine Studies* no. 69 [1988]:300–302). It must be recalled here that the two countries had signed, in April 1985, an agreement instituting a free trade zone between them, the first agreement of its kind ever signed by Washington (Ateya 1987).

Our overview of the areas of American-Israeli cooperation would be incomplete if we did not mention the joint maneuvers which have been taking place between the two countries' armed forces since 1983. Although information on this point is scarce because of the American wish to remain discreet, at least in the earlier period, we may cite the following cases.

In June 1984, the two countries held their first joint maneuvers for the evacuation of "wounded" troops to Israeli medical facilities using vessels of the U.S. 6th Fleet in the Mediterranean. The exercise was also intended to test communications between the two parties and the Israeli system of air traffic control (Wingerter 1985:84). In December of the same year, the two marine corps held their first joint maneuvers in the area of antisubmarine warfare (ibid.; Spiegel

1986:493; Blitzer 1985:80). Since that time, the port of Haifa has been frequently used by the 6th Fleet for visits and repairs. Indeed, a "Master Repair Agreement" was signed in June 1986 (Ryan 1987:14). It also appears that aircraft belonging to the 6th Fleet performs training exercises in the Negev (Gold 1988:92; Cobban 1991:88).

The Israeli author Benny Morris (1989:14) provided in August 1989 some supplementary details concerning the American-Israeli maneuvers. Invoking "secret details" divulged by Rabin to a limited group of American Jewish leaders, he writes: "In April, 1989, Israel and the United States carried out their first joint military maneuvers at the batallion level, with the participation of Marines from the 6th Fleet, assault helicopters and artillery. It was merely the 28th exercise of its kind, but up to now they had been conducted only at the company level."

We may conclude with the question of prepositioning of American military equipment in Israel. Interesting information on this point was provided in November 1989 by the Assistant Secretary of State for Political-Military Affairs, Richard Clark, who represented the American side in the above-mentioned Joint Political Military Group. In testimony before the Senate Foreign Affairs Committee, Clark noted that in 1985, negotiations had taken place between the two parties concerning the stocking of military equipment in Israel and a memorandum was drawn up on this subject. Several depots were accordingly constructed and some equipment was placed there in 1987 (Maalouf 1989). The Assistant Secretary of State added that, in accordance with an earlier American promise, the administration was examining the possibility of concluding a new agreement which would allow Israel to use the materiel stored in the "prepositioning sites" for its own needs in case of emergency. This agreement would be comparable to the one existing between the United States and Thailand and South Korea.

*The Risks Involved in Strategic Cooperation.*It may be concluded from the preceding section that American-Israeli strategic cooperation presents a set of tangible advantages for both parties, and for Israel in particular. We must, however, consider the direct risks or disadvantages that this cooperation has implied for each because of the other's initiative.

Regarding the risks originating from the American side, we have already noted that the Israelis' initial reaction to the American offer contained in NSDD 111 was mixed, since they apprehended the costs involved in this generous offer. This apprehension justly reflected the double dimension of strategic cooperation, as we have inferred it from the analysis of the asset doctrine at the beginning of this study. We observed that strategic cooperation placed Israel in an intermediate position between the ideas of intrinsic and extrinsic asset, that is, between the idea of an autonomous Israeli role which would at the same time serve American interests, and the idea of a direct American use of Israeli territory, facilities, and capacities, regardless of the problem of converging or diverging interests between the two countries. Was there not the danger for Israel that the strategic cooperation relaunched in 1983 might involve "instrumentalizing" Israel as an extrinsic asset?

To answer this question, it should first be pointed out that American-Israeli strategic cooperation (concerning joint maneuvers and prepositioning of American equipment) does not occur in the institutional framework that replaced the RDJTF in January 1983, that is, the CENTCOM (Central Command). The establishment of CENTCOM promoted the American military apparatus in charge of Southwest Asia to the same rank as EUCOM (European Command) and PACOM (Pacific Command). We have already noted that the RDJTF's area of responsibility, Southwest Asia, included neither Israel nor Jordan nor Egypt. This time, Egypt, Sudan, and Jordan were included in the CENTCOM area, whereas Israel's place did not change: like Syria and Lebanon, Israel was kept within the EUCOM's traditional area of responsibility. This way of redrawing the map would have made no difference had there not been a new element in the picture: American-Israeli strategic cooperation in the form it had taken since 1983, with joint maneuvers and the prepositioning of equipment. This cooperation was taken charge of on the American side by EUCOM (Gold 1988:38, 92).

According to Dore Gold, a researcher at the Jaffee Center for Strategic Studies at the University of Tel Aviv, who in 1986 conducted a series of interviews with State Department, Pentagon and National Security Council officials, the noninclusion of Israel in CENTCOM is justified in the following manner. First of all, there are the well-known political reasons, relating to the difficulty of associating Israel with American-Arab strategic cooperation, which is already, in itself, difficult to implement. Next, Israel has had relations with EUCOM for a long time, and this organization "was responsible for past resupply missions in 1973 and would be responsible for any resupply efforts in a future war" (Gold 1988:85). Finally, strategists determine theaters of operation according to the criterion of naval access, and "Israel as a Mediterranean country belongs in EUCOM, whereas Southwest Asia and the Gulf are an extension of the Indian Ocean and therefore belong to a separate theater. Egypt is also a Mediterranean country, but by virtue of its location along the Red Sea, it belongs to the Indian Ocean area as well."

Above and beyond these American justifications, the exclusion of Israel from the CENTCOM zone and its inclusion in that of EUCOM had implications from the standpoint of actual American doctrine. First, Washington was allowing Israel to benefit, for its survival (thus in some sense considering it as a burden) from the tangible present or future windfalls of strategic cooperation. Secondly, Israel was not treated as an asset contributing to the struggle against regional instability in its hinterland, whether of Soviet inspiration or otherwise. Thirdly, Israeli power was put forward as an extrinsic asset to counter the Soviet Union in the eastern Mediterranean, since the main objective of EUCOM was to plan European defense (Gold 1988:94–95).

For Israel, the latter two implications of the effective U.S. doctrine were not necessarily satisfactory. While Israel's own interest was to play a political-strategic role in its own zone, the Middle East, in cooperation with the United States, it was now being herded into an anti-Soviet struggle of a purely military nature, as a participant in the defense of NATO's southern flank. Positive side-effects notwithstanding, this situation was not in conformity with the vision of all Israeli strategists. Gold (1988:95) expressed this dissatisfaction by proposing that *"at least a mechanism should be created that gives Israel a role in CENTCOM without removing it entirely from EUCOM"* (Gold's emphasis). In other words, instead of being a "subject" excluded from CENTCOM and a mere "object" (extrinsic asset) within EUCOM, Israel should have, in Gold's view, a status of subject in both; it should be able to intervene in the CENTCOM area with the prestige conferred on it by its belonging to EUCOM.

There was thus, in American-Israeli strategic cooperation, at least a potential dimension of Israel as an extrinsic asset. Indeed, the possibility of using the Jewish state in this manner, politically rather than militarily, was first seen in 1984, when Tel Aviv had to reply to a pressing demand to install broadcasting facilities for the Voice of America on its territory. Israeli leaders, worried about the future of Soviet Jewish emigration, had reservations about facilitating this "war of the airwaves" against Moscow. However, after several months of indecision, Israel bowed in February 1985 to the American request. According to Amnon Rubenstein, Israeli Communications Minister, "beggars cannot be choosers" (*International Herald Tribune* 2/9–10/85). This was, however, the only such episode of an American demand for Israel to participate in an anti-Soviet effort against its will.

Let us now consider the risks related to Israeli strategic initiative. Such risks could originate from repeated claims on both sides regarding the quality of strategic cooperation, since this could lead Israeli decisionmakers to express an exaggerated confidence in themselves. We may take, for example, the case of the intensified consultations and the personal contacts between the leaders of the two countries at all levels. According to Thomas Dine, director of the official pro-Israel lobbying organization AIPAC (1987:96), "over 1200 officials of the U.S. Department of Defense and the services visited Israel on official business" in 1986, not to mention, of course, political visits in both directions and those of Israeli military envoys to the United States.

These contacts allow Israeli leaders to find, among American officials, ears receptive to their analyses of regional developments (Cobban 1991:97). In so doing, the Israelis contribute to molding American perception to serve their own interests. But this Israeli advantage involves a liability for Washington. One significant example is provided by the role of active and persuasive intermediary played by Israeli officials in the secret sale of American weapons to Iran in 1985/86 (Pincus 1985). Washington's secret diplomacy was in a certain sense a victim of what Israeli leaders saw as their regional interests (Pincus and Woodward 1988; Hooglund 1988; Green 1988:212–218). The Tower Commission, which was assembled to investigate the Irangate scandal, stressed in its report that Israel "had longstanding interests in a relationship with Iran and in promoting its arms export industry. . . . Elements in Israel undoubtedly wanted the United States involved for its own sake so as to distance the United States from the Arab world and ultimately to establish Israel as the only real strategic partner of the United States in the region" (President's Special Review Board 1987:III-4).

If the intimacy of the Israeli-American relationship contributed to common strategic visions, it also increased the risks of Israeli errors in its relations with the United States. Behavior which, under other conditions, would express only a short-sighted calculus of interest and relations of suspicion between two states took on much more gravity because of the Israeli-American intimacy and could be considered as betrayals of mutual confidence. This was the case, for example, in the Jonathan Pollard affair, in which an American citizen of Jewish origin was implicated in spying activity for Israel in November 1985 (Richard Cohen 1987; Safire 1987; Woodward and Pincus 1988; McConnell 1986). During a period of 14 months, Pollard provided Israel with 1800 secret documents, or about 500,000 pages, relating among other things to air defense, Soviet strategic arms, and codes used in American diplomatic communications. According to one author, "some of the most important Pollard documents were retyped and sanitized by Israeli intelligence officials and then made available to the Soviet Union as a gesture of Israeli goodwill, at the specific instructions of Yitzhak Shamir" (Hersh 1991:286).

Let us finally add that, throughout the 1983–89 period, Israel's confidence in the role it played in American strategy caused it to attribute little importance to the disagreements of a political nature that sometimes pitted it against Washington. The Palestinian uprising that began in the occupied territories at the end of 1987 resulted in one such disagreement, since it provoked the rise of Israeli repression, the announcement in March 1988 of the Shultz plan for a phased settlement of the Palestinian question, and the Israeli refusal of this plan.

However, neither the Israeli blunders concerning the American-Iranian arms sales scandal, nor the Pollard affair, nor Tel Aviv's refusal of the Shultz plan were considered sufficient by the Reagan administration to warrant calling into question the strategic cooperation between the two countries. American decisionmakers and commentators treated Israel's part in the Irangate scandal very gingerly. The Pollard case, which burst into public attention in November 1986, did not prevent a meeting of the JMPG during the same month and the designation of Israel as a non-NATO ally a few weeks later (Cobban 1991:91; Black and Morris 1991:426). Nor did the Israeli refusal of the Shultz plan in the least perturb the signing of the memorandum of strategic cooperation in April 1988. Was the upheaval on the international and regional scenes under the presidency of George Bush (1989–1992) to prove a challenge to the American-Israeli strategic relationship?

The Bush Administration and the New World Order, 1989–1992

When George Bush succeeded Ronald Reagan in January 1989, the situation in the world and in the Middle East was already much different from what it had been just a year earlier. At the international level, the Soviet-American détente and the arms reduction process were taking effect and it was already clear that Soviet power no longer wanted, or was no longer able, to forcibly repress popular movements in Eastern Europe or even within its own borders. In the Middle East, a secular Iraq, encouraged by the West, had very recently—in July 1988—practically imposed a cease-fire on Khomeinyist Iran and was perhaps preparing to play a more active role in the region. In the field of the Palestinian-Israeli conflict, the PLO, motivated by the confidence afforded it by the uprising in the occupied territories and by international détente, had, in November and December of 1988, launched a peace initiative by calling for the coexistence of two states recognizing each other in mandate Palestine, while satisfying the American conditions stipulated in the American-Israeli memorandum of September 1, 1975 regarding the opening of American-Palestinian negotiations. These negotiations were finally inaugurated by the Reagan administration in its last weeks, on December 16, 1988.

In facing these international and regional changes, the new administration surely lacked vision, even though it was the heir to an administration whose main attribute had perhaps been Reagan's ability to project the image of a visionary leadership. The Bush team, in which Secretary of State James Baker occupied a dominant position, had as its asset, but also as its shortcoming, its pragmatism. It would not exclude, for instance, conducting several courses of action at once, even if their implications were contradictory. Thus, it was ready to pursue strategic cooperation with Tel Aviv at a time when the end of the Cold War was undermining one of its very foundations, when in fact it was not very receptive to the idea of an Israeli strategic role in the Middle East (Cockburn and Cockburn 1991:352), and when it found itself in the unprecedented situation of having to give substance to the first official dialogue with the PLO.

It was in this last area that the potential contradiction in the Bush administration's political choices was most apparent. For if it wished to use détente with Moscow in order to accomplish in the

Middle East what it had been led to do in other areas of the world (arms reductions in Europe, settlement of conflicts in Afghanistan, Angola, Mozambique, and Namibia), and if it sought to move toward a settlement of the Israeli-Palestinian and Israeli-Arab conflicts, then the agenda of its contacts with a reinforced PLO (strengthened by its popular base, by the support of all the Arab states as well as the international community for its peace initiative) could be nothing other than the establishment of a Palestinian state in the occupied territories. This choice would have called into question the strategic role of Israel, brought back into the center of debate the idea of an American guarantee to the Jewish state, and implied on the latter's part territorial and symbolic concessions to Palestinian nationhood and identity. It would have run up against the refusal of the Israeli government, which considered these concessions too exorbitant a price to pay for the intangible advantages of recognition and peace promised to it.

The new administration did not follow this route, which would of course have been difficult from the point of view of its strategic and political relations with Israel, and yet in conformity with changes under way and the expectations of the Palestinians, the Arabs, and international opinion. It was receptive to the suggestions of advisers such as Dennis Ross and Richard Haass, who had taken part in the drafting of a 1988 report sponsored by the pro-Israeli Washington Institute for Near East Policy entitled "Building for Peace," on the desirable American policy in the Middle East. It thus pursued the traditional policy of supporting Tel Aviv, with minimal adjustments to take into account new international and regional conditions. Thus, although it insisted that Prime Minister Yitzhak Shamir take a step toward the Palestinians and present a peace plan, it took care, in exchange, to provide Israel with all the necessary assurances. During Bush's first 18 months in office, these included maintaining strategic cooperation as instituted by the previous administration (consultations, R&D, prepositioning, joint maneuvers); accepting the Shamir plan of May 1989 on autonomy in the Palestinian occupied territories as a basis of discussion with none other than the Egyptians; downgrading the discussions with the PLO, acting as if this dialogue were being maintained only to avoid accusations that it was not respecting the previous administration's commitments; and finally, at a moment when Soviet Jews' requests to emigrate were much more easily accepted by Moscow, suddenly closing the United States' traditionally hospitable gates in order to channel immigration toward Israel. And when, in March 1990, the Shamir government caused the Baker plan to fail—a plan based on Israel's own project—an act which provoked the Labor Party's departure from the coalition government, the Secretary of State went no further than to express his frustration by reminding the Israelis leaders of the White House telephone number in case they ever became serious about peace (Hadar 1990–91:106).

This mixture of cooperation and friction in the relations between the two countries presented no novelty with respect to earlier periods and might have endured in the same form had changes in the international environment proven superficial or reversible. However, what occurred in the last quarter of 1989 was an authentic overturning of the world strategic configuration: with the collapse of Soviet influence in Eastern Europe and upheaval in the Soviet republics, the bipolar world was coming to an end. Of course, questions were still raised about the shape of the new world system, the comparative relevance of economic power and military strength, and, by extension, the place the United States would occupy in the new system with respect to the EEC or Japan; but developments in the Middle East, which culminated in the Gulf War, were to contribute to clarifying and reorienting the response.

Certain aspects of these developments should be noted. The first of these, although not of a military nature, nonetheless involved a most important security dimension, at least in the eyes of the parties involved: the immigration of Soviet Jews. The number advanced, from 500,000 to 1,000,000 immigrants, was not only imposing in itself, but also truly monumental in the Israeli-Palestinian context. For the Israeli Prime Minister Yitzhak Shamir, the influx of immigrants legitimated "Greater Israel" and allowed him to declare, in January 1990: "Around us, the Arabs are in complete disarray, in a state of panic . . . ; they are submerged by a feeling of defeat because they see that the Intifada is useless; they cannot stop the natural flow of the Jewish people toward its homeland—and after all, that is what this conflict is all about" (*Le Monde* 1/16/90). For their part, the Palestinians noted that the historic concessions they had made at the end of 1988 had gone for naught in terms of the Israeli response and the American attitude. Graver still, they perceived the further development of colonization in the occupied territories resulting from the new immigration as implying a repeat of their mass expulsion (known, in the euphemistic terminology of Israel's far right, then apparently in expansion, as "transfer").

The next set of Middle East developments to be noted is of a military nature. Iraq, which had supported the PLO's peace initiative, also aspired to occupy a central position in the region, pursuing its military effort and in particular the development of nuclear and chemical weapons and ballistic missiles. Limiting ourselves to the Israeli-Arab context, we may note that the Iraqi effort, which could be considered as coming within the framework of a quest for mutual deterrence, in fact increased the risks of destabilization. In order for mutual deterrence to exercise a stabilizing influence, it must, following a long race for parity punctuated by dangerous crises and a difficult political learning process, be recognized as such by the parties concerned, preferably in a treaty (such as the SALT and ABM treaties of 1972). But in the present case, Iraq was still at the beginning of the race, while Israel did not wish to lose its dominant strategic position and its unilateral deterrence capability: conventional superiority; the possession of nuclear weapons and perhaps tactical ones (Hersh 1991:120, 200, 216, 220, 312); the ability to strike Iraqi or Arab objectives selectively and discriminatingly; its advanced research program on Jericho ballistic missiles and the more hesitant Israeli-American program of Arrow anti-missile missiles; and effective protection against chemical weapons. From a strict point of view of strategic balance, Israel might have been tempted (and was thus perceived as being actually tempted) to engage in a first strike before the Iraqi threat became truly credible. While the absence of a common border between the two countries made accidental confrontations unlikely, it also made it extremely difficult (unlike in the Syrian-Israeli case) to manage possible crises by controlling the escalation at its lowest level.

Even if a preventive strike was not on the Israeli agenda, and even if a realistic scenario for triggering a crisis was barely imaginable, the perception that the Israeli strike was possible, and above all the fear of an inevitable escalation in the event of any crisis, were nourished by Iraqi declarations about the destruction of half of Israel in the event of an Israeli attack on Iraq, by the attention given by the media and the U.S., British and Israeli governments to the Iraqi military effort (for example the "super cannon" affair), and by American acquiescence to (if not participation in) the comparable Israeli effort (as in the Arrow missile project). When one considers that all this fed into the exacerbation of the Israeli-Palestinian conflict, the freezing of the Baker initiative, the PLO-Iraq rapprochement and the suspending of the American-Palestinian dialogue following an anti-

Israeli operation by the Palestinian group of Abu Abbas, one can imagine the diffuse but nevertheless very strong tension that gripped the Middle East by the end of spring 1990 (Diehl and Murphy 1990).

By his decision to invade Kuwait on August 2, and whatever the factors involved (immoderate Iraqi ambitions, Kuwaiti obstinacy, planned American provocation), Iraqi President Saddam Hussein himself undermined one of the foundations of the Iraqi-Israeli mutual deterrence to which he aspired. While the invasion, other things being equal, had the effect of increasing Iraq's power with respect to Israel without provoking it in its space of vital interest (as would have been the case, if Iraqi troops had been sent to Jordan, which would have provoked an Israeli response and caused mutual deterrence to fail), it also had the effect of bringing U.S. military power into the regional equation. Even if one supposes that the rules of mutual deterrence—and fragile ones at that—already governed Iraqi-Israeli relations, they could only function in a strictly regional framework. But the involvement of the United States was already threefold: as a power concerned by the oil stake, as an unfailing ally of Israel, and as a world power with an interest in the fate of any region in the world. For the Americans, not to respond seriously to the invasion of Kuwait would have meant losing a part of their mastery over oil and resigning themselves to facing later, and under much more difficult and perhaps uncontrollable conditions, the test of their alliance with Israel, either as a result of an Israeli-Iraqi and Israeli-Arab military confrontation (Schiff 1991), or because this very risk would have imposed a settlement process clearly unfavorable to Israel; and finally, it would have been to admit that the end of the Cold War led to the neutralization of the American military instrument and to the increased freedom of maneuver for any state wishing to modify a regional status quo or seize a place left vacant locally by the USSR.

The American decision to intervene militarily had implications for Israel's place in American strategy. At the most elementary and obvious level, it was a spectacular negation of the idea, long held by some in the United States, that Israel was a strategic asset for the United States in the Gulf region: Tel Aviv was in no position either to prevent the invasion or to punish its perpetrators. On the contrary, the enthusiasm with which Israel welcomed the deployment of American troops in Saudi Arabia, and its clear preference for a military rather than political outcome in the crisis, leading not only to the Iraqi withdrawal from Kuwait but also to the military destruction of Iraq's strategic potential (Cockburn and Cockburn 1991:353) showed that Israel was counting, for the first time, on American troops to neutralize a danger located in the area of the Israeli-Arab conflict itself. Following the defeat of Iraq, Zeev Schiff (1991:21) wrote that the way in which the war had taken place had been "almost a miracle for Israel," thus suggesting that the difficulties faced by Israeli deterrence in the area of the Israeli-Arab conflict prior to the invasion were much more serious than had been recognized.

If the sending of American troops into the Gulf thus revealed the weakening of Israel's status as an intrinsic asset for the United States, one must ask whether strategic cooperation between the two countries, which had been quite active in the 1980s and which represented an intermediate level between the ideas of intrinsic and extrinsic assets, was still in any way a viable idea during the crisis. It must be recognized that this aspect of the crisis, perhaps more than any other, was remarkably managed by Washington. Schiff (1991:22) asserts that the day before the hostilities began, cooperation between the intelligence agencies of the two countries was "minimal" and that there had been no consultation on operational questions. This may be so, but it must be recalled that the chief of staff of the U.S. Air Force, Michael Dugan, was forced to resign in September 1990 after disclosing certain aspects of Israeli-American cooperation (and of military strategy in the campaign being prepared). In fact, Washington wanted to dissociate Israel as much as possible from the anti-Iraqi coalition and associate the Arab states as much as possible, in order not to expose itself to the Iraqi accusation that the American military threat and that of Israel were linked. Whatever secret cooperation may have existed between the United States and Israel, what was important politically was the public attitude of these two countries and of the Arab states contributing to the mobilization against Iraq. Politically, Israel was a burden in this mobilization, while Egypt and, paradoxically, Syria, were now assets for the United States.

Given the risks of instability and anti-American explosions in the Arab world, Israel was now so much a liability that president Bush asked Yitzhak Shamir in December 1990 not to respond to an Iraqi attack (Cockburn and Cockburn 1991:356) Shamir could not, of course, accede to such a demand and thereby make a general promise that would have broken all the rules of Israeli military doctrine. But it is known that as soon as the first Iraqi missiles fell on Israeli territory, Washington firmly persuaded Tel Aviv not to respond and, in compensation, sent batteries of Patriot missiles to Israel with American soldiers to operate them. This case, in which the United States took responsibility for protecting Israel and asked it to remain inactive, illustrated precisely the opposite of the asset idea, in which Israel protects American interests and requests the latter's inaction. It must be admitted that this scenario was exceptional and had not been foreseen, even by those who had always seen Israel as a burden and warned against actively associating Israel with the Rapid Deployment Force established by Carter in 1980.

In any event, Iraq's defeat and the process of eliminating its strategic weapons meant that there was no longer any Arab power capable of defying Israeli superiority. Does this mean that Israel thus regained the place it had earlier occupied in American strategic doctrine? Could Israel be perceived and treated as if it had become once again the U.S. asset in the Middle East? The answer can only be negative for several reasons. First, the coalition that had to be constructed against Iraq showed that the United States, in protecting its interests, might have to seek the support of allies other than Israel, such as Saudi Arabia and Egypt, and find circumstantial allies such as Syria, while having to tolerate the "betrayal" of some traditional allies such as Jordan. Also, the dislocation of the Soviet Union made it impossible to speak of Israel as a rampart against a danger originating in Moscow. Not only did this danger no longer exist, but also, perhaps as direct outcomes, other dangers emerged, such as the Iraqi invasion of Kuwait. The disappearance of the "structuring" (and frequently moderating) influence of the Soviet Union, and now the defeat of Iraq, left a vacuum in the Middle East that only Washington could fill. Finally, the risk of proliferation of arms of massive destruction could be countered only by the United States.

Of course, the Israelis and the defenders of the asset idea could still speak of an Israeli role in countering the rise of anti-Western Islamic fundamentalism. But Islamic fundamentalism, even more than oil interests, overflowed by far the geographic area in which Israel could play a role; now, more than ever, this role, if recognized, had to remain limited to the area of the Palestinian occupied territories, Jordan, Syria, and Lebanon. Furthermore, and above all,

Islamic fundamentalism, like any ideological current with a voca-
tion for mobilizing masses, could not be deterred or foiled by military superiority; it might even be strengthened if this superiority
was brandished against it. In fact, Islamic fundamentalism posed
the more general problem of stability in the Middle East. In this new
era in which the United States had become the only world superpower, the real question was whether it could tolerate instability in
the region. It could be thought, after the war against Iraq, that disorder would leave the United States indifferent, precisely because
there was no other great power to exploit it to the U.S. disadvantage.
However, by taking the initiative of generating an Israeli-Arab peace
process just after the war, the American administration showed that
it preferred order to disorder in a region that had just proven its
strategic importance, or at least that disorder there had to be kept
within certain limits. The American message to the Israelis could
be summed up as follows: you wish to contribute to American interests, you can do so only by contributing to regional stability, and
this now implies your commitment to the peace process (Friedman
1992).

In the framework of this preference for order and stability, the
administration devoted its efforts to convening the Madrid conference in late October 1991 and bringing the Arabs and the Israelis to
the table of bilateral negotiations in Washington. To pose the terms
of reference of the negotiation, Washington took Israeli demands at
their letter and imposed them at the outset on the Arabs, especially
on the Palestinians, now weakened by the consequences of the Gulf
War: the refusal of a separate Palestinian delegation, of PLO participation, or that of Palestinians from Jerusalem or outside the occupied territories; the refusal of active UN participation; the requirement of a five-year interim period for the occupied Palestinian territories, with a postponing of negotiations on their definitive status;
and the non-inclusion, in the letter of invitation to the conference,
of the principle of land for peace. By accepting these Israeli conditions as the point of departure for the process, Washington hoped to
stimulate a dynamic of negotiation in which Israel would agree at
each stage, and without much pressure, to make concessions it
would have refused in the preceding stage. As we know, the Shamir
government had another strategy, and the Bush team, in order to
prevent the negotiations from collapsing, had to refuse to guarantee
a loan of $10 billion as long as the Israeli government did not cease
its settlement activities in the occupied territories. The Likud's

defeat in the elections of June, 1992 by the Labor Party under the leadership of Yitzhak Rabin were probably due, at least in part, to American resolve.

The Labor victory allowed the U.S. administration to show, if it were necessary, that the search for regional stability and Israeli-Arab peace did not imply lukewarm pursuit of American-Israeli relations. If there were reservations during the time of Shamir, they were directed to the old meaning of the asset idea, since it seemed to require the continuation of Israeli-Arab hostility. Rabin's victory was apparently that of acquiescence to the American strategic vision and Israel's place in it. Just before the elections, Leslie Gelb wrote that "Israel's future value to the United States, in Mr. Rabin's view, should be as a peacemaker." Gelb reports that Rabin had dismissed the idea that the United States should use Israeli weapons to face the anti-Western fundamentalist threat, but insisted on the fact that "whatever happens in this area, Israel will always be on the same front as the U.S." (Gelb 1992).

Finally, it should not be thought that the American strategic vision in the post-Cold War and post-Gulf War period excludes American-Israeli military cooperation in the directions pursued in the 1980s (prepositioning, joint maneuvers, cooperation in R&D as in the Arrow missile). Cooperation could continue, short of a joint American-Israeli armed intervention against an Arab party. Thus, Secretary of Defense Richard Cheney declared, during a visit to Israel in late May 1991, that the United States was just about to preposition "significant stockpiles of military equipment" in Israel (*International Herald Tribune* 6/1–2/91). Even at the height of tension with the Shamir government in April 1992, the armed forces of the two countries held important joint maneuvers and, significantly, this news was announced by the U.S. ambassador to Israel, William Harrop (*Ha'aretz* 5/6/92).

Balance Sheet and Conclusion

We have now reached the current end-point of the evolution of American strategic doctrine with respect to Israel. We hope that from this examination of the past 45 years, guided by the concepts and categories drawn from the first two chapters of this work, has emerged not necessarily a coherent and functioning doctrine, but at least a coherent effort to reconstruct and render explicit the evolution of such a doctrine. We must now take stock of the situation, that is, specify the place Israel occupies today in American strategy with respect to the place it occupied just after the state's founding.

What is remarkable first of all in American policy is the constancy of support to Israel at the diplomatic and financial levels. Diplomatic support has never failed, even in the event of disagreements. We do not wish to suggest by this that past disagreements between the two countries have been merely apparent ones, deliberately magnified in order to hide the collusion of their objectives. Our point is rather that the two countries, each time their differences were in danger of becoming tangible disagreements about the actions to undertake or the decisions to adopt, have made it a point not to let these differences become aggravated and to resolve them rapidly through negotiation. This was true even before 1967, during the period that observers consider to be that of nonprivileged relations. An example of this is the aftermath of the Suez war of 1956, when the Israeli and American leaders, whatever may have been the recriminations uttered by the former and the pressure exercised by the latter, sought together to repair what was harmful to their relations as a result of Israeli participation in that war.

American financial support to Israel is also stable. From the quantitative point of view (see table 5.1), it traces a rising curve punctuated by "plateaus" (in particular from 1952 to 1965), and rarely undergoes substantial drops. The crest in 1966 is due to the Skyhawk aircraft supply agreement and signals the predominance of the military dimension in American aid in the following years. The year 1975 does not mark a spectacular fall but rather a strong progression with respect to 1973, since the pinnacle of 1974 is explained by the airlift set up during the October war. The crest in 1979 may be explained by the financing of Israeli military redeployment (from the Sinai toward the Negev in particular) following the peace treaty with Egypt. It should further be noted that after the 1973 war, the order of magnitude of American aid underwent an important leap and grants began replacing loans (a trend that prevailed after 1984).

In the absence of a formal treaty of guarantee, is this American diplomatic and financial support to Israel equivalent to a de facto

Table 5.1
American Aid to Israel, 1949-1990
(In millions of dollars)

Year	Military Assistance		Economic Assistance		Total
	Loans	Grants	Loans	Grants	
1949	-	-	100.0	-	100.0
1950	-	-	-	-	-
1951	-	-	35.0	0.1	35.1
1952	-	-	-	86.4	86.4
1953	-	-	-	73.6	73.6
1954	-	-	-	74.7	74.7
1955	-	-	30.8	21.9	52.7
1956	-	-	35.2	15.6	50.8
1957	-	-	21.8	19.1	40.9
1958	-	-	74.1	11.3	85.4
1959	0.4	-	42.0	10.9	53.3
1960	0.5	-	42.3	13.4	56.2
1961	-	-	59.6	18.3	77.9
1962	13.2	-	73.0	7.2	93.4
1963	13.3	-	68.6	6.0	87.9
1964	-	-	32.2	4.8	37.0
1965	12.9	-	47.3	4.9	65.1
1966	90.0	-	35.9	0.9	126.8
1967	7.0	-	15.1	1.6	23.7
1968	25.0	-	75.0	6.5	106.5
1969	85.0	-	74.7	0.6	160.3
1970	30.0	-	50.7	12.9	93.6
1971	545.0	-	86.5	2.8	634.3
1972	300.0	-	124.9	56.0	480.9
1973	307.5	-	80.5	104.8	492.8
1974	982.7	1500.0	72.3	91.3	2646.3
1975	200.0	100.0	96.0	407.0	803.0
1976	850.0	850.0	410.3	544.9	2655.2
1977	500.0	500.0	277.9	509.6	1787.5
1978	500.0	500.0	272.2	550.4	1822.6
1979	2700.0	1300.0	358.8	554.2	4913.0
1980	500.0	500.0	591.9	554.1	2146.0
1981	900.0	500.0	217.4	791.0	2408.4
1982	850.0	550.0	24.0	821.5	2245.5
1983	950.0	750.0	-	800.6	2500.6
1984	850.0	850.0	-	926.6	2626.6
1985	-	1400.0	-	1971.7	3371.7
1986	-	1722.6	15.0	1920.9	3658.5
1987	-	1800.0	-	1235.2	3035.2
1988	-	1800.0	-	1234.9	3034.9
1989	-	1800.0	-	1239.9	3039.9
1990	-	1792.3	400.0	1235.7	3428.0
TOTAL	11212.5	18214.9	3941.0	15943.8	49312.2

SOURCE: Computed from Clyde R. Mark, Israel: U.S. Foreign Assistance, CRS Issue Brief, Congressional Research Service, Washington DC: Library of Congress, January 5, 1993, p.6–7.

guarantee? As far as the post-1973 period is concerned, one may answer in the affirmative: since the emergency airlift established during the October war, the American guarantee, although de facto, has become explicit for the actors concerned and for observers. With the memoranda of agreement of 1975 and 1979, it began to be codified. It is nonetheless difficult to answer with the same assurance for the years prior to 1973, since a possible guarantee did not have to pass the reality test. In the wars waged by Israel in 1948, 1956, and 1967, Israeli military superiority was such that the U.S. administration did not even have to answer the question of whether it was committed to a possible guarantee. And if the United States seemed rather open to a guarantee in 1967, it was not to protect Israel against an impossible Arab victory, but rather to counter the improbable eventuality of a Soviet response to the expected defeat of the Arab armies.

The history of the idea of guarantee cannot, however, be reduced to these key but relatively short moments of combat. The question remains whether Israel, before 1973, enjoyed a de facto guarantee between one war and another, that is, in periods during which the Israeli-Arab conflict took place in the form of truces, and in which uncertainty regarding new hostilities continued, with ongoing questions based on the possibility that the balance of forces might be eroded or even reversed in the foreseeable future. Faced with an uncertain future, even a strong Israel might wish to benefit from an American guarantee, and the United States might look upon this eventuality favorably.

What have the previous chapters taught us in this regard? It appears that at the beginning of the 1950s, Washington considered it could not abandon Israel in case of danger and was ready to sign a treaty of guarantee. It is true that this guarantee was conditional, that is, it hinged on the prior or concomitant settlement of the Israeli-Arab conflict, and in this sense it corresponded to what we have called the GLS (an idea flirted with by Kissinger and Carter after 1973). This American readiness to sign a treaty of guarantee, albeit a conditional one, confirms that for American leaders, Israel already enjoyed a de facto guarantee, and it was preferable to regulate the latter by codifying it and linking it to some quid pro quo. We may thus advance the hypothesis that since the moment of its founding, Israel enjoyed at least an implicit de facto guarantee, and after 1973, this guarantee became explicit.

In any event, what Washington was ready to offer did not corre-

spond to what Tel Aviv had in mind. The conditional guarantee
implied, already in the 1950s, that Israel would have to make concessions that would facilitate the settlement of the Israeli-Arab conflict. Tel Aviv, of course, was not so inclined. What the Israelis first
proposed, however, was a mutual defense treaty which, though
implying an American guarantee, had the advantage of calling not
for concessions leading to a settlement of the Israeli-Arab conflict,
but for Israeli participation in the "defense" of the United States. In
other words, what Tel Aviv desired was that the United States make
the shift from the idea of Israel as a burden (as implied in the GLS
idea) to that of Israel as an asset (as implied in the treaty of mutual
defense).

After reviewing the idea of guarantee, we must now sum up the
evolution of the American attitude toward Israel as an asset. It
would seem that at the outset, in the framework of the policy of
"containment," Washington placed value on the new state's advantages in terms of location and infrastructure. The Israeli territory
could be considered as a possible extrinsic asset from which advantages could be derived in time of a serious international crisis. But
up to 1956, the United States did not appear to want to go beyond
this. Its priority was to establish a system of regional security in the
framework of the doctrine of containment and it was forced to
exclude Israel from this, fearing Tel Aviv's participation might lead
to a rebuff by the Arab countries, whose support was considered
indispensable. It may be noted that Washington faced the same
dilemma and the same impossibility about 30 years later with the
idea of strategic consensus regrouping Israel and the Arab countries.

After the war of 1956, several factors converged to modify Israel's
status in effective American doctrine: the idea that the Arab countries as a whole were no longer necessarily won over to the Western
side and that certain of them had a Soviet option; the idea that Arab
nationalism and Nasserism converged "objectively" with Soviet
interests; and the fact of Israel's overwhelming superiority, as
proven by the Suez war. Without seeking to sign a mutual defense
treaty with Israel nor, probably, to coordinate its defense policy
with Israel's, the United States began to integrate that country into
its strategic vision of the region: Israeli power was perceived as a
possible counterweight to Nasserism. Provided that it kept to a
moderate policy, the Jewish state was no longer a burden, but it was

still only a potential strategic asset. This balancing point between burden and asset is illustrated by the fact that neither Washington nor Tel Aviv sought seriously, during the 1956–67 period, to sign either a treaty of guarantee or a mutual defense treaty.

Israel displayed such a regional superiority during the 1967 war that the United States was scarcely preoccupied with the potentially negative effects of Israeli activism following the war. Even if Israel was not yet explicitly considered to be an asset, the U.S. administration's effective policy (arms supplies, absence of pressure for a settlement of the conflict or for a more moderate Israeli behavior in the region) to all intents and purposes accorded this status to the Jewish state. With the Jordanian crisis of 1970, another stage was reached: the asset idea became explicit American doctrine. But the shock of the October 1973 war called this idea into question: the GLS returned to the agenda and the United States was tempted to use certain territories occupied by Israel as an extrinsic asset in their negotiations with the Arabs (i.e., the promise that the territories would be returned in exchange for an improvement in Arab-American relations).

The new U.S. policy succeeded so well, the Arab states played their cards so badly, and Israel played its cards with such skill that the Jewish state progressively obtained (with the 1975 and 1979 memoranda) the equivalent of an American guarantee with only a minimum of the conditions it feared. It is true that Israel eventually withdrew from the Sinai, but in exchange it reinforced itself on its eastern front and made possible Washington's reconversion to the idea of Israel as a strategic asset. This American reconversion took symbolic form in the strategic cooperation memorandum of 1981 and was consolidated between 1983 and 1989 with the pooling of intelligence, military experience and technological knowhow. However, even if the Reagan administration liked to repeat that Israel was a precious strategic asset, its effective attitude toward Israeli autonomy in decision-making at the regional level was marked by a certain uneasiness.

With the major changes in Eastern Europe and the ex-Soviet Union, and the emergence and then the fall of Iraq as a strategic factor, the idea of Israel as an asset faced a serious challenge. The Islamic "danger" is by no means equivalent to the Soviet "danger" and does not require Washington to reserve the same strategic role for Israel. Moreover, the importance accorded by the United States to a certain regional order, and thus the Israeli-Arab peace process, may call into question one of the correlates of the idea of Israel as an intrinsic asset: Israeli-Arab hostility. The American-Israeli strategic relation would then consist above all in technical cooperation.

6 | The Instrumental Explanation

In the first part of this work, we tried to sum up the debate within the American political elite about the place Israel should occupy in U.S. Middle Eastern policy. This has provided us with a battery of categories and concepts that allowed us to study, in a second stage, the evolution of Israel's place in Washington's strategic doctrine in the past 45 years. But this is not sufficient, for we must still explain why this doctrine is as we have described it. More precisely, we must attempt to answer the following two sets of questions:

Why do all the advocacies agree that there is a privileged Israeli-American relationship? Why does the doctrine of asset predominate among them? How is it that even those who consider Israel to be a burden propose to accord that country a guarantee, albeit a conditional one?

Why do American leaders, whatever their individual perceptions or convictions, conduct a policy that favors the development of this privileged relationship? Why do they tend to conduct a policy congruent with the idea of Israel as asset, even when this presents risks for American interests? Why do they exclude the possibility of abandoning Israel in the event that support to this country appears detrimental?

What we need to explain, just as much as American strategic doctrine with respect to Israel, is the privileged character of the Israeli-

American relationship, its solidity and permanence. This is the object of the two chapters that follow. We shall ask, in the present chapter, whether the instrumental explanation allows for a satisfactory answer to the two series of questions raised above. We shall observe that it is insufficient and that we must resort, in order to complete it, to an explanation that takes into account internal American realities (the pro-Israeli lobby and the ideological-cultural instance). This line of inquiry will be developed in chapter 7.

The main difficulty in examining the validity of the instrumental explanation is determining what instrumentality means and does not mean. The instrumental explanation could indeed be associated with certain objectionable meanings—objectionable because they are too simplistic or inoperative. Not to dismiss them would be to condemn in advance the instrumental explanation of American-Israeli relations. We shall thus, first, point out the dangers of an instrumental explanation in terms of imperialism, which we see as an overly broad, "macrodimensional" perspective. We shall, second, indicate the weaknesses of explanations based on decision-making rationality, which we consider to be an overly narrow or "microdimensional" perspective. This will lead us to define what we see as the most reasonable and fruitful meaning of the idea of instrumentality, that is, the one that can give it the best chances of validity, and will permit us to verify whether American doctrine regarding Israel can be understood within an instrumental framework.

The Explanation in Terms of Imperialism

The instrumental explanation in terms of imperialism is a macrodimensional one, modern imperialism being a worldwide phenomenon, several centuries old. In popular perception in the Arab world, in the Third World more generally, and in anticolonialist and anti-imperialist ideology, the privileged relations between the United States and Israel are explained by the idea that Israel, today an instrument of the United States, is essentially a base implanted by imperialism in the heart of the Arab world in order to maintain the area in a situation of dependency, division, and weakness and to exploit its natural resources.

To substantiate this view, a number of facts are cited: the circumstances of the birth of the Zionist movement alongside the European imperial expansion in the second half of the nineteenth century; the attempts by Zionist leaders to convince one or another

European power at the beginning of the twentieth century of the advantages of helping to establish a Jewish state in Palestine; Great Britain's support to the Zionist project as soon as it had gained control over a substantial portion of the Arab provinces of the Ottoman empire in 1917; the active policy of the United States, new world power after World War II, in favor of the establishment of the state of Israel; the tripartite Suez expedition; the various American attempts to foil Nasser's policy of Arab unity and independence; the "green light" given to the Israeli attack of 1967; the repeated declarations by American leaders to the effect that Israel is an ally and a strategic asset.

In order to account for privileged American-Israeli relations, what could seem more logical than to adopt the instrumental explanation in terms of imperialism? The concept of imperialism enjoys, after all, an honorable scientific status. Nonetheless, this explanation involves unjustified generalizations and hazardous simplifications.

A Concept to be Handled with Care

Let us state at the outset that we have no intention of denying the importance of imperialism as a historical phenomenon. For the requirements of our analysis, we will note here simply that modern imperialism is constituted by the totality of facts that express European expansion and domination from the sixteenth century on, and their acceleration in the second half of the nineteenth century. These include economic, technological, social, demographic, cultural, military, and political factors that have marked this expansion and contributed to it, as well as economic forces and groups, ruling classes and states that have objectively taken part in it. European colonization of extra-European territories should be considered as a part of the imperialist drive when it manifests itself through the institution of a lasting domination over them. Whatever the differences between schools of thought about the origins and dynamics of imperialism, the necessary (though not sufficient) role of a dynamic capitalist social formation should be pointed out, since it alone gives a certain permanence and solidity to imperialist domination and distinguishes the latter from the necessarily more ephemeral military expansion. That is what allows us to consider the world leadership of the United States since 1945 and in the wake of the relative decline of Europe as a manifestation and continuation of modern imperialism, in spite of the new features it obviously includes (Amin 1976; Arendt 1966; Hobson 1965:41–59; Langer 1935:95; Lenin 1939; Magdoff 1969; Schumpeter 1955:84; Staley 1935:361–362).

Although modern imperialism is to be grasped as a whole phenomenon with a certain unity of meaning, one must not neglect the diversity or the contradiction of the factors that are related to it. The history of imperialism is not a unilinear one in which all facts converge harmoniously toward a single objective. Certain facts that form a part of the imperialist drive may in the end have negative effects on this thrust. The same factors that, at certain moments and in certain places, may serve that drive, may at other moments and in other places hinder it. The forces that take part in this thrust may ally together and coordinate their actions, but they may also oppose each other in armed conflict. The motivations of actors may be the pursuit of material interests and prestige, but they may also involve a sincere "mission civilisatrice" (Aron 1984:88–89; Miège 1973:157–166).

Some precautions have thus to be taken: one should base the analysis on objective criteria and not consider everything that is "malevolent" to be part of imperialism (Koebner and Schmidt 1964:233, 249). In addition, one should include in the analysis the diverse and contradictory motivations of actors. By taking such precautions, one is likely to avoid a conspiratorial vision of history, although they make it difficult to determine, in the short term, whether a given fact is part of or independent from the imperialist drive, whether it has contributed to or hindered it.

Dangers of the Thesis of Israel as an Instrument of Imperialism

In the light of these remarks, one could assess the dangers of using the concept of imperialism to account for American-Israeli relations, and unveil the more or less implicit assumptions that are made by those who adopt without reservation the viewpoint that Israel is a base of imperialism.

Asserting that Israel is a base of imperialism may first imply that imperialism is the single cause of the birth of the Jewish state and that everything that has its geographical source in Europe or America belongs to the imperialist phenomenon. Now, the Zionist idea that sprang up in the second half of the nineteenth century was the result of a conjunction of three major factors: "Jewish memory" in the European Jewish communities; the aggravation of the Jewish condition in Eastern Europe due especially to the rise of nationalism in that region; and the imperialist drive (Corm 1989; Halperin 1961; Hertzberg 1969; Herzl 1967). If these three factors had Europe and only Europe as their theater and if, as the Arabs have rightly claimed, Europeans are responsible for the genesis and the implementation of the Zionist project, it must, however, be added that everything that is European (or American) does not belong to an imperialist "essence." Jewish collective memory and the aggravation of the Jewish question in Eastern Europe in the nineteenth century do not arise from imperialism, any more than does the emergence of Jewish nationalism in reaction to the Eastern European nationalisms. What the imperialist drive did do was to offer, conceptually and practically, an extra-European outlet to the idea of European Jewish nationalism. To this extent, one of the dimensions of Zionism, the program of colonizing Palestine, formed a part of the imperialist drive without necessarily serving it.

The European-American—let us say Western—support to the Zionist project and then to Israel constitutes one of the three major facets of relations between the West and European Jews (and Jews of European origin). The pogroms of the nineteenth century and the Nazi massacres (as well as the silence that surrounded them) form another facet. The assimilation of the Jews, through French-style integration or through American-style liberal pluralism, constitutes the third facet. These three facets may be considered as expressing the vicissitudes, in terms of both humanism and dehumanization, of relations between European and American societies and the Jewish communities that have lived within them for centuries. These facets are to be analyzed as independent, in their essence, from the framework of imperialism.

It should be added, however, that one cannot be entirely content with analyzing the first facet of Western-Jewish relations factor independent of the problem of imperialism. For Western support to the Zionist project and to Israel must also be understood as forming a part of the imperialist expansion of the West into the Middle East—as at least being congruent with it—since the Zionist-Israeli phenomenon transposes, in part, the relations between the West and the Jews from the internal Euro-American theater onto the Palestinian and Middle Eastern terrain, one of the primary areas of the imperialist expansion. But this congruence between imperialism and Western support to the Zionist-Israeli phenomenon is by no means a guarantee of the utility of the latter to the former. We shall further explore the question of utility below.

The assertion that Israel is an imperialist base may imply a second assumption. This assertion tends to "personify" the historical phenomenon of imperialism and leads one, indeed, to emphasize the idea of the unity of imperialism and to neglect its diversity and its contradictions. Considered as a unit over a very large time and space, it becomes imperialism with a capital "I" and is treated as if it were an actor, a monolithic center of decision, and a pure intentionality embracing the entire time and space in question. As an instrument of imperialism, Israel would be so since its origin. It would be seen as having been established and sustained by the same spirit once embodied at an earlier time by Great Britain, and later transmigrating to the United States.

There cannot be intentionality at the macrodimensional level because there can be no actor that embraces this level. In order to study the intentionality, the free and thought-out choice of an actor, one must analyze shorter spans of time and the actor must be identifiable as a decisionmaker. The new problems this poses (the degree of determinism in decisions, identifying decisionmakers as individuals, organized groups, or states) will be examined below when we discuss the instrumental explanation at the micro-dimensional level.

The statement that Israel is a base for imperialism seems to imply a third assumption. That assumption concerns the dynamism and the omnipotence of imperialist decisions. In other words, nothing that happens can be a failure, but can only accomplish the design of the concerned imperialist actor or actors. According to this perspective, all the British, then American, decisions as well as all Zionist, then Israeli, actions, can only have contributed to the strengthening of imperialism. As to victory over imperialism, it becomes no more than a "historical necessity" indefinitely postponed.

While waiting for this inevitable but constantly delayed victory, the facts are explained as resulting from the watchfulness of the imperialist actors, their ability to foil the forces that resist them, and to choose the best alternatives in every situation. When Great Britain becomes weakened as a result of World War II, the United States comes along to take care of Israel; when Nasser raises his head, the punitive response is readily carried out; when the PLO gains strength, its liquidation is already planned and ready to be executed. . . . Pushed to its extreme limits, this approach may lead to assertions such as: it was imperialism that allowed Nasser or the PLO to gain strength in order to better strike blows at them through the intermediary of Israel; it was imperialism that inspired the Arab attack and the oil embargo of 1973 in order to better control the Arab world afterward.

In other words, the "macrodimensional" explanation claims to account not only for major phenomena over the long term, but also for particular facts that in reality only a microdimensional analysis can attempt to explain. A serious analysis might determine, for example, that in a given particular case, what is interpreted as a British, American, or Israeli success is in fact only the result of an intrinsic weakness on the Arab side. It might determine, conversely, that a given rapprochement between Washington and an Arab capital concerning the settlement of the Israeli-Arab conflict is not necessarily an Arab submission to American-Israeli diktats, but in fact represents an American concession to the Arabs.

Counter to the idea of imperialist omnipotence in all particular facts, it must be pointed out that imperialism at any given moment is just as much a *state of affairs* (or perhaps a status quo) as a *project*. As a state, it is a dense network of acquired resources and strengths, but also of weaknesses. As a project, it possesses a dynamic that not only causes the actors that constitute its core to go on the offensive but may also lead them, when faced with strong resistance, to remain on the defensive. When they go on the offensive, it cannot be automatically determined whether they do so on the basis of planning (imperialism as a project) or whether the local reality they face has offered unexpected opportunities—a "soft underbelly" (in which case imperialism must be considered as a state). And when they appear on the defensive, it is equally difficult to determine whether the local reality against which they are applying their force is offering a strong and costly resistance (imperialism as a project) or whether, more gravely, they themselves are experiencing an internal crisis (imperialism as a state). Once again, only serious observation of the case under study can produce answers to these questions.

Israel is a mere plaything of imperialism. This fourth assumption pushes the idea of instrumentality to the extreme. In this extremely mechanistic interpretation, Israel becomes a docile hand in the service of a thinking and deciding brain. In other words, the instrumental explanation, while raising imperialism to the rank of a conscious actor, lowers its instrument, Israel, to the status of an object. Not only is the convergence of interests between Israel and imperialism assumed, but it is also assumed that the interests of the former cede automatically to those of the latter (today the United States, yesterday Great Britain). The disagreements often mentioned in the media and sometimes confirmed by official declarations are seen as nothing more than a distribution of roles orchestrated by the imperialist center.

Against this perspective, it must be stressed that even if we assumed Zionism to be a pure product of imperialism, with no intrinsic specificity, interests proper to Zionism and then Israel have formed over time. These interests are no longer determined solely by interaction with the center and supplier of support, but now are constituted as well according to the internal societal and political balance within Israel, the latter's relations with the Jewish communities in the world, and the evolution of its relations with the different Arab countries. Even in the case of relations between a settler colony and a single, clearly identifiable metropole, a major contradiction is not impossible, as was shown by the conflictual relations between Rhodesia under Ian Smith and Great Britain in the 1960s and 1970s.

The possibility of such a contradiction militates against any mechanistic explanation of imperialism and requires us to postulate, as a methodological premise of our search for an instrumental explanation of privileged American-Israeli relations, not just one center of decision (the United States) but two (the United States and Israel). Each of these two countries must be considered as enjoying, although of course to different degrees, the attribute of free choice; at the same time, each must be seen as subject to specific societal and other types of determinisms (including those of the physical environment and the regional and international strategic setting) that limit its freedom of choice.

Nothing should prohibit us from thinking that in the pursuit of its own interests, Israel may undertake actions the effects of which are to harm imperialist expansion or, in a more current and precise formulation, American interests. The very fact of support to Israel by a protecting power may provoke the mobilization of resistance in the region against this power and thus hinder its interests. The same Israel that could not emerge or develop without imperialism may nonetheless become quite costly to it. The possibility that Israel may be a burden for the United States indicates that no a priori judgment can replace the actual study of areas of convergence and divergence of interests and attitudes between the two countries.

The idea that Israel in its genesis and development has been a mechanistic instrument of imperialism is thus not convincing. Would the same idea be true if imperialism were understood as a historical phenomenon (rather than an actor) and if the concept of instrumentality at the macrodimensional level were understood in a global and relative sense rather than a total and absolute one? In other words, can we say, today, more than a century after the beginning of Jewish colonization in Palestine, that Zionism and Israel have, on the whole, been useful to the imperialist phenomenon? It is extremely difficult to answer this question for the obvious reason that nothing, outside professions of faith, allows us to say, for such a long period, what sort of influence the West, and the United States in particular, would have had in the Middle East if Zionism had not existed and Israel had never been founded. We can say only that as long as the balance of forces is favorable to Israel in a situation of hostility with the Arab world, or as long as Israel does not consider itself, and is not considered by the Arabs and the West, as being an integral part of the Middle East, the Jewish state will be the tangible sign of an Arab failure in the face of one of the main vestiges of imperialism in the region.

Here, then, are the assumptions implied by the statement that Israel is an imperialist base. These assumptions have provided us the paths by which to criticize the instrumental explanation in terms of imperialism. We have shown that this type of explanation is often simplistic, overambitious, or erroneous. One could, of course, say that some of the assumptions examined are so crude that no analyst could succumb to them. But this is not necessarily true, for these assumptions are often only implicit; and the instrumental explanation offers the undeniable attraction, if not of realism, then of a certain internal coherence and of elevating social phenomena to the rank of rational actors.

The imperialist explanation is attractive also because it continually forces the analyst to deal with the central slogan of the predominant political discourse in the Arab world and among Third World supporters. However, this slogan is not just one of political mobilization, for it also allows certain actors to justify themselves and deny the responsibility for their own failures. If imperialism is omnipotent and constitutes absolute Evil, then such and such an Arab actor is in no way responsible, whatever errors he makes, for the consequences of the blows dealt to him by Imperialism, either directly or through the intermediary of Israel. Iraq's behavior from 1990–1992 is a case in point.

For a Contextual and Non-Instrumental Use of the Concept of Imperialism

Does all this mean that the concept of imperialism is itself useless for understanding the privileged relations between the United States and Israel? We do not think so. Israel, a colonial-settler entity, as Maxime Rodinson so clearly demonstrated more than twenty years ago (Rodinson 1973), would not have existed in the absence of the imperialist drive of modern times. Nor would it have developed itself effectively had it not been supported by the successor of the European colonial powers, the United States. But contrary to the debatable formula about Israel as a base of imperialism, these two assertions do not claim to explain everything. They recognize in imperialism a necessary, but not sufficient, condition. They allow us only to put forward a contextual perspective on imperialism, not an instrumental one. According to this perspective, imperialism is the context, the environment, in which Israel established and developed itself.

What does this imply for our search for a convincing explanation of privileged American-Israeli relations? The instrumental explanation in terms of imperialism is "self-sufficient" and claims to hold the key that makes these relations immediately intelligible, but as we have seen is often misleading. As for the contextual perspective, although it corrects the instrumental one, it remains inadequate to account for these relations. It is too broad to allow at this point an explanation of the data assembled in the previous chapters concerning policy advocacy and the actual American doctrine regarding Israel. Other steps need to be taken in this and the following chapters before the contextual perspective on imperialism proves its usefulness.

Other lessons can be drawn from our discussion of imperialism. It has allowed us to clarify certain traps to be avoided in the use of the very idea of instrumentality. We have shown that this idea cannot be used fruitfully at the macrodimensional level, because it assumes the impossible: the existence of monolithic actors covering large spans of time and space. We have also shown that the concept of instrumentality must be understood in a relative rather than an absolute sense, since we must allow for the autonomy of two centers of decision (the United States and Israel)—whereby what is instrumental for one power is not necessarily the other power, but its own relations with that power. We have shown, finally, that instrumentality does not necessarily mean conformity of the result to the initial design.

If the macrodimensional version of the instrumental explanation is not satisfactory, does recourse to the microdimensional version (involving the rationality of the decision-maker) succeed in avoiding the traps mentioned? That is what we shall now explore.

The Explanation in Terms of Decision-Making Rationality

If the idea of instrumentality is not applicable to the macrodimensional level (imperialism), this is above all, as we have seen, because one cannot speak of an actor or a decision-maker at this level. It could thus be thought that wherever there is an actor bearing an intentionality, capable of conceiving a design and taking a decision "here and now"—that is, at the microdimensional level—instrumentality has a better chance of being exercised and thus of taking on meaning. To consider the instrumental explanation at this level is tantamount to examining what some authors have called rational decision-making or the rational actor model. As we shall see, this model does not escape criticism.

Critique of the Rational Decision Model

In the most extreme formulation, the process of rational decision-making aims to maximize the utility of an action. When confronted with a given problem, the rational decisionmaker begins by clarifying his objectives and ranking them from the most to the least desirable. He then makes a list of all the possible paths or alternatives for realizing his objectives. Next he examines the consequences that could arise from each of the alternatives identified in the previous stage. He can then compare the potential consequences with the objectives sought. Finally, the decisionmaker chooses the decision or the alternative whose consequences are the most likely to lead to the objectives pursued (Russet and Starr 1981:268; Snyder and Diesing 1977:340; Janis and Mann 1977; Carley 1982:61). Applied to U.S. policy toward Israel, the rational process would mean that the decisionmaker adopts, each time, the most fruitful decision from the point of view of American interests, after having weighed the consequences of all the alternatives.

The criticisms that have been formulated against this definition of rationality are well known. First, one cannot assume the decisionmakers are omniscient (Braybrooke and Lindblom 1963:ch. 4), that is, that they have immediate and perfect access to the totality of the information that would allow them to evaluate their own capacities, the physical constraints, and, above all, the reactions of the other "players" to each alternative considered. It flows from this that the execution of the best-informed decision—the one based on the most precise information—does not necessarily lead to the objective sought, but may have unexpected consequences that may even be contrary to what has been aimed for at the outset. Finally, to assume that all the alternatives and all their potential consequences can be considered and analyzed before the decision is made is to assume that the decisionmaker has the capacity for making a virtually infinite number of calculations (Snyder and Diesing 1977:341), as is suggested by the great number of possible outcomes of a chess game (estimated at 10^{120}) that would have to be taken into account by each player in a given game (Allison 1971:286).

To give rationality such a mathematical rigor is to render it sterile in the social sciences, even if one considers it as an ideal to be attained, and even if one makes it more flexible by integrating probability calculations as in games theory. Since Herbert Simon (1957:241–260), authors have preferred with good reason to speak of bounded rationality. The decisionmaker does not seek so much to maximize as to avoid going below a certain level of acceptability (recall Simon's neologism: to "satisfice," as opposed to "satisfy"). He considers only a few alternatives that appear most obvious or most promising and eliminates others that seem too risky or too costly. When a negative consequence threatens to occur, he modifies his choice to avoid this occurrence. Most often, the decisionmaker does not make abrupt decisions but prefers to operate with small "touchups," in a progressive, marginal or incremental manner (Braybrooke and Lindblom 1953:71–79; Lindblom 1979:517–526).

However, these few correctives to the idea of rationality, which remove its caricatural aspect, are insufficient; there are other problems than the limits to omniscience and the capacity for calculation of the most rational mind. For decisionmakers are not disembodied minds. Reason does not provide them with the key allowing them to define their objectives and to arrange them in a pyramidal hierarchy. The definition of objectives is often a matter of subjective values and objectives do not necessarily compose a coherent whole; they are not linked together by a transitive relation and thus cannot become the object of a pyramidal rank of preferences. In other words, what are usually called the interests of an actor are not always logically deducible. Pure rationality does not dictate what must be the nature of an interest in the short, middle, or long term, nor which objective should be preferred at a given moment. The intentionality of the decisionmaker contains a lesser or greater measure of subjectivity.

The idea of the subjectivity of the decisionmaker is made more complex by the fact that he or she is not necessarily a single individual but may well be a social group, one or several organizations or structures whose respective members have different visions and different interpretations of the interests they are pursuing. The decision that emerges from their interactions may thus express the victory of one vision over another, or an awkward compromise, or a paralysis due to the reciprocal neutralization of the contradictory visions. The fact that the decision is an outcome means that intentionality (with its measure of subjectivity) aiming toward an end intervenes only in varying degrees in the decisions taken here and now by the collective decisionmaker. The decision is not a simple expression of an intentionality, even of a collective nature.

All these remarks refer to fairly common knowledge and do not require any further explanation. But as in the case of our remarks about imperialism, the observer tends to neglect them when studying concrete situations. After reviewing several examples of foreign policy analysis by authors such as Hans Morgenthau, Thomas Schelling and Herman Kahn, Graham Allison (1971:13) reached the following conclusion:

> Each assumes that what must be explained is an action, i.e., behavior that reflects purpose or intention. Each assumes that the actor is a national government. Each assumes that the action is chosen as a calculated solution to a strategic problem. For each, explanation consists of showing what goal the government was pursuing when it acted and how the action was a reasonable choice, given the nation's objective.

In other words, the analyst more or less implicitly attributes to the decisionmaker the analyst's own definition, his own hierarchy of objectives, and projects his own rationality on the behavior observed as if it were the guiding principle of explanation. Any instance of political behavior (and its opposite) can thus find its argumentation and its rational justification.

It is therefore clear that, even if we understand the idea of rationality in the limited sense evoked above, it is futile to hope for the validity of a pure instrumental explanation at the microdimensional level—a level at which analysts of decision-making processes propose other kinds of explanations based on taking into account bureaucratic maneuvers, organizational routine (Allison 1971; Halperin 1974) or subjectivity of perception (Brecher 1972; Jervis 1976). But this is not the place to review them.

What is the relevance of these remarks for our search for an operational meaning of the idea of instrumentality? Must we methodologically condemn all explicit recourse to this idea? Obviously not. Between pure rationality and pure subjectivity or pure determinism, there has to be a space for individual or collective choices that are free and calculated. These can be identified only through what could be called *assumed rationality*. In order to be intelligible, all behavior must first be apprehended as if it were rational, at least in the sense of limited rationality. But assumed rationality must be no more than a working hypothesis among others; it must serve to ask the right questions about reality, to seek its own confirmation or negation in the most pertinent sources of information (Dougherty and Pfaltzgraff 1981:477–478). Otherwise, the assumption of rationality that is self-justifying is a facile solution and, of course, a source of error.

However, in spite of all these limitations and precautions, the recourse to assumed rationality remains insufficient if one understands it as an instrument of verification of a microdimensional instrumental rationality, because the object to be studied—the explanation of American support to Israel—concerns a period of more than 45 years. Even if one is certain to find certain American decisions that verify the hypothesis of instrumentality (one is reminded for example of several decisions by Kissinger during and after the 1973 war), one must inevitably recognize that other decisions will not verify this idea. What is the minimal proportion of decisions conforming to the instrumental explanation above which one may say that this explanation is globally valid? Can such a "threshold" be measured or only identified, given that not all decisions have the same importance and that behavior is made up not only of a set of decisions, but also of "non-decisions"? (Bachrach and Baratz 1963; Parry and Morriss 1974) The absurdity of such an approach is evident.

It thus appears that to limit the use of the hypothesis of rationality to the microdimensional level (i.e., trying to verify instrumentality in each decision and in the totality of decisions), would condemn in advance any search for an explanation of American policy toward Israel based on this hypothesis. In the following pages, we will argue that the hypothesis of rationality finds a more adequate application at the intermediate level, in the medium term (for periods that may last several years rather than several days), concerning relatively durable behavior by a state—behavior that constitutes the substratum of a series of decisions (and nondecisions) rather than being constituted by the sum of particular decisions. We shall note in what follows that this shift to the intermediate level is more fruitful, even if it greatly relativizes the idea of rationality.

For an Intermediate Use of the Concept: The Idea of Utility

In order to establish the appropriateness of the hypothesis of rationality at an intermediate level, we shall consider, in turn, the ideas of interest, intentionality, and state actor.

Interest. Although, for the process of a particular decision in foreign policy, the immediate definition of the interests at stake and their hierarchical ranking for a given country is an operation often characterized by subjectivity on the part of decisionmakers as well as the analysts observing them, it is easier, when dealing with the medium term, to reach a consensual and objective delimitation of certain general, durable, and essential interests. These interests, which must be distinguished from ideals without operational character, are "those purposes which the nation, through its leadership, appears to pursue persistently through time" (Seabury quoted by Holsti 1967:125; Krasner 1978:43). These purposes, or rather interests, are determined, in the period considered, by relatively stable conditions such as the geopolitical situation, economic and military power, regional and international balance. They are usually identifiable within a perspective of "Realpolitik," that is, in terms that "cold" and "calculating" strategists would accept.

Duration makes it possible to overcome the dilemma of ranking essential interests—a dilemma faced by all decisionmakers when they have to deal "here and now" with immediate constraints and opportunities. Let us take the well-known example of the two interests of peace and security in the nuclear era. While they may be in conflict when a short-term decision is to be made, especially in time of crisis (such as the Cuban missile crisis), and which may then become the object of disagreements within the decision-making group as to the priority of one or the other, over the medium term these issues are easier for decisionmakers to agree upon. Similarly, the difficulties that a decisionmaker encounters in evaluating the risks linked to each choice lose their acuteness over time.

Over time, the essential interests of a state in foreign policy are those to which decisionmakers and observers can willingly sub-scribe—those which are directly implied by the continued existence of the state (territorial integrity, sovereignty, etc.) and its durable achievements at the regional and international level (rank in the world, blocking the expansionism of enemy forces, defense of over-seas military bases, protection of economic markets, and so on). To this should be added those interests related to the recovery of stable and important attributes that may have been abruptly lost to adver-sary forces (the occupation of a part of the national territory, the loss of a traditional foreign base of control, whether economic, diplo-matic or military).

It follows that these essential interests, which are not objects of disagreement, must be understood above all in the sense of con-serving the status quo, unless they involve recovering attributes abruptly lost, in which case they express the will to return to the status quo ante. Essential interests are those minimal ones whose neglect implies damage to the state; we may call them "non-dam-ages." That is why we prefer not to call these interests "objectives" or "purposes," for these terms always have a dynamic connotation. It does not follow, however, that the means used to safeguard these "static" interests may not become altogether dynamic, or even destabilizing (as in the use of force to protect these interests).

It is, once again, the test of time that allows us to "purify" the essential interests of the state, or cleanse them of such subjective determinations as the "preferences" of decisionmakers (Krasner 1978:43) and to verify their operative, objective, and consensual character. Time allows us in particular to distinguish them from what decisionmakers claim to be "the national interest." Caught in the struggle for power and seeking sometimes to inscribe their action in the framework of a mission, a great project, a "grand design," as opposed to "policy" (Harkabi 1988:2), decisionmakers tend to understand the National Interest in a programmatic sense, and to go beyond essential interests of the state. When carried to the extreme, a grand strategy can be the cause of great successes or serious failures, or even can result in the establishment of a new regional or international order, in which the essential interests of the state concerned are set at a new mark, higher or lower. Thus, Hitler's grand strategy brought about, along with his own fall, a radical modification of the essential interests of Germany (a lower mark). The new international order established as a result of World War II signified an alteration of the essential, minimal interests of the United States (a higher mark). However, apart from the upheavals that result in a modification of essential interests, these usually remain relatively stable, even when they are embodied in policies and perceptions that change in many respects.

Intentionality. With the idea of changing policies and perceptions, we approach the question of the intentionality (or design) of decisionmakers. Intentionality is the second foundation, after the idea of interest, of any instrumental explanation of behavior. Here we have to ask how duration over time allows us to overcome the limits of intentionality noted above: the fact that the decisionmaker's actions are due not solely to an intentionality but also contain a measure of determinism; the fact that this intentionality often contains, in turn, a measure of subjectivity and nonrationality; the fact that the decision, in the most usual instances of collective decisionmaking, is a result of multiple and possibly contradictory intentionalities.

If the essential interests, in the sense we have proposed, constitute "non-damages" and do not necessarily dictate precise and voluntaristic programs, intentionality that conforms durably to these interests may be only negative, more or less implicit, and accordingly subject to being induced only over time. In other words, if a positive and explicit design at the origin of a behavior aiming for the protection of the essential interests of the state cannot be found, because of the lack of adequate sources or for any other reason, it should be possible to interpret longer term behavior conforming to, or congruent with, the essential interests of the state, as constituting the functional equivalent of an instrumental intentionality. We shall try to clarify these points.

Unless there is a radical internal break (such as a revolution), decisionmakers consciously avoid harming the essential interests of their state. Thus, when an opposition party comes to power, it is usually led to reconcile the ideological program to which it apparently owes its rise with the (often implicit) pragmatic necessities involved in conducting the foreign affairs of the state—necessities originating in the latter's essential interests. However broad may be the spectrum of different and often contradictory perceptions of national interest among the members of the decision-making group, it does not include certain obviously impossible choices (such as valuing defeat or the loss of a market) but does include durable elements that are common to the different perceptions.

This does not mean, of course, that all decisionmakers and all governmental programs are of equal value in a given country, nor that the means adopted effectively serve its essential interests. It simply means that decisionmakers behave and make decisions in foreign policy in accordance with their own personality, their world-view, their political program, their electoral interests, the interests of given socioeconomic classes, and the necessities of the struggle for power; but they generally stop short of reaching a situation in which they perceive themselves and may be perceived as having purposely damaged the state's essential interests. Since decisionmakers must be accountable for the consequences of their actions, their own viability as decisionmakers depends on the viability of their policy. When certain limits are not violated for a long time, however diverse the decision-making groups and programs have been, and when a minimal, durable common policy that does not contradict the state's essential interests appears to emerge from the diversity, one may then speak, at the least, of an implicit intentionality that underlies this behavior or of a negative intentionality (a concern not to cause damage). We say "at least" because often the constant respect of certain limits throughout a whole period of time is equivalent to (or even leads to) a more or less explicit intentionality on the part of the decisionmakers.

However, damage is always possible in spite of the constant respect of the limits. A positive design governing the conduct of the most rational decisionmaker is not yet a guarantee that there will be an adequate relation between the goal pursued, the means adopted, and the consequences actually obtained. Damage is even less to be excluded in other cases, that is, where the particular decision is nothing more than the outcome of multiple subjective purposes. In these cases, when damage is observed after the fact, decisionmakers may seek to impute it to other causes, such as the errors of their predecessors, the malevolence of another state (perhaps the enemy), the arising of unforeseeable circumstances, the "technical" difficulties of executing a decision, and so on; but they are also driven to modify their policy or program sufficiently so as to prove their capacity to learn lessons from experience. They cannot easily claim twice or several times that they "didn't know." The learning process is equivalent to the process of making intentionality explicit.

We may deduce from the preceding remarks that incidental damage affecting the essential interests of the state and originating from the acts of decisionmakers are inevitable no matter how rational their designs are. But we must also deduce that damage originating from the decisionmakers that is repeated over time, though possible, is improbable, even in the absence of a rational decisionmaker enjoying a constant, explicit, and positive intentionality. Conversely, this means that the spectrum of diverse policies (due to the multiplicity and the succession of decisionmakers) may be compatible in its consequences with the essential interests of the state, in spite of inevitable incidental failures, if it contains durable and stable elements of a minimal common policy: (a) The elements of a policy common to the entire spectrum allow us, as we have seen, to postulate at least the idea of negative and implicit intentionality, or that of a functional equivalent of intentionality. (b) The overall compatibility between the common policy, its effective consequences, and the essential interests of the state allow us to qualify this intentionality (which is, once again, at least negative and implicit) as utilitarian if not instrumental.

However, the utility we speak of cannot be observed until after the fact. Only after having verified that a constant policy has been roughly compatible with nondamage can we qualify it as utilitarian; it is because the constancy of this utility cannot be due to chance that we propose to say that it is underlain by an intentionality that is at least negative and implicit, or by an implicit instrumentality. One cannot say the same of the utility, observed after the fact, of a single and particular decision; one cannot speak in this case of instrumentality—even implicit—because this utility may be due to all sorts of reasons, even to chance, and thus not necessarily to the rationality of the decisionmaker. As we have noted previously, the rationality of the decisionmaker in a particular decision can only be a working hypothesis; it must be checked in the sources, not inferred from the reasoning. But when the matter concerns the established utility of a durable policy that is the result of a series of decisions and nondecisions, the difficulty of proving the existence of an explicit and credible design underlying the policy must not prevent us from seeing in it at least the effect of a negative and implicit instrumental design.

State actor. What is the relevance of these ideas of implicit instrumentality and intentionality over time for the third pillar of any instrumental explanation, that is, the notion of actor? It seems to us that the state actor, or the state as actor, is rehabilitated by these ideas. If one allows that the behavior of a multiplicity of successive individual actors over the medium term can be considered as a resultant underlain by a design—at least a negative and implicit one, compatible with nondamage—then one must also allow the notion of state actor, to which this behavior and this design can be attributed. The state is the factor that unifies the multiplicity and the succession of individual decisionmakers by transcending them over time, in the medium term. Let us recall that if we are speaking of the short term, that is, the comprehension of a particular decision, it is difficult to be satisfied with posing the state as an actor. In this case, the analyst must rather attempt to identify the individual decisionmaker(s), with their specific characteristics, and then face an often insoluble dilemma: must one impute the decision to a fictional actor—the state—or must one attribute it to one or several particular people?

What conclusion may we draw from these remarks about the notion of instrumentality for our investigation of the instrumental explanation of American support to Israel? It is now clear, even before applying the notion of instrumentality to American policy toward Israel, that it can only have, in the best of cases, an imperfect and approximate validity; we can only use it in a relative sense and under certain conditions. This means that verification of the validity of the instrumental explanation for American support to Israel must obey certain rules. First of all, we must avoid focusing on particular decisions, even the most important ones, and verifying whether the place accorded to Israel is in accordance, each time, with American interests, for it is futile to look for a positive and explicit instrumentality in each and every case. The exercise would in any case be over-fastidious because it would repeat a number of the developments of previous chapters. We must thus place ourselves in a global perspective. The particular decisions we shall mention will be cited only as illustrations. And in order to judge the utility of American support to Israel, we will begin with the essential interests of the United States in the sense defined above. The utility we will have to verify will be located between two poles: at one pole will be the utility observed after the fact of American support to Israel (congruence of its interests with an implicit design); at the other pole will be the accordance of this utility with an explicit and constant intentionality on the part of the decisionmaker (i.e., instrumentality). And in order to make it clear that positive and explicit intentionality is not indispensable in order to affirm the possibility of a congruence between behavior and essential interests over the medium term, we have entitled the third section of this chapter "The Utilitarian Explanation," rather than the "instrumental" one.

The Utilitarian Explanation

In order to verify the validity of the utilitarian explanation concerning American support to Israel, it is thus necessary first of all to define Washington's essential interests in the Middle East and the Arab world since the 1950s. These interests are determined by the importance of the stakes constituted by the wealth of the region, its geographical extension from the Atlantic to the Persian Gulf via the Mediterranean, the proximity of the Soviet Union and Europe, the structure and dynamics of the Arab system (distribution of influence between the different states, the internal and foreign policy of the predominant center(s), and trends toward unification or divisiveness. . .) These different stakes allow us to enumerate, with little risk of error, the main American interests in the Middle East since the 1950s. These interests involve:

- maintaining Western and especially American influence in the region;
- being able to prevent military control of the region by adversary forces, in particular those of the Soviet Union (at least until the mid-1980s);
- weakening the Soviet Union's political and diplomatic influence;
- preventing the region's oil wealth from being controlled by enemy forces and assuring the flow of oil according to appropriate conditions and with appropriate prices;
- securing control and stability of economic markets;
- weakening local forces (states, movements, parties) that seek to acquire a status of leadership and/or work to overturn the regional status quo through transnational ideological mobilization (such as pan-Arabism or Islam).

To work for the protection of these interests, the United States, as a world power, has at its disposition a multitude of means and instruments, direct and indirect. These range from diplomatic activity to the use of force, and include economic pressure, subversion, manipulation of internal social or political forces and also, under certain circumstances, making use of Israeli power. Among these possible means and instruments, it is mainly Israel that will be considered here. To this end, and contrary to the classic American enumeration, we have not mentioned support to Israel in the list of American interests, for to do so would have been to assume the problem to be already resolved. Only if the utilitarian explanation succeeds in establishing that Israel serves American interests can support to Israel be elevated to the rank of an interest.

The Convergence of Interests and Risks

The first reason that can be proposed to support the utilitarian explanation is the contribution of Israel to intelligence on the region and to American R&D and the technical services (in terms of infrastructure and logistics) it can render to U.S. intervention forces in the region or in the Mediterranean. We will not insist, however, on this sort of contribution since it is relatively modest (Cobban 1991:95–100) and is the necessary and obvious corollary of massive American military assistance to Israel. What interests us most here is the strategic justification that can be given for this assistance, that is, the idea that Israel's military superiority, translated into intervention and deterrence on the regional level, serves American interests.

The idea that Israel is a strategic asset for the United States raises first of all the question of the congruence of the respective interests of the two countries. It is reasonable to see the interests that Israel aims to defend as likely to converge, roughly and with some nuances, with many American interests. Thus the Jewish state, because of Moscow's longtime military and diplomatic support to the Arab countries of the front, could only subscribe to the objective of weakening Soviet influence. The same Israeli-American convergence of interests persists after the recent upheaval, since its consequences have been Moscow's withdrawal from the Middle East and the spectacular growth of Jewish immigration to Israel.

Moreover, concerning the local forces that aspire to regional preeminence or that challenge the status quo, Israel can only applaud their weakening and work toward it (Gold 1988:89–90). The Jewish state is even more interested in this than the United States, since the future of the Zionist project depends on it. Let us not forget that Zionism's appropriation of Palestine could only engender hostility between Israel and the Palestinians and neighboring Arab states. Given that Israel is perceived historically by the Arabs as an entity that fundamentally challenges their integrity and identity, no transnational Arab-Islamic force can hope to attain a role of regional leadership unless it at least appears to adopt this basic Arab perception; this has been the case since the 1940s and will be true for an indeterminate time in the future.

This was true, for example, of Nasser's Egypt, Ba'athist Syria, Iran under Khomeini, and Iraq under Saddam Hussein after 1988. It was true for Sadat's Egypt after the peace treaty with Israel, since Egypt by the very fact of this treaty lost its regional leadership status. It has always been true for the Palestinian movement, for two reasons: First, because it is a symbol of a central Arab cause and is thus adopted by Arab political parties and popular forces and by the concert of Arab nations in the form of the Arab League and the successive summits of Arab chiefs of state, even if a part of Arab support to the Palestinian movement may consist of manipulation. Secondly, because the political and military action of the Palestinian movement, owing to the Palestinian's dispersion among several states, involves a dynamic that implicates these states in a way that challenges any regional status quo.

Israeli-Arab hostility thus generates Israeli hostility to "Arab-Muslim political projects" (mobilization, independence, unification, nonalignment, control of resources). Israeli military initiative and superiority, when they succeed in causing the failure of such projects, can also be considered in many respects as serving ipso facto the American interests enumerated above. In other words, it is as if the United States were profiting from the effects of Israeli-Arab hostility and, in a sort of "indirect strategy," had no need always to invest their own forces directly against "Arab-Muslim political projects."

None of this necessarily means that Israel is pushed by the United States, knowingly or secretly, toward an activist attitude. Israeli activism does not need the encouragement of Washington and accommodates very well to Washington's passivity; it can be content with Washington's permissiveness. In the climate of Israeli-Arab hostility, the Israelis, as we have said, have a tendency to privilege military means (Roberts 1973:121–124). Faced with this situation, the Americans, who have after all the advantage of enjoying some distance, do not have the same tendency as Israel to interpret the Arabs' anti-Israeli attitude as an anti-American attitude, nor do they have the same propensity to counsel the use of force. They may sometimes prefer, not only for themselves but also for Israel, that diplomatic means first be tried.

In this perspective, not investing itself directly means, for Washington, having the possibility to play the attractive role in the Arabs' eyes (sincerely or otherwise, but that is not the question), or at least to maintain an ambiguous attitude regarding Israeli actions. It is, after all, Israel that uses the "stick" rather than the "carrot," and the United States that is able to back off if necessary while "objectively" profiting from its effects. Even if things are not planned in advance, it may seem after the event that there had been a "distribution of roles" between the two countries. This is frequently, for Washington, an excellent means of pressure on the Arabs—one that John Sigler (1983:567) and Claudia Wright (1984) have suggestively called a "protection racket." By threatening to unleash the Israelis, or, on the contrary, by promising to try to moderate them, while explaining that Israel is not a docile partner, Washington places itself in an advantageous negotiating position for imposing its conditions and winning concessions from the Arabs. Let us recall, for example, Kissinger's remarks (1982:483–484, 1057) as we have quoted them in chapter 4, regarding his step-by-step diplomacy.

One might perhaps object here that there is a danger that the Israeli "stick" might strike too hard, or even be broken, and that in either case there would be negative effects for American interests. In the first case, an overly audacious Israeli policy may provoke a disastrous destabilization (of the Iranian type) (H. Brown 1983:149), the rise of Arabism (as was the case with Nasserism after 1956), recourse to Soviet aid (as after 1967) (Chubin 1987:257, 271), the revival of anti-American ideological themes, the multiplication of "terrorist" operations against American interests or outside the Middle East region. In the second case, Israel may find itself dangerously confronting an upsurge of Arab military determination (as in the campaign of 1973), and the United States may be either directly confronted with the Soviet Union or subjected to Arab pressure (as in the oil embargo) rather than exercising such pressure itself. All of this is true and causes some Americans to state that Israel is a burden rather than an asset, but the utilitarian explanation may, in turn, resort to the following counterarguments.

First, the dangers inherent in Israeli activism are perhaps only short-term ones. In the medium term, tangible Israeli military superiority has more weight in the divided Middle East than ex-Soviet attempts to exercise influence or than Arabist "myths"; these are seen as precarious and volatile. The reversal of Egypt's position from a pan-Arabic policy and a pro-Soviet attitude (justified, after all, by the struggle against Israel) to a narrowly Egyptian horizon and a pro-American attitude, and the evolution of the PLO toward an attitude of realism after the defeat of 1982, prove that the power of the Jewish state is, in the end, profitable. Further, even if Israel were responsible for the weakening of pro-American regimes, for their internal instability, or for the rise of popular anti-Americanism with its destabilizing effects, it would be too late for the Americans to treat the cause (Israeli activism); their concern in such circumstances would be simply to treat the effects (Kissinger 1979:569). And in order to do this, the surest remedy, if not the best one, would still be to support Israel, that stable rock in an ocean of instability. Finally, if the precariousness of pro-Western regimes is not to be wished for from the point of view of American interests, it is not necessarily disastrous; it can offer Washington means of internal manipulation and pressure on regimes in difficulty.

In any event, there is no policy without risk and there is nothing to indicate that the United States could have avoided the negative effects of a direct confrontation with the "Arab political projects," without the mediation of the Israeli "buffer" and without the flexibility provided by the indirect strategy. It might even be thought that without Israel, the risks for the Americans would have been much worse and the costs of preventing or treating these risks would have been much higher. It is true that all of this remains quite hypothetical, since Israel is there, in the Middle East, and Washington's regional policy cannot abstract from it. The real problem for the United States is not to choose between integrating Israel into its Middle Eastern policy and ignoring it but rather, while integrating it, to decide whether this can be done in any other way than by supporting it unconditionally and treating it as an asset, when its activism is in danger of harming American interests.

American Pressure on Israel and its Useful Limits

Apparently this other way has existed and has consisted of fruitful pressure on Israel. Several examples can be cited: the 1956–57 episode in which Eisenhower forced Ben-Gurion to withdraw his troops from the Sinai; the aftermath of the 1973 war when Kissinger required Israel to return pieces of territory to the Arabs ("a parcel of territory for a parcel of peace"). Later examples are Reagan's pressure on Begin in September 1982 to withdraw the Israeli army from Beirut after the massacres of Sabra and Shatila and Bush's pressure on Shamir not to respond to Iraqi missile launches against Israeli territory during the Gulf War in 1991. Since these pressures have aimed at safeguarding the American position in the Arab world, one could think that they were exercised essentially at the expense of the Jewish state and that the United States was paying the Arabs in Israeli coin. Since Israel is no longer, at these moments, an autonomous asset rendering services to the United States by its own choosing—and indeed runs the risk of becoming a burden—it may be seen as transformed against its will into an extrinsic political asset by a great power concerned with its regional interests. One would even be tempted to induce from these examples that the Americans would be prepared in the future to abandon Israel if the cold consideration of their interests required it.

However, these assumptions, and in particular the latter one, are exaggerated. American pressure on Israel is, when necessary, quite real, but it remains within certain limits. In order to trace these limits, let us first say that in the search for a type of support to Israel other than unconditional, two options, rather than one, theoretically present themselves. The first would consist of exercising a certain pressure on Israel while offering it compensation and assuring it of the continuation of the policy of support. The second would combine pressure with threats to abandon Israel and would in fact consider the idea of no longer supporting it. Washington has not confused these two options, which have presented themselves in periods when Israel has appeared manifestly to be hurting American regional interests. It has clearly chosen the first option and totally excluded the second. In other words, the American response has always been located within the will to support Israel and maintain privileged relations with that country, even while exercising pressure on it when the regional stakes made Israeli concessions unavoidable.

Thus, in the examples cited above, the limits that pressure must not exceed are clearly drawn: it must be minimal and moderate; the most serious—and effective—applications of pressure must be confidential (such as Kissinger's injunction to Israel to respect the cease-fire on the Egyptian front following the nuclear alert of October 1973), as opposed to the lightest and most artificial applications, which may be aired in public (such as the verbal condemnation of the annexation of the Golan in 1981, the establishment of settlements in the occupied Palestinian territories, or the repression in these territories); persuasion must be used more than threats; Israel has to be offered credible compensation in the areas where its vital interests are affected (such as supplying it with arms, rejecting the PLO and not supporting a Palestinian state); and pressure has to be justified by the desire to "save Israel despite itself" and assure it the best conditions for peace. Even most of those who consider Israel a strategic burden would subscribe to these limits. Can one consider these limits to be fruitful and that exceeding them, that is, threatening to abandon Israel, would be more harmful to the United States than the activism or even the intransigence of Israel? American strategists may propose the following justifications to this effect.

To aggravate the pressure on Israel to the point where it would consider its vital interests threatened, and where it would have nothing to lose, would provoke a "desperado" attitude that would lead it to lower the ceiling of its conditions for resorting to preventive war and even to the use of nuclear weapons. The regional interests (such as oil wells) that would be the source of intense American pressure on Israel could themselves become the target of Israeli desperation. Such eventualities were evoked several times in the 1970s to explain the moderation of American pressure and the increase, simultaneous with such pressure, in military and financial assistance.

Israel is perceived in any event by the Arabs as enjoying the unshakable support of the United States and as having privileged relations with it. According to popular perception in the Arab world, the Jewish state is the creation of the West and of imperialism; an important sector of the Arab-Muslim intelligentsia continues to think so. Whether these perceptions are correct or not is not the point here; what is important is that they have consequences for the U.S. attitude toward Israel. Washington may indeed fear that choosing to abandon Israel or to reduce its level of economic or military aid might be understood by the Arabs as an important sign that

Washington is willing to disavow its ally and protégé, allows it to become weakened politically and perhaps, in time, militarily as well (Quandt 1977:12; Reich 1984:181). This would constitute a loss of American credibility and a "historic" Arab victory, even if it were limited at first, because it would make it possible for the Arabs to demand even more American concessions in the future in areas that do not even concern Israel. The regional damage caused by Israeli activism or even intransigence are, according to this point of view, nothing compared to the damage that would come from an American-Israeli divorce.

One must add to these reasons that the cessation of support to Israel or American-Israeli divorce would be useless. There is no reason for Washington to give the Arabs an easy victory when, in terms of the military balance of forces, Israel still enjoys superiority, even at times when it goes through a crisis in the definition of its strategic choices, as was the case after 1973, after 1982, or after 1988 (the Palestinian uprising). The basic Arab perception of Israel as the enemy hopefully to be defeated, and the cessation of American support to Israel as the objective hopefully to be attained, do not have to be gratuitously encouraged when they cannot be translated into an effective Arab policy. For a long time already, victory over Israel has been absent from the practical, "operative" agenda of the Arab governments. Since 1967 at least, and even during the few months of triumphalism after 1973, the Arab consensus has been reduced, at the very most, to the idea of obtaining a "just" settlement of the conflict—an idea that implies calling into question neither Israeli military superiority nor privileged American-Israeli relations. The Palestinian movement itself converted officially to these perspectives—and adjusted to this given state of things—when it adopted its peace initiative of November 1988 and engaged in the Madrid process in 1991.

Of course, the American image in Arab public opinion suffers from the United States multiplication of signs of support to Israel, but that negative image may be compensated for by the Arabs' impotence, most of the time. It matters little whether this impotence is attributable to exogenous causes, Israeli or otherwise, or to endogenous ones, or to an interaction of the two types of factors. In any event, there would be little damage for the United States in pursuing a policy of support to Israel. If, indeed, Arab impotence is due to the intervention of external forces (Israeli and American above all), Washington can only wish to pursue such intervention. If, on the other hand, Arab incapacity is endogenous, then there is no hurry to change the course of Israeli-American relations. And if, in spite of everything, an upsurge of Arab determination sometimes occurs, the fact that Israel is accused before the United States gives Washington enough reaction time to offer the Arabs, without panicking, the minimal concessions compatible with the range of possible choices from unconditional support to conditional support of Tel Aviv.

The Validity of the Utilitarian Explanation

All things considered, American support to Israel could thus be seen as reasonable, and more useful than harmful. What it requires in terms of U.S. investment in favor of Tel Aviv is calculated only in dollars, not in American lives. This investment has lasted for more than 45 years, in spite of changing decisionmakers in Washington and in Tel Aviv—an indication that it involves no indisputable damage to American interests. When Lucius Battle, an Assistant Secretary of State for Middle Eastern and Southern Asian affairs, advised President Johnson not to accede to an Israeli demand for arms supplies (50 F-4 planes) toward the end of 1967, the President replied: "You have to give me more reason *not* to do it" (quoted in Tivnan 1987:66, our emphasis). The idea of overall utility, or at least overall nondamage, or again, viability, thus seems to have a certain explanatory value as regards American-Israeli relations.

The reader will have noted, however, that we have sometimes used the conditional to account for the utilitarian explanation. This is the case because, first of all, the instrumentality this explanation seeks to account for expresses an intentionality that is most often implicit, and secondly, because no one can really say what would have become of American interests in the region if Washington's policy toward Israel had been different. All that can be said with assurance is that the detractors of this policy cannot prove positively that other choices would have been preferable from the point of view of American interests.

Although the utilitarian explanation has a relative validity, one can also say that it is insufficient. This is true because it is an explanation in terms of "effect" rather than "cause." It observes the effect (one of overall nondamage) of American behavior toward Israel but cannot account for the causes of this behavior (rationality, motives, motivations and the like). At the most one can say that it is "as if" a rational intentionality were commanding this behavior, but one cannot affirm the existence of this rational intentionality in all decision-making processes. Is it possible, following the order of the questions we earlier proposed, to go beyond the idea of an implicit utilitarian intentionality underlying American support to Israel and say that an explicit utilitarian design—a causality of an instrumental nature—is commanding this support? In other words, can we establish the validity of an explicit instrumental explanation? This is what we shall now proceed to examine.

An American or an Israeli Design?

In order to verify the validity of the instrumental explanation at an intermediate level (that is, neither the macro- nor the microdimensional level), we shall ask if, given that Washington profits (more or less) from Israeli dependence on the United States in terms of arms and money, from Israeli military superiority over its neighbors, and from the state of hostility between Israel and the Arabs, it is correct to say that Washington consciously maintains and incites this triad of dependence-superiority-hostility with little concern about the fate of Israel as a "subject." Is there an American "project" in this sense? We shall try to answer this question by considering each of the three terms of the triad. Let us note at the outset, however, that this will lead us to ask whether the instrumentality sought for is not to be found on the Israeli side rather than the American one, and whether American-Israeli relations are not underlain by an Israeli "project" rather than an American one.

Is There an American Project Regarding Israel?

Let us consider first of all the idea of Israeli dependence on the United States. Israel's belonging to the Western camp and its not being able to play East against West were, from 1948 on, the object of an American resoluteness—a resoluteness verified in 1950 during the Korean crisis when Israel was asked to make clear its position in the Western camp (Brecher 1972:272). That the Israelis could not take advantage of a real competition between Washington and its European allies was confirmed by the energetic American attitude during the Suez war of 1956–57. It can be said, however, as we shall see further on, that Israel's belonging to the American camp "goes without saying" and that, as a result, with the exception of the Suez war, an American resoluteness in this area has been unnecessary since at least 1950. One cannot, however, extrapolate from the fact of Israel's pro-American orientation the idea that the United States has a constant and conscious policy of aggravating Israeli dependence so that it will be politically more and more obliged to follow. To attempt this analytical jump is to fall into the trap of the "conspiratorial" explanation.

The same is not true of Israeli's military superiority. Ensuring it (indirectly through French arms until 1967) or directly (since the mid-1960s) is the expression of a constant American watchfulness, although the objective has been to maintain Israeli superiority rather than to build it from scratch. In my view, there is an explicit American intentionality in this area, whatever its justification may be: either the necessity of this superiority for the survival of the Jewish state or its utility for its regional role as a strategic asset of the United States. American leaders have never concealed their commitment to ensuring this superiority, even if few among them have explained whether this commitment, as Leonard Binder says (1983:1–2), "is a necessary prerequisite to other goals, an adjunct but separate goal, or merely one part of more generally stated goals."

A comparative quantitative study of three variables (American aid to Israel; allocation of resources by the Arab states for the military effort; and allocation of resources by Israel for the military and civilian effort) during the 1960–79 period confirms the rationality of the curve of American military assistance to Israel. For Martin C. McGuire who has made this study (1982:233),

> the signals which the United States seems historically to have emitted suggest a more logical pattern than what one might have expected. There have been both efficiency and equity objectives operating with respect to U.S. aid allotments—efficiency, because the United States has augmented its defense support to offset (in part) Arab arms increases, and equity, because the United States has cut back its defense support as Israel has grown richer (*other factors being held constant*) (McGuire's emphasis).

Another quantitative study (Beenstock 1992:94) has similarly concluded that "U.S. assistance to Israel appears to be systematically influenced by Israel's defense burden and by Israel's indebtedness to the United States."

There remains the question of Israeli-Arab hostility. Nothing allows us to state that there is a thought-out and constant American policy aiming to resolutely stir up this conflict in order to utilize

Israeli regional supremacy and threaten the Arab countries with the Israeli "stick." This means, not that the United States must be seen as a state morally devoted to peace and determined to resolve the Israeli-Arab conflict come what may, but only that American policy regarding the conflict is often reactive, little disposed to truly commit itself to realizing peace, engages in a process of settlement (always partial and incomplete) when there is no other alternative, and does not hesitate to stir up the conflict at other times.

However, because Washington engages in the settlement process only when its interests are clearly and directly threatened—that it is concerned above all and always about Israeli military superiority rather than about a settlement (often because of Israeli reluctance or pressure), the overall consequence is that Israeli-Arab hostility is perpetuated and sometimes aggravated. Although one cannot say that Washington plays expressly with Israel's fate and treats it as an object, American permissiveness toward Israel's regional activism carries this meaning implicitly. This is, at least, how the Israel "doves" understand it when they beg the American leaders to prove that they have the peaceful destiny of Israel at heart by ceasing to consider the country as a strategic asset (Tivnan 1987:264), by making sharp cuts in the amounts of economic aid (234–235) and by putting pressure on the Israeli government to make the necessary concessions for an overall settlement (210–211). The changes that have taken place in the world and the Middle East since 1990 have given more weight to these arguments in U.S. calculations.

In any event, it is probably only in the "superiority" portion of the triad dependence-superiority-hostility that a truly constant and thought-out American policy toward Israel is expressed. That is not sufficient to cause us to move from a utilitarian explanation (with implicit intentionality) to an instrumental explanation (with explicit intentionality) of the place occupied by Israel in American regional strategy. If this is true, and given that there are two actors in the relation, might not the instrumentality be found on the side of the other actor concerned, Israel? Rather than the idea of an American design or project in which Israel is an "object," might it not be possible to consider the idea of an Israeli design or project oriented toward the development and exploitation of a strategic relation with the United States? We shall try to answer these questions in the following section.

An Israeli Project?

The reader will have noted in this study, and in particular in this chapter, my reservations regarding the idea of state design or calculation. I have tried, on the contrary, to favor the idea of implicit intentionality, observed after the fact. Yet one must recognize that regarding the actions of Israel there is a higher coefficient of explicit intentionality in political behavior. This is due, as we shall see, to the conditions under which the state of Israel was born.

The birth of the state of Israel is not the outcome of the long sociopolitical evolution of an indigenous community established in the towns and villages of Palestine and that became progressively self-conscious as a nation in the face of an Ottoman empire dominating it and an Arab population living by its side. With the exception of the small historic (and Arabic-speaking) Jewish community of Palestine, the "Yishuv" that was to make up Israel under the protection of the British mandate was essentially a community of European immigrants. Israel thus owes its birth to a phenomenon external to the region. This phenomenon is, of course, Zionism.

To make Palestine the place of Jewish immigration, to appropriate it and to prepare the establishment of a state there, European-born Zionism could only be a fundamentally voluntaristic phenomenon—a project. Of course, Zionism had roots in the Jewish memory and in the perception of a Jewish specificity with respect to its European environment; these aspects had nothing programmatic about them and, besides, involved a tragic dimension. But from the moment when, because of circumstances mentioned above (Eastern European nationalisms, the imperialist drive of the nineteenth century), the idea of a Jewish state in Palestine began to crystallize (and this current was neither the only one nor the most popular one within the European Jewish communities), it took the form of a movement or "project." From this project and its voluntarism (Jamous 1982) flowed its great choices: the first Zionist congresses, the establishment of the World Zionist Organization, the launching of immigration toward Palestine, the modes of organization of the Yishuv; and the latter included the setting up of a military wing of the movement, the fixing of priorities for the colonization of lands, the dispossession of the Palestinians and, most important for the present discussion, the establishment of alliances with European actors.

It was thus within the framework of a project that the genesis of the state of Israel must be located. We do not mean at all to suggest that everything that has occurred in Palestine for the past 75 years or more is the product of a grand Zionist-Israeli design that has been able to anticipate all possible dynamics and command all events; nor do we mean to deny the importance of contradictions within the Yishuv and later the state, nor the sometimes unexpected and paralyzing effects of these contradictions on the political decisions of the leadership. What we do mean by our insistence on the idea of a project or design is that, above and beyond the contradictions, the reversals, the structural constraints and the resistance of other actors, the leaders of the Zionist movement made important choices, which all derived from a voluntarism born in Europe. This was expressed very well by the founding father, Theodore Herzl, in his introduction to *A Jewish State* (1967:7–9): "The Jews who wish for a state shall have it and it will not be a 'phantasy.' "

Among the choices made by the Zionist movement and that concern us here, we must especially note, once again, its alliances. In accordance with Zionist doctrine regarding the necessity of support from a great power (Klieman 1979:101–102), it was in Europe, in the countries displaying the greatest imperial prowess (Great Britain and France) or imperial aspirations (Germany), and in which Jewish elites had long enjoyed respectable status, that the necessary alliance was sought and finally found. As is well known, it was Great Britain that officially adopted in 1917 the project of a "Jewish national home" in Palestine (the Balfour declaration), and wrote it into its Mandate over that country in 1922 at the League of Nations. Between 1917 and 1922, the legal and practical measures taken in favor of the "national home" represented the convergence of two different projects, one Zionist and the other British-imperial. In the 20 years that followed, what counted most for the Zionist movement was the attitude of the mandated power, which was, of course, a world power as well.

In the period between the two world wars, finding a source of support other than British was not of crucial importance for the Zionist movement. Of course, the movement did have some activities in Washington; thus, in October 1917, the young Zionist leader Louis Brandeis obtained from President Woodrow Wilson, a personal friend of his, support for the draft of a British text that was to become, only a few days later (November 2, 1917) the Balfour Declaration (Feis 1969:13). American Zionists succeeded in September 1922 in having the two houses of Congress adopt a joint resolution expressing their support to the project for a National Jewish home-land in Palestine (Manuel 1949:282). In 1924, Washington and London signed an agreement concerning the rights of Americans in Palestine; in the preamble, the United States agreed to include an explicit reference to the Balfour Declaration in exchange for British guarantees concerning the protection of the economic and mission-ary interests of American citizens in Palestine (Safran 1978:35). But none of this had much strategic importance for the Zionist move-ment, especially if one takes into account the isolationist tendency of American foreign policy after World War I (Klieman 1979:102).

It was not until the beginning of the 1940s, and in particular the "Biltmore Conference," a meeting held by Zionist leaders from the United States and Palestine (including Ben-Gurion) in a New York hotel, in May 1942, that "the center of Zionist political activities . . . shifted to the United States" (Schechtman 1966:64). Disappointed by the White Paper of 1939 that included British concessions to the Arabs, and cognizant of the emerging global role of the United States since it had entered the war to help Great Britain and other powers, the Zionist leaders justly saw international predominance as belonging to Washington rather than London. They knew the realization of their objectives now depended much more on the for-mer than on the latter (Ben-Gurion 1963:17–18; Bar-Zohar 1978:105). The Zionists thought that even if Great Britain—in the best of cases for that power—maintained its influence throughout the Middle East, it would now require Washington's approval to retain its regional assets. In particular, they "felt that Great Britain could not afford to disregard intervention by the United States in favor of the Zionist cause and hoped that the U.S. Government might be induced by aroused public opinion to intercede with the British Government" (Schechtman 1966:65).

Thus, through political farsightedness or thanks to the influence of the American Jewish community under the circumstances of the period (including the various reactions to the Nazi massacres), the Zionist leaders were not handicapped by the inertia of their multi-ple ties of dependence with Great Britain; they were able to antici-pate the new international reality and redirect their alliances to ful-fill their objectives. For the Zionist movement in the 1940s, as in earlier periods, the forging of alliances was not a mere supplement to other assets it already possessed; it was truly a necessary condi-tion for the survival and the development of the Zionist project in an Arab environment that was hostile because it refused to endure the consequences of this project. As Samuel Roberts explains (1973:79, 111): "Leading Zionists, despite their public emphasis on the necessity for self-reliance, were, like their Israeli successors, fully aware that the success of the Zionist effort did not and had never depended solely upon Jewish resources, as these resources had been, were presently, and would for a long time in the future remain inadequate to the task. The Zionist leadership knew that a great power of imperial dimensions had to be induced to serve as patron of the Zionist cause." Aaron Klieman explains (1980:45, 48) that Zionist, later Israeli, doctrine, concerning the necessity of support from a single great power ("the one great power doctrine") had three motivations: legitimacy (not being diplomatically isolated); protection (receiving economic and military aid); and deterrence (deterring the Arabs).

One cannot help contrasting the Zionists' initiative and determination with respect to the American administration with the latter's hesitation and vacillation. Likewise, one cannot help comparing British behavior in 1917–1922 with U.S. conduct in 1947–48. British support for the Jewish Home was integrated into the overall British vision for the Middle East. In the American case, support for a Jewish state was due mainly to the pressure of public opinion and from Congress, and was not an expression of an American strategic "project" for the Middle East (Roberts 1973:77). In sum, if one examines the relationship between the Zionist-Israeli side and the American side during this constitutive period, one will notice that it was the former rather than the latter that constructed the relationship as a project or an explicit instrumentality.

It is important, concerning this constituting period, to distinguish the Zionist-Israeli strategic orientation toward the United States from the policy it followed toward the Soviet Union, in spite of an apparent parallelism. It is often pointed out that Soviet support to the United Nations' partition plan and the supplying of Czech weapons to the new state constituted counterweights to the Israeli-American relationship and found their expression in the Israeli policy of "nonidentification" with the East or West, advanced by Ben-Gurion in September 1948 and formally included in the program of the Israeli government the following March (Brecher 1972:39–40). It is noted as well that the socialist ideals held by an important wing of the Zionist movement, along with the Eastern European origins of many of its leaders, gave rise to a special "emotional" attitude, an "ideological empathy," toward Moscow (Brecher 1972:164,

244–245; Bialer 1990:135–136). Finally, one may recall the confidential American reports from that period in which Israel is seen as a fertile ground for Soviet expansion (Bialer 1990:208).

In spite of some elements of truth in these arguments, one cannot speak of a pro-Soviet Israeli policy during these crucial years, nor even of an American-Soviet parallelism in Israeli strategy. The Zionist leaders were the first to be astonished by the Soviet position in favor of the partition; they in fact interpreted it as a purely tactical attitude on Moscow's part, in which the will to eject Great Britain from Palestine played a significant role (Michael Cohen 1982:261–262; Horowitz 1953:272; Bialer 1990:142). The fact is that neither a socialist internal structure nor certain scattered elements of socialism, as was the case in Israel, necessarily signify an "internationalist" choice or a pro-Soviet policy (Rodinson 1973:83–84). If socialist ideals could theoretically draw the Israelis closer to Moscow, one must also note a sentiment of cultural community with the West, the key role of the American Jewish community starting in the 1940s (Bialer 1990:211), and an indifference to the Third World (Brecher 1972:561). Furthermore, the quest for the support of a single great power, which caused Israel to favor the United States over the Soviet Union, was probably aimed at preventing the "insecurity and risks" involved in maneuvering between two great powers "without the assurance of consistent support from either side" (Klieman 1980:48). Finally, Israeli dependency on the United States was already too great to allow it to take any distance: in 1949–50, between 30 and 40 percent of its imports and 60 percent of its foreign exchange currency came from the U.S. (Bialer 1990:221–222).

Thus "nonidentification" with either the East or the West as proclaimed by Israel in fact expressed not so much a distance from the two blocs as an attempt not to lose the good graces of the Soviet Union (mainly with respect to Jewish emigration) while identifying with the West (Bialer 1990:206). The decision to put an end to the "illusion" of nonidentification when the Korean war broke out in July 1950 (Brecher 1974:36) showed that this effort to conciliate the two considerations was a pious wish and that the less vital interest had to be sacrificed in a period of international tension. With this development, Israeli rhetoric now coincided with its strategic choice to be on the side of the West. The solidity of this choice is confirmed by the speed with which Israel tried to integrate itself into the Western system of defense of the Middle East, starting at the end of the year 1950, by proposing to make its territory a logistical base for the U.S. Army and to conclude a defense treaty with Washington.

This analysis is congruent with the hypothesis put forward by Uri Bialer regarding the responsibility for the deterioration of Soviet-Israeli relations. Observers have tended to place the responsibility on Moscow. Bialer, using Israeli archive sources (1990:179), shows with great care that in 1948 the Soviet leadership was prepared to be content with an independent Israeli position concerning the East-West conflict, but changed its attitude toward Tel Aviv "only when Israel publicly supported the American position on Korea late in 1950, and when signs of her growing reliance on the U.S. became unmistakable." As proof, the author cites the fact that Czech arms sales to Israel continued up to early 1951, and not only to October or December of 1948, as scholars had believed up to now.

If, between 1950 and 1956, Israel sought to develop its strategic relations with the United States, it was in order to be in a position to have an active policy in the region—so active that it "would push the Arabs into fighting a war they could never win" (Tivnan 1987:45; Bar-Siman-Tov 1988:336). Moshe Sharett, Foreign Minister and then Prime Minister of Israel, explains in the pages of his memoirs covering the years 1953–54, and not without disapproval and a personal sense of impotence, that the Israeli army was planning "war in order to occupy the rest of Western Eretz Israel" (quoted in Rokach 1980:17); that Chief of Staff Moshe Dayan was proposing to multiply provocations against Egypt in order to pull it into a war (ibid.:18); and that Pinhas Lavon, Defense Minister, saw in a coup d'état in Damascus the opportunity to "occupy Syrian border positions beyond the demilitarized zone" (ibid.:19). Confidential American reports drawn up in Tel Aviv or in Washington did not fail to emphasize that "Israel was obviously spoiling for a fight" (Green 1984:118).

In 1955–56, Israel's regional activism, confronted with American reservations and the Czech-Egyptian arms deal of September 1955, led it to turn toward another Western power, France, since that country's interest converged for the moment with that of Tel Aviv and consisted of using force against Egypt, the leading country of the Arab world. Although Israel stayed within the framework of the West and did not seek, like Nasser's Egypt, to play a balancing game between the two world camps, it nonetheless committed an error of evaluation about what was acceptable to Washington when it chose to launch the Sinai campaign in coordination with France and Great Britain. The price paid by Israel for this error convinced it that it was no longer able to manipulate its alliances to accord with its regional strategy in a way that would largely overstep the limits of what was acceptable to the world's foremost power; for example, it had to obtain a green light before waging the 1967 and 1982 campaigns, and it had always to stop short of blackmailing the United States with the threat of divorce.

One must hasten to add that these limits have most often been quite broad and that short of them, Israel has continued as before to place its relations with the United States in the service of its own regional strategy. Even Israel's wish to develop its own atomic bomb in cooperation with France may be interpreted as fitting within this framework, as François Perrin, former French High Commissioner for Atomic Energy explains: "We thought the Israeli bomb was aimed at the Americans; not to launch it against America but to say: 'If you don't want to help us in a critical situation we will require you to help us, otherwise we will use our nuclear bombs'" (quoted in Milhollin 1987–88:115–116).

In any event, Israeli dependence on the United States for arms and money and Israeli-Arab hostility, two phenomena structurally linked to Israel's very existence, are mutually reinforcing because of the Israeli will to play a regional role. In the effort to escape the docility that would ordinarily be the consequence of their dependence, the Israelis want so much to prove to their benefactor their role as a strategic asset that they are led to adopt ambitious and daring regional policies that are prone to aggravating Israeli-Arab hostility. Hostility in turn increases the need for weapons, arms, money, and diplomatic support.

This mutual reinforcement would not, of course, be possible without the "mediation" of Israeli military superiority, the third term of the triad presented above. To assure its own survival and to lead an audacious regional policy, military supremacy is a sine qua non. Israeli military superiority is thus at once a product and a factor of Israeli-Arab hostility. Military superiority also has perhaps the same type of relation with dependence toward the United States since it is both a product of it and a factor tending to aggravate it.

It must be said, however, that Israel (like Zionism before it) is, in spite of its dependence on external aid, the craftsman of its own supremacy. It is in this sense that we must understand the idea of "self-sufficiency" (or "self-reliance") constantly enunciated by

Zionist or Israeli leaders (Roberts 1973:68, 113; Peri 1983:20). Israel has shown that it possesses a great capacity for mobilizing, utilizing, and "digesting" the resources provided by the European and American powers and the Jewish communities in the world. In other words, while one may doubt that Israel could have survived since 1948 without enormous outside aid, this aid alone clearly has failed to guarantee Israel's survival, its military supremacy, and its place in the Middle East. One need only consider the extreme example of South Vietnam, which fell in spite of all the American assistance provided to it.

Israel's capacity to take measures, both internal and external, to assure its regional supremacy, provides a complementary explanation for the weakness of U.S. pressure in return for dependence. It is customary to think, in a utilitarian perspective, that American propensity not to exercise pressure is due to the services rendered by Israeli power. It is often forgotten, however, that this power itself gives Israel the means to resist possible pressure or to exercise pressure on Washington in turn (Nachmias 1987:16–17). Even if there were no privileged relations between the two countries, the United States, like any other outside power, would have to take into account first of all the balance of forces in the region and the possible reactions of the most powerful state there, which is Israel. In a situation of regional conflict, it is usually the weakest party that is led to make the most concessions if a process of calming the conflict is initiated.

Conclusion

If there is an area in which the idea of an Israeli project manifests itself unambiguously, it is that of military power. The mobilization of resources to perpetuate that power, added to the will to play a regional role and to place the relation with the United States in the service of this role, allocates to explicit Israeli intentionality a preponderant place in the spiralling up and mutual reinforcement of the terms of the triad (Israeli-Arab hostility, dependency toward the United States, regional supremacy)—terms which are, from the point of view of their genesis, already consubstantial with the very situation of the state of Israel. This fact, compared with what we stated above about the secondary role of an explicit American project in this triad, leads us to the paradox that, in the relation between the two parties, a world power and a dependent state, it is the latter more than the former that "instrumentalizes" the relation with its regional interests in view. There is a dissymmetry in the comparative situation of the two states: with respect to the Americans, the Israelis have what could be called "instrumentality surplus."

In saying this, we do not mean that Israel is the party that most profits from the relationship. In any event, the respective profits and costs are not comparable because they are not of the same nature for the two parties, and a distinction must be made between short-term and long-term profits and costs. Nor do we wish to minimize the importance of the effect of American policy—and the status of the United States—on the fate of Israel (Efrat and Bercovitch 1991:18). What we do want to emphasize is that, in contrast to the preponderant role of calculation and planning in the Israeli attitude (doubtless because Israel has what it considers its vital interests at stake), a large place must be allotted in the American attitude to the dimension of permissiveness and reactive behavior. It is this permissiveness that allows us to speak of an American policy congruent with the idea of strategic asset even at time when decisionmakers think the opposite.

The Israeli-American dissymmetry confirms that, regarding the United States, there is no satisfactory instrumental explanation (in the sense of explicit instrumentality) of its policy of support to Israel and that one must be content with a utilitarian (or implicitly instrumental) explanation. Can we identify the reasons for the relative validity of the utilitarian explanation and the extreme difficulty of establishing the validity of the instrumental (explicit) one? In addition to the general reasons evoked earlier, regarding the limits of the decisionmakers' rationality, the subjectivity of their motives, and the difficulty in establishing an adequate relation between the objectives pursued and the results obtained, we believe there is another answer: the utilitarian explanation and the explicit instrumental explanation do not claim to account for exactly the same object.

The utilitarian explanation, a post facto perspective, accounts for the privileged character of American-Israeli relations by observing that the constant American support for Israel, even when this country is a burden, is not really harmful to the United States. Its validity claims to be no more than relative and its object (the privileged relations and the support) requires no major coherence because it is content to constitute a common denominator between the fact that

Israel is sometimes an asset and sometimes a burden and the fact that American support is sometimes permissive and sometimes conditional.

The explicit instrumental explanation claims, for its part, to account for American-Israeli relations by resorting to the idea that Washington supports Tel Aviv because of the current and potential services it can render as a strategic asset. Being an explanation in terms of "cause" (rather than in terms of "effect," as is the case of the utilitarian explanation), the explicit instrumental explanation is naturally more demanding and more coherent: the "cause" is assumed to be located in the intentionality and the minds of the decisionmakers (hence the need for coherence) while the "effect" is located in reality (hence the possibility for at least secondary contradictions). Consequently, the explicit instrumental explanation cannot simultaneously admit one thing (Israel as asset) and its opposite (Israel as burden). But these two things indeed coexist both in reality and in the minds of American decisionmakers. The explicit instrumental explanation, since it accounts only for the idea of asset, cannot be valid.

It is interesting to note in passing that the argumentation of the explicit instrumental explanation is essentially the same as the coherent advocacy of the asset doctrine. It is no coincidence that this advocacy converges with the "instrumentality surplus" of the Israelis, that is, with their effort to make Washington admit that their country is a strategic asset, since this implies that Israel needs support in arms and money without requiring blind docility. We might add that this Israeli instrumentality surplus and the asset advocacy constitute two convergent efforts to convert American decisionmakers and analysts to the explicit instrumental explanation. When addressed to American decisionmakers, this effort is quite legitimate (and quite successful) since it is an integral part of politics. When addressed to analysts, however, it is at best an ideological argument claiming to bear the mantle of science.

We have now established that the utilitarian explanation (implicit instrumentality) is valid but insufficient, since it succeeds less in considering the causes than the effects of American policy. The explicit instrumental explanation, which could have been sufficient since it claims to identify the causes, is unable to prove its validity. We must thus search elsewhere for the causes of American support to Israel, among causes which are not of a strategic and instrumental nature. This is the aim of the following chapter.

7 | The Domestic Dynamics Explanation

Since the strategic-utilitarian perspective does not suffice to explain United States' constant support to Israel and the predominance of the idea of Israel as asset, we must now turn to the internal factors of U.S. policy-making. The first of these that comes to every observer's mind is the influence of what is customarily called the Jewish lobby, the pro-Israeli lobby, or even simply "the lobby." It is this influence that we shall consider first in this chapter. This influence goes well beyond the "normal" dimension of a lobby and must in turn be explained, and we will try to show that its basis lies in American society itself, in what we propose to call the ideological-cultural instance of the society. This will constitute the second section of the chapter.

Finally, since it does not suffice to state that each of these two instances (strategic-utilitarian and ideological-cultural) contains a portion of validity, or that one complements the other, we shall conclude by trying to articulate their respective places in a unified explanation.

Explanation Through the Pro-Israeli Lobby

Since the end of World War II, it has been impossible to analyze the United States' Middle East policy without taking into account the role of the American Jewish community. Moreover, this role, recognized to one degree or another by all the actors concerned (Americans, Jewish-Americans, Israelis, and Arabs), enjoys an honorable scientific status thanks to models of explanation popularized by many American foreign-policy specialists, who emphasize that the decision-making process is determined less by decisionmakers' endeavors to conform objectively to the strategic interests of their country, than by the effective advocacy of bureaucratic, sectoral, or ethnic pressure groups. Indeed, we ourselves insisted in the previous chapter on the limits of decisionmakers' rationality and on decisions as resultants of multiple points of view in which motives such as maintaining popularity in the polls or reelection come into play. Next we will determine to what extent and why Washington's policy of supporting Israel is influenced by the organized action of the American Jewish community.

A Review of the Lobby

A rapid review of the pro-Israeli lobby is necessary at the outset. By this expression, and in accordance with the broad sense of the term (*Legislators and the Lobbyists* 1968:4), we mean the organized political action of American Jews directed at decisionmakers with the aim of causing them to maintain and promote a pro-Israeli American policy. Neither the community life of American Jews, nor even their direct support to Israel, can be considered as lobbying, however important these factors may be. Since the 1950s, lobbying has been the responsibility of two institutions: the Conference of Presidents of Major Jewish Organizations and AIPAC.

The Conference of Presidents of Major Jewish Organizations (also known as the Presidents' Conference or Club) is a relatively unstructured body whose primary objective is to define by consensus the grievances of the Jewish community concerning American Middle East policy and to present them to the White House or the Department of State. The Conference of Presidents was created in 1954 by Nahum Goldmann in reaction to a remark by a high State Department official who complained about having had to face contradictory demands by different Jewish groups and wished to hear them speak with a single voice (Tivnan 1987:40–41; Reich 1984:200). In 1966, the Conference decided to consider itself as representative of the affiliated organizations, not just of their leaders (L.

O'Brien 1986:191). Slightly fewer than 40 organizations belong to the Conference today.

The Conference has an office and a budget. It elects a president from among its members every two years. The president is an important figure in the community and has access, with his peers, to the highest officials of the U.S. administration, including the President. Although the Conference seeks only to reach a consensus among its members on questions concerning Israel rather than impose a line, there is no doubt that it enjoys the same high prestige among decisionmakers as the community itself. The Conference of Presidents is, so to speak, the diplomatic arm of the community not only in its relations with the U.S. government, but also with the Israeli government, occasionally playing an intermediary role between the two to moderate their possible contradictions (L. O'Brien 1986:192–193).

AIPAC (The American Israel Public Affairs Committee) is the pro-Israeli lobby in the strict sense (*Legislators and the Lobbyists* 1968:4): it is officially registered as a lobby with the Senate and the House of Representatives and has the rights and obligations stipulated by existing regulations on lobbies (for example, it must submit a quarterly financial report; donations to the organization are not tax-deductible; it is prohibited from contributing to candidates' electoral campaign funds) (L. O'Brien 1986:161–162). Having operated under an ambiguous legal status from 1951 to 1954, the lobby was officially founded in 1954 when the effort was made to place it in harmony with the law. It was then called the American Zionist Committee for Public Affairs (the current name and acronym date from 1959). As a lobby in the strict sense, AIPAC's field of action is the Congress (Goldberg 1990:16, 19). Since its inception, AIPAC's principal difficulty has been in demonstrating that it is not the agent of a foreign government; if it were, it would have to register under a different legal status, which would be less favorable to its activities and, especially, to the image it seeks to project (Kenen 1981:66–69, 106–110). As we shall see, however, AIPAC does coordinate its actions very closely with the Israeli government.

Unlike the Conference of Presidents, AIPAC is not a loosely structured grouping but a highly centralized organization. It includes a supervisory board made up of leaders of Jewish organizations. Its chief officer, the executive director, is a salaried professional. As of 1989, the executive director commanded a staff of more than 100 persons (compared to about 20 in 1981) (Bard 1991:12;

Findley 1985:32; Babcock 1986a; Shipler 1987; *Congressional Quarterly Weekly Report* 1989:298). Among the members of this staff are specialists "who represent a broad range of expertise on the U.S. political process—particularly the workings of Congress—foreign affairs, communications, and the operations of the U.S. Jewish community" (Laufer 1987:147). Moreover AIPAC, which aspires to be a "mass movement," has had, since the end of 1984, more than 50,000 dues-paying members; there were only 11,000 in 1981 (Tivnan 1987:202, 284; Fredet and Gilson 1991:10). Its budget, approximately $250,000 in 1973 (L. O'Brien 1986:162), reached $11,00,000 in 1989 (Bard 1991:12).

Because of its day-to-day organized work with the two houses of Congress, AIPAC has come to supplant the Conference of Presidents and become, as Tivnan states, "the de facto leader of the American Jewish community" (Tivnan 1987:215; also Goldberg 1990:19). Considered at first as the servant of the community before Congress, AIPAC is now perceived as its "spearhead," to the chagrin of other American Jewish organizations, in particular the American Jewish Committee and B'nai B'rith. AIPAC's dominance in the community brings great prestige to its director; this was indeed the case for Thomas Dine, who prior to 1981 "had never worked for a Jewish organization in his life" (Tivnan 1987:164).

How the Lobby Operates

In order to exercise its influence on the executive and legislative branches of government and cause them to support Israel unconditionally, the lobby in the broad sense, but above all AIPAC and its "grassroots" network, makes use of the following means and mechanisms:

First of all, the lobby maintains contacts on a daily basis with members of the administration, senators, and representatives, in particular those who sit on committees concerned with foreign affairs, the armed forces and the budget. It is reported that between March 1981 and April 1983, Jewish personalities and groups obtained some 350 meetings with officials of various levels at the White House and the Departments of State and Defense, that is, a meeting every two days (L. O'Brien 1986:156). AIPAC, for its part, tries to stay informed on the stances and votes of members of Congress; it sends its representatives to all the meetings of relevant committees (ibid.:170; Bloomfield 1983:19). Close ties are established with legislative aides who, of course, play a crucial role in setting the agenda and directing the legislative process since their task is to prepare the speeches of their Congressperson and to treat the demands of constituents and pressure groups. It is they, in fact, who "draft the legislation, prepare the amendments, organize the hearings, write the reports and help plan the strategy" (Bloomfield 1983:22).

Maintaining these close contacts is doubly useful for the pro-Israeli lobby. The contacts serve first of all to gain information about projects in gestation before any official announcement or media coverage; this allows AIPAC "to identify key elements, issues and personalities before formulating its strategy" (Laufer 1987:148). The possibility is thus open for intervening at an early stage, discreetly and effectively, either to harmonize American positions with those of Israel or to counsel Israel on what it can or cannot reasonably hope from Washington. Secondly, daily contacts facilitate the application of pressure in the most appropriate way for modifying administration decisions judged unfavorable to Israel and obtaining favorable votes from Congress. When, in 1985, the administration envisioned a sale of arms to Jordan and Saudi Arabia, AIPAC "started the attack long before the administration even announced its intention to sell the arms. It used a time-tested formula: get insider information on the proposals, give them to the press or friendly Congressmen and use the resulting publicity to generate opposition" (Babcock 1986a).

Collecting information may, however, cross the line into espionage, especially when it involves technology and the military. Paul Findley, a 22-year member of Congress for whose electoral defeat in 1982 the lobby claims credit (L. O'Brien 1986:186; Findley 1985:22), even goes so far as to accuse "U.S. citizens" of penetrating government services for the benefit of a foreign power. He adds: "The practical effect is to give Israel its own network of sources through which it is able to learn almost everything it wishes about decisions or resources of the U.S. government. When making procurement demands, Israel can display better knowledge of Defense Department inventories than the Pentagon itself" (Findley 1985:140–141). It must be added, however, that mainstream opinion in the Jewish community is not ready to admit espionage as a legitimate instrument for expressing identification with Israel, as the Pollard case has shown (Goshko 1987).

In order to fulfill its function, the lobby must not only store information; it must also supply it. A study by the Congressional Research Service on sources of foreign policy information available to members of Congress states that "AIPAC and the other groups comprising the Israeli lobby are as effective as they are in part because of the services they supply to members of Congress and their staffs. These principally involve the production of carefully crafted and packaged information, designed to be of maximum value to a busy legislator" (quoted in Laufer 1987:149). The same study emphasizes that in a situation perceived as a crisis, AIPAC "can put a carefully researched, well-documented statement of its views on the desk of every Senator and Congressman and appropriate committee staff within four hours of a decision to do so" (ibid.; Reich 1984:199). The late senator Frank Church is cited in an AIPAC appeal as having declared: "When I needed information on the Middle East, it was reassuring to know that I could depend on AIPAC for professional and reliable assistance" (L. O'Brien 1986:170).

Douglas Bloomfield, an AIPAC staff member, has written (1983:18–19): "It is common for members of Congress and their staffs to turn to AIPAC first when they need information, before calling the Library of Congress, the Congressional Research Service, committee staff or administration experts." Unable to suppress his pride, Bloomfield continues, "We are often called upon to draft speeches, work on legislation, advise on tactics, perform research, collect co-sponsors and marshal votes."

AIPAC publishes 60,000 copies of a weekly bulletin, *The Near East Report,* which is distributed to members of Congress, among other readers; it covers Middle East events and related congressional activity. This contributes, along with all the other publications of pro-Israeli groups and the near-absence of other sources of information, to fashioning perceptions favorable to unconditional support for Israel. The country is described as the only democracy in the Middle East and as sharing American values; the image attributed to the Arabs and the Palestinians is negative (they are portrayed as anti-Western, feudal, corrupt, and terroristic). In the early 1980s, AIPAC, assimilating the conservative and strategy-oriented attitude of the Reagan administration, published a series of studies glorifying the place of Israel in American strategy and the services Israel could render to Washington, emphasizing the instability of pro-American Arab regimes and the futility of strategic cooperation with them. The lobby's effort to promote a positive image of Israel is supplemented by organized visits to the country for members of Congress and their aides (L. O'Brien 1986:167).

The lobby's efforts to model a favorable perception of Israel further involves formulating value judgments about American individuals and groups. The distribution of labels, such as "great friend of Israel," "enemy of Israel," "Israel's worst adversary in Congress" (used to describe former Senator Charles Percy) (Tivnan 1987:190), "purveyor of Arab propaganda," or even "anti-Semite" (ibid.:54) is a powerful weapon that the lobby sometimes abuses (Rubenberg 1986:336–338). Exploiting negative labels has even become an organized action of the lobby with the publication of a pamphlet entitled *The Campaign to Discredit Israel* (Goott and Rosen 1983), essentially a Who's Who (or blacklist) of American personalities and organizations considered anti-Israeli, which allows grassroots activists to identify them and develop appropriate arguments against them during public debates (Tivnan 1987:183). In a similar vein, we may cite *The AIPAC College Guide: Exposing the Anti-Israeli Campaign on Campus* (Kessler and Schwaber 1984). What is perceived as an anti-Israeli attitude in these two publications is defined in a very broad sense and the methods they use recall, for some, those of McCarthyism (A. Lewis 1984; Findley 1985:35). According to the authors of the first publication mentioned, "promotion of Arab interests becomes an anti-Israeli activity when the main policies being advanced would reduce the security of Israel or weaken the bonds between the United States and Israel" (quoted by L. O'Brien 1986:182).

The application of pressure is organized to a very high degree. As soon as a senator or representative votes against the perceived interests of Israel or shows any hesitation in his or her support to that country, that person can be sure to be flooded, according to the description of Senator Charles Mathias (1981:993), with a "large number of letters and telegrams, or visits and phone calls from influential constituents." The lobby in fact maintains, for each member of Congress, a computerized list of persons who can be mobilized, following an "Action Alert" procedure, in a matter of hours or even minutes, to address a reprimand to a member of Congress or require him or her to reaffirm abiding support to Israel in the terms suggested by the lobby (Laufer 1987:150; L. O'Brien 1986:177; Findley 1985:35). Addressing, in April 1986, the participants of the annual AIPAC conference, Thomas Dine told them about the cancellation of an arms sale to Jordan (1986:136–137):

This did not happen by accident. It came about because you and thousands more like you all around this country worked very hard. You spoke and wrote and phoned and visited your representatives and senators. . . . You articulated your views in an effective manner to your elected officials. That is the essence of the democratic process and it is the essence of AIPAC. It is the essence of America.

The lobby does not always mobilize with the aim of expressing disapproval or applying pressure; it also seeks to reward at the polls attitudes judged favorable. According to a former senatorial aide, "If you vote with them, or make a public statement that they like, they get the word out fast through their own publications and through editors around the country who are sympathetic to their cause. It's an instantaneous reward with immediate positive feedback." (quoted in L. O'Brien 1986:175). In principle, the Conference of Presidents and AIPAC hold to a "bipartisan" policy and do not endorse presidential or congressional candidates. However, the lobby makes it well understood who is considered a "friend" of Israel and who is not, unless the candidates themselves compete for the most fervent pro-Israeli professions of faith. Is it possible to calculate the electoral performance of the lobby? To answer this question, we shall begin by considering two sets of data which are quantitative by nature: the financing of electoral campaigns and the Jewish vote.

The Financing of Electoral Campaigns

AIPAC, as an official lobby, is not authorized to solicit donations for the financing of electoral campaigns. The same is true of any tax-exempt charitable organization, including those of the Jewish community. However, financing can occur, within the limits of the law, through the gifts of persons and of institutions created expressly for this purpose: the political action committees (PACs). A PAC—and AIPAC is not one—is any committee sponsored by a corporation, a labor union, a trade association, or any group of persons that receives contributions and makes expenditures relative to federal elections in excess of $1000 per year (Tivnan 1987:85).

There is no doubt that, as Stephen Isaacs notes, American Jews, thanks to their tradition of contributing to charitable causes, their motivations, their incomes (which are above the national average), and their tendency (again above the national average) to work in professions rather than as wage workers, display an exemplary generosity for the financing of their favorite candidates' campaigns

(Isaacs 1974:115–122). Isaacs also observes a "predominance" of Jewish contributors to the Democratic Party at the national level (121–122). He estimates that two-thirds of the largest contributions (more than $100,000 each) to the presidential campaign of 1972 came from Jewish personalities. According to Earl Raab and Seymour Lipset who wrote in 1985, "more than a majority of Democratic funds on a national level and as much as a quarter of Republican funds have come from Jewish sources" (quoted in Sifry 1988:8).

Since 1974, the date when the Congress voted the Campaign Financing Act among other measures intended to moralize public life after the Watergate scandal, a drastic limit has been placed on the contributions an individual may make for a candidate: $1000 (Tivnan 1987:85). One might have thought that this legislative reform, which was to put an end to the large contributions of certain Jewish donors, would at the same time diminish the influence of the lobby. But nothing of the sort happened; in fact, by all accounts the opposite occurred.

It quickly appeared, indeed, that the PAC system, which had been conceived in the 1940s by labor organizations precisely to counterbalance the influence of the large donors, now made it possible to escape several restrictions imposed by the new law. Although each PAC can give only a limited amount to a given candidate ($5000), nothing prevents the creation of as many PACs as desired, or rather as many as possible. Thus, a single candidate can be financed by several PACs, often located far from his or her home state, and one PAC can finance several candidates at once; as a result, campaign funds may exceed those provided by large contributors in the earlier system. Much depends on the organizational and mobilizing capacities of the groups concerned, especially since the amount each individual is authorized to give is not as unsubstantial as one might first think. If the $1000 limit per candidate is imposed on an individual, that individual may nonetheless give up to $25,000 per year to an array of national candidates. He or she may further give $5000 to a PAC and $20,000 to a party during that same period. Each member of a household, children included, may make equivalent contributions (Tivnan 1987:85, Rubenberg 1986:430). Furthermore, certain types of spending easily escape legal restrictions: for example, spending $1 million in a campaign *against* a candidate perceived as anti-Israeli, while taking care not to espouse the cause of the targeted candidate's rival. This was the case of the campaign against former senator Charles Percy (Babcock 1986b; Tivnan 1987:191).

If organization and mobilization of human resources constitute the two necessary conditions for making PACs an effective financing instrument, it is obvious that the pro-Israeli lobby excels at both. The creation of PACs made it possible for the lobby to reinforce its organization and the degree of mobilization of its activists, and to greatly increase the number of the latter. With the heightened activity of the PACs, which have constituted since the early 1980s one of the main priorities of the lobby, one author could write that there had not been "a better instrument of power for the American Jewish community than the PAC" (Tivnan 1987:85).

By 1982, the lobby had contributed to the constitution of more than 80 PACs; by 1984, there were 75 of them. According to observers, the number of pro-Israeli PACs is perhaps greater still, but the actual number is difficult to determine since in many cases there is no reference to Israel or the Middle East in their name. Here are the names of some of the pro-Israeli PACs that contributed more than $100,000 each to the 1983–84 campaigns: Americans for Good Government, Citizens Organized PAC, Delaware Valley PAC, Desert Caucus, Florida Congressional Committee, Hudson Valley PAC, Joint Action Committee for Political Affairs, NATPAC (which is the most important pro-Israeli PAC and the first among the ideologically oriented PACs), Roundtable PAC, San Franciscans for Good Government, St. Louisans for Better Government, and Washington PAC (L. O'Brien 1986:189–190; Novik 1986:61). The sums offered to electoral campaigns (presidential and congressional) by these PACs have more than doubled during the same period: from $1.87 million in 1982 to $4 million in 1984. In 1988, the pro-Israeli PACs contributed about $5 million (Bard 1991:9). However, in the 1991–1992 election cycle, their contributions declined to about $4 million (Lorenz 1993:27). The recipients included 403 candidates, 264 incumbents and 139 challengers (ibid.).

Although the sums of money contributed by the pro-Israeli PACs are relatively limited, representing only 4 percent of those contributed by the 3000 existing PACs on the American scene in 1984 (Fialka 1985), it seems that the total of donations allocated by American Jews to election campaigns, directly and through PACs, surpasses that rate. But aside from their amount, what makes them effective is the manner in which they are contributed. Financing for a campaign is often introduced early, in favor of a relatively unknown candidate (this is particularly true for presidential elections), at a stage when smaller sums have the most impact; if the candidate succeeds, he or she will be all the more grateful (Tivnan 1987:55, 188). Money is allocated by priority to "sensitive" seats, that is, potential members of the foreign affairs, armed forces, or budget committees (Novik 1986:62). Moreover, given that the lobby already enjoys a majority that is beholden to it in Congress, its finances serve more to punish than to reward. Thus in 1982, to prevent the eleventh re-election of Paul Findley, accused of having met with Yasser Arafat, the lobby mobilized the funds of nearly all the existing pro-Israeli PACs and offered more than $100,000 to a nearly unknown candidate (Halimi 1989:14). There is no need, on the other hand, to finance campaigns for "friendly" candidates whose victory is practically a foregone conclusion (L. O'Brien 1986:184).

Furthermore, the lobby makes use of its officially bipartisan attitude, even though the majority of American Jews tends to vote for the Democrats. To fight against the re-election of Republican Senator Charles Percy in 1984, the lobby co-coordinated both the financing of a Republican rival in the primaries and that of the Democratic candidate in the general election (Halimi 1989:15). Some funds are expressly allocated to districts where the Jewish electorate is practically nonexistent, the aim being to demonstrate that sanction by money can replace sanction by the vote (Findley 1985:44; Novik 1986:62). The lobby concentrates on a single issue—support to Israel—that does not concern the daily lives of voters. The lobby needs, therefore, to make only a marginal financial effort in order to tip the balance on election day (Findley 1985:45). Dine (1986:137) explains the effectiveness of the lobby in the following way: "We are the watchdogs of one key issue, the U.S.-Israel partnership."

Furthermore, the lobby does not arouse the opposition of other influential groups. Morris Amitay, a former director of AIPAC, wrote in 1983: "So far there are no pro-Arab PACs operating. When the oil interests and other corporate interests lobby, 99 percent of the time they are acting in what they perceive to be their own self-interest—they lobby on tax bills, but we rarely see them lobbying on foreign policy issues. In a sense we have the field to ourselves. I think we should take advantage of this" (quoted in L. O'Brien 1986:184). Richard Curtiss, writing a few years later (1989:25), reached the same conclusion, although he contradicts Amitay on certain details: "Arab-American and Muslim-American groups, Jewish peace activists and U.S. business groups seeking to stimulate

trade with Middle East countries have generated over a 12-year period only nine PACs. The only one that has ever made significant
donations is the National Association of Arab Americans PAC
(NAAAPAC). It contributed $17,350 to candidates in 1984, $49,225
in 1986 and some $25,000 in 1988."

The "Jewish Vote"

If money is a key factor in preselecting candidates and reducing
their ranks to the most "respectable" ones, the ballot itself is
nonetheless the decisive test. What is the place of the "Jewish vote"
in the strength of the lobby? Observers agree that considering only
the percentage of Jews with respect to the general population (5.5
million, constituting 3 percent of the total population) does not provide an accurate reading of the actual weight of the American Jewish vote. There are several reasons why:

The American Jewish population is not equally distributed
throughout the states of the union. In, for example, New York, California, and New Jersey, their proportion is significantly greater
than the national average, making their electoral influence greater.
Thus, 12 percent of the eligible voters of New York are Jewish; they
represent about 3 percent in California and 6 percent in New Jersey
(Novik 1986:59–60). Moreover, they are concentrated in the urban
zones of these states, which are the politically most important
areas. New York City is the home of more than 90 percent of the
Jewish population of New York state; Philadelphia is where more
than 70 percent of the Jews of Pennsylvania live; and in Massachusetts, 68 percent of the Jews reside in Boston (ibid.). These states
have a greater weight than many others because of their large number of electoral votes in presidential elections. These factors have a
multiplier effect on the influence of the Jewish vote locally and
nationally (Brenner 1986:120).

American Jews are generally very politicized. More than 90 percent of them actually vote whereas nearly half of all eligible American voters do not take the trouble to cast their ballot (Tivnan
1987:54; Novik 1986:59). This increases the percentage of Jewish
voters by at least one percentage point. This increase is, of course,
greater in the states where Jews are highly concentrated: it rises to
between 2 and 6 percent in New York (Isaacs 1974:6). But the importance of the Jewish vote is even greater at the stage of primary elections. Jews make up fully a quarter of voters participating in the

Democratic primaries of New York, and half of those in New York City (ibid.). According to Raab and Lipset, one must "apply a factor of at least three to the Jewish voting population to find the proportion of Jewish voters in the Democratic primaries" (quoted in Sifry 1988:8). Thus, the choices of Jewish voters in the presidential primaries often determine the name of the Democratic candidate who will enter the race against the Republican.

The Jewish vote gains further influence because it is located at the center of the electoral configuration. Jewish voters tend to be in the center (or more precisely, the center-left), for many reasons related to the history of their integration into American society and the low degree of polarization between right and left. Had they been more peripheral to the configuration (as was the case of the blacks until recently), their electoral weight would have been much weaker. But because American Jews are located at the center of a weakly polarized formation while continuing to vote—despite recent signs of hesitation—for the Democratic party, they are motivated to become a swing vote in favor of one candidate or another. The decisive importance of the swing vote in a close competition is well known: a minimal percentage of votes can often assure victory and thus encourage candidates to make whatever promises necessary to attract the precious votes of the center.

The fact that American Jews are strongly mobilized in favor of Israel often leads them to vote as a bloc for candidates perceived as pro-Israeli and thus gives much credibility to their status as a swing vote. Polls indicate that more than 70 percent of all Jews believe that "the Jews should not vote for candidates who have a hostile attitude toward Israel" (Novik 1986:64). Carter, who in 1976 captured 70 percent of Jewish votes, drew less than 50 percent (the worst score for a Democratic candidate in 56 years) in his reelection bid of 1980 because he was perceived as anti-Israeli by a portion of the Jewish voters (ibid.).

By all indications, in the cases where competing candidates do not appear to have the same attitude regarding Israel, a clear Jewish majority manifests itself and, given the multiplier effects we have mentioned, can be decisive for the results of the election. It must be added, however, that there may be instances where Jewish voters do not have the same perception of the candidate's attitude toward Israel; an example would be that of Carter, hailed by some for his success at Camp David and rejected by others for his position on the Palestinian question. It should also be added that Jewish voters may express a certain weariness when faced with some candidates' pro-Israeli "pandering" (Tivnan 1987:197); the paradoxical effect of this is to neutralize the effectiveness of the Jewish vote. It should finally be mentioned that compared to the highly organized financing of campaigns, the Jewish vote has, and will continue to have, only a relative effectiveness. Financing can be meticulously coordinated by the lobby because it involves a relatively limited number of donors and considers only the candidate's attitude toward Israel. The vote, however, involves millions of Jewish voters whose concerns are not totally centered on Israel and who are not automatons that blindly carry out the directives of the lobby. As Micah Sifry writes (1988:8), "Jewish money is more conservative than the Jewish electorate and does not reflect the debate that takes place within the Jewish community."

We cannot conclude these remarks without noting certain changes whose effects may become apparent in the long term. Because of low birth rates, intermarriage, and "assimilation," the number of Jews in the United States is in constant decline (L. O'Brien 1986:7; Sheffer 1987b:40). In addition, they are leaving the politically important states and the districts of dense Jewish population and becoming dispersed into states and cities where their concentration is low (this often takes the form of migration from the East coast to the "Sun Belt"), and this may diminish their local and national electoral power and lessen their cohesion as a community (Novik 1986:78). With the passing of time, their values (which have traditionally caused them to lean toward the Democratic party), may begin to coincide with their material interests (which would steer them toward voting Republican). That would dissolve a part of their voting power (ibid.:65–67). All this could only constitute a brake, in the long term, on their pro-Israeli mobilization and their effectiveness.

The Electoral Effectiveness of the Lobby

If we understand the idea of electoral effectiveness in a narrow sense, according to which campaign financing and the Jewish vote make a direct difference in a given election, then the only indicators available to us are those concerning the battles the lobby explicitly chooses to wage. Here are a few examples. Of the 31 candidates for the Senate that NATPAC, the most important pro-Israeli PAC, sought to aid in 1982, 28 were elected; for the House of Representatives, the rate of success was 57 out of 73 candidates (Findley 1985:43). That year, the lobby contributed in particular to the defeat of representatives Paul Findley, as we have seen, and Paul McCloskey (L. O'Brien 1986:186; Findley 1985:55–56). In 1984, it waged a successful campaign against the re-election of senator Charles Percy and Roger Jepsen, whom it accused of having voted in favor of the sale of AWACS aircraft to Saudi Arabia in the fall of 1981 (Fialka 1985; Tivnan 1987:188–192). However, the lobby's efforts did not succeed in defeating three other senators, Jesse Helms, Thad Cochran, and Gordon Humphrey, all accused of the same deed (Fialka 1985). Nor did the lobby succeed in bringing about the reelection of representative Clarence Long of Maryland, in spite of exceptional PACs donations amounting to $155,000 (Findley 1985:39).

However, such indicators of the lobby's electoral effectiveness may be misleading, since effectiveness cannot be reduced merely to the cases in which the lobby itself decides to wage campaigns for or against a given candidate. Those candidates the lobby seeks to punish are most often guilty only of committing one or a few mistakes in the context of an overall pro-Israeli attitude. The objective of the lobby in such cases is to deter other members of Congress from succumbing to similar temptations. For this deterrence to work, it need not be effective in every case where the lobby expresses its preferences; it need only be effective in a single, carefully chosen case that serves as an example. This was the case in 1984, with the defeat of Senator Percy, about which AIPAC director Thomas Dine made the following comment: "All the Jews in America, from coast to coast, gathered to oust Percy. And the American politicians . . . got the message" (Tivnan 1987:191).

The electoral effectiveness of the lobby thus goes beyond such cases and must rather be understood in a larger sense that includes cases in which elected officials and candidates, however far away the next elections may be, seek to be in the good graces of Jewish community representatives or defer to the views of the lobby, out of fear or respect. Can one measure electoral effectiveness in this larger sense by correlating senators' and representatives' degrees of support to Israel (as expressed by their voting record on measures concerning Israel) with the size of the Jewish population in a district or the size of Jewish financial contributions? Several authors have attempted to apply this method.

Robert Trice (1977:461), studying the votes of senators between

1970 and 1973, found only a moderate correlation between the index of support to Israel and the size of the Jewish electorate in a given state. According to his findings, the correlation was even weaker between this index and Jewish financial support. David Garnham (1977:32–35), in a study of the 93rd Congress (1973–74), observed that the correlation between support to Israel and the size of the Jewish electorate was positive for representatives but not for senators. This was true, according to Garnham, because a senator represents an entire state, which is more likely to contain a Jewish electorate than a representative's district. Of these 435 districts, at least 50 have no Jewish voters, and in these 50, the representatives have a lower index of support to Israel than the general average. In the case of senators, the size of the Jewish electorate is less relevant because Jewish voters exercise their influence mostly through the intermediary of well-known personalities who lead Jewish associations; because senators are more oriented toward national and foreign policy than toward local politics; and because the Senate, whose members are elected for six-year terms, includes more than a few potential aspirants to the presidency. Representatives, elected every two years, are concerned above all by the tangible (and narrow) interests of their district.

A more recent study by A. F. K. Organski (1990:74) found that the size of the Jewish electorate (for the period 1969–1982) and the rate of campaign contributions from Jewish sources (for the period 1977–1982), "appear strongly connected" to the index of senatorial support to Israel. However, Organski, like the previous authors, observes the presence of a substantial group of senators that strongly support Israel in spite of receiving little Jewish support. The liberal "internationalism" of certain senators (to be distinguished from their "security concerns") would seem a better way to explain their support for Israel than would the Jewish vote or Jewish money (ibid.:75). Does this mean that the influence of the lobby should be sharply minimized? Organski seems to think so. I do not think, however, that this influence can be reduced to the quantitative variations of the Jewish electorate or Jewish financial contributions; the influence of the lobby is also exercised through its organized force as an apparatus.

As an apparatus, it is apparent that the lobby enjoys enormous strength. We could cite innumerable examples, even excepting those that do not explicitly involve a direct submission to the lobby. Here, then, are some recent ones.

In the spring of 1983, AIPAC coordinated the passage of a resolution in the Senate and the sending of a letter from members of the House of Representatives to the President in the aim of stopping an arms sale to Jordan. The scope of this coordination, or rather of this managing role, is expressed in a directive from the lobby to those of its members who were called upon to put pressure on members of Congress: "Both the letter and resolution are being held until after the AIPAC Policy Conference in order to get the maximum number of signatures. The House letter will be sent to the President at the end of this week. The Senate Resolution will be dropped in the hopper at the same time" (quoted in L. O'Brien 1986:178).

In September 1983, Representative Clarence Long proposed an amendment calling for an interruption of funding to the U.S. Marines' mission in Lebanon within 60 days, which would in effect have meant their withdrawal. To one journalist who, surprised at his initiative, asked him if it would not bring him trouble, Long is reported to have replied: "I cleared it with AIPAC" (Findley 1985:39).

In March 1984, Under-Secretary of State for Political Affairs Lawrence Eagleburger negotiated with AIPAC director Thomas Dine a compromise in which the administration would withdraw its project to sell Stinger missiles to Jordan, in compensation for Congressional backing off from a resolution to transfer the American embassy in Israel from Tel Aviv to Jerusalem (Tivnan 1987:198–199). This meant that the lobby was practically negotiating in Congress's name and committing it to a compromise formula. Although such a direct relation between the administration and the lobby generated some tension on the Hill, members of Congress did not publicly display any annoyance (*Congressional Quarterly Weekly Report* 1989:299).

In July 1987, 16 months before the 1988 presidential election, Thomas Dine boasted that almost all the candidates (13 in all, Democrats and Republicans) had personally met with AIPAC officials to present their respective positions on the Middle East (Shipler 1987; Halimi 1989:15). Dine added that any candidate, before making a speech, "could ask our view on the way it would be received in the Jewish community." The AIPAC director further reported that a candidate came to the lobby to ask its view about naming a certain person to a position of high responsibility in his campaign (Shipler 1987).

Finally, in March 1991, 50 senators and 100 representatives felt the need to be present at at least one session of AIPAC's 32nd convention (Fredet and Gilson 1991:11).

The Influence of the Lobby on Foreign Policy

Is it possible to go beyond our examination of the effectiveness of the lobby in the electoral process, largely in the legislative branch, and evaluate the extent to which its influence determines the overall policy of the United States regarding the Middle East and Israel? This question raises the general problem of the relation between the legislative and executive branches and the former's actual participation in determining American foreign policy. Without attempting to treat this general problem here, we may note that it is customarily the executive branch that initiates foreign and defense policy and that Congress participates in a mainly "reactive" way by using (and occasionally increasing, as in the 1970s) its prerogatives in the areas of treaties, arms sales, supervising the conduct of covert operations, war powers and approval of the budget (in particular the defense and foreign aid budgets) (Blechman 1990; Franck and Weisbank 1979; Kegley and Wittkopf 1979:313–324). Congress may also exercise control by holding hearings on foreign policy issues, by demanding that the executive branch submit reports—sometimes periodical ones—on such issues and by provoking public debate on certain subjects, thus shaping public opinion in ways favorable to its views (Collier 1988; Wolfinger 1988:8–11; Rusonik 1990:33). Having noted this, we will limit the following exposition to that which, in the U.S. Middle East policy, appears to result from the influence of the lobby, either on the legislative branch or on the executive branch directly.

It is above all via the budget and the vote on funds for foreign aid that Congress, under the impetus of the lobby, takes part in determining American Middle East policy. The Congress always approves, with a crushing majority, any proposal for aid to Israel and frequently decides to increase the amount asked for by the administration. Between 1969 and 1976, "an average of about 80 percent of the Senate and 86 percent of the House cast votes favorable to Israel" in questions of aid to that country (Feuerwerger 1979:28).

The budget voting process not only provides opportunities for pro-Israeli bidding among members of Congress; it also allows them to address political and diplomatic directives to the administration in the disguise of restrictions imposed on certain expenditures. This was the case, for example, of the Anti-Terrorism Act of 1987, which was included in the credit authorization bill for the State Department and American missions abroad and which enjoined the administration to close the PLO bureaus in Washington and at the United Nations (Abu-Khadra 1988). A refusal by the president to sign the budget authorization bill in order not to comply with such an injunction would have by the same token paralyzed the State Department itself. As is well known, the administration, in spite of objections concerning the international legality of Congress's action, acquiesced and asked the PLO in March 1988 to close its New York mission. Later, however, a federal judge in that city reversed the administration's decision.

Another means by which Congress, urged by the pro-Israeli lobby, intervenes actively in American Middle East policy derives from its capacity to contest arms sales, for which a prior notification by the administration (30 days before the final decision) is required for transactions exceeding $50 million in toto or $14 million for a single type of weapon (Blechman 1990:121). Since the second half of the 1970s, Congressional opposition has manifested itself especially when the arms were destined for Jordan or Saudi Arabia. The only two "fights" waged to the end and won (barely) by the White House over Congressional challenge concerned the sale to Saudi Arabia of F-15 aircraft in 1978 (under Carter) and of AWACS in 1981 (under Reagan). Since that date, the executive has always chosen, at the last minute, not to confront Congress, even if it was already committed to a sale toward the country concerned.

Here, then, are the main channels by which Congress prints its stamp on Washington's Middle East policy at the prodding of the pro-Israeli lobby, and contributes at the same time to "legitimizing" the latter's activities within the American political system (Trice 1977:446). Does the lobby have the same direct influence on Middle Eastern policy-making at the executive level?

It is difficult to cite political initiatives adopted by the executive branch that were directly inspired by the lobby, but one may observe since the 1980s a convergence between the points of view expressed by pro-Israeli think tanks (such as WINEP) and ideas defined by the administration. The Baker Plan of 1989 is one example. If the lobby has a positive, "inspiring" impact on the executive, it is in a broad sense and over the long term, by contributing to the shaping of a "world view" favorable to Israel among future presidents (such as the candidate Reagan) or future administration officials, among other things by edging out the "Arabist" point of view of certain State Department officials.

But it is mainly by sanctions or fear of these that the lobby exercises direct and selective influence on the executive. Administration officials are often forced to retract their words or else suppress certain projected initiatives at the last minute so as not to have to confront the lobby's reactions, which would not fail to manifest themselves in the media, via Congress, and through the mobilization of the Jewish community. Among the examples of the administration's backpedalling as a result of lobby pressure, we may cite president Carter's retreat three days after the signing of the joint Soviet-American communiqué by his Secretary of State on October 1, 1977. There was also the administration's claim that its delegate had voted by mistake in favor of U.N. Security Council Resolution 465 of March 1, 1980 on Israeli colonization of the occupied territories, and that he had intended to abstain (Reich 1984:76).

It should not be thought, however, that the lobby's influence paralyzes the administration in every circumstance. If the White House decides to challenge Congress, the direct pressure it can exert on many members of Congress makes it the most powerful "lobby," as the battle over AWACS shows (Bard 1991:19; Tivnan 1987:161). And when the administration considers that American interests are clearly at stake, it disregards the preferences and wishes of the lobby with relatively little difficulty. This brings us back to our analysis in the previous chapter about the utilitarian perspective: the limits of American permissiveness with regard to Israel (in this case, the limits of the lobby's influence), are constituted by the harm this influence can indisputably provoke under given circumstances. But short of these, that is, if the external (strategic or diplomatic) costs of permissiveness are nonexistent, not manifest, or questionable, nothing induces the decisionmaker to suffer the domestic costs (in electoral or public image terms) of putting pressure on Israel.

Is it possible to make a quantitative measure of the lobby's direct influence on U.S. Middle East policy, just as some have tried to do for its electoral influence? Mitchell Bard (1991) has made such an attempt. Having selected for the 1945–1984 period 782 positions taken by the U.S. government on Middle East affairs (legislative texts, actions, executive declarations), he found that in 60 percent of the cases they were in accordance with those of the lobby. He concludes, rather arbitrarily, that the lobby "wins" 60 percent of the time (1991:267). He recognizes, however, that the best proof of the

lobby's influence in foreign policy resides in the cases where it succeeds in spite of the opposition of the president. If only these cases,
of which there are 297, are taken into account, then the lobby wins
in 27 percent of the cases, and much more frequently on economic
issues than on political ones (270, 278).

Although the methodology employed by Bard is not very convincing, his conclusions confirm that the pro-Israeli lobby, either
directly or via Congress, has a real influence on Middle East policy.
Because of the restrictions the lobby has succeeded in imposing, the
executive's policy is more rigid, its room for maneuver narrower, its
credibility with the Arab states questioned, its pressure on Israel difficult to exercise and its initiatives in favor of a settlement generally timid.

The Validity of the Lobby Explanation

We may now ask whether the lobby constitutes a valid explanation
of American-Israeli relations. It is obvious at the outset that the limits, however slack, of its influence make it impossible to attribute
to it "all" American policy concerning Israel, since cases of American pressure on Israel, disagreements between the two countries,
and certain arms sales to Arab countries must be excluded. The real
question is whether the lobby's influence alone explains the positive and privileged aspect of American-Israeli relations. Although it
is not certain that the information in the previous section allows us
to answer yes, it at least indicates that the influence of the lobby
contributes greatly to the explanation. We know, in particular, that
it helps to explain the more than generous support to Israel; the perception that Israel is an asset for the United States; the timorous
conduct of the executive branch in treating the Israeli-Arab conflict;
and the fact that pressure on Israel must remain within very severe
limits and be exercised in the name of that country's welfare. But it
is hardly possible to impute all this to the lobby.

Why do we have such reservations when, in our earlier exposition, we reached the conclusion that the lobby's electoral effectiveness and its influence on political decisions are impressive? This is
the case because there is a remarkable disproportion between the
intrinsic dimension of the lobby, limited after all in demographic
and even financial terms, and its considerable power. The lobby's
admirable organization, the multiplier factors of Jewish financial
power, and the Jewish vote are not sufficient in themselves to estab-

lish this power. What would be the point of explaining American-Israeli relations by the power of the lobby if this power itself remained unexplained or unexplainable?

It is because the justification of the lobby's power by intrinsic or essentially quantitative criteria is difficult to defend that it is often complemented, more or less explicitly, by an exaggerated idea of conspiracy or threats to American politicians, and by recourse to short-term explanations that anecdotally privilege single events. This point of view has some followers among American, Arab and Israeli leaders because it fulfills a useful function for them (Organski 1990:27ff). For American leaders in their contacts with Arabs, exaggerating the intrinsic role of the lobby makes it possible to dissociate themselves from the pro-Israeli attitude of their administration and to ask their interlocutor for concessions that may help them in their "struggle" against the lobby. When Arab leaders adopt the exclusively lobby-based explanation, it becomes possible for them to defend their pro-American attitude before their constituencies and to sustain the illusion that it would suffice to finance a counter-lobby in Washington, advised by American public relations consultants. As for Israeli leaders, their belief in the omnipotence of the lobby allows them to think that whatever they do, they will always have defenders in Washington to neutralize the administration's attempts to exercise pressure.

The explanations of the lobby's power based on anecdotal and short-term evidence, or on the idea of conspiracy or threat, have no scientific validity, whatever political or ideological function they might fulfill. They cannot explain, for example, the extraordinary competition among senators or representatives to prove who among them is the closest to Israel, the bidding between the two major parties over pro-Israeli electoral platforms, enthusiastic expressions of presidential loyalty to the Jewish state, or media glorification of Israeli military prowess.

The power of the lobby, rather than explaining the privileged character of American-Israeli relations, needs itself to be explained. And it can be explained only by factors external to the lobby—factors that not only constitute reasons for its great success but also contribute in turn to explaining directly the special relationship between the United States and Israel. These exogenous factors may be found in three places: the prestige of the state of Israel, the great-power role of the United States and the ideological and cultural dimension of American society.

There is no doubt that the lobby derives a part of its power from Israel's prestige. Israel has been for the American Jews a mobilizing and unifying cause, a reason for pride, and an object of identification. At the same time, paradoxically, it has been a channel for active integration into American society. The fact that the lobby follows orientations decided by the government of Israel is a source of influence. It is important to note in this regard that just prior to the birth of Israel, a certain power balance reigned within the Jewish Agency between the Yishuv (the Jewish community in Palestine) and the Jewish communities in the rest of the world. But the creation of Israel in 1948 rapidly brought about a total reversal of these institutional relations within world Jewry by giving a preponderant weight to the new state. Today, the lobby's leaders wage their campaigns in Washington in accordance with the agenda, the orientations, and the tactics of the Israeli leaders themselves (Tivnan 1987:60, 71, 174). These campaigns, supported by a prestigious and determined Israel, thus have added impact on American decisionmakers.

This does not mean that the American Jewish community has everything dictated to it, including its most spontaneous reactions and the intensity of its mobilization, by Israeli injunction; that vision would be sociologically absurd. It does mean, however, that the organized action in favor of Israel by a lobby constituted expressly for that purpose is coordinated with Israeli representatives. After all, the lobby's leaders do their work in accordance with their declared objectives when they support whatever Israeli government is in office, right or wrong (Tivnan 1987:175–176; Reich 1984:200–201). As for the American Jewish community, it is led, in spite of its diversity and the reservations of many of its members regarding Israeli policy and the methods of the lobby, to stifle its criticisms before the "united front" constituted by the Israeli government and the lobby so as not to offer arguments to the "enemies of Israel." The American press has often written about this malaise, but its impact on the lobby can manifest itself, under certain circumstances, only over the long term.

If Israel's prestige is a factor in reinforcing the lobby and acts on the United States by this channel, it must also be noted that the Jewish state as a regional power has a direct and unmediated influence on American decisionmakers, as we saw in the previous chapter. To ignore this double track in the relation between the two governments and to amalgamate the two would lead to further exaggeration of the autonomous influence of the lobby on American decisionmakers. Arab and American leaders often complain, for example, that it is not the United States that commands Israel but the opposite, because of the lobby. According to this point of view, without the lobby Israel would have no means of pressure on Washington. I believe, rather, that the American decisionmakers submit to (at least) two types of influence in formulating their Middle East policy. One arises from external strategic determinants, that is, Israel's regional power (and the corresponding weakness of the Arab world), and the other arises from the internal American dynamic in which the intrinsic role of the lobby, reinforced in turn by Israeli prestige, intervenes.

Furthermore, the pro-Israeli lobby derives—or appears to derive— its strength from the superpower status of the United States. A victory by the lobby, even a minute one, in a domestic American battle is multiplied many times when translated into foreign policy because it is then carried forward by all the power of the United States. Not only the lobby's domestic victory, but also its external effects, are attributed to the lobby itself whereas in fact the effects in question are the expression of the world role of the United States. This was true of the period between the two world wars for the influence of the British Jewish community on the great power of that time, the United Kingdom.

There remains a third important factor that tends to strengthen the lobby and that acts directly on decisionmakers to favor a privileged Israeli-American relation: the predominant culture and ideology in the United States. If the lobby has been and remains successful, it is because it plays advocate for Israel in the name of a mutual American-Israeli identification—and because, in so doing, it persuades the public.

The Ideological-Cultural Explanation

The mutual identification of the United States and Israel involves, on the one hand, a perception in American society of the place of the Jewish community within it and is related, on the other hand, to the ideological and cultural basis of the American attitude toward the state of Israel. Before considering these two dimensions, which are of course linked, we shall define the notion of culture (and that of ideology as well), emphasizing only those aspects necessary to our own inquiry.

The Ideological-Cultural Instance

Following Guy Rocher (1968:88), we see culture as "a related set of more or less formalized ways of thinking, feeling and acting which, having been learned and shared by a plurality of persons, serve, objectively and symbolically, to constitute these persons as a particular collectivity." This definition focuses on "ways" of thinking or acting rather than an on enumeration, such as the one attempted by E. B. Tylor, of elements including "knowledge, beliefs, law" and so on (quoted in ibid.:84). Indeed, the explicit contents of beliefs and rules of conduct are not always the most important components of culture. More significant are the common "structures of meaning" (Leca 1988:35) accorded by the members of the collectivity to things and actions. More significant as well is what is "latent" in culture, what refers within it to "implicit structuring models" (Badie 1983:18; J. B. Thompson 1990:136).

Understood in this manner, that is, as implying ways of being and as bearing values, and in a rather latent and implicit sense, culture is what gives the members of a collectivity the spontaneous sentiment that they have a particular identity, a "we" to which the others do not belong (Walker 1984:3–4). It is in the name of this "we" that decisions are taken by those invested with authority in the collectivity. For the members of this collectivity, cultural identity serves to determine what is "moral" and what is not, who is a friend and who an enemy (Booth 1979:24–27), in whose name decisions are made, and for whom or against whom they are made. For analysts and observers, the reference to culture serves to emphasize the relevance of the particular (sometimes expressed with the term ethnocentricity) to the detriment of the universal, and subjectivity to the detriment of rationality. Applied to international relations, this reference serves to suggest that in order to understand the foreign policy of a state, explanations in terms of strategic interests or economism are insufficient.

We do not mean to suggest that we adhere to what is known as the culturalist explanation, understood in an absolute sense: a form of idealism that considers culture as an autonomous sphere influencing economic or power processes without itself undergoing the influence of these. Nor do we wish to adhere to a "reductionism" that sees culture as only an epiphenomenon or mechanical subproduct of economic or power relations. The idea of a "first causality" appears artificial and poses theoretical problems that go well beyond our scope. It is better to speak of a complex, multilevel causality or of "secondary" causalities in the framework of a total social system in which the same element (cultural or "material") can be in one instance a cause and in another an effect, depending on the span of time in question and its degree of stability during (or beyond) that span of time. It is within these limits and following this perspective that we shall try, regarding the American attitude toward Israel, to identify some of the "secondary" causalities at work and to track the connection between culture and strategic rationality.

What we can conclude for the moment is that if the factors that command the historical genesis of cultural identity are not the same for all collectivities (since the respective roles of religion, the mode of production, internal or external coercion, and free choice, may vary in the historical formation of the cultural identity of a group) (Ronen 1979; Ross and Cottrell 1980), and if a collectivity is not necessarily constituted as an autonomous strategic or economic actor by the mere fact of having a cultural identity, it is in any case through this identity that it manifests itself as an actor. Furthermore, the distinction we made above between the "latent" dimension of culture and the explicit content of beliefs and ideas allows us to go beyond what is usually a futile debate between culturalism and reductionism. In Christian or Muslim societies, for example, traditional sacred beliefs clearly are autonomous from modes of production and domination; they even influence these in a way that varies in importance according to the period. But the modes of production and domination in turn mold (or re-mold), in a specific manner for each period, the way in which people experience these beliefs, if not their content as well.

To make this idea more concrete, let us say that what distinguishes two social groups from each other is not so much the differences between their respective beliefs (religious beliefs in particular) as the different modes by which they apprehend these beliefs, even if they happen to have an identical content. Conversely, two religious communities living side by side may, at a certain moment, take part in the same culture. A Sunni Muslim of Lebanon is, from the cultural point of view, probably closer to a Christian of that country than to an Indonesian Sunnite. Maxime Rodinson (1981:99), following the American sociologist Will Herberg, writes, for example, that "the American way of life has changed the very content of the three major religions in the United States: Catholicism, Protestantism and Judaism. Their dogmas and precepts have been reinterpreted so that the three religions have become three languages or three formulations, very close to one another, expressing basically the same ideology." In another passage, Rodinson characterizes an ideology that "transforms the existing ideologies from the inside and makes them compatible even if they are not logically compatible," as an "implicit" ideology (ibid.:69).

Implicit ideology, the latent but essential dimension of culture, must therefore be distinguished from ideology in the usual sense, that is, a set of discourses that can be defined, according to Rocher (1968:100–101), as "an explicit and generally organized system of ideas and judgments that serve to describe, explain, interpret or justify the situation of a group or a collectivity and that, being inspired to a great degree by values, indicates a precise orientation for the historical actions of this group or collectivity" (also Donald and Hall 1986:ix-x). Although the ideology of a collectivity is in certain respects (but not exclusively) an expression of the culture, it is suitable to distinguish the two concepts. Ideology has as one of its functions to justify the stable interests of a social class or group; as a discourse, it makes a claim to be coherent and rational; and it is programmatic. A culture, for the members of the collectivity that claim it, is a "given" condition, so self-evident that it does not need to be justified.

Another dimension of the distinction between culture and ideology must be examined. In the framework of a total society, ideology is often that of the dominant class—the one that controls, as Marx would say, the "spiritual" means of production since it also controls the "material" means of production. Without going as far as certain Marxist authors such as Gramsci or Althusser, who attribute to "dominant ideology" the durable success of capitalism thanks to the dominant class's ability to ideologically integrate the working class, we think that dominant ideology does have the capacity to "inhibit and confuse the development of the counter ideology of a subordinate class" (Bottomore 1980:x) and that it alone enjoys a status of legitimacy and respectability in the overall society. The role of the elite in elaborating the dominant ideology must be stressed here.

These observations do not apply in the same way to culture because it is possible to speak of a "common culture" beyond classes, and of "subcultures" for classes or minorities in the overall culture (whereas the idea of "subideology" makes no sense). If one wishes to speak of a dominant culture, the expression refers less to the domination of a class (in the Marxist sense) than to the extension of the culture from the center toward a periphery that may lie inside or outside the overall society, as in the case of an infra- or trans-state ethnic or religious minority.

The articulation of these common points and distinguishing traits between culture and ideology allows us to understand the notion of *cultural identification* that we will call upon later on. If ideology has an explicit dimension and sees itself as voluntarist and rational, one collectivity may seek to draw closer to another or, on the contrary, underscore its irreducible differences—leaving aside the "objective" proximity or distance between the respective cultures. For ideological reasons (including religion and a certain kind of rationality), a Lebanese Christian, although culturally close to his fellow Sunni citizen, will seek to identify with the West from which he is separated by his very culture of origin. We believe, contrary to the appearance created by terminology, that cultural identification is more a part of the ideological register (an explicit, voluntarist and rational phenomenon) than of the cultural one (latent and implicit). Let us add, however, that generally speaking, it cannot be determined a priori whether a collectivity will seek to identify with another culture or will refuse to do so; whether it will consider it as its "culture of reference" (we allude here to Merton's notion of "reference group" [Merton 1957:225]) or will refuse to do so; and whether it will be permeable to "acculturation" or will resist this process.

What is the relevance of these remarks for explaining American support to Israel and the special relationship between these two countries? The culture and ideology of a group must be considered as a determinant, a cause of decisions—as being able to orient decisions in a direction that might not be expected by observers basing themselves only on the criterion of the apparent "interest" of the group. In this regard, it must be noted that culture and ideology, in the senses defined here, cannot be reduced to arguments, to opportunistic discursive tools to which decisionmakers resort in order to disguise in "warm" terms "cold" interests, seen as the only real causes of a decision. Culture and ideology *as determinants of action* must be distinguished from the effort to "rationalize" or justify decisions after the fact (Morgenthau 1978:121). But if the ideological-cultural instance is a determinant of decision, what exactly is its place with respect to interest? We shall try to answer this question at the end of this section.

American Society and the Jewish Community

The relation between American society and the Jewish community is one of adoption and integration. The Jewish community is considered as sharing all the values of dominant American culture. Its leaders are part of the social and political elite of the United States, and the Jewish community is well-placed in the social scale of religious or ethnic communities in the country. Its respectability is recognized in a way that is not true of the black or Hispanic communities, for example.

Because of the nature of the American political system, weakly polarized between right and left, integrative and at the same time open to religious or ethnic distinctiveness, and for reasons linked to their own history, American Jews are, in turn, satisfied with the fact that the entire political system has historically allowed them to experience socioeconomic mobility and that is has always acted in ways congruent with their interests and values. Although they react with great cohesion on central questions (such as their attachment to Israel), they do not make up a marginal community, turned in on itself, from the political point of view, nor do they feel the need to consider themselves as a minority group concerned above all to elect its own representatives to the legislative bodies in order to protect their group interests.

Of course, if one calculates the proportion of Jewish members of Congress, one will observe that the Jews are now beginning to be "over-represented": 10 senators out of 100 and 33 representatives out of 435 in 1992 (Cohler 1992:15); there were respectively only 3 and 12 in 1974 (computed from Isaacs 1974:235–238). But this "over-representation" has come about quite normally, for it faithfully reflects the difference in socioeconomic status between the "average" American Jew and the "average" American in general. It is above all the sign of a more direct mode of integration of the Jews into political society, after a long period of reticence about elective office and a preference for participating in politics at a lower level (ibid.:198–235).

Another noteworthy, though obvious, fact is that Jewish members of Congress owe their victory to the electorate of their district as a whole, not principally to their co-religionists. They are not perceived—or at least, not so much as blacks—as representatives in Congress of an ethnic minority. It is symptomatic in this regard that the pro-Israeli lobby sometimes does not hesitate to endorse a non-Jewish candidate over a Jewish one (Findley 1985:47; Tivnan 1987:253; Halimi 1989:14; Bloomfield 1983:20). This does not mean that the Jewish community fails to react as such to foreign events, nor that Jewish elected representatives fail to identify strongly with the values of their community, and in particular to Israel. It does mean that, for American voters, Jewish candidates are preferred or rejected according to their positions on a wide range of questions; the fact of being Jewish and identifying with Israel has no more than a marginal incidence on the people who vote for them (Wolfinger 1988:11).

In any event, Jews, as they participate in the political process, are becoming more and more confident and self-assured. It is because they are so confident in the system that they can allow themselves to add to their socioeconomic and ideological preferences the requirement that candidates adopt a positive attitude toward Israel. Further, the Jewish community, in appealing for defense of the Israelis as survivors of Nazism, encounters a favorable echo with Americans, who have the collective memory of having fought the war to save the Jews from Nazi massacres—which was not exactly true historically, as David Wyman demonstrated in *The Abandonment of the Jews* (1984). This echo is perhaps, by reaction, more favorable among those who believe that the United States did not do enough for the Jews during the war.

One cannot stress enough the importance of the American (and Western) experience during World War II—the massacre by the Nazis of the European Jewish communities, the civilian and military losses suffered by the Allies in combat, but also the final victory—as a factor explaining extreme sensitivity in American society regarding anti-Semitism. This sensitivity is especially marked in veterans of the war and in certain "philo-Semitic" Christian groups deeply attached to the Old Testament (Sheffer and Hofnung 1987a:11–12). Members of the American sociopolitical elite are imbued with this sensitivity, which has become a central and even sacralized value within the political system; it manifests itself positively in the fear of a return of the "demons" of Nazism and negatively in the fear of being labeled anti-Semitic.

It must be added, however, that the American and Western rejection of anti-Semitism (as this rejection has manifested itself since

World War II) belongs more to the ideological (voluntarist and explicit) register than to the cultural (spontaneous) one. Although questioning the respectability of the Jewish community has no legitimacy whatsoever, this does not mean that anti-Semitism has disappeared in the United States. The rejection of anti-Semitism by the elite is limited in many cases to public life. One need only recall, to illustrate this point, the "private" expression of anti-Semitism by Richard Nixon, who nonetheless granted, in the five years and seven months of his presidency, more aid than all his predecessors combined over the previous 20 years. The American and Western rejection of anti-Semitism is thus not yet totally spontaneous and serene. Might this explain a certain compensatory attitude that leads Americans to acquiesce without criticism to the pro-Israeli appeals of the lobby? Whatever the case may be, and as the two Israeli authors Sheffer and Hofnung write (1987a:12), "it is undeniable that guilt feelings, pro-Israeli tendencies and philo-Semitism are closely related" (also Reich 1984:186; Safran 1978:572).

American Society and the State of Israel

Numerous polls show that American public opinion is much more favorable to Israel than to the Arab countries (Rosen and Abramowitz 1984; Gilboa 1987). It would be of little interest here to review the questions asked in these polls and the answers they elicit, particularly since public opinion polls raise theoretical and methodological problems that fall outside the domain of this study (Moughrabi 1988:134–136; Zureik and Moughrabi 1987). It is especially difficult to attach the same meaning to propositions as different as having a positive image of Israel (the most pertinent question for our inquiry); considering Israel as an ally; considering it as a "friendly state"; acquiescing to economic and military aid; supporting the idea of a military intervention to defend Israel against the Arabs, and so on. Finally and above all, one might ask whether the answers given, and their variations over time, do not reflect a great vulnerability of public opinion to the influence of governmental and media attitudes and opinions. Is public opinion, as expressed in the polls, the cause of the product of the attitudes of decisionmakers?

To avoid these pitfalls, it is preferable to pay more attention to "informed" opinion, that of "leaders in government, in the Foreign Service, and the military, as well as non-governmental ones in the media, labor unions, corporations, universities, churches and elsewhere" (Holsti and Rosenau 1984:20). It is not original to observe that this elite is traditionally and spontaneously pro-Israeli, but more precise data on this subject are provided in a survey conducted by Ole Holsti and James Rosenau in 1976 and 1980 about the elite's attitudes toward the lessons of the Vietnamese experience. The authors' objective was to establish a correlation between the opinions that 2500 respondents held about the Vietnam war and their political and ideological affiliations. They succeeded in establishing such a correlation, but discovered (1984:97) that "a notable exception to this pattern concerns the survival of Israel. Not only did a strong majority approve of an American commitment to this end" but "the issue of Israel appears to cut across rather than along the lines of cleavage." Whatever their opinion may have been on other questions, three quarters of the respondents considered that the United States had "a moral obligation to prevent the destruction of the state of Israel" (ibid.:239). The authors have planned to renew the same inquiry every four years. The 1988 study shows the same results for Democrats or "liberals" (75 percent) but a lesser proportion of Republicans or "conservatives" (66 percent) (Holsti and Rosenau 1990:586–587).

This answer, expressing the respondents' values, should be compared with that expressing their perception of American interests. To a question about what American policy in the Middle East should put its primary emphasis on, only 7 percent of this elite— one learns with astonishment—mention safeguarding Israeli security, whereas 51 percent wish to maintain an effective balance of power in the region, 21 percent to prevent expansion of Soviet influence, 7 percent to ensure the friendship of oil-exporting states, and 6 percent to procure a homeland for the Palestinians (Holsti and Rosenau 1984:238–239). For these "opinionmakers," perhaps more than for Americans as a whole, the pragmatism that guides them in determining (or changing opinions about) the interests of their country in the region does not preclude a spontaneous expression of pro-Israeli attitudes. This fact confirms our earlier observations about the concern not to abandon Israel on the part of the same people who consider that country a strategic burden.

As a value, the favorable attitude toward Israel is based on the ideological-cultural instance. Several elements of this register contribute to shaping the pro-Israeli attitude of the American social and political elite.

First of all, Israel perceives itself and is perceived as being a part of European and Western culture. It identifies and is identified with the West and its Judeo-Christian heritage. It is interesting to note in this regard that although Zionism and the creation of Israel signified in a certain sense the rejection of the Jews by the Europeans and concomitantly, the refusal of Jews to assimilate in Europe, the Yishuv and Israel are nonetheless seen as belonging to Western civilization. This phenomenon is also found in South Africa, where the Afrikaaners, although their departure from the Netherlands in the eighteenth century is justified by the idea of a distinct "mission," and despite the Boer war against Great Britain, have never ceased to feel an integral part of the white Western world. Perhaps the perception of the Arab-Muslim world in one case and the African world in the other as different and hostile helps them rediscover points in common with the culture they thought they had rejected.

This identification with European culture, civilization, and political and social values is not exclusively Israeli or South African; it embraces other extra-European countries governed by people of European origin, or considered as European. What seems to be most important in the distinction between European and non-European is not only the historical belonging to one or another ensemble, but also (and perhaps especially) the self-perception and perception by others of this belonging (Singer 1972:130). In particular, and regarding the United States and Israel, the feeling of being a part of a European "we," although it contains many cultural elements in common, does not so much express a common and uniform culture (Rubenberg 1986:335) as a cultural identification which is, as we have seen, of an "ideological" nature, that is, voluntaristic and explicit. This remains true even when one considers that perhaps 60 percent of the Jews of Israel originate from Arab or Muslim countries (Patai 1970). This is the case because Israel was founded and remains under the leadership of a mainly Ashkenazi elite and because the "Orientals" have only gradually—and insufficiently—been recruited to the leadership ranks. This accession to the elite has taken place so far in more of an individual than a "community" manner and has tended to lead Oriental Jews in turn to internalize an identification with the West. Another factor reduces the extent of the "Orientalization" of Israel: the progressive Americanization of society, as manifested in film, television, modes of consumption and the liberalization of the economy (Roshwald 1974:85; Sheffer 1987b:37).

If we now turn to the United States, we will observe along with

William Quandt (1977:16) that "a predisposition no doubt exists in American political culture that works to the advantage of the Israelis." The conquest of the Western frontier of North America is seen as analogous to the Zionist colonization of Palestinian lands (Safran 1978:572). "The Israeli," writes Zweig (1969:261), "is a frontier man like the American once was. Both had to fight against hostile indigenous population, although both came with good intentions" (also Reich 1984:186). We have noted in chapter 2 how Aaron Wildavsky, describing pro-Israeli American values, remarked that they were not necessarily based on universal moral principles. Peter Grose (1983:316) described the American perception of Israel very suggestively:

> Liking it or not, Americans who are willing to look see something of themselves in Israel. . . . As the Judaic heritage flowed through the minds of America's early settlers and helped to shape the new American republic, so Israel restored the vision and the values of the American dream. Each, the United States and Israel, grafted the heritage of the other onto itself.

The American-Israeli "congruence of values" manifestly excludes the Arabs. Here is how Michael Hunt (1987:177) describes the exclusion of those who are considered outside the American "we": "The paternalism and contempt evident in the Vietnam 'adventure' testifies to the continuing influence of culture-bound, color-conscious world view that still positions nations and peoples in a hierarchy defined at the extremes by civilization and barbarism, modernity and tradition. It renders us sympathetic to forward-looking Israelis, seen largely as Europeans, at loggerheads with swarthy, bearded, polygamous, fanatical Arabs. It supports empathy with civilized white South Africans rather than a black underclass barely removed from their 'primitive' tribal origins."

The elites of the United States and Israel thus have a spontaneously "Orientalist" attitude toward Muslims and Arabs. And American opinion sides spontaneously with Israel in its conflict with its neighbors. What is perceived by the Arabs and Third World peoples as Israeli intransigence is spontaneously seen by Americans as an Israeli struggle for survival. Israel is like a piece of the West in the Middle East; it symbolizes the possibility of a continuing world role for the West after the proclaimed end of colonialism. The favorable image of Israel is reinforced by the media and by Israeli success in the area of communication (Rubenberg 1986:15; Curtiss 1986:307–326).

American identification with Israel is even more marked in certain specific social sectors such as the Christian fundamentalists and evangelists, for whom Israel is fulfilling an eschatological mission (Drinan 1977; Halsell 1986; Mouly 1982). The most renowned figure of the Christian fundamentalists in the 1980s, was Jerry Falwell, leader of the "Moral Majority," a far-rightist whose televised sermons broke all records for audience appeal (Falwell 1980; Falwell, ed. 1981). These "Zionist Christians," even support the idea of "Greater Israel," that is, the annexation of the West Bank, because the restoration of Biblical lands to Israel announces, in their view, the second coming of Christ (Tivnan 1987:181; Sheffer and Hofnung 1987a:12–13; Stockton 1987).

What is surprising is that these Christians have in their ranks many anti-Semites or persons imbued with an anti-Semitic "cultural heritage." What is even more astonishing is that the director of the Anti-Defamation League of B'nai B'rith, Nathan Perlmutter, has criticized Rabbi Alexander Schindler for having warned against relying on the pro-Israeli attitude of Christian fundamentalists (Stockton 1987:243). Perlmutter has come to prefer the intolerance of the fundamentalists, combined with their pro-Israeli attitude, to the tolerance of the more liberal Protestants, combined with their critical attitude toward Israel. He writes (1983:14): "Liberal Protestantism's tolerance is not so helpful to us as its political hostility to Israel is damaging to us. Fundamentalist religious conceit is currently not so baneful as its friendship for Israel is helpful."

It is interesting to note that fundamentalist support to Israel converges with that of the "new right" of the Republican party, which contributed to the electoral successes of Ronald Reagan and George Bush. The new right, of course, justifies its pro-Israeli stance on the grounds that Israel constitutes a strategic asset for the United States. The point of departure of the "strategic" discourse of this wing of the Republican party is eminently ideological and subjective, by no means based on a pragmatic evaluation of the complex Middle East situation. The tendency to expound a military-strategic discourse must thus be considered as belonging sometimes to the ideological-cultural register. This tendency reached its zenith in the first years of the Reagan presidency. The "demonization" of the Soviet Union, the faith in "resurgent (and re-armed) America," identification with the self-confident and omnipotent Israeli ally, all came together with élan.

This type of identification with Israel competed, for the first time with so much force, with another theme in American dominant ideology, and one that was traditionally rooted in the Democratic party: identification with the Jewish state as a matter of "moral obligation." Whether the discourse defines itself as strategic or as humanist, the valorization of Israel is in any case affirmed. As we shall see, however, each of these discourses carries within it the seeds of a more critical attitude toward Israel.

The Ideological-Cultural Factors Unfavorable to Israel

In the American ideological-cultural register, there are not only elements favorable to Israel. Culture and even ideology, in spite of the latter's pretensions of coherence, contain contradictory values or values whose implications for action may be in opposition as soon as a concrete situation arises. In a society, values may be in contradiction with each other not only between conflicting social groups (classes, ethnic minorities, etc.), but also within a group, however homogeneous it may be, or within a single individual. Here we may speak of a latent and possibly intense competition of values.

Some examples will help to illustrate this point. The discourse that claims to be humanist and universalist and is developed by a trend within the Democratic party, although it justifies its pro-Israeli attitude by a "moral commitment," must necessarily contain the seeds of a commitment to human rights or to the right of self-determination in the occupied territories. A pro-Palestinian humanistic sensibility was already perceptible among party activists during the presidential primaries of 1988 (Sifry 1988:9–10). As for the strategic-ideological discourse of a wing of the Republican party, it may also find itself in perilous competition with another strategic discourse that invokes the priority to be accorded to American "national interest" over that of Israel, or even "national pride," as during the struggle over the AWACS sale in 1981 between President Reagan and the lobby. To make the opponents of the sale of these aircraft to Saudi Arabia yield, the allies of the president called on senators to choose between "Reagan or Begin" (Tivnan 1987:135–161).

If we now turn to the American groups that question the idea of blind support to Israel because of their "universalist, humanitarian tendencies" (Sheffer and Hofnung 1987a:21), we will find that it includes certain sectors of the Catholic community (in particular a portion of the hierarchy), the Protestant community (such as the Quakers), and even members of the Jewish community (Jailer and McAlistair 1989:275–299). We can also cite Arab-Americans, whose influence, while still minimal, is no longer seen as illegitimate. However, it is the black community that is the most notable here. It has a quite ambiguous view of Israel; it is not very sensitive to the dominant Western position on the question of anti-Semitism and a great number of its members identify more easily with the fate of the Palestinians.

It must be recognized that these elements of challenge to the identification with Israel are mostly latent or situated at a low rank in the scale of values within the American elite or are expressed only by groups that do not belong to the elite, or are at least not at its core. We shall inquire further as to whether the emergence and the reinforcement of these values are possible and under what conditions. For the moment, we must observe that the ideological-cultural elements favorable to Israel remain predominant in the final analysis. The members of the Democratic party taken as a whole are quite distant from a pro-Arab sensibility; and in the event that their proclaimed universalism leads them to a recognition of Palestinian rights, they will do this in the name of protecting the long-term interests of Israel. As for the ideologues of the Republican party, they have not ceased during the 1980s and early 1990s to speak of Israel as a strategic asset, in spite of the misfortunes of that idea in actual Middle Eastern practice (in Lebanon, on the West Bank, in the Gulf, etc.).

As for nonidentification with Israel in non-elite groups, such as the black or Arab communities, two examples help to demonstrate its limited importance. When leaders of the black community succeed in being co-opted by the elite, their new respectability requires them to moderate their pro-Arab attitude and to make a step toward Israel: because Jesse Jackson was more credible as a candidate in the presidential campaign of 1988 than in that of 1984, he also distanced himself more from Arab positions (Sifry 1988:5). This was also the case of John Sununu, an American of Arab origin, who had to declare that he harbored no anti-Israeli sentiments as soon as he was chosen as a candidate for the position of White House chief of staff under president-elect Bush (*International Herald Tribune* 11/18/88). These two examples illustrate quite clearly the relevance of the idea of dominant ideology.

The Ideological-Cultural Instance and the Lobby

Since it contains many decisive elements that explain the American identification with Israel and with the American Jewish community, the dominant culture and ideology explain at the same time the inordinate influence of the lobby, that is, the disproportion between its intrinsic dimensions and its apparent power. If candidates to elective office attempt to outbid each other in declaring their support for Israel, and if, at certain times, politicians feel their electoral future threatened because of their failure to take pro-Israeli positions, it is not only because the lobby threatens sanctions or decides to use them, but especially because the dominant culture and ideology generally permit and legitimate such action. For similar reasons, there has not been a durable consolidation of interest groups (e.g., the Arab-American community, oil companies, business circles) more favorable to the Arabs and capable of gaining the support of a respectable portion of the political elite, in the name of Arab identification with the United States or of American values. An ideological-cultural environment favorable to the lobby is a necessary if not a sufficient condition for its development.

One cannot deduce from this, however, a mechanistic and always harmonious relationship between the legitimation accorded to the lobby by the social system and the means of action the lobby utilizes. At a given moment, the ideological-cultural instance is a condition under which the lobby, as a hierarchical organization operates. Because the lobby is an organization, its decision-making process, which can be analyzed from the viewpoint of the sociology of organizations, takes place in the framework of a "system" that enjoys a certain autonomy within its environment. Its internal decision-making may or may not be adapted to the requirements of the environment—dysfunction is possible—and readaptation acceptable to the environment may not occur before a more or less lengthy series of negative feedbacks. Additionally, since the pro-Israeli lobby is hierarchical, its leaders are liable to make bad calculations, follow their passions, or conform to directives that have their source neither within the Jewish community nor in the American environment, but rather in Israeli contingencies. It is thus not possible for all the resulting decisions to be acceptable to the ideological-cultural environment.

Therefore, while the power of the lobby may be explained in terms of American identification with Israel and the Jewish community, this does not mean that the decisions and the means of action of the lobby are always and automatically adapted to what constitutes the very base of that identification. It is not certain, in particular, that the threats and sanctions the lobby may institute against those who do not follow its injunctions are always in harmony with the dominant American culture and ideology. The media reported news of sanctions relative to cases that in Israel itself would have been the subject of debate. It has often been said in this regard that it is easier to criticize the official policy of the Israeli government in the Knesset than in the United States Senate (*Congressional Quarterly Weekly Report* 1989:298–299).

The gap between American values and the lobby's excessive recourse to threats is suggested by an American legislative aide in these terms: "Too many senators are playing along out of fear or expediency. If I were the Israelis, or the lobby, I would not want my support built on fear and political expediency" (quoted in Tivnan 1987:257). Because of its extravagant quest for technical professionalism and short-term effectiveness, AIPAC, as the major apparatus of the lobby, has become a machine detached from the pro-Israeli roots of American society. For one former Pentagon and White House official, the problem is "not that AIPAC has become too powerful. The problem is that it's out of control. It is a self-stimulating machine with no corrective device" (quoted in Tivnan 1987:255).

For some American Jews, the lobby, seen in this way, is becoming a stranger to its own community base. By justifying solidarity with Israel with arguments that are more "strategic" than "moral," and by turning to the right in its themes and alliances, and by discouraging all criticism of Israel within the community, the lobby does not appear to be respecting the traditional diversity of American Jewry, the basic motives of their support for Israel, and the identification of many of them with American humanistic causes such as the rights of minorities and equal opportunity (Tivnan 1987:252; *Congressional Quarterly Weekly Report* 1989:297).

Arthur Hertzberg, former president of the American Jewish Congress and vice president of the World Jewish Congress, has even declared that the lobby is no longer an expression of Jewish or Judeo-American values: "The AIPAC people are hardly Jewish. They certainly don't know anything about Judaism, or Zionism for that matter. What kind of Jewish education do they have? They're lobbyists who could lobby for just about anything, except perhaps the Arabs."

Hertzberg adds that the lobby "is creating more anti-Semites than it's scaring away" (quoted in Tivnan 1987:165). The same Jewish leader explains elsewhere that this is the case because the lobby "pushed the American consensus beyond its limits" (ibid.:256). A former AIPAC director, Morris Amitay, involuntarily acknowledges that such American Jewish critics are right when he says of the lobby's action: "Moral authority has very little influence in politics" (ibid.:193).

In conclusion, let us say that if the ideological-cultural instance in American society contributes (along with other factors examined above, such as Israel's regional power or the United States' world power) to explaining the excessive influence of the lobby, this does not mean that it explains the sometimes reckless use of that influence. This reckless use, which can only be explained with recourse to a sociology of organizations, may indeed, in the long term, undermine the lobby's societal foundations. It has in any event provoked tensions and even resignations from AIPAC, such as that of Douglas Bloomfield, whom we quoted earlier in this chapter, in late 1988 (*Congressional Quarterly Weekly Report* 1989:297–301). A lobby such as AIPAC, whatever its specific means of action may be, cannot long remain powerful and organized if it becomes isolated from the values of society and if its image deteriorates durably. For the moment, however, and in spite of the criticisms that have been addressed to it by many Americans including Jewish Americans, it appears to be applying minimal corrective measures so as not to stray too far from the limits of the acceptable in the ideological-cultural environment. It is too early to tell whether these minimal efforts will suffice.

The Ideological-Cultural Instance and the Idea of Interest

All in all, it may be said that certain elements at the heart of the American ideological-cultural register, as well as the action of the lobby, engender a predisposition or spontaneous attitude in favor of Israel and thus do not fail to influence political decision-making. These elements may account for the privileged character of American-Israeli relations and Washington's permissiveness and unwavering support to Tel Aviv—but to what extent? Does the influence of the pro-Israeli predisposition make itself felt *in spite of* what is commonly called interest, or at least without taking it into consideration? The question being raised here is that of the relation between the ideological-cultural instance and interest, that is, between the domestic dynamics explanation and the instrumental explanation examined in the previous chapter.

Let us state at the outset that culture belongs to the register of "being," whereas interest belongs to that of "having." Even if we consider decisionmakers as rational actors, capable of making decisions that maximize their advantages, and even if we reduce interests to what we have called "essential interests" or "nondamages," it is through their identity that the decisionmakers perform and make choices as strategic actors. The centrality of the ideological-cultural instance is all the more manifest when we recall that decisionmakers are not purely rational beings and are not merely pursuing "essential interests"; they have a subjective vision of these and must take into account "immaterial" interests such as prestige, the credibility of their own declarations, and the support of public opinion (which can be manipulated only within certain limits). The ideological-cultural instance is the enduring "matrix" in which their behavior evolves and their decisions (or strategy, that is, a whole set of decisions) germinate (Atkinson 1981:24).

The pro-Israeli predisposition as a central element of the ideological-cultural instance seems therefore to be a stubborn and enduring given that "precedes" any consideration of interest, any concern with cost or damage. Its object—Israel—is intimately linked to the European and Western history of a world role that has lasted several centuries. Moreover, if strategy is tied to the identity of a social group as a whole, one may say as well that cultural identification causes people to perceive that those with whom they identify are also contributing to their own strategy. By taking part in the "being" of American society, Israel also participates in its integrity and its defense. Does one think spontaneously of costs when the problem is to defend one's being, one's space, one's border?

It is because this is true—because strategy is tied to cultural identity—that it can remain, like the policy that it inspires, relatively stable, even if material interests are ephemeral. Moreover, when interest is difficult to evaluate objectively from the point of view of pure rationality and becomes the object of debate and uncertainty, as in the debate between the idea of Israel as a strategic asset and that of Israel as a burden, political actors follow the strategy most in conformity with their identity and ideology. This idea accords with that of Alexander George, who writes (1987:7) that "one of the functions of ideology generally in decision-making is to help policymakers to cope with critical uncertainties that stem from the well-known 'cognitive limits' on rationality." Since they cannot decide rationally whether supporting Israel against its neighbors promotes or undermines American interests, they follow their spontaneous pro-Israeli sentiments and the persuasive force of the lobby.

However, decisions are not mere mental acts and cannot be separated from their positive or negative effects on reality. What is remarkable in the American-Israeli case is that the pro-Israeli policy, decided upon in spite of the uncertainty as to its fruitfulness, proves most often, after the fact, not to be harmful to the United States overall (that is, it is "utilitarian" in the sense we discussed in the previous chapter). The ideological-cultural identification is not only not challenged, but is in fact comforted in its original "good conscience" and optimism. Allusion is made here to the optimism of American liberalism, to what is called American "exceptionalism" (Hoffmann 1980:6). Two sets of factors, one domestic and ideological-cultural (to which the lobby should be added) and the other external and utilitarian, coincide in producing, over time, an effective American policy favorable to Israel. These two sets of factors are thus congruent, but if they must be arranged in an acceptable conformation, it seems to me that primacy belongs to the ideological-cultural instance. The reason is that this instance contributes to the validity of an explanation by the "cause" (the internal American dynamic, cause of the support to Israel) whereas the utilitarian instance establishes only, as we noted at the end of the last chapter, the relative validity of an explanation by the "effect."

If the ideological-cultural instance and the utilitarian instance remain congruent, instrumentality (and no longer just utility) may, over time, affirm itself in turn, at least for a portion of the decision-makers and members of the elite who gravitate around them. American support to Israel which, at its origin, was caused by a pro-Israeli predisposition may, in certain periods, be integrated into an explicit doctrine and an instrumental practice by the decisionmakers. This idea is illustrated by the following reflections of Kissinger and Shultz—reflections that appear to correspond partially to their actual behavior. For Kissinger (1982:203–204), "Israel's security could be preserved in the long run only by anchoring it to a strategic interest of the United States, not to the sentiments of individuals." As for Shultz, he is reported by AIPAC director Dine (1986:139) to have said (possibly in 1985 or 1986) that the objective of the American-Israeli strategic cooperation relaunched in 1983 was to "build institutional arrangements so that eight years from now, if there is a Secretary of State who is not positive about Israel, he will not be able to overcome the bureaucratic relationship between Israel and the United States that we have established."

Kissinger and Shultz are perhaps expressing here the fear that the pro-Israeli predisposition in the United States is precarious (which I do not believe to be true, as I have tried to demonstrate in this chapter). But they seem also to recognize that it is this predisposition, and not an "objective" strategic interest, that is at the origin of the "strategic" content of their policies. In any event, what emerges clearly from these statements by two Secretaries of State and from the preceding paragraphs is that the lobby, ideological-cultural identification, utility (including, sometimes, instrumentality) and bureaucratic ties mutually reinforce each other. However, this idea of mutual reinforcement does not constitute in our view an explanation of the basis of privileged American-Israeli relations, but rather a partial explanation of their constant perpetuation.

The partial and incomplete character of the explanation in terms of the mutual reinforcement of the different factors becomes apparent if we try to account for the (usually marginal) opposition that may occur between identification with Israel and protection of American interests in the Arab world, that is, when the utility of a pro-Israeli policy is not verified. It seems to us that to the idea of mutual reinforcement between the ideological-cultural instance and the utilitarian one should be added that of mutual "control" or mutual limits. In other words, each of the two instances imposes limits on the other when, outside their common area, a marginal opposition appears to manifest itself between them. These reciprocal limits would appear to work as follows. Because of cultural identification, American policy in the Middle East must never have—and has in fact never had—the alternative of ending support to Israel; pressure on Israel must be a last resort; it must remain moderate and be applied in the name of the welfare of the Jewish state itself. Because of the utilitarian concern (fear of damage to U.S. Arab interests), support to Israel must sometimes be tempered with an effort to persuade or apply pressure; permissiveness must give way to control. As Lily Feldman has written (1984:270), the essential characteristic of the special relationship between two countries is "their ability to overcome crises in which the interests of the two partners seem opposed."

Let us state in passing that the reasonable explanations proposed by authors such as Stanley Hoffman (1980:296), Abraham Ben-Zvi (1984:5–7) and William Quandt (1977:24) are located at this level of

analysis. These three authors bring into play strategic considerations and the internal dynamic simultaneously. The first two speak
of mutual American-Israeli deterrence, while the third speaks of
"external limits" imposed by the American societal dynamic on the
president's freedom of action.

The idea of reciprocal limits within the framework of the conformation proposed (primacy of the ideological-cultural instance over
the utilitarian one and complementarity between the two) raises the
question of the consequences of change in one of the instances for
the other, and more fundamentally, the possibilities for change in
American policy. How can American-Israeli relations, rooted as
they are in a cultural identity, remain privileged if American interest comes to require the contrary? Or conversely, can there be a
change in ideological-cultural values that would lead to a change in
the quality of relations between the two countries and the nature of
American political decisions affecting Israel?

In response to the first question, let us say that there can be a
change in policy only if the perceived interest that opposes ideological-cultural values emerges from the area of uncertainty and
debate. The interest that causes cultural values to be sacrificed
must appear not only *indisputable* and *clear-cut* but also *of major
import, unavoidable,* and *irreversible.* Cultural values resist policy
changes longer and more fiercely than could be expected from the
prospect of a change of interest understood in terms of material cost
and benefit. In France, for example, identification with the idea of
"French Algeria" did not cease to predominate in political decision-
making until the loss of Algeria began to appear inevitable, after
several years of deep internal crisis—and even then it remained very
much alive.

A change in policy, which thus cannot occur unless a profound
and unavoidable change in interests occurs, can further lead to the
conciliation of values earlier considered contradictory, to an amendment to the hierarchy of values, or even, but with greater difficulty,
a change in values. In every society, a major change of strategy must
be legitimized in moral terms; the justifying values must come from
within the culture itself. In this process, the values that up to now
have been marginal or remained at the bottom of the scale and
defended only by "nonrespectable" groups, will be favored. This
process, which may involve a real intrasocietal struggle, may lead
for some to a political defeat and the marginalization of the values
they have defended and for others to an opportunistic conversion to

the newly dominant values—a conversion ascribable to rationalizing.

Thus a change in American policy made imperative by a decline in the United States' world status (comparable to that of Great Britain after World War II or the Soviet Union at the beginning of the 1990s), or an irreversible modification in the balance of forces between Israel and the Arab countries, or the perception that the establishment of a Palestinian state in the occupied territories was inevitable, would bring the American political system to "rediscover" universal values it had neglected—at least where the Arabs were concerned: the legitimacy of reparations for a historical injustice, the self-determination of a people, the recovery of occupied territories and so on. It must be added, however, that even in the extreme case of a modification of the balance of forces, American support to Israel would always be considered as a moral commitment, but in practice it would become conditional and take the form of vigorous American action in favor of a final settlement of the Israeli-Arab conflict combined with the granting of a treaty of guarantee to Israel. As for the consequences of a decline of the U.S. world status, we shall not hazard to speculate about it, even though the upheavals in the former Eastern bloc show that nothing is permanent in this world.

Could one envision the opposite case, that is, a change in policy that did not originate from the imperious necessity of a vital interest but from the modification of dominant values? In theory it could be imagined, but in practice it is to be excluded for the United States. Only revolutions can modify dominant values abruptly. All that could be envisioned regarding the U.S. policy in the Middle East would be a slow evolution of values within the American Jewish community itself. An evolution within this community concerning the centrality of Israel—the emergence, for example, of a greater diversity of views and greater understanding of the cost for the Palestinians of the founding of the Jewish state—might cause the influence of the lobby to erode, the ideological-cultural instance of American society to change course, and American policy, thereby, to support Israel on a more conditional basis (Slater and Nardin 1991:93).

Conclusion

Several conclusions can be drawn from the preceding development. First of all, we may note that the ideological-cultural instance, through the certainties it engenders, is the matrix in which strategy is defined, especially when the interest linked to it is rationally uncertain. Next, we may state that interest prevails over the ideological-cultural instance only in the final analysis—only if it is a major and imperious interest. Finally, we may affirm, concerning American policy toward Israel, that the ideological-cultural and utilitarian instances go more or less in the same direction, but each one imposes on the other limits that must not be exceeded. Generally, however, and probably as long as Israeli regional superiority endures, instrumentality and cultural identification reinforce each other. That is why the instrumental interpretation of events and the ideological-cultural one are both possible, and that is why it is difficult for the observer to determine the nature of the special relationship between the two countries.

To state that the cultural instance is the matrix in which American policy favorable to Israel is determined, is not to require a belief in a culturalist explanation of the American role in the world or the Middle East. We noted earlier how a change i.n the world status of the United States, a change in interest—albeit major and ineluctable—could lead to a change in policy and even a change in values. But more systematically, we can now say that the ideological-cultural instance is itself the "product" of a superior instance, relative to the status, or world stature, of the United States. We shall call this the "statural" instance. It is constituted by the internal societal history of the United States, its political system, the culture imparted by the European immigrants, and the world role of the United States as heir to European imperialism since 1945. In other words, the imperialism, the world role, the status, and the stature of the United States (commanded historically by a series of economic, military, political and ideological-cultural factors), constitute the condition of development of a dominant culture and ideology in which support to Israel is considered a value. Any major modification of this "statural" instance cannot help having an effect, over time, on the ideological-cultural instance. This perspective is, by the way, in conformity with what we stated in the previous chapter regarding imperialism: it does not provide an instrumental explanation of American support to Israel, but rather a contextual explanation.

More precisely, we propose the following articulation between the U.S. world role, the cultural instance and utility-instrumentality:

- At a first level (the statural instance), we place the general U.S. society, with its political system, its history, the imperialism to which it is heir, and its world role. All this constitutes the matrix of the following level.
- At a second level (the ideological-cultural instance), we place the dominant culture and ideology in the U.S., with its "Eurocentrism" and certain of its current characteristics, including the recognized status of the Jewish-American community and identification with Israel. This culture is the "product," over a long period of time, of the previous level; it is through the mediation of this level that imperialism, as the context of the world role of the United States, can be congruent with the idea of support to Israel. That is why the ideological-cultural instance constitutes, in turn, the matrix of the third level.
- At a third level, the utilitarian instance, we place the utility (nondamage) of American support to Israel, and its possible instrumentality. There is utility (and sometimes instrumentality) because there is prior support. In other words, if one must in any case engage in support to Israel, it is good that this engagement be profitable to the United States and its world role.

It remains that these three levels suggest that only the superior one imposes limits on that which follows it and thus do not allow for an explanation of the mutual limits evoked above. In order to account for these limits as well as the conformation of the three levels, we propose to represent the latter through figure 7.1.
The United States, represented by I, has a world role delimited by the angle AIB; the arc AB would express the scope of this role. The American ideological-cultural instance begins at point O (the "locus" of decision), normally situated within AIB, because culture is, over the long term, the "product" of U.S. society and its world role. But its extension CD is broader than AB, because any culture contains representations, has pretensions of universality (such as the idea of a "civilizing mission" accompanying imperialism) that exceed the material possibilities (and contradictions) of the society in the exercising of its world role, from economic, military, and political viewpoints. The ideological-cultural instance, the angle COD, contains an area slightly narrower, the angle MON, which represents American identification with Israel. This means that the angles MOC and NOD represent ideological-cultural fringes

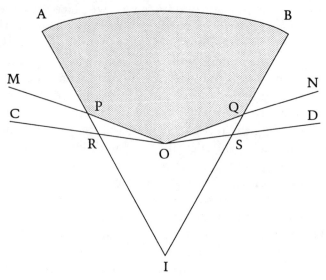

Key:
AIB: Statural Instance (U.S. world role)
COD: Ideological-Cultural Instance
MON: U.S. Ideological-Cultural Identification with Israel
APOQB: Utilitarian Instance (Utility of U.S. Support to Israel)

Figure 7.1
Ideological-Cultural Instance and U.S. World Role

(respectively the far left and the far right) unfavorable to Israel in American society.

The area representing the world role of the United States, the angle AIB, and that representing cultural identification with Israel, the angle MON, mutually delimit a common field APOQB, within which actual American support to Israel occurs, that is, in which support proves its utility (nondamage) and can sometimes be justified by its instrumentality. In practice, U.S. policy tries to avoid being located outside "mutual limits," that is, in the external zones, which are of two types. On the one hand there are POR and QOS, the zones of nonsupport; U.S. decisionmakers avoid being located in these narrow zones (containing ideological-cultural values unfavorable to identification with Israel), although they are not harmful to U.S. interests in the Middle East; we shall not even speak of MPRC and NQSD, which express simultaneous nonsupport and damage. On the other hand, there are APM and BQN, zones of support to

Israel because of identification, but harmful from the point of view of utility; decisionmakers also avoid being located there.

If the balance of forces in the Middle East region becomes irremediably favorable to the Arabs, it is of course AB that is likely to shrink, not MN; or at least, MN can shrink only very gradually and over the long term. The more AB shrinks, the more actual support to Israel becomes conditional, but the support is nonetheless present (for example, a U.S.-Israeli treaty of guarantee in exchange for Israeli withdrawal from the occupied territories in the framework of a settlement of the Israeli-Arab conflict).

It is thus in the common field APOQB, congruent with utility and nondamage, that the spectrum of U.S. attitudes relative to Israel, ranging from conditional support to permissiveness, is in practice located. It is within this field that implicit intentionality and the subjectivity of the decisionmakers may be placed, along with presidential initiatives or noninitiatives (reference to Quandt 1977:28ff; Spiegel 1985:10), bureaucratic arbitration or organizational routine (Allison 1971). We may note in particular, regarding Graham Allison, that while this author appears to superimpose the bureaucratic and organizational models on the rational one, we think it would be more fruitful to integrate the three models in a "simultaneous" explanation. But such an explanation can be formulated only if the idea of rationality is reduced not only to that of "limited rationality," but also to that of utility and nondamage. These remarks imply that the figure we propose and the explanation underlying it can be generalized.

General Conclusion

The initial aim of this work was to account for the basis of the special relationship between the United States and Israel, given the various and divergent interpretations concerning this phenomenon and the important stake it represents for all the actors concerned. The fact that many of the current interpretations are based, or claim to be based, on the idea of rationality as the foundation of the special relationship led us to propose an analysis of the place of Israel in U.S. strategic doctrine as the central theme of this study and to take the idea of instrumental rationality as its point of departure. We may now observe that in spite of all the methodological "chances" accorded to the strategic-instrumental perspective throughout this work, it has shown itself to be quite insufficient in accounting for the U.S.-Israeli relationship.

The very approach we have adopted in this study has allowed the instrumental perspective an ample opportunity to prove its validity. Thus, in the first part, nearly all the advocacies examined, whether they plead for considering Israel as an asset or whether they propose to accord Israel a guarantee (except of the kind based on a "moral commitment"), refer largely if not primarily to the concern of protecting U.S. interests. In the second part, the official doctrine is induced from an essentially instrumental interpretation of the history of U.S. policy in the Middle East, or at least the indices of an

American rationality are sought in this policy. Finally, chapter 6 in the third part is entirely dedicated to discussing the rational-instrumental perspective.

In spite of all this, however, we have been led, at different stages of this study, to call on factors that have little or nothing to do with strategic instrumentality. For example, the advocacies in favor of the doctrine of asset, although they refuse to resort to the argument of "moral commitment" toward Israel so as not to recognize the latter's dependency and indebtedness, cannot avoid appealing to the argument of an American-Israeli cultural identification, from which the Arabs are excluded. It may even be that these advocacies' insistence on strategic instrumentality has as its main goal to spare Israel the price of dependency. As for the authors who consider Israel as a burden, they do not go so far as to propose that Israel be abandoned, because they recognize the prior existence of an American "moral obligation"; the appeal for a U.S. conditional guarantee to Israel is their compromise solution between identification with Israel and U.S. interest. Further, our reading of the evolution of U.S. doctrine over the past 45 years of Israel's existence has not been able to avoid taking into account, at certain moments, nonstrategic factors such as Congressional pressure or the spontaneous pro-Israeli sentiment of decisionmakers or public opinion, in order to explain a given orientation of U.S. policy.

But it is in the third part of this study that we were led to give nonstrategic factors the full place they deserve. We did so, first of all, by "unraveling" the instrumental explanation in order to reveal its insufficiency and the difficulty of going beyond a "utilitarian" explanation, or beyond implicit intentionality on the part of decisionmakers. We did so, secondly, by establishing the validity—albeit incomplete—of an explanation in terms of the internal dynamics of U.S. society and the primacy of the U.S.-Israeli cultural identification over the utilitarian explanation. Finally, the instrumentality of the lobby in the U.S. political arena could only be explained with reference to the internal dynamics of U.S. society.

If these factors, which have apparently nothing to do with U.S. strategic interests in the Middle East nonetheless broadly determine Washington's policies toward this region and toward Israel, and take precedence over strategic (instrumental or utilitarian) considerations, we may then ask why the question of the conformation of these two sets of factors has given rise to so many disagreements among "commentators" (journalists, intellectuals, politicians), that is, more or less engaged observers, mainly but not exclusively non-

Americans, and whose advocacies are not destined, like those examined in the first part of the study, to influence American decisionmakers. Are these divergences due only to the "situation" of these commentators, that is, to their ideological affiliations ("left" or "right"), of their ethnic-national identity (Arab, Israeli, American, Jewish American)? It seems to us that the existence of an overall congruence between the ideological-cultural instance and the utilitarian one (nondamage) generates ambiguity in evaluating the relative weight of the factors at work, favoring the expression of divergent interpretations. Thus, certain authors will minimize one of these two instances while privileging elements of the other, while others will take the opposite approach with the same claim to rigor and coherence. Let us take a closer look.

Certain commentators (Arabs of the "left," Marxist or Third-Worldist analysts), noting the overall utility (nondamage) of U.S. support to Israel, will ignore the possibility of Israel as a burden; instead of being content to acknowledge utility, they will infer from it the idea that U.S. policy is always instrumental, totally based on interest, and capable of programming an effective relationship between means (support to a militarized Israel) and ends (control of the Middle East). This leap from the idea of utility to that of instrumentality is facilitated by the American (private and/or official) discourse in favor of the doctrine of asset. These commentators see in this strategic discourse the "admission" by the decisionmakers of their "actual" intentions, and concomitantly, see in the discourse of ideological-cultural identification ("moral obligation" toward Israel) nothing more than a smokescreen or rationalization. The manifest influence of the lobby is seen as an illusion, intentionally magnified by U.S. decisionmakers in order to soften the aggressive character of their own strategic aims. Let us call this type of interpretation type I.

Conversely, other commentators (Arabs of the "right," "centrist" Israelis, American analysts traditionally close to those known as the "Arabists" of the State Department and business circles) take note of the importance of internal U.S. dynamics and deny any relevance to the idea of strategic instrumentality in U.S. support to Israel. Let us call the resulting interpretation type II. If certain authors in this category (particularly among liberal American Jews) accord a great deal of importance to the idea of a U.S.-Israeli cultural identification (type IIa), it would seem that most commentators of type II, especially among Arabs, take little interest in the idea of cultural identification and attribute the pro-Israeli effects of the internal U.S. dynamic to the omnipotence of the lobby (type IIb). Both subcategories believe that U.S. support to Israel is likely to endanger, at least potentially, U.S. interests in the Middle East. While they are prepared to allow that the actual damage caused to these interests by U.S. support of Israel has not yet proven extensive and indisputable, the overall nondamage is considered accidental and is seen to exist in spite of, not because of, this support. For these commentators, the strategic discourse of the lobby or certain decisionmakers, to the effect that Israel serves U.S. interests, is only a smokescreen or rationalization to justify generous aid or rather to justify the submission of decisionmakers to the pressure of public opinion and Congress and to the threats of the lobby. In other words, since decisionmakers cannot admit publicly that they bow to electoral necessity or to the injunctions of the lobby, they justify their support to Israel with strategic pretexts.

If these diverging types of interpretation are espoused by advocates with equally strong convictions, it is because the overall congruence of the factors in play (strategic-utilitarian factors, the lobby, ideological-cultural identification) allows each category of commentators to argue that the factor it chooses to privilege has solid roots in reality. Following our conclusions in the preceding chapter, we would say that the truth is not located at the midpoint between these types of interpretation, but rather in a correct conformation of the relative weight of the factors cited, or better still, in the conformation we have proposed of the three factors—statural, ideological-cultural, and utilitarian. Let us explain why this conformation cannot be reduced to a simple "middle term" between the interpretations presented.

First and above all, these interpretations seem to confuse, explicitly or implicitly, that which for us must be separated out, that is, the statural instance (the context of the world role of the United States) and the utilitarian instance (nondamage as a consequence of decision or behavior). Next, if we consider types I and IIb, so different in many respects, we will observe that they nonetheless have a common dimension. Indeed, both lay stress on the voluntarism of the actor: the state in the first case, the lobby in the second. The instrumental rationallty of the actor is not affirmed only in type I, but also in type IIb (although the instrumentality attributed in this type to the lobby belongs to the domestic political order rather than to the strategic one). These two types thus are in agreement insofar as they privilege one decisionmaker (the state or the lobby) to whom a flawless design is attributed, whereas the other actors are reduced to secondary players or passive receptacles; and insofar as they both shun any logic not that of an actor, thus excluding the spontaneity of ideological-cultural identification as an explanatory factor.

Against this instrumental "cynicism" (or rather, against this attitude which consists of attributing an instrumental cynicism to an actor one chooses to privilege), we hope to have firmly established that the ideological-cultural identification indeed occupies a central and durable place in the explanation of U.S.-Israeli relations. But we also hope not to have fallen into the "naïveté" of type IIa interpretations, which accord no relevance to the strategic consequences of the ideological-cultural identification, nor to its global context. If support to Israel is part of the United States' "being," it is not seriously challenged by negative effects on this great power; the United States sometimes profits from its support to Israel, generally does not suffer damage, and reacts most often to its own permissiveness when the damage occurs, in order to prevent aggravation of the damage.

All the preceding observations shed light on the margin of maneuver of the two parties whose fate is linked to the future of U.S.-Israeli relations, that is, the Israelis and the Arabs. The former are apparently the main beneficiaries of their special relationship with a great power. If one is tempted to conclude from this study that whatever they do, the Israelis are always sure of U.S. support and draw from it the means (military, financial, and diplomatic) of their margin of maneuver, it must be added that they pay the price of dependency, and sometimes, the feeling of being smothered in an exaggeratedly friendly embrace. In spite of the broad margin of maneuver regarding what Washington will tolerate (and we have had ample occasion to observe this), it is probable that, beyond the rare American applications of pressure, the Israelis sometimes impose limits on themselves, imperceptibly and immediately. In other words, it is probable that at certain times certain options are excluded from the Israeli governmental agenda, not only because of submission to American persuasion or pressure, but also spontaneously, as if this exclusion were self-evident, taken for granted, because—implicitly—of the very system of special relations with Washington.

This exclusion by Israel of certain actions from its agenda, whether spontaneous or deliberate, and whether accepted willingly or reluctantly, concerns those actions that would call into question, first, the foundation of the special relationship, and secondarily its "perpetuation." The foundation of this relationship, it is now well understood, concerns the first two instances, i.e. the statural and the ideological-cultural ones. Israeli actions cannot, of course, affect the status of the United States as a great world power, but during the Cold War period Israel saw itself as obliged to avoid being seen as the cause of a direct U.S.-Soviet military confrontation and avoid betraying U.S. confidence by moving too close to the Soviet Union. With the end of the competition between the two superpowers, these risks no longer exist, although, by the same token, the United States is less interested than before in developing certain aspects of its strategic cooperation with Israel. On the other hand, the Jewish state must refrain from bringing harm to the ideological-cultural identification of U.S. society with itself; that is, it must refrain from going too far in undermining its legitimacy as a "Western" state and the image Americans have of it, or from overly straining its relations with the American Jewish community. Finally, on the utilitarian level and regarding the perpetuation of relations, Tel Aviv must make certain that the United States does not attribute to it the responsibility for unquestionable damage to U.S. regional interests.

Short of these limits which are, as we can see, either extreme or very relaxed, the special relationship between the two countries implies an American permissiveness that gives Israel a very broad freedom of action, including freedom to assert differences of interest on many regional questions. However, the special relationship, through the reaffirmation of Israel's belonging to the West and the U.S. permissiveness it implies, and through the means it provides to Israel to express its freedom of action and even its regional ambitions, may have the consequence of gravely hindering Israel's integration into its regional environment. It is possible, on the other hand, that an overall Arab-Israeli peace settlement, bearing with it promises of durability and regional stability would result in a reduced Israeli dependence on the United States and signal the beginning of a long, gradual process of trivialization of U.S.-Israeli relations.

Now let us consider the U.S.-Israeli relationship from the standpoint of the Arabs' margin of maneuver. If the special character of the relationship between the U.S and Israel is a given, then it is vain to think that the Arabs might be able to do anything to qualitatively transform it in the foreseeable future. They can have only a very marginal impact on the status of the United States as a great power and on the U.S.-Israeli ideological-cultural identification. On the first point, the Arabs are above all themselves, one of the "objects" upon which (or against which) the world role of the United States is exercised. Even during the period of East-West competition, the alliances between certain Arab countries and the Soviet Union never appeared durable, "special," and irreversible and had at best the effect of irritating the United States, while provoking a strengthening rather than a weakening of the Israeli-American alliance. Further, because of the Arabs' divisions, the pro-American orientation of the majority of the Arab states, Arab oil, and the necessity of their integration into the international economic system, the Arabs themselves have contributed, and continue to contribute, to the reinforcement of the world role of the United States, and thus have not challenged the global context in which the U.S.-Israeli special relationship has taken shape. The only challenge that has occurred was that of Iraq in 1990–91, but instead of calling into question the U.S. world role, it has resulted in the enhancement of this role and brought about the near-demise of the challenger.

Concerning the second point, that is, the U.S.-Israeli identification, it must be said that the Arabs, whatever they do, cannot change their "being," become "Western," and replace Israel in the ideological-cultural instance of U.S. society, or even occupy the same rank as Israel in that instance. There is, undeniably, a practically unbridgeable gap, which media images of political Islam, of the anti-Westernism of Arab peoples, and of Middle Eastern terrorism, only help to widen. Neither the Westernized image attributed to certain Arab leaders artificially cut off from their societal roots, nor U.S.-Arab cooperation (which, in the case of Saudi Arabia, even preceded the creation of the state of Israel), nor the constitution of an official Arab lobby in Washington, can bridge this cultural gap. The fringe of the ideological-cultural instance whose gradual extension could offer some elements favorable to the Arabs (as in the case of American and Jewish-American reactions to repression in the Palestinian occupied territories) perhaps concerns only what is universal in American values, but this extension (or its opposite) does not depend only on Arab behavior; it depends as well on Israeli actions and on internal developments in U.S. society, independent of what happens in the Middle East.

It is mainly on the level of the "perpetuation" of the U.S.-Israeli relationship, that is, on the level of the utilitarian instance in the Middle East arena, that the Arabs can intervene, by acting or failing to act. This by no means calls into question the special character of the relationship, but it could have the effect of enlarging (or, quite the opposite, of diminishing) the costs of U.S. permissiveness and Israel's regional margin of maneuver. This judgment will be valid, it seems to us, as long as a final Israeli-Arab peace settlement has not been achieved. In this respect, the negotiation process that began in Madrid in the fall of 1991 must be considered—as long as it does not result in an overall settlement—as one of the forms of the Israeli-Arab conflict and as one of the theaters in which the classic tug-of-war between the Arabs, the Israelis, and the Americans takes place, against the constant backdrop of the special American-Israeli relationship.

But if the Madrid process leads to durable peace and regional stability, it would mean that new sets of rules concerning the American-Israeli-Arab triangular game are being established. It is useless to make predictions about these new rules. Let's only say that the exclusiveness of U.S.-Israeli ties might then erode to the extent that Israel integrates politically, economically and culturally in its environment.

References

Abu-Khadra, Rajai M. 1988. "The Closure of the PLO Offices." *Journal of Palestine Studies* no. 67 (Spring).

Allen, Harry S. and Ivan Volgyes, eds. 1983. *Israel, the Middle East and U.S. Interests*. New York: Praeger.

Allison, Graham T. 1971. *Essence of Decision: Explaining the Cuban Missile Crisis*. Boston: Little, Brown.

Amin, Samir. 1976. *L'impérialisme et le développement inégal*. Paris: Editions de minuit.

Arendt, Hannah. 1966. *The Origins of Totalitarianism*. New York: Harcourt Brace.

Aron, Raymond. 1984. *Paix et guerre entre les nations*. Paris: Calmann-Lévy.

Ateya, Moustafa N. 1987. "Israël/Etats-Unis: la zone de libre-échange." *Revue d'études palestiniennes* no. 23 (Spring).

Atkinson, Alexander. 1981. *Social Order and the General Theory of Strategy*. London: Routledge and Kegan Paul.

Avruch, Kevin. 1981. *American Immigrants in Israel: Social Identities and Change*. Chicago: The University of Chicago Press.

Babcock, Charles R. 1986a. "Why the Balance of Power Favors Israel." *International Herald Tribune*. August 8.

—— 1986b. "Pro-Israelis Force Congressmen to Remember 'the Percy Factor.' " *International Herald Tribune*. August 8.

Bachrach, P. and M.S. Baratz. 1963. "Decisions and Non-Decisions: An Analytical Framework." *American Political Science Review* 57, no. 3 (September).

Badie, Bertrand. 1983. *Culture et politique*. Paris: Economica.

Ball, George W. 1975. "The Looming War in the Middle East." *Atlantic Monthly* (January).

———— 1977. "How to Save Israel in Spite of Herself." *Foreign Affairs* 55, no. 3 (April).

———— 1978. An Interview with, "American Policy on Trial." *Journal of Palestine Studies* no. 27 (Spring).

———— 1979–1980. "The Coming Crisis in Israeli-American Relations." *Foreign Affairs* 58, no. 2 (Winter).

———— 1984. *Error and Betrayal in Lebanon: An Analysis of Israel's Invasion of Lebanon and the Implications for U.S.-Israeli Relations.* Washington, D.C.: Foundation for Middle East Peace.

Bard, Mitchell G. 1988. "The Turning Point in United States Relations With Israel: The 1968 Sale of Phantom Jets." *Middle East Review* 20, no. 4 (Summer).

———— 1991. *The Water's Edge and Beyond: Defining the Limits to Domestic Influence on United States Middle East Policy.* New Brunswick, N.J.: Transaction Publishers.

Barrett, Laurence I. 1983. *Gambling With History: Reagan in the White House.* New York: Doubleday.

Bar-Siman-Tov, Yaacov. 1980. "Alliance Strategy: U.S.-Small Allies Relationships." *Journal of Strategic Studies* 3, no. 2 (September).

———— 1988. "Ben-Gurion and Sharett: Conflict Management and Great Power Constraints on Israeli Foreign Policy." *Middle Eastern Review* 24, no. 3 (July).

Bar-Zohar, Michael. 1978. *Ben-Gurion: A Biography.* London: Weidenfeld and Nicolson.

Battle, Lucius. 1974. "Peace—Inshallah." *Foreign Policy*, no. 14 (Spring).

Beenstock, Michael. 1992. "The Determinants of US Assistance to Israel." *Jerusalem Journal of International Relations* 14, no. 1 (March).

Ben-Gurion, David. 1963. *Israel: Years of Challenge.* New York: Holt, Rinehart and Winston.

Ben-Zvi, Abraham. 1984. *Alliance Politics and the Limits of Influence: The Case of the U.S. and Israel, 1975–1983.* Tel Aviv: Jaffee Center for Strategic Studies, Tel Aviv University.

Bergus, Donald C. 1988. " 'Forty Years On'—Israel's Quest for Security." *Middle East Journal* 42, no. 2 (Spring).

Between Two Administrations: An American-Israeli Dialogue. 1989. Washington, D.C.: The Washington Institute for Near East Policy.

Bialer, Uri. 1990. *Between East and West: Israel's Foreign Policy Orientation, 1948–1956.* Cambridge: Cambridge University Press.

Binder, Leonard. 1983. "U.S. Policy in the Middle East: Exploiting New Opportunities." *Current History* 82 no. 480 (January) .

———— 1984. "Failure, Defeat, Debacle: U.S. Policy in the Middle East." *World Politics* 36, no. 3 (April).

Black, Ian and Benny Morris. 1991. *Israel's Secret Wars: A History of Israel's Intelligence Services.* New York: Grove Weidenfeld.

Blechman, Barry M. 1990. *The Politics of National Security: Congress and U.S. Defense Policy.* New York: Oxford University Press.

Blitzer, Wolf. 1981. "No AWACS, no Strategic Deal With Israel—Pentagon." *Jerusalem Post*. September 13.

—— 1985. *Between Washington and Jerusalem: A Reporter's Notebook*. Oxford: Oxford University Press.

Bloomfield, Douglas M. 1983. "Israel's Standing in the Congress: Will Foreign Aid Be Spared?." in Novik, ed. (1983).

Blumenthal, Sidney. 1986. *The Rise of the Counter-Establishment: From Conservative Ideology to Political Power*. New York: Times Books.

Booth, Ken. 1979. *Strategy and Ethnocentrism*. London: Croom Helm.

Bottomore, Tom. 1980. "Preface" in Nicholas Abercrombie, Stephen Hill and Bryan S. Turner, *The Dominant Ideology Thesis*. London: George Allen and Unwin.

Braun, Aurel, ed. 1987. *The Middle East in Global Strategy*. Boulder, Colorado: Westview Press.

Braybrooke, David and Charles E. Lindblom. 1963. *A Strategy of Decision*. New York: The Free Press.

Brecher, Michael. 1972. *The Foreign Policy System of Israel: Setting, Images, Process*. New Haven: Yale University Press.

—— 1974. *Israel, the Korean War and China: Images, Decisions and Consequences*. Jerusalem: The Jerusalem Academic Press.

—— 1980. *Decisions in Crisis: Israel, 1967 and 1973*. Berkeley: University of California Press.

Brenner, Lenni. 1986. *Jews in America Today*. London: Al Saqi Books.

Brooks, Charles D. 1986. "S.D.I.: A New Dimension for Israel." *Journal of Social, Political and Economic Studies* 11, no. 4 (Winter).

Brown, Harold. 1983. *Thinking About National Security: Defense and Foreign Policy in a Dangerous World*. Boulder: Westview Press.

Brown, L. Carl. 1984. *International Politics and the Middle East: Old Rules, Dangerous Game*. Princeton: Princeton University Press.

Bruzonsky, Mark A. 1976. "American Thinking about a Security Guarantee to Israel." *International Problems* 15, no. 3–4 (Fall).

Brzezinski, Zbigniew. 1974. "A Plan for Peace in the Middle East." *New Leader*. January 7.

—— 1983. *Power and Principle: Memoirs of the National Security Adviser, 1977–1981*. New York: Farrar, Straus, Giroux.

—— François Duchêne and Kiichi Saeki. 1975. "Peace in an International Framework." *Foreign Policy*, no. 19 (Summer).

Buheiry, Marwan R. 1978. "The Saunders Document." *Journal of Palestine Studies* no. 29 (Autumn).

—— 1980. *U.S. Threats of Intervention Against Arab Oil: 1973–1979*. Beirut: Institute for Palestine Studies.

Carley, M. 1982. "Analytic Rationality." in Anthony G. McGrew and M.J. Wilson, eds., *Decision Making: Approaches and Analysis*. Manchester: Manchester University Press.

Carter, Jimmy. 1980. "The State of the Union." *Weekly Compilation of Presidential Documents*. January 28.

—— 1982. *Keeping Faith: Memoirs of a President*. New York: Bantam Books.

Carus, W. Seth. 1983. *Israel and the U.S. Navy*. Washington, D.C.: AIPAC Papers on U.S.-Israel Relations.

Chadda, Maya. 1986. *Paradox of Power: The United States in Southwest Asia, 1973–1984*. Santa Barbara, CA: ABC-CLIO.

Chomsky, Noam. 1984. *The Fateful Triangle: The United States, Israel and the Palestinians*. Boston: South End Press.

Christison, Kathleen. 1989. "The Arab-Israeli Policy of George Shultz." *Journal of Palestine Studies* no. 70 (Winter).

Chubin, Shahram. 1987. "Soviet Policy in the Middle East." in Samuel F. Wells, Jr. and Mark A. Bruzonsky, eds., *Security in the Middle East: Regional Change and Great Power Strategies*. Boulder: Westview Press.

Churba, Joseph. 1977. *The Politics of Defeat: America's Decline in the Middle East*. New York: Cyrco Press.

——— 1980. "The Eroding Security Balance in the Middle East." *Orbis* 24, no. 2 (Summer).

Cline, Ray S. 1980. *World Power Trends and U.S. Foreign Policy for the 1980s*. Boulder: Westview Press.

Cobban, Helena. 1991. *The Superpowers and the Syrian-Israeli Conflict: Beyond Crisis Management?* New York: Praeger.

Cockburn, Andrew and Leslie Cockburn. 1991. *Dangerous Liaison: The Inside Story of the U.S.-Israeli Covert Relationship*. New York: Harper-Collins.

Cohen, Michael J. 1982. *Palestine and the Great Powers, 1945–1948*. Princeton: Princeton University Press.

Cohen, Raymond. 1978. "Israel and the Soviet-American Statement of October 1, 1977: The Limits of Patron-Client Influence." *Orbis* 22, no. 3 (Fall).

Cohen, Richard. 1987. "Israelis Are Endangering the Israeli-U.S. Alliance." *International Herald Tribune*. March 9.

Cohler, Larry. 1992. "Bound by a Common Thread: New Jewish Congressmen Proud of Their Roots." *Washington Jewish Week* 28, no. 48 (November 26).

Coker, Christopher, 1983. *U.S. Military Power in the 1980s*. London: MacMillan.

Collier, Ellen C. 1988. "Foreign Policy by Reporting Requirement." *Washington Quarterly* 11, no. 1 (Winter).

Congressional Quarterly Weekly Report. 1989. "AIPAC Working to Shore Up Its Clout With Congress." 47, no. 7 (February 18).

Cordesman, Anthony H. 1984. *The Gulf and the Search for Strategic Stability: Saudi Arabia, the Military Balance in the Gulf, and Trends in the Arab-Israeli Military Balance*. Boulder: Westview Press.

Cordier, Sherwood, 1983. *U.S. Military Power and Rapid Deployment Requirements in the 1980s*. Boulder: Westview Press.

Corm, Georges. 1989. *L'Europe et l'Orient, de la balkanisation à la libanisation: histoire d'une modernité inaccomplie*. Paris: La Découverte.

Curtiss, Richard H. 1986. *A Changing Image: American Perceptions of the Arab-Israeli Dispute*. Washington, D.C.: American Eudcational Trust.

—— 1989. "Pro-Israel PACs: Still Unique." *Washington Report on Middle East Affairs*. July.

Dayan, Moshe. 1976. *Story of my Life*. London: Weidenfeld and Nicolson.

—— 1981. *Breakthrough: A Personal Account of the Egypt-Israel Peace Negotiation*. London: Weidenfeld and Nicolson.

Deibel, Terry L. 1980. *Commitment in American Foreign Policy*. Washington, D.C.: The National Defense University.

Diehl, Jackson and Caryle Murphy. 1990. "The Saber Rattling in Mideast: Despite Hot Rhetoric, a New Arab-Israeli War Is Doubted." *International Herald Tribune*. July 3.

Dine, Thomas A. 1986. "The Revolution in U.S.-Israel Relations." reproduced in *Journal of Palestine Studies* no. 60 (Summer).

—— 1987. "Achievements and Advances in the United States—Israel Relationship." reproduced in *Journal of Palestine Studies* no. 64 (Summer).

Dinstein, Yoram. 1980. "International Guarantees and the Middle East Conflict." in Shaked and Rabinovich, eds. (1980).

Donald, James and Stuart Hall, eds. 1986. *Politics and Ideology: A Reader*. Milton Keynes: Open University Press.

Dougherty, James E. and Robert L. Pfaltzgraff, Jr. 1981. *Contending Theories of International Relations: A Comprehensive Survey*. New York: Harper and Row.

Dowty, Alan. 1974. *The Role of Great Power Guarantees in International Peace Agreements*. Jerusalem: The Leonard Davis Institute for International Relations, The Hebrew University of Jerusalem.

—— 1984. *Middle East Crisis: U.S. Decision-Making in 1958, 1970, and 1973*. Berkeley: University of California Press.

Draper, Theodore. 1975. "The United States and Israel: Tilt in the Middle East." *Commentary* 59, no. 4 (April).

Drinan, Robert F. 1977. *Honor the Promise: America's Commitment to Israel*. Garden City, NY: Doubleday.

Duncan, Andrew 1982.. "The Military Threat to Israel." *Survival* 24 (May–June).

Eban, Abba. 1977. *An Auto-Biography*. London: Weidenfeld and Nicolson.

Efrat, Moshe and Jacob Bercovitch. 1991. *Superpowers and Client States in the Middle East: The Imbalance of Influence*. London: Routledge.

Eisenhower, Dwight D. 1965. *The White House Years: Waging Peace, 1956-1961*. Garden City, NY: Doubleday.

Ennes, James M. 1979. *Assault on the Liberty*. New York: Random House.

Evensen, Bruce J. 1992. "Truman, Palestine and the Cold War." *Middle Eastern Studies* 28, no. 1 (January).

Eytan, Walter. 1958. *The First Ten Years: A Diplomatic History of Israel*. New York: Simon and Schuster.

Falwell, Jerry. 1980. *Listen America*. New York: Doubleday.

——, ed. 1981. *The Fundamentalist Phenomenon: The Resurgence of Conservative Christianity*. Garden City, N.Y.: Doubleday.

Feis, Herbert. 1969. *The Birth of Israel*. New York: Norton.

Feldman Lily Gardner. 1984. *The Special Relationship Between West Germany and Israel*. Boston: George Allen and Unwin.

Feldman, Shai. 1981. "Peacemaking in the Middle East: The Next Step." *Foreign Affairs*. Spring, 59, no. 4.

⸺ and Heda Rechnitz-Kijner. 1984. *Deception, Consensus and War: Israel in Lebanon*. Tel Aviv: The Jaffee Center for Strategic Studies.

Feuerwerger, Marvin C. 1979. *Congress and Israel: Foreign Aid Decision Making in the House of Representatives, 1969–1976*. Westport, Connecticut: Greenwood Press.

Fialka, John. 1985. "Pro-Israel Lobby: Jewish PACs Emerge as a Powerful Force in U.S Election Races." *Wall Street Journal*. February 26.

Findley, Paul. 1985. *They Dare to Speak Out: People and Institutions Confront Israel's Lobby*. Westport: Lawrence Hill and Co.

Ford, Gerald. 1979. *A Time to Heal: The Autobiography of Gerald Ford*. New York: Harper.

Franck, Thomas M. and Edward Weisbank. 1979. *Foreign Policy by Congress*. New York: Oxford University Press.

Fraser, T. G., 1989. *The USA and the Middle East Since World War 2*. London: Macmillan.

Fredet, Jean-Gabriel and Martine Gilson. 1991. "De Roosevelt à Bush: l'Amérique et les juifs." *Le Nouvel observateur*. March 28–April 3.

Friedman, Thomas L. 1984. "Israel Gets Aid on Jet From U.S.: Weinberger Grants Requests for Technology." *International Herald Tribune*. October 18.

⸺ 1992. "Israel Scrambles to Define Its Post-Cold War Ties With U.S.." *International Herald Tribune*. March 23.

FRUS [Foreign Relations of the United States]. 1948, 5, pt 2, Washington, D.C.: United States Government Printing Office.

⸺ 1949, vol. 6.

⸺ 1950, 5.

⸺ 1951, 5.

⸺ 1952–1954, 9.

⸺ 1955–1957, 12.

⸺ 1958–1960, 13.

Fulbright, J. William. 1972. *The Crippled Giant: American Foreign Policy and its Domestic Consequences*. New York: Random House.

⸺ 1975. "Getting Tough with Israel." *Washington Monthly*. February.

Fuller, Graham E. 1990/91. "The Strategic Irrelevance of Israel." *National Interest*, no. 22 (Winter).

Garfinkle, Adam M. 1985. "U.S. Decision Making in the Jordan Crisis: Correcting the Record." *Political Science Quarterly* no. 100 (Spring).

Garnham, David. 1977. "Factors Influencing Congressional Support for Israel During the 93rd Congress." *Jerusalem Journal of International Relations* 2, no. 3 (Spring).

Gazit, Mordechai. 1983. *President Kennedy's Policy Toward the Arab States and Israel*. Tel Aviv: The Shiloah Center for Middle Eastern and African Studies, Tel Aviv University.

⸺ 1987. "Israeli Military Procurement from the United States." in Sheffer, ed. (1987a)

Gelb, Leslie H. 1983. "Shultz Emerges as Policy Tough Guy." *International Herald Tribune.* November 8.

——— 1992. "Rethinking U.S.-Israeli Relations." *International Herald Tribune.* June 16.

Gendzier, Irene L. 1989. "The United States, the USSR and the Arab World in NSC Reports of the 1950s." *American-Arab Affairs* no. 28 (Spring).

George, Alexander L. 1987. "Ideology and International Relations: A Conceptual Analysis." *Jerusalem Journal of International Relations* 9, no. 1.

Geyelin, Philip. 1983. "A New Strategic Agreement Between U.S. and Israel." *International Herald Tribune.* November 10.

Gilboa, Eytan. 1987. *American Public Opinion Toward Israel and the Arab-Israeli Conflict.* Lexington, Massachusetts: Lexington Books.

Glick, Edward Bernard. 1982. *The Triangular Connection: America, Israel and American Jews.* London: George Allen and Unwin.

Golan, Matti. 1976. *The Secret Conversations of Henry Kissinger.* New York: Quadrangle Books.

Gold, Dore. 1988. *America, the Gulf and Israel: CENTCOM Central Command and Emerging U.S. Regional Security Policies in the Middle East.* Tel Aviv: The Jaffee Center for Strategic Studies, Tel Aviv University.

Goldberg, David Howard. 1990. *Foreign Policy and Ethnic Interest Groups: American and Canadian Jews Lobby for Israel.* Westport: Greenwood Press.

Goott, Amy Kaufman and Steven J. Rosen. 1983. *The Campaign to Discredit Israel.* Washington, D.C.: AIPAC Papers on U.S.-Israel Relations.

Goshko, John M. 1987. "U.S. Jewry Assails Israel in Spy Case." *International Herald Tribune.* March 14–15.

Grayson, Benson Lee. 1982. *Soviet Intentions and American Options in the Middle East.* Washington, D.C.: National Defense University Press.

Green, Stephen. 1984. *Taking Sides: America's Secret Relations With a Militant Israel.* New York: William Morrow.

——— 1988. *Living by the Sword: America and Israel in the Middle East, 1968–1987.* London: Faber and Faber.

Griffith, William E. 1975. "It's our Move in the Middle East." *Reader's Digest.* February.

Grose, Peter. 1983. *Israel in the Mind of America.* New York: Knopf.

Gwertzman, Bernard. 1983. "Reagan Turns to Israel." *New York Times Magazine.* November 27.

——— 1984. "U.S. Intermediary Held Secret Talks With Arafat." *International Herald Tribune.* February 2.

Haber, Eytan. 1981. "A Useless War." *Yediot Aharonot.* May 14 in Hebrew.

Hadar, Leon T. 1990–91. "Reforming Israel—Before It's Too Late." *Foreign Policy* no. 81 (Winter).

Haffa, Robert P. 1984. *The Half War: Planning U.S. Rapid Deployment Forces to Meet a Limited Contingency, 1960–1983.* Boulder: Westview Press.

Haig, Alexander M. 1984. *Caveat: Realism, Reagan and Foreign Policy.* London: Weidenfeld and Nicolson.

Halimi, Serge. 1989. "Le poids du lobby pro-israélien aux Etats-Unis." *Le Monde diplomatique.* August.

Halperin, Morton H. 1974. *Bureaucratic Politics and Foreign Policy*. Washington, D.C.: The Brookings Institution.

Halpern, Ben. 1961. *The Idea of the Jewish State*. Cambridge: Harvard University Press.

Halsell, Grace. 1986. *Prophecy and Politics: Militant Evangelists on the Road to Nuclear War*. Westport: Lawrence Hill.

Handel, Michael. 1983. "Israel's Contribution to U.S. Interests in the Middle East." in Allen and Volgyes, eds. (1983).

Hanks, Robert. 1982. *The U.S. Military Presence in the Middle East: Problems and Prospects*. Cambridge: Institute for Foreign Policy Analysis.

Hargrove, John. 1975. "Guaranteeing Israel's Borders." *Washington Post*. January 14.

Harkabi, Yehoshafat. 1988. *Israel's Fateful Hour*. New York: Harper.

Hassner, Pierre. 1966. *Les alliances sont-elles dépassées?* Paris: Centre d'études et de recherches internationales.

Heikal, Mohamed Hassanein. 1988. *Years of Turmoil*. 1, Cairo: al-Ahram in Arabic.

Hentsch, Thierry. 1987. *L'Orient imaginaire: la vision politique occidentale de l'Est méditerranéen*. Paris: Editions de minuit.

Heren, Louis. 1970. *No Hail, no Farewell*. New York: Harper.

Hersh, Seymour M. 1991. *The Samson Option: Israel's Nuclear Arsenal and American Foreign Policy*. New York: Random House.

Hertzberg, Arthur, ed. 1969. *The Zionist Idea: A Historical Analysis and Reader*. New York: Atheneum.

Herzl, Theodor. 1967. *The Jewish State: An Attempt at a Modern Solution of the Jewish Question*. London: H. Pordes.

Herzog, Haim. 1981. "Like Blind People in Lebanon." *Ma'ariv*. May 8 in Hebrew.

Hobson, John A. 1965. *Imperialism: A Study*. Ann Arbor: University of Michigan Press.

Hoffmann, Stanley. 1975. "A New Policy for Israel." *Foreign Affairs* 53, no. 3 (Spring).

—— 1980. *Primacy or World Order: American Foreign Policy Since the Cold War*. New York: McGraw-Hill.

—— 1981. "Requiem." *Foreign Policy* no. 42 (Spring).

Holsti, K.J. 1967. *International Politics: A Framework for Analysis*. Englewood Cliffs: Prentice-Hall.

Holsti, Ole R. and James N. Rosenau. 1984. *American Leadership in World Affairs: Vietnam and the Breakdown of Consensus*. Boston: Allen and Unwin.

—— 1990. "The Emerging U.S Consensus on Foreign Policy." *Orbis* 34, no. 3 (Fall).

Hooglund, Eric. 1988. "Reagan's Iran: Factions Behind US Policy in the Gulf." *Middle East Report*. March-April.

Horowitz, David. 1953. *State in the Making*. New York: Knopf.

Hunt, Michael H. 1987. *Ideology and U.S. Foreign Policy*. New Haven: Yale University Press.

Huth, Paul and Bruce Russett. 1984. "What Makes Deterrence Work: Cases from 1900 to 1980." *World Politics* 36, no. 4 (July).

Inbar, Efraim. 1982/1983. "The American Arms Transfer to Israel." *Middle East Review* 15, no. 1–2 (Fall-Winter).

Indyk, Martin. 1985. "Faulty Assumptions, Failed Policy: The Arabists and the PLO During the First Reagan Administration." in Paul Marantz and Blema S. Steinberg, eds., *Superpower Involvement in the Middle East: Dynamics of Foreign Policy.* Boulder: Westview Press.

Indyk, Martin, Charles Kupchan and Steven J. Rosen. 1983. *Israel and the U.S. Air Force.* Washington, D.C.: AIPAC Papers on U.S.-Israel Relations.

Insight Team of the *Sunday Times.* 1974. *Insight on the Middle East War.* London: André Deutsch.

Isaacs, Stephen D. 1974. *Jews and American Politics.* Garden City, N.Y.: Doubleday.

Jailer, Todd and Melani Mcalistair. 1989. "The Israeli-Palestinian Conflict and the US Peace Movement." in Zachary Lockman and Joel Beinin, eds., *Intifada: The Palestinian Uprising Against Israeli Occupation.* Boston: A Merip Book, South End Press.

Jamous, Haroun. 1982. *Israël et ses juifs: Essai sur les limites du volontarisme.* Paris: Maspero.

Janis, Irving and Ralph Mann. 1977. *Decision Making.* New York: Free Press.

Jervis, Robert. 1976. *Perception and Misperception in International Politics.* Princeton: Princeton University Press.

Johnson, Lyndon Baines. 1971. *The Vantage Point: Perspectives of the Presidency 1963–69.* New York: Holt, Rinehart and Winston.

Johnson, Maxwell Orme. 1983. *The Military as an Instrument of U.S. Policy in Southwest Asia: The Rapid Deployment Joint Task Force, 1979–1982.* Boulder: Westview Press.

Johnstone, Diana. 1976. "Une stratégie trilatérale." *Le Monde diplomatique.* November.

Joyner, Christopher and Shafqat Ali Shah. 1981. "The Reagan Policy of 'Strategic Consensus' in the Middle East." *Strategic Review.* Fall.

Kalb, Marvin and Bernard Kalb. 1974. *Kissinger.* New York: Dell.

Kegley, Charles W. and Eugene R. Wittkopf. 1979. *American Foreign Policy: Pattern and Processes.* New York: St. Martin's.

Kemp, Geoffrey. 1980. "Defense Innovation and Geopolitics: From the Persian Gulf to Outer Space." in Thompson, ed (1980).

——— 1981. "Military Forces and Middle East Oil." in David A. Deese and Joseph S. Nye, eds., *Energy and Security.* Cambridge: Ballinger Publishing Company.

Kenen, I. L. 1981. *Israel's Defense Line: Her Friends and Foes in Washington.* Buffalo, N.Y.: Prometheus Books.

Keohane, Robert O. 1971. "The Big Influence of Small Allies." *Foreign Policy* no. 2 (Spring).

Kerr, Malcom H. 1971. *The Arab Cold War: Gamal 'Abd al-Nasir and his Rivals, 1958–1970.* New York: Oxford University Press.

——— 1980. *America's Middle East Policy: Kissinger, Carter and the Future.* Beirut: Institute for Palestine Studies.

Kessler, Jonathan S. and Jeff Schwaber, eds. 1984. *The AIPAC College*

Guide: Exposing the Anti-Israel Campaign on Campus. Washington, D.C.: AIPAC Papers on U.S.-Israel Relations.

Khalidi, Rashid. 1986. *Under Siege: P.L.O. Decisionmaking During the 1982 War*. New York: Columbia University Press.

Kissinger, Henry. 1979. *White House Years*. Boston: Little, Brown.

—— 1982. *Years of Upheaval*. Boston: Little, Brown.

Klieman, Aaron S. 1979. "Zionist Diplomacy and Israeli Foreign Policy." *Jerusalem Quarterly* no. 11 (Spring).

—— 1980. "Israeli Diplomacy in the Thirtieth Year of Statehood: Some Constraints and Discontinuities." in Asher Arian, ed., *Israel: A Developing Society*. Tel Aviv: Tel Aviv University.

—— 1985. *Israel's Global Reach: Arms Sales as Diplomacy*. New York: Pergamon-Brassey's.

Koebner, Richard and Helmut Dan Schmidt. 1964. *Imperialism: The Story and Significance of a Political Word, 1840–1960*. New York: Cambridge University Press.

Krasner, Stephen D. 1978. *Defending the National Interest: Raw Materials Investments and U.S. Foreign Policy*. Princeton: Princeton University Press.

Krauthammer, Charles. 1991. "What's the Point in Waltzing With Assad on a Road to Nowhere?." *International Herald Tribune*. August 3–4.

Kuniholm, Bruce R. 1983. "Carrots or Sticks? The Question of United States Influence Over Israel." *International Journal* 38, no. 4 (Autumn).

Kupchan, Charles A. 1987. *The Persian Gulf and the West: The Dilemmas of Security*. Boston: Allen and Unwin.

Lakoff, Sanford. 1987. "Power and Limit: U.S. Strategic Doctrine in the Middle East." in Braun, ed. (1987).

Lalande, André. 1976. *Vocabulaire technique et critique de la philosophie*. Paris: Presses universitaires de France.

Langellier, Jean-Pierre. 1989. "Cher lobby . . . ", *Le Monde*. July 6.

Langer, William L. 1935. *The Diplomacy of Imperialism, 1870–1914*. New York: Knopf.

Laufer, Leopold Yehuda. 1987. "U.S. Aid to Israel: Problems and Perspectives." in Sheffer, ed. (1987a).

Leca, Jean. 1988. "L'économie contre la culture dans l'explication des dynamiques politiques." *Bulletin du CEDEJ*. no. 23.

Legislators and the Lobbyists. 1968. Washington, D.C.: Congressional Quarterly Services.

Lenczowski, George. 1990. *American Presidents and the Middle East*. Durham, North Carolina: Duke University Press.

Lenin, V.I. 1939. *Imperialism: The Highest Stage of Capitalism*. New York: International Publishers.

Lesser, Allen. 1975. "Letter to the Editor." *Foreign Affairs* 53, no. 3 (April).

Lewis, Anthony. 1977. "A Preemptive Strike." *New York Times*. May 12.

—— 1984. "Protocols of Palestine." *New York Times*. January 15.

Lewis, Samuel W. 1988. "The United States and Israel: Constancy and Change." in Quandt, ed. (1988).

Lindblom, C.E. 1979. "Still Muddling, not Yet Through." *Public Administration Review*. 39.

Liska, George. 1968. *Alliances and the Third World*. Baltimore: The Johns Hopkins Press.

Lorenz, Andrea W. 1993. "Pro-Israel Political Action Committee Contributions to Congressional Candidates in the 1991–1992 Election Cycle." *Washington Report on Middle East Affairs* 11, no. 8 (March).

Luttwak, Edward N. 1989. "Strategic Cooperation: A Strategist's View." in *Between Two Administrations* (1989).

Maalouf, Rafik. 1989. "Israel Seeks to Sign a New Accord With Washington For Weapons Use in Emergency." *al-Hayat*. November 20 in Arabic.

Macdonald, Charles G. 1984. "U.S. Policy and Gulf Security." in Robert G. Darius, John W. Amos II and Ralph H. Magnus, eds., *Gulf Security into the 1980s: Perceptual and Strategic Dimensions*. Stanford, CA: Hoover Institution Press.

Madison, Christopher. 1984. "Reagan Links Middle East Disputes to Global East-West Struggle." *National Journal*. January 28, no. 4.

Magdoff, Harry. 1969. *The Age of Imperialism*. New York: Monthly Review Press.

Mansour, Abdul Kasim [pseud.]. 1980. "The American Threat to Saudi Arabia." *Armed Forces Journal International*. September.

Mansour, Camille. 1982. "Palestine and the Gulf: An Eastern Arab Perspective." in Rashid Khalidi and Camille Mansour, eds. *Palestine and the Gulf*. Beirut: Institute for Palestine Studies.

Manuel, Frank E. 1949. *The Realities of American-Palestine Relations*. Washington, D.C.: Public Affairs Press.

Mathias, Charles. 1981. "Ethnic Groups and Foreign Policy." *Foreign Affairs* 59, no. 5 (Summer).

McConnell, Jeff. 1986. "Israeli Spies in the U.S." *Middle East Report*. January-February.

McFarlane, Robert C. 1989. "Introduction." in *Between Two Administrations* (1989).

McGuire, Martin C. 1982. "U.S. Assistance, Israeli Allocation, and the Arms Race in the Middle East." *Journal of Conflict Resolution* 26, no. 2 (June).

McNaugher, Thomas L. 1985. *Arms and Oil: U.S. Military Strategy and the Persian Gulf*. Washington, D.C.: The Brookings Institution.

Merton, Robert K. 1957. *Social Theory and Social Structure*. Glencoe, Illinois: The Free Press.

Middleton, Drew. 1981. "Israel Hopes to Speed U.S. Military Accord." *New York Times*. October 9.

Miège, Jean-Louis. 1973. *Expansion européenne et décolonisation de 1870 à nos jours*. Paris: Presses universitaires de France.

Milhollin, Gary. 1987–88. "Heavy Water Cheaters." *Foreign Policy* no. 69 (Winter).

Morgenthau, Hans J. 1978. "The Organic Relationship Between Ideology and Political Reality." in George Schwab, ed., *Ideology and Foreign Policy: A Global Perspective*. New York: Cyrco Press.

Morris, Benny. 1989. "Coup de froid sur les relations entre Jérusalem et Washington." *Le Monde diplomatique*. August.

Moughrabi, Fouad. 1988. "The U.S.-Israel Relationship." *Journal of Palestine Studies* no. 68 (Summer).

Mouly, Ruth W. 1982. "Israel: Darling of the Religious Right." *The Humanist* no. 42 (May-June).

Nachmias, Nitza. 1987. "U.S.-Israel Relationships, 1968–1986." *International Problems* 26, no. 3–4 (Winter).

Neff, Donald. 1981. *Warriors at Suez: Eisenhower Takes America Into the Middle East*. New York: The Linden Press / Simon and Schuster.

—— 1984. *Warriors for Jerusalem: The Six Days That Changed the Middle East*. New York: The Linden Press / Simon and Schuster.

—— 1987. "The Beginnings of U.S. Strategic Cooperation With Israel." *American-Arab Affairs* no. 21 (Summer).

—— 1988. "Palestine, Truman and America's Strategic Balance." *American-Arab Affairs* no. 25 (Summer).

Newhouse, John. 1971. *U.S. Troops in Europe: Issues, Costs and Choices*. Washington, D.C.: The Brookings Institution.

Nixon, Richard. 1978. *The Memoirs of Richard Nixon*. New York: Grosset and Dunlap.

Novik, Nimrod. 1984. "The United States in Lebanon: Unfulfilled Expectations." in Joseph Alpher, ed., *Israel's Lebanon Policy: Where To?* Tel Aviv: The Jaffee Center for Strategic Studies, Tel Aviv University.

—— 1986. *The United States and Israel: Domestic Determinants of a Changing U.S. Commitment*. Boulder: Westview Press / Tel Aviv: The Jaffee Center for Strategic Studies, Tel Aviv University.

——, ed. 1983. *Israel in U.S. Foreign and Security Policies*. Tel Aviv: Jaffee Center for Strategic Studies, Tel Aviv University.

O'Brien, Lee. 1986. *American Jewish Organizations and Israel*. Washington, D.C.: Institute for Palestine Studies.

O'Brien, William. 1982. "Reflections on the Future of American-Israeli Relations." *Jerusalem Quarterly* no. 22 (Winter).

Organski, A. F. K. 1990. *The $36 Billion Bargain: Strategy and Politics in U.S. Assistance to Israel*. New York: Columbia University Press.

Park, Chang Jin. 1975. "The Influence of Small States Upon the Superpowers: United States-South Korea Relations as a Case Study, 1950–1953." *World Politics* 28, no. 1 (October).

Parry, G. and P. Morriss. 1974. "When is a Decision not a Decision?" *British Political Sociology Yearbook*, vol 1.

Patai, Raphael. 1970. *Israel Between East and West: A Study in Human Relations*. Westport: Greenwood.

Paul, Roland A. 1973. *American Military Commitments Abroad*. New Brunswick: Rutgers University Press.

Pelcovits, N. A. 1976. *Security Guarantees in a Middle East Settlement*. Beverly Hills, California: Sage Publications.

Peri, Yoram. 1983. *Between Battles and Ballots*. Cambridge: Cambridge University Press.

Perlmutter, Amos. 1983. "The Parameters of U.S Policy in the Persian Gulf and the Middle East." in Allen and Volgyes, eds. (1983).

——, Michael Handel and Uri Bar-Joseph. 1982. *Two Minutes Over Baghdad*. London: Transworld Publishers, Corgi Books.

Perlmutter, Nathan. 1983. "Domestic Realignments and a Changing Jewish Community: Implications for US Policy." in Novik, ed. (1983).

Phillips, James. 1986. *America's Security Stake in Israel*. Washington, D.C.: Heritage Foundation.

Pincus, Walter. 1985. "Israeli Request Called Key to U.S.-Iran Arms Deals." *International Herald Tribune*. September 30.

Pincus, Walter, and Bob Woodward. 1988. "Pressed on Iran Deal, Bush Blames Israelis." *International Herald Tribune*. January 28.

Podhoretz, Norman. 1980. *Breaking Ranks: A Political Memoir*. London: Weidenfeld and Nicolson.

Pollock, David. 1982. *The Politics of Pressure: American Arms and Israeli Policy Since the Six Day War*. Westport: Greenwood Press.

Pomerance, Michla. 1974. *American Guarantees to Israel and the Law of American Foreign Relations*. Jerusalem: The Leonard Davis Institute for International Relations, The Hebrew University of Jerusalem.

President's Special Review Board. 1987. *Report of the President's Special Review Board*. Washington, D.C., February 26.

Quandt, William B. 1975. "Kissinger and the Arab-Israeli Disengagement Negotiations." *Journal of International Affairs*. Spring.

—— 1977. *Decade of Decisions: American Policy Toward the Arab-Israeli Conflict, 1967–76*. Berkeley: University of California Press.

—— 1984. "Reagan's Lebanon Policy: Trial and Error." *Middle East Journal*, no. 38 (Spring).

—— 1986. *Camp David: Peacemaking and Politics*. Washington, D.C.: The Brookings Institution.

——, ed. 1988. *The Middle East: Ten Years After Camp David*. Washington, D.C.: The Brookings Institution.

Rabin, Yitzhak. 1979. *The Rabin Memoirs*. Boston: Little, Brown.

Rabinovich, Itamar. 1984. *The War for Lebanon, 1970–1983*. Ithaca: Cornell University Press.

Ray, James Lee. 1985. *The Future of American-Israeli Relations: A Parting of the Ways?* Lexington: The University Press of Kentucky.

Reagan, Ronald. 1979. "Recognizing the Israeli Asset." *Washington Post*. August 15.

—— 1990. *An American Life*. New York: Simon and Schuster.

Reich, Bernard. 1977. *Quest for Peace: United States—Israel Relations and the Arab-Israeli Conflict*. New Brunswick: Transaction Books / Tel Aviv: The Shiloah Center for Middle Eastern and African Studies, Tel Aviv University.

—— 1980. "United States Interests in the Middle East." In Shaked and Rabinovich, eds. (1980).

—— 1984. *The United States and Israel: Influence in the Special Relationship*. New York: Praeger.

Reston, James. 1989. "Clear the Air With a U.S.-Israeli Security Treaty." *International Herald Tribune*. January 16.

Riad, Mahmoud. 1981. *Memoirs, 1948–1978: Searching for Peace and the Middle East Conflict*. Beirut: The Arab Institute for Studies and Publishing in Arabic.

Roberts, Samuel J. 1973. *Survival or Hegemony? The Foundations of Israeli Foreign Policy*. Baltimore: The Johns Hopkins University Press.

Rocher, Guy. 1968. *Introduction à la sociologie générale.* T. 1, Montreal: Editions HMH.

Rodinson, Maxime. 1973. *Israel: A Colonial-Settler State?* New York: Monad Press.

―――― 1981. *Marxism and the Muslim World.* New York: Monthly Review.

Rokach, Livia. 1980. *Israel's Sacred Terrorism: A Study Based on Moshe Sharett's Personal Diary and Other Documents.* Belmont, Massachusetts: AAUG.

Ronen, Dov. 1979. *The Quest for Self-Determination.* New Haven: Yale University Press.

Rosen, Steven J. 1982. *The Strategic Value of Israel.* Washington, D.C.: AIPAC Papers on U.S.-Israel Relations.

―――― and Yosef I. Abramowitz. 1984. *How Americans Feel About Israel.* Washington, D.C.: AIPAC Papers on U.S.-Israel Relations.

Rosecrance, Richard. 1980. "Objectives of U.S. Middle East Policy." in Shaked and Rabinovich, eds. (1980).

Roshwald, Mordecai. 1974. "America and Israel." *Social Science* 49, no. 2 (Spring).

Ross, Jeffrey A. and Ann Baker Cottrell, eds. 1980. *Mobilization of Collective Identity.* Lanham, Maryland: University Press of America.

Rostow, Eugene V. 1977. "The American Stake in Israel." *Commentary* 63, no. 4 (April).

Rothstein, Robert. 1968. *Alliances and Small Powers.* New York: Columbia University Press.

Rubenberg, Cheryl A. 1986. *Israel and the American National Interest: A Critical Examination.* Chicago: University of Illinois Press.

Rubin, Barry. 1981. *The Arab States and the Palestine Question.* Syracuse, N.Y.: Syracuse University Press.

Rubinstein, Alvin Z. 1978. "Israel in NATO: Basis for a Middle East Settlement." *Orbis* 22, no. 1 (Spring).

Rusonik, Anthony. 1990. "On the West Bank of the Potomac: Debating the Sources of US Support for Israel." *Jerusalem Journal of International Relations* 12, no. 4 (December).

Russet, Bruce and Harvey Starr. 1981. *World Politics: The Menu for Choice.* San Francisco: Freeman and Co.

Ryan, Sheila. 1982. "Israel's Invasion of Lebanon: Background to the Crisis." *Journal of Palestine Studies* no. 44–45 (Summer/Fall).

―――― 1987. "U.S. Military Contractors in Israel." *Middle East Report* January-February.

Safire, William. 1987. "Why Israelis Are Losing in America." *International Herald Tribune.* September 10.

Safran, Nadav. 1974. "The War and the Future of the Arab-Israeli Conflict." *Foreign Affairs* 52, no. 2 (January).

―――― 1978. *Israel: The Embattled Ally.* Cambridge: The Belknap Press of Harvard University Press.

Saïd, Edward. 1978. *Orientalism.* New York: Random House.

Schechtman, Joseph B. 1966. *The United States and the Jewish State Movement: The Crucial Decade, 1939–1949.* New York: Herzl Press.

Schelling, Thomas C. 1960. *The Strategy of Conflict*. Oxford: Oxford University Press.

Schiff, Zeev. 1983. "The Green Light." *Foreign Policy* no. 50 (Spring).

—— 1991. "Israel After the War." *Foreign Affairs* 70, no. 2 (Spring).

Schiff, Zeev, and Ehud Ya'ari. 1984. *Israel's Lebanon War*. London: George Allen and Unwin.

Schumpeter, Joseph. 1955. *Imperialism and Social Classes*. New York: Meridian Books.

Shaked, Haim and Itamar Rabinovich, eds. 1980. *The Middle East and the United States: Perceptions and Policies*. New Brunswick: Transaction Books / Tel Aviv: The Shiloah Center for Middle Eastern and African Studies, Tel Aviv University.

Sharon, Ariel with David Chanoff. 1989. *Warrior: An Autobiography*. New York: Simon and Schuster.

Shaw, Harry J. 1985/1986. "Strategic Dissensus." *Foreign Policy* no. 61 (Winter).

Sheehan, Edward. 1976. *The Arabs, Israelis and Kissinger: A Secret History of American Diplomacy in the Middle East*. New York: Reader's Digest Press.

Sheffer, Gabriel, ed. 1987a. *Dynamics of Dependence: U.S.-Israeli Relations*. Boulder: Westview Press / Jerusalem: The Leonard Davis Institute for International Relations, The Hebrew University of Jerusalem.

—— 1987b. "The United States-Israeli Relationship." *Jerusalem Journal of International Relations* 9, no. 4 (December).

Sheffer, Gabriel and Menachem Hofnung. 1987a. "Israel's Image." in Sheffer, ed. (1987a).

Shipler, David K. 1981. "Israel's Desire for a Strategic Relationship With U.S. Is Taken More Seriously Than Ever." *New York Times*. October 2.

—— 1983. "A Precarious Harmony: Divergent Priorities of U.S and Israel Could Revive Differences at Summit." *International Herald Tribune*. November 29.

—— 1987. "Potent U.S. Lobby for Israel Bends Politicians and Generals." *International Herald Tribune*. July 7.

Sicherman, Harvey. 1978. *Broker or Advocate? The U.S. Role in the Arab-Israeli Dispute, 1973–1978*. Philadelphia: Foreign Policy Research Institute.

—— 1983. " 'A Perilous Partnership': Israel's Role in U.S. Strategy." in Novik, ed. (1983).

Sifry, Micah L. 1988. "Jesse and the Jews: Palestine and the Struggle for the Democratic Party." *Middle East Report* no. 155. (November-December).

Sigler, John H. 1983. "United States Policy in the Aftermath of Lebanon: The Perils of Unilateralism." *International Journal* 38 no. 4 (Autumn).

Simon, Herbert A., ed. 1957. *Models of Man: Social and Rational*. New York: Wiley.

Singer, Marshall R. 1972. *Weak States in a World of Powers: The Dynamics of International Relationships*. New York: The Free Press.

Slater, Jerome. 1991. "The Superpowers and an Arab-Israeli Settlement: the Cold War Years." *Political Science Quarterly* 105, no. 4 (Winter).

Slater, Jerome, and Terry Nardin. 1991. "Interests vs. Principles: Reassessing the US Commitment to Israel." *Jerusalem Journal of International Relations* 13, no. 3 (September).

Slonim, Shlomo. 1974. *United States—Israel Relations, 1967–1973: A Study in the Convergence and Divergence of Interests.* Jerusalem: Jerusalem Papers on Peace Problems, The Hebrew University of Jerusalem.

Smith, James A. 1991. *The Idea Brokers: Think Tanks and the Rise of the New Policy Elite.* New York: The Free Press.

Snyder, Glenn H. and Paul Diesing. 1977. *Conflict Among Nations: Bargaining, Decision Making and System Structure in International Crisis.* Princeton: Princeton University Press.

Snyder, Jed C. 1985. "Strategic Bias and Southern Flank Security." *Washington Quarterly* 8, no. 3 (Summer).

Spiegel, Steven L. 1980. "Does the United States Have Options in the Middle East?" *Orbis* 24, no. 2 (Summer).

——— 1983. "Israel as a Strategic Asset." *Commentary* 75, no. 6 (June).

——— 1985. *The Other Arab-Israeli Conflict: Making America's Middle East Policy from Truman to Reagan.* Chicago: The University of Chicago Press.

——— 1986. "U.S. Relations with Israel: The Military Benefits." *Orbis* 30, no. 3 (Fall).

——— 1990/91. "America and Israel: How Bad Is It? Will It Get Worse?" *National Interest* no. 22 (Winter).

Springborg, Robert. 1981. "U.S. Policy Toward Egypt: Problems and Prospects." *Orbis* 24, no. 4 (Winter).

Staley, Eugene. 1935. *War and the Private Investor.* Garden City, N.Y.: Doubleday.

Starr, Joyce R. 1986. " 'Star Wars' and Israel: A Celestial Attraction." *International Herald Tribune.* March 22–23.

"Statement of the Committee on U.S. Interests in the Middle East." 1992. *New York Times.* February 26 and March 5.

Stein, Janice Gross. 1987. "Extended Deterrence in the Middle East: American Strategy Reconsidered." *World Politics* 39, no. 3 (April).

Steinberg, Gerald M. and Steven L. Spiegel. 1987. "Israel and the Security of the West." in Braun, ed. (1987).

Stockton, Ronald R. 1987. "Christian Zionism: Prophecy and Public Opinion." *Middle East Journal* 41 (Spring).

Stork, Joe. 1982. "Israel as a Strategic Asset." *Merip Reports.* May.

——— and Martha Wenger. 1983. "US Aid to Israel: The Censored GAO Report." *Merip Reports.* September.

Tamir, Avraham. 1988. *A Soldier in Search of Peace: An Inside Look at Israel's Strategy.* London: Weidenfeld and Nicolson.

Teveth, Shabtai. 1972. *Moshe Dayan.* London: Weidenfeld and Nicolson.

Thompson, John B. 1990. *Ideology and Modern Culture.* Stanford: Stanford University Press.

Thompson, W. Scott, ed. 1980. *National Security in the 1980s: From Weakness to Strength.* San Francisco: Institute for Contemporary Studies.

Tillman, Seth. 1980. *American Interests in the Middle East.* Washington, D.C.: Middle East Institute.

Tivnan, Edward. 1987. *The Lobby: Jewish Political Power and American Foreign Policy.* New York: Simon and Schuster.

Toward Peace in the Middle East: Report of a Study Group. 1975. Washington, D.C.: The Brookings Institution.

Trice, Robert H. 1977. "Congress and the Arab-Israeli Conflict: Support for Israel in the U.S. Senate, 1970–1973." *Political Science Quarterly* 92, no. 3 (Fall).

Tucker, Robert W. 1975. "Israel and the United States: From Dependence to Nuclear Weapons?" *Commentary* 60, no. 5 (November).

——— 1981. "The Middle East: Carterism Without Carter?" *Commentary* 72, no. 3 (September).

Ullman, Richard. 1975a. "After Rabat: Middle East Risks and American Roles." *Foreign Affairs* 53, no. 2 (January).

——— 1975b. "Alliance With Israel?" *Foreign Policy* no. 19 (Summer).

U.S. General Accounting Office. 1983. *U.S. Assistance to the State of Israel.* Washington, D.C., June 24, GAO/ID-83–51.

Walker, R.B.J., ed. 1984. *Culture, Ideology and World Order.* Boulder: Westview Press.

Weinberger, Caspar. 1990. *Fighting for Peace: Seven Critical Years in the Pentagon.* New York: Warner Books.

Wildavsky, Aaron. 1977. "What's in it for Us? America's National Interest in Israel." *The Middle East Review* 10 no. 1 (Fall).

Wilson, Evan M. 1979. *Decision on Palestine: How the U.S. Came to Recognize Israel.* Stanford: Hoover Institution Press.

Wingerter, Rex B. 1985. "Israel's Search for Strategic Interdependence and the 1983 U.S.-Israeli Strategic Cooperation Agreement." *American-Arab Affairs* no. 14 (Fall).

Wolfinger, Raymond. 1988. "Structural and Generational Changes in Congress, and the Role of Congress in US Foreign Policy." in Shai Feldman, ed., *U.S. Middle East Policy: the Domestic Setting.* Tel Aviv: The Jaffee Center for Strategic Studies, Tel Aviv University.

Woodward, Bob and Walter Pincus. 1988. "U.S. Spy Hunters Are Stalking Israel's 'Mr. X'." *International Herald Tribune.* February 20–21.

Wright, Claudia. 1982. "The Turn of the Screw: The Lebanon War and American Policy." *Journal of Palestine Studies* no. 44–45 (Summer/Fall).

——— 1984. "Reagan Arms Policy, the Arabs and Israel—Protectorate or Protection Racket?" *Third World Quarterly* 6, no. 3 (July).

Wyman, David S. 1984. *The Abandonment of the Jews: America and the Holocaust, 1941–1945.* New York: Pantheon Books.

Yaniv, Avner. 1987. *Deterrence Without the Bomb: The Politics of Israeli Strategy.* Lexington, Massachusetts: Lexington Books.

Yatsiv, Gadi. 1982. " Peace of the Galilee, Peace of Israel and Peace of the United States." *Hotam. al-Hamishmar Supplement.* June 18 in Hebrew.

Zureik, Elia and Fouad Moughrabi. 1907. *Public Opinion and the Palestine Question.* London: Croom Helm.

Zweig, Ferdynand. 1969. *Israel: The Sword and the Harp.* London: Heinemann.

Index